AMERICAN BAR ASSOCIATION
Defending Liberty
Pursuing Justice

The Criminal Lawyer's Guide to Immigration Law

Questions and Answers
Second Edition

Robert James McWhirter

Criminal Justice Section

Cover design by ABA Publishing.

Printed in the United States of America.

10 09 08 5 4 3 2

Library of Congress Cataloging-in-Publication Data

McWhirter, Robert James, 1961-
The criminal lawyer's guide to immigration law : questions and answers / by Robert James McWhirter.—2nd ed.
p. cm.
Includes index.
ISBN 1-59031-602-9
1. Emigration and immigration law--United States. 2. Alien criminals—United States. 3. Defense (Criminal procedure)--United States. I. Title: Guide to immigration law. II. Title.

KF4819.M39 2005
342.7308'2--dc22 05-26426

www.ababooks.org

Chapter 2: Immigration Law for Criminal Lawyers

Chapter 3: Border Stops

Table of Contents

Summary of Contents

Chapter 5: Aggravated Felonies

Part III: Immigration Crimes

Chapter 6: Alien Employment Crimes

Chapter 7: Marriage Fraud

Chapter 8: Alien Smuggling and Hostage Taking

Part IV: Reentry After Deportation and Illegal Entry

Chapter 10: Illegal Entry and Reentry — Pretrial and Trial

Part V: Alien Witnesses and Defendants

Chapter 12: Getting Witnesses and Evidence from Abroad

Chapter 13: International Extradition

Chapter 14: Treaty Transfers — Aliens There and Citizens Here

Table of Questions

To my boys, Robert Anthony, Ryan Alexander, and Gabriel Adam — and to my wife, Gina, who gave them to me.

About the Author

Robert J. McWhirter has been an Assistant Federal Public Defender for the District of Arizona since 1989. He received his Juris Doctorate from Arizona State University College of Law in 1988 and, after graduation, clerked for then-Vice Chief Justice Stanley G. Feldman of the Supreme Court of Arizona.

Since joining the Office of the Federal Public Defender, McWhirter has represented Native Americans and other clients in a broad range of federal cases involving homicide, sexual abuse, and bank robbery, and developed a specialty in criminal immigration law. He has published articles in the Georgetown Immigration Law Review and Criminal Practice Law Report.

McWhirter also teaches nationally and internationally. In the U.S., he has taught seminars on criminal immigration law and immigration consequences of criminal convictions for the Criminal Justice Act program, sponsored by the Administrative Office of the U.S. Courts. He was a visiting professor of law at the Catholic University of Chile and the University of Chile, where he taught Spanish-language seminars on free speech, privacy and the Internet, and American criminal procedure. McWhirter has taught trial practice skills to new public defenders and judges in Venezuela as part of the country's judicial reform. Under U.S. Information Agency sponsorship, he served as an advisor for the recently ratified Venezuelan Constitution. He has since given trainings in Nicaragua, Chile, and Colombia on oral advocacy skills.

McWhirter is currently still fighting for his clients at the Federal Public Defenders office and has begun work on a new book, to the gentle dismay of his loving wife and three small sons, telling the "story behind the story" of the Bill of Rights.

Foreword

The topics in Robert McWhirter's book, *A Criminal Lawyer's Guide to Immigration Law: Questions and Answers*, have perhaps not gotten the attention they deserved. But, with drastic immigration consequences, the continued criminalization of immigration law, and the global nature of criminal prosecutions Robert's book is ever more pertinent.

I have known Robert since he was a "baby Federal Public Defender" some 16 years ago when I had the privilege of working with him at the National Criminal Defense College in Macon, Georgia. He has made both the College and me proud. He has represented a great number of people from other countries charged with immigration crimes. In the Federal system he has the reputation of being an innovator in criminal immigration cases. He has also extensively trained Latin American lawyers in trial techniques. In fact, he confessed to me that he "stole" my Killer Cross Examination lecture, translated it into Spanish, and presented it all over South America. I don't know whether to be flattered or offended but I want to see the Spanish version!

His extensive work has uniquely qualified him to write this book. Robert writes from the perspective of a practicing lawyer. His straightforward organization gives answers to everyday practice questions. I am very happy that the ABA Criminal Justice Section published Robert's book because it helps us fulfill our mission to serve the practicing lawyer. As a long-time member of the Criminal Justice Section Council, of which Robert is also now a member, I am delighted that we have this resource to offer.

The first edition "sold out," necessitating this second edition. But, this second edition is not just an update but literally a whole new book. The reader will find not just expanded coverage but more chapters, topics, answers, and resources.

As director of the Federal Defender's of Chicago, one of my responsibilities is to see that my lawyers have the resources they need. That is why we have many copies of The Criminal Lawyer's Guide to Immigration Law: Questions and Answers in our library. Indeed, several of my lawyers, as well as Assistant Federal Defenders across the country have been known to buy their own copies. Attorneys "on the front lines" use this book as their "first grab."

One of the most fulfilling moments for a teacher is when he sees a student contributing to the profession and improving the quality of justice. I have had this pleasure many times among the Assistant Federal Defenders I trained in cross-examination and other trial skills. Thus, it makes me proud to see Robert's contribution to this important area of our practice. I know you find this book as useful as I do.

Terence MacCarthy
Chicago — Fall 2005.

Introduction and Acknowledgments

This is a *waay* better book than the first edition!

In fact, it is a whole new book — completely rewritten and organized. The law in this area changes so fast that a simple revision would not do. I needed to re-conceptualize many of the chapters and overall organization. Also, many people have said nice things about the book over the last few years and were generous with their ideas. I have tried to incorporate them. A few said they did not like the book, sometimes in print, and were also generous with their ideas. I have tried to steal their ideas as well.

One of the main reasons this book is better is that I have a whole new crowd to thank for their help. Thanks again to several colleagues and friends at the Federal Defender Office who reviewed various chapters including Milagros Cisneros, Lee Titterington, Douglas Passon, Donna Elm, Jeanette Alvarado, and Gregory Bartolomei. I also thank Jon Sands, the Federal Public Defender for the District of Arizona for the support he gives to projects like this book. I hope this book reflects well on the office but, of course, the Federal Defender Office is not responsible for any mistakes I have made in the book. I thank my friend Reid Pixler from the United States Attorney's Office in Phoenix for his review of the Extradition chapter. Regina Jeffries and Keith Hilzendeger were a great help as my law clerks.

My gratitude again goes to the staff of the Federal Court's library in Phoenix, Arizona: Tim Blake, Margaret Ackroyd, and Mary Bailey. The Federal Court library in Phoenix is an underappreciated treasure trove and these people are the key. Anyone who says that librarians are becoming less relevant in the "new information age" does not know much about the information they seek. This book would not have been possible without Tim and his staff.

I am flattered (shall I admit surprised) that the ABA wanted another edition and that the first one sold out. But, I must thank my editor, Tim Brandhorst at the ABA. He does a great job and was an intelligent and calming influence during the whole process. Also, Barb Leff, who markets the book, is tireless and no doubt is one of the main reasons this book is in its second edition. Thank you also to the entire Publications Committee of the ABA Criminal Justice Section, formally headed by Paul

Rashkind and now by Amie Clifford. I now serve on this committee and can attest that you are all a great group of bibliophiles. I really enjoy and learn from our meetings. Thank you.

Since the first edition, I have been blessed with a wife and three small boys, explaining why this edition did not come out earlier. My wife Gina Huerta, an intelligent and practical lawyer in her own right, reviewed most of the chapters. My twin boys, Robert Anthony and Ryan Alexander also edited the chapters whenever they could get their hands on my pencils and drafts. But because they are three years old, I generally did not incorporate their suggestions in this edition. Our baby, Gabriel Adam, also helped by generously waking me up in the middle of the night for his supper, usually provided by his mama, after which I was free to write. Thank you all for your contribution and love.

Robert James McWhirter
Tempe, Arizona — June 2005

PART I

ALIENS AND GOVERNMENT

CHAPTER 1

STRANGERS IN AN EVEN STRANGER LAND: ALIENS AND IMMIGRATION LAW AFTER SEPTEMBER 11, 2001

Introduction

I. Aliens in a Time of "Patriots": Immigration Policy After 9/11

II. The Patriot Act and Other Statutes

- **A. Legislation**
- **B. "Terrorism" — Do We "Know It When We See It?"**
- **C. "Foreign Terrorist Organizations"**
- **D. The Patriot Act and Foreign Governments**

III. Immigration Consequences and Terrorism

- **A. New Grounds of Inadmissibility and Deportation**
- **B. Secret Deportations and Evidence**
- **C. Excluding the Family of "Terrorists"**
- **D. Aliens and Fund-raising**
- **E. Aliens and Money Laundering**

IV. Detention of Aliens on Terrorist Allegations

V. How 9/11 Affected Various Types of Immigrants

- **A. Men from Muslim Countries: "Let's Try Racial Profiling Again"**
- **B. Alien Students**
- **C. Refugees**

VI. Alien Terrorism Victims

VII. Alien Informants

VIII. Military Commissions

IX. Punishing Terrorists

Other Resources:

DAVID COLE, ENEMY ALIENS: DOUBLE STANDARDS AND CONSTITUTIONAL FREEDOMS IN THE WAR ON TERRORISM (2003).

Rebecca L. Sigmund, *Chapter 8: Immigration and Border Security*, HOMELAND SECURITY LAW HANDBOOK, ABS Consulting/Government Institutes (Rockville, Md. 2003).

Introduction

This chapter focuses on how September 11, 2001 (9/11) changed the legal landscape for aliens. Immigration law became the most visible tool in the war on terror as the Attorney General stated on October 25, 2001:

> Let the terrorists among us be warned: If you overstay your visa — even by one day — we will arrest you. If you violate a local law, you will be put in jail and kept in custody as long as possible.

Department of Justice, Office of the Inspector General, *The September 11 Detainees: A Review of the Treatment of Aliens Held on Immigration Charges in Connection with the Investigation of the September 11 Attacks* 12 (Apr. 2003), *discussed in The Child Status Protection Act: Is Your Child Protected?*, 80:28 INTERPRETER RELEASES 977 (July 21, 2003). *See* Daniel Kanstroom, *Criminalizing the Undocumented: Ironic Boundaries of the Post-September 11th "Pale of Law,"* 29 N.C.J. INT'L L. & COM. REG. 639 (2004); Lindsay N. Kendrick, Comment, *Alienable Rights and Unalienable Wrongs: Fighting the "War on Terror" Through the Fourth Amendment*, 47 HOW. L.J. 989 (2004); Teresa Miller, *Blurring the Boundaries Between Immigration and Crime Control After September 11th*, 25 B.C. THIRD WORLD L.J. 81 (2005); John S. Richbourg, *Liberty and Security: The Yin and Yang of Immigration Law*, 33 U. MEM. L. REV. 475 (2003).

I. Aliens in a Time of "Patriots": Immigration Policy After 9/11

§ 1.1. *How has the war on terror affected immigration policy?*

Before 9/11 the discussion of immigration policy included a comprehensive amnesty program for the millions of aliens illegally in the United States, new procedures to allow for speedy adjustment of employment-based visa applications, and a general campaign to facilitate the flow of people across borders. Businesses need workers, and organized labor views these workers as potential members. *See generally* Margaret D. Stock, *United States Immigration Law in a World of Terror*, 7:10 BENDER'S IMMIGR. BULL. 559 (May 15, 2002); Steven S. Miller & Laurie Bernbaum, *Immigration Law and Civil Rights: Where Do Aliens Stand After 9/11?*, WASH. ST. BAR NEWS, Mar. 2002, at 19. Today, one does not even hear such discussion and suggestions for reform are more restrictive to aliens. *See Administration Formulates "Patriot II" with Harsher Immigration Provisions*, 80:8 INTERPRETER RELEASES 270 (Feb. 24, 2003); Tom Barry, *Anti-Immigrant Backlash on the Home Front*, 38:6 NACLA REPORT ON THE AMERICAS 28 (May/June 2005); Michele Waslin, *Immigration Policy in Flux*, 35:3 NACLA REPORT ON THE AMERICAS 34 (Nov./Dec. 2001); David Cole, *Enemy Aliens*, 54 STAN. L. REV. 953 (2002); Kevin R. Johnson, *The End of "Civil Rights" As We Know It?: Immigration and Civil Rights in the New Millennium*, 49:5 UCLA L. REV. 1481 (2002); Karen C. Tumlin, Comment, *Suspect First: How Terrorism Policy Is Reshaping Immigration Policy*, 92 CAL. L. REV. 1173 (2004).

But, room for positive policy changes still exists. *See* Quinn H. Vandenberg, Note, *How Can the United States Rectify Its Post 9/11 Stance on Non-citizens' Rights?*, 18 NOTRE DAME J. L. & PUB. POL'Y 605 (2004).

§ 1.2. *What immigration laws concern aliens more than ever?*

Aliens must be more aware than ever of little-known provisions of the law such as every alien must "carry with him and have in his possession any certificate of alien registration or alien registration receipt card issued to him," 8 U.S.C. § 1304(e), and every alien must notify the Bureau of Citizenship and Immigration Services (CIS) within 10 days of a change of residence. 8 U.S.C. § 1305(a). *See generally* Asli U Bali, *Changes in Immigration Law and Practice After September 11: A Practitioner's Perspective*, 2 CARDOZO PUB. L. POL'Y & ETHICS J. 161 (2003). Also, aliens now face more scrutiny and obstacles when returning to the United States after travel abroad. *See* Stanley Mailman & Stephen Yale-Loehr, *Documentation and Travel Tips for Immigrants After September 11*, 7:1 BENDER'S IMMIGR. BULL. 1 (Jan. 1, 2002); see *also* Angelo A. Paparelli & John C. Valdez, *September 11 Ushers In a New Era in Immigration Law and Procedure*, 7:7 BENDER'S IMMIGR. BULL. 379 (Apr. 1, 2002); Angelo A. Paparelli & John C. Valdez, *September 11 Ushers In a New Era in Immigration Law and Procedure — Part II*, 7:8 BENDER'S IMMIGR. BULL. 427 (Apr. 15, 2002); Theresa Sidebothom, *Immigration Policies and the War on Terrorism*, 32 DENV. J. INT'L L. & POL'Y 539 (2004). Various other rights of aliens in the United States have been limited or curtailed. *See, e.g.*, Lory Diana Rosenberg, *Right to Protest and Immigration Status*, 9:19 BENDER'S IMMIGR. BULL. 1169 (Oct. 1, 2004).

§ 1.3. *Has the war on immigrants made us safer?*

Not likely. Though the United States can remove terrorist suspects without a trial by extradition, rendition or deportation, Nora V. Demleitner, *How Many Terrorists Are There? The Escalation in So-Called Terrorism Prosecutions*, 16:1 FED. SENT'G REP. 38 (Oct. 2003), the war on immigrants has led to no quantifiable victories in the "war" on terror. As Doris Meissner, former INS Commissioner, stated, "[t]he government is trying to engage in ill-conceived immigration clean-up activities in the name of anti-terrorism and perhaps in the belief that these are effective anti-terror tools. However, there is very little to show that they have made us safer." Presentation by Doris Meissner, Briefing Issued by the National Immigration Forum (March 6, 2003). *See also* Nora V. Demleitner, *Immigration Threats and Rewards: Effective Law Enforcement Tools in the "War" on Terrorism?*, 51 EMORY L.J. 1059 (2002) (immigration sanctions and rewards are flawed tools for fighting terrorism); Alexander L. Mounts, Note, *A Safer Nation?: How Driver's License Restrictions Hurt Immigrants and Noncitizens, Not Terrorists*, 37 IND. L. REV. 247 (2003); *but see* Jan Ting, *Immigration Law Reform After 9/11: What Has Been and What Still Needs To Be Done*, 17 TEMP. INT'L & COMP. L.J. 503 (2003).

America has tried this approach before with the Alien and Sedition Acts of 1798. *See* Ch. 58, 1 Stat. 570 (allowing the President to deport dangerous aliens); *see also* ch. 66, 1 stat. 577 and ch. 130, 2 Stat. 781. Perhaps learning from history would give us a better start in fighting terrorism. *See* James Bacchus, *Turning to Tacitus*, 37 VAND. J. TRANSNAT'L L. 631 (2004); Michael P. O'Connor & Celia M. Rumann, *Into the Fire: How To Avoid Getting Burned by the Same Mistakes Made Fighting Terrorism in Northern Ireland*, 24 CARDOZO L. REV. 1657 (2003).

§ 1.4. *Since 9/11 have any aliens been removed as "terrorists"?*

No. Though being a "terrorist" is a basis for deportation, the government has not deported a single person after 9/11 on this ground.

Nora V. Demleitner, *How Many Terrorists Are There? The Escalation in So-Called Terrorism Prosecutions*, 16:1 FED. SENT'G REP. 38 (Oct. 2003). In a sample of the 761 aliens arrested as a result of 9/11 terrorism investigations, the FBI exonerated almost all of any terrorism connection. Department of Justice, Office of the Inspector General, *The September 11 Detainees: A Review of the Treatment of Aliens Held on Immigration Charges in Connection with the Investigation of the September 11 Attacks* (Apr. 2003). Despite this, the Justice Department claims to have removed suspected terrorists for immigration status violations — begging the question of how giving up custody of suspected terrorists accomplishes the goal of fighting terrorism.

II. The Patriot Act and Other Statutes

A. Legislation

§ 1.5. *What did Congress do after 9/11?*

On October 26, 2001, Congress passed the Uniting and Strengthening America by Providing Appropriate Tools Required to Intercept and Obstruct Terrorism Act of 2001 (Patriot Act). Pub L. No. 107-56. On the same date, Congress also passed the Crimes Against Charitable Americans Act of 2001, Pub. L. No. 107-56, Title X, § 1011, 115 Stat. 396 (Oct. 26, 2001) (codified at 15 U.S.C. §§ 6101 note, 6102, 6106; 18 U.S.C. §§ 917, 2325), the Critical Infrastructures Protection Act of 2001, Pub. L. No. 107-56, Title X, § 1016, 115 Stat. 400 (Oct. 26, 2001) (codified at 42 U.S.C. § 5195c), the First Responders Assistance Act, Pub. L. No. 107-56, Title X, § 1005, 115 Stat. 393 (Oct. 26, 2001) (codified at 28 U.S.C. § 509 note), and the International Money Laundering Abatement and Anti-Terrorist Financing Act of 2001, Pub. L. No. 107-56, Title III, 115 Stat. 296 (Oct. 26, 2001) (codified at 12 U.S.C. §§ 248, 1828, 1829b, 1842, 1953, 3412, 3414, 3420; 15 U.S.C. §§ 1681u, 1681v; 18 U.S.C. §§ 470 to 474, 476 to 484, 493, 981, 982, 983 note, 1029, 1956, 1960, 2466; 22 U.S.C. § 262p-4r; 28 U.S.C. § 2467; 31 U.S.C. §§ 310, 311, 5311 note, 5312, 5313 note, 5314 note, 5317, 5318, 5318A, 5319, 5321, 5322, 5324, 5326, 5328, 5330, 5331, 5332, 5341). Congress has followed these with several other acts including the Enhanced Border Security and Visa Entry Reform Act of 2002, Pub. L. No. 107-173, 116 Stat. 543, which the President signed into law on May

14, 2002. *See President Signs Border Security Bill, Promises Swift Action on § 245(i)*, 79:21 INTERPRETER RELEASES 769 (May 20, 2002).

The Patriot Act never went through the standard committee process. The Senate Bill went straight to the floor and the Senate and House versions never went to a conference committee to resolve the conflicting provisions. Rather, differences between the two bills were worked out informally among the House and Senate leadership. *See* Rebecca L. Sigmund, *Chapter 8: Immigration and Border Security*, HOMELAND SECURITY LAW HANDBOOK, ABS Consulting/Government Institutes (Rockville, Md. 2003).

§ 1.6. *What did the Patriot Act and other legislation do?*

The Patriot Act is the most expansive antiterrorism measure in history and encompasses the following among many other provisions:

Expands the common definition of terrorism to include premeditated, politically motivated violent acts against civilians;

Defines grounds for barring admission to the United States and for deporting aliens already in the country;

Gives law enforcement broad new powers to search, employ electronic surveillance, and detain suspected terrorists;

Imposes stricter controls on countries participating in the Visa Waiver Program;

Requires interagency information sharing;

Calls for quick implementation of the entry-exit and foreign student tracking systems of the Illegal Immigration Reform and Immigrant Responsibility Act of 1996 (IIRAIRA).

The Enhanced Border Security and Visa Entry Reform Act (Border Security Act) followed the Patriot Act and provides for the following:

Greater information sharing between agencies;

An electronic immigration data system;

The implementation of entry-exit and foreign student tracking systems;

Limitations and enhanced security measures on visa applications from countries designated as state sponsors of terrorism;

The establishment of "terrorist lookout committees" in embassies and consulates.

Congress then passed the Homeland Security Act of 2002, reorganizing the government and abolishing the Immigration and Naturalization Service. *See* **Chapter 2: Immigration Law for Criminal Lawyers**.

§ 1.7. *How did the Patriot Act specifically affect aliens?*

The Patriot Act mandated detention of aliens suspected of terrorist activity, limited judicial review, increased protection of the northern border, and implemented modern technology to track aliens. For the criminal lawyer these changes raise serious implications including First, Fifth, and Sixth Amendment considerations. *See generally* STANLEY MAILMAN ET AL., UNITING AND STRENGTHENING AMERICA BY PROVIDING APPROPRIATE TOOLS REQUIRED TO INTERCEPT AND OBSTRUCT TERRORISM (USA PATRIOT ACT) ACT OF 2001: AN ANALYSIS (2002); David Cole, *Enemy Aliens*, 54 STAN. L. REV. 953 (2002). Title VI also preserved the immigration benefits for alien victims and families of the 9/11 attacks.

§ 1.8. *What previous anti-terrorist legislation existed?*

Modern anti-terror legislation started in the early 1960s with the air piracy statute implementing an international convention against hijacking commercial airlines. Nora V. Demleitner, *How Many Terrorists Are There? The Escalation in So-Called Terrorism Prosecutions*, 16:1 FED. SENT'G REP. 38 (Oct. 2003). Responding to the attack on the World Trade Center in 1993, Congress passed the Anti-Terrorism and Effective Death Penalty Act of 1996 (AEDPA) and the Illegal Immigration Reform and Immigrant Responsibility Act of 1996 (IIRAIRA). *See generally* Jason Binimow & Amy Bunk, Annotation, *Validity, Construction, and Operation of "Foreign Terrorist Organization" Provision of Anti-Terrorism and Effective Death Penalty Act (AEDPA), 8 U.S.C.A. § 1189*, 178 A.L.R. FED. 535 (2002).

At least one commentator argues that had these laws been implemented properly, they would have prevented the 9/11 attacks and we should not make "war on immigrants" part of the "war on terrorism." Margaret D. Stock, *United States Immigration Law in a World of Terror*, 7:10 BENDER'S IMMIGR. BULL. 559 (May 15, 2002).

B. "Terrorism" — Do We "Know It When We See It?"

§ 1.9. *Is "terrorism" easily defined?*

No, though the Patriot Act legally defines "terrorism," this does not solve the problem. In fiscal year 2002, federal prosecutors charged over 1,200 people with terrorism or national security crimes, an increase of over 100 percent. Different U.S. Attorney's offices, however, classify different crimes as "terrorism," raising "truth in labeling" concerns. Nora V. Demleitner, *How Many Terrorists Are There? The Escalation in So-Called Terrorism Prosecutions*, 16:1 FED. SENT'G REP. 38, 40 (Oct. 2003). For example, the New Jersey U.S. Attorney's Office classifies cases of foreign students who pay others to take the English language proficiency exams as "international terrorism." *Id.* The unavoidable conclusion is that the increase in "terrorism" prosecutions is not necessarily improving our security. *Id.* at 42. *See generally* Aaron J. Noteboom, *Terrorism: I Know It When I See It*, 81 OR. L. REV. 553 (2002) (a study of international and national "terrorism" definitions).

§ 1.10. *What is "terrorism"?*

The Patriot Act did not add new crimes but instead expanded the definitions of "terrorism," "terrorist activity," "engaging in terrorist activity," and "terrorist organization":

> **"Terrorism"** — is the "premeditated, politically motivated violence perpetrated against noncombatant targets by subnational groups or clandestine agents." 22 U.S.C. § 2656f(d)(2).
>
> **"Terrorist Activity"** — is any unlawful activity done anywhere including high-jacking, sabotage, assassination, or the use of firearms, explosives, biological or chemical agents, or nuclear or other weapons, with the intent to endanger safety or to cause substantial damage. Terrorist activity also includes threatening, attempting, conspiring, or using a "weapon or dangerous device" to commit the above listed crimes. To distinguish it from ordinary crimes, terrorist activity must be "other than for mere personal monetary gain." 8 U.S.C. § 1182(a)(3)(B)(iii)(V)(b).

"Engaging In Terrorist Activity" — includes committing, or inciting another to commit, a terrorist activity. It also includes planning, gathering information for, or soliciting funds or members for terrorist activity. Finally, it includes offering material support for the commission of terrorist activity, including providing a safe house, transportation, funds, weapons, or false documents. Thus, one can be guilty of engaging in terrorist activity for soliciting money or members for any "terrorist organization" even if the organization has other valid political or humanitarian ends. 8 U.S.C. § 1182(a)(3)(B)(iv)(IV)(bb), (IV)(cc), (V)(bb), (V)(cc), (VI)(cc).

The Patriot Act also provides a mechanism for defining a "foreign terrorist organization," outlined in the next subsection.

§ 1.11. *Do any of these terms encompass mens rea and actus reus?*

"Terrorism" under the statute may be the *mens rea* or the *actus reus* or the jurisdictional element of a crime. Nora V. Demleitner, *How Many Terrorists Are There? The Escalation in So-Called Terrorism Prosecutions*, 16:1 FED. SENT'G REP. 38 (Oct. 2003).

§ 1.12. *Could these terms include drug trafficking?*

If an action endangers the "national security" it could be "terrorist activity." Title 8 U.S.C. § 1189(c)(2) defines "national security" as "the national defense, foreign relations, or economic interests of the United States." The "War on Drugs" has often been phrased in terms of "national security," which raises the question of how far we are from defining common drug traffickers as "terrorists."

§ 1.13. *Does the Patriot Act mention the PLO?*

Yes. The Patriot Act specifically states that an "alien who is an officer, official, representative, or spokesman of the Palestine Liberation Organization is considered, for purposes of this chapter, to be engaged in a terrorist activity." 8 U.S.C. § 1182(a)(3)(B)(i).

C. "Foreign Terrorist Organizations"

§ 1.14. *What is a "terrorist organization"?*

Under the Patriot Act, the following is a terrorist organization:

> An organization the Secretary of State designates as such (upon notice to Congress and publication in the Federal Register);
>
> An organization otherwise so designated in consultation with the Attorney General; and
>
> Two or more individuals "whether organized or not" who engage in terrorist activities.

8 U.S.C. 1182(a)(3)(B)(vi)(I)-(III).

§ 1.15. *What criteria designates a "foreign terrorist organization"?*

The Secretary of State must find all of the following:

> The organization is a foreign organization;
>
> The organization engages in terrorist activity (as defined in 8 U.S.C. § 1182(a)(3)(B)) or terrorism (as defined in the Foreign Relations Authorization Act (22 U.S.C. § 2656f(d)(2)), or retains the capability and intent to engage in terrorist activity or terrorism; and
>
> The terrorist activity or terrorism of the organization threatens U.S. nationals or national security.

8 U.S.C. § 1189(a)(1).

§ 1.16. *Can an organization challenge the designation?*

Yes. The Secretary of State must notify the "foreign terrorist organization" of the impending designation and give the organization the chance to present contrary evidence. Nat'l Council of Resistance of Iran v. Dep't of State, 251 F.3d 192 (D.C. Cir. 2001).

§ 1.17. *Would the "foreign terrorist organization" designation support a later criminal charge?*

Given that the State Department's designation procedure has a very low standard, it might violate due process to use the designation as a predicate in a criminal prosecution. *See* Nat'l Council of Resistance of Iran v. Dep't of State, 251 F.3d 192 (D.C. Cir. 2001).

§ 1.18. *How long does the foreign terrorist organization designation last?*

Two years, and the State Department may redesignate it for another two years. Congress may block or revoke a redesignation at any time.

As of December 5, 2001, the State Department, at the Attorney General's request, had designated 39 groups as "terrorist organizations." Rebecca L. Sigmund, *Chapter 8: Immigration and Border Security*, HOMELAND SECURITY LAW HANDBOOK, ABS Consulting/Government Institutes (Rockville, Md. 2003) (*see* note 15 for a listing); Designation of 39 "Terrorist Organizations" Under the "PATRIOT USA Act," 66 Fed. Reg. 63,620 (Dec. 7, 2001); John W. Whitehead & Steven H. Aden, *Forfeiting "Enduring Freedom" for "Homeland Security": A Constitutional Analysis of the USA Patriot Act and the Justice Department's Anti-Terrorism Initiatives*, 51 AM. U. L. REV. 1081 (2002).

§ 1.19. *What does the designation mean for U.S. citizens and banks?*

Citizens may not support designated terrorist organizations and U.S. financial institutions must freeze their assets.

The AEDPA already prohibited assisting designated organizations and required financial institutions to block these organization's funds. *See Naturalization, Dual Citizenship and Retention of Foreign Citizenship: A Survey*, 73:16 INTERPRETER RELEASES 521 (Apr. 22, 1996), *cited in Giving Voice to the Vulnerable: On Representing Detained Immigrant and Refugee Children*, 78:39 INTERPRETER RELEASES 1604 (Oct. 8, 2001).

See generally Randolph N. Jonakait, *The Mens Rea for the Crime of Providing Material Resources to a Foreign Terrorist Organization*, 56 BAYLOR L. REV. 861 (2004).

D. The Patriot Act and Foreign Governments

§ 1.20. *Does the Patriot Act allow the U.S. government to give foreign governments access to records?*

Yes. Our government can now provide another country State Department records to prevent, investigate, or punish terrorism. 8 U.S.C. § 1202(f)(2). Before the Patriot Act, only U.S. law enforcement agencies could get State Department records relating to issuing or refusing visas. Our government can now share this information with any country regardless of whether it is democratic or respects human rights.

Other countries, of course, had their own responses to 9/11. *See generally* Kim Lane Scheppele, *Other People's Patriot Acts: Europe's Response to September 11*, 50 LOY. L. REV. 89 (2004).

III. Immigration Consequences and Terrorism

For a more complete presentation of immigration consequences of criminal conviction, see **Chapter 6: Alien Employment Crimes.**

A. New Grounds of Inadmissibility and Deportation

§ 1.21. *Can a terrorist enter the country?*

Not legally. The Patriot Act amended 8 U.S.C. § 1182(a)(3)(B)(i) to provide that an alien who meets one of the following conditions is not admissible:

1. Has engaged in a terrorist activity;
2. A consular officer or the Justice Department knows, or has reasonable ground to believe, is engaged in or is likely to engage after entry in any terrorist activity (as defined in 8 U.S.C. § 1182(a)(3)(B)(iv));
3. Has, under circumstance indicating an intention to cause death or serious bodily harm, incited terrorist activity;
4. Is a representative (as defined in 8 U.S.C. § 1182(a)(3)(B)(v)) of —
   a. a foreign terrorist organization, as designated by the Secretary of State under 22 U.S.C. § 2656f, or
   b. a political, social or other similar group whose public endorsement of acts of terrorist activity the Secretary of State has determined undermines United State efforts to reduce or eliminate terrorist activities;
5. Is a member of a foreign terrorist organization, as designated by the Secretary under 22 U.S.C. § 2656f, or which the alien knows or should have known is a terrorist organization;
6. Has used the alien's position of prominence within any country to endorse or espouse terrorist activity, or to persuade others to support terrorist activity or a terrorist organization, in a

way that the Secretary of State has determined undermines U.S. efforts to reduce or eliminate terrorist activities; or

7. Is the spouse or child of an alien who is inadmissible under this section, if the activity causing the alien to be found inadmissible occurred within the previous five years.

§ 1.22. *Can an alien be excluded just for what he believes?*

Now yes. Aliens can be excluded for "endorsing" terrorism. The Patriot Act amended 8 U.S.C. § 1182(a)(3) (2000) to prohibit any alien from entering the United States who represents a "foreign terrorist organization," is a member of "a political, social, or other similar group whose public endorsement of acts undermines U.S. efforts to reduce or eliminate terrorist activities." USA Patriot Act, Pub. L. No. 107-56, § 411(a), 115 Stat. 272, 346 (2001). "Material support" includes such activities as transportation, operating safe houses, and communications. Indeed, even those who only support or encourage others to support such organizations are subject to exclusion. USA Patriot Act, Pub. L. No. 107-56, § 411, 115 Stat. 272, 346 (2001).

§ 1.23. *What about free speech?*

Aliens may not have it. The United States has frequently deported aliens upon suspicion that they support unpopular political positions. *See, e.g.*, Galvan v. Press, 347 U.S. 522, 74 S. Ct. 737 (upholding deportation of 30-year resident for brief Communist Party membership), *reh'g denied*, 348 U.S. 852, 75 S. Ct. 17 (1954); Harisiades v. Shaughnessy, 342 U.S. 580, 72 S. Ct. 512 (upholding deportation for former Communist Party membership), *reh'g denied*, 343 U.S. 936, 72 S. Ct. 767 (1952); *see also* Lory Diana Rosenberg, *Right to Protest and Immigration Status*, 9:19 BENDER'S IMMIGR. BULL. 1169 (Oct. 1, 2004); John W. Whitehead & Steven H. Aden, *Forfeiting "Enduring Freedom" for "Homeland Security": A Constitutional Analysis of the USA Patriot Act and the Justice Department's Anti-Terrorism Initiatives*, 51 AM. U. L. REV. 1081 (2002).

§ 1.24. *Is there any defense to this ground of inadmissibility?*

Only if the alien can "demonstrate that he did not know and should not reasonably have known, that the [above acts] would further the organization's terrorist activity."

§ 1.25. *Were "terrorists" deported before the Patriot Act?*

Yes, IIRAIRA gave the former INS power to deport anyone whom it believed was engaged in terrorist activities and limited an alien's possible deportation relief. *See* Nathan W. Gordon & Louis A. Gordon, *Discretionary Relief from Deportation Curtailed*, LOS ANGELES LAW., Mar. 2002, at 52. Also, IIRAIRA's "expedited removal" provision granted INS inspectors broad and unreviewable authority to deny entry and prevent aliens from getting a visa for at least five years.

B. Secret Deportations and Evidence

§ 1.26. *Can the government conduct secret deportations?*

Yes. After 9/11 the Justice Department barred the press from all "special interest" removal proceedings. The Justice Department can designate a removal hearing as "special interest" if it alleges the case poses national security concerns. Immigration judges cannot easily challenge the prosecutors' decisions, 8 C.F.R. §§ 1003.27, 1003.31, 1003.46, and neither the judges nor the parties can publicize the cases. 8 C.F.R. § 1003.46(f)(2)(i). *See* Gabriel Hasti Fakhrai-Bayrooti, Comment, *Denial of Public Access to Deportation Hearings: Is It Protecting National Security or Violating Fundamental Liberties?*, 25 WHITTIER L. REV. 203 (2003); Jonathan L. Hafetz, *The First Amendment and the Right of Access to Deportation Proceedings*, 40 CAL. W. L. REV. 265 (2004); Heidi Kitrosser, *Secrecy in the Immigration Courts and Beyond: Considering the Right to Know in the Administrative State*, 39 HARV. C.R.-C.L. L. REV. 95 (2004); S. Oberfield, Note, *Press Rights in Peril: The Department of Justice Infringes upon Press Liberties by Conducting "Special Interest" Removal Proceedings*, 13 FORDHAM INTELL. PROP. MEDIA & ENT. L.J. 1209, 1212 (2003); Alice Cole Ortiz, Comment, *Our "Eternal Struggle Between Liberty and Security:" A First Amendment Right of Access to Deportation Hearings*, 55 BAYLOR L. REV. 1203 (2003).

Before 9/11, immigration judges decided whether to close their courts only if the situation warranted it. *Compare* 8 C.F.R. § 3.27 (1997) *with* 8 C.F.R. § 1003.27 (2003).

§ 1.27. *Have secret deportation hearings been challenged?*

Yes, resulting in a split between the Third Circuit upholding closed deportations, North Jersey Media Group v. Ashcroft, 308 F.3d 198 (3d Cir. 2002), *cert. denied,* 538 U.S. 1056, 123 S. Ct. 2215 (2003), and the Sixth Circuit, Detroit Free Press v. Ashcroft, 303 F.3d 681 (6th Cir. 2002), *motion granted in part,* 2002 U.S. Dist. LEXIS 19991 (E.D. Mich. Oct. 7, 2002), *reh'g en banc denied,* 2003 U.S. App. LEXIS 1278 (2003). *See* Shirley C. Rivadeneira, Comment, *The Closure of Removal Proceedings of September 11th Detainees: An Analysis of* Detroit Free Press, North Jersey Media Group *and the Creppy Directive,* 55 ADMIN. L. REV. 843 (2003). The Supreme Court denied certiorari and the Supreme Court has not considered a press access case since 1986. *See* Press-Enterprise Co. v. Super. Court of Cal., 478 U.S. 1, 13–14, 106 S. Ct. 2735 (1986) (press has qualified First Amendment right of access to preliminary hearings); *see generally* Rashad Hussain, *Security with Transparency: Judicial Review in "Special Interest" Immigration Proceedings,* 113 YALE L.J. 1333 (2004); Andrew J. Walkup, Comment, *Please Take Back Your Huddled Masses: A Look at the First Amendment Right to Access Deportation Hearings After September 11, 2001,* 22 ST. LOUIS U. PUB. L. REV. 593 (2003).

§ 1.28. *What about secret evidence?*

The Patriot Act authorizes secret evidence in immigration court. Previously, secret evidence was allowed only in deportation hearings before the Alien Terrorist Removal Court. *See* 8 U.S.C. §§ 1531 to 1537. The former INS, however, long took the position that it could use secret evidence in detention hearings. *See generally* Kelley Brooke Snyder, *A Clash of Values: Classified Information in Immigration Proceedings,* 88 VA. L. REV. 447 (2002).

§ 1.29. *Has the Justice Department closed the deportation hearings of many detainees?*

Yes. The Department of Justice has subjected roughly 800 detainees to closed deportation hearings. *Counterterrorism and Immigrant Rights Two Years Later,* 80:39 INTERPRETER RELEASES 1404 (Oct. 13, 2003).

C. Excluding the Family of "Terrorists"

§ 1.30. *What about the family members of aliens thought to be terrorists?*

If a spouse or parent commits a terrorist act within five years, the spouse or child is barred from entry into the United States. 8 U.S.C. § 1182(a)(3)(B)(i)(VII).

Attorney General Ashcroft justified the exclusion of family by stating that the "ability of terrorists to move freely across borders and operate within the United States is critical to their capacity to inflict damage on the citizens and facilities in the United States." *Homeland Defense Before the Senate Comm. on the Judiciary*, 107th Cong. (2001) (Sept. 25, 2001), *cited in* John W. Whitehead & Steven H. Aden, *Forfeiting "Enduring Freedom" for "Homeland Security": A Constitutional Analysis of the USA Patriot Act and the Justice Department's Anti-Terrorism Initiatives*, 51 AM. U. L. REV. 1081 n.91 (2002).

§ 1.31. *Can a spouse or child of a terrorist still argue for entry?*

Yes. If the spouse or child can show that he or she "did not know or should not reasonably have known of the activity causing the alien to be found inadmissible," he or she may gain entry. Also, if a "consular officer or Attorney General has reasonable grounds to believe [the alien spouse or child] has renounced the activity causing the alien to be found inadmissible ...," the Patriot Act provides an exemption from exclusion. 8 U.S.C. § 1182(a)(3)(B)(ii)(I), (II).

D. Aliens and Fund-raising

§ 1.32. *Can political fund-raising get an alien removed?*

Yes, any solicitation of "funds or other things of value" for "terrorist activity" or a "terrorist organization" is a ground for deportation. 8 U.S.C. § 1182(a)(3)(B)(iv)(IV)(aa), (bb), (B)(iv)(V). *See* Sahar R. Aziz, Note, *The Laws on Providing Material Support to Terrorist Organizations: The Erosion of Constitutional Rights or a Legitimate Tool for Preventing Terrorism?*, 9 TEX. J. C.L. & C.R. 45–92 (2003).

§ 1.33. *What if the alien was only supporting a "humanitarian" purpose?*

The alien's purpose is immaterial, even if the alien only raises funds for the humanitarian division of a listed terrorist organization. 8 U.S.C. § 1182(a)(3)(B). The State Department lists the terrorist organizations, but also supporting persons engaged in terrorist conduct is grounds for removal. 8 U.S.C. § 1182(a)(3)(B)(vii)(III).

§ 1.34. *Does the alien have a defense?*

If the alien can "demonstrate that he did not know, and should not reasonably have known, that the act would further the organization's terrorist activity," 8 U.S.C. § 1182(a)(3)(B)(iv)(IV)(cc), (V)(cc), (VI)(dd), he may have a ground to seek admission. This defense is available only to aliens who solicited for the terrorist organizations described in clause (iv)(III).

§ 1.35. *Do these new rules apply retroactively?*

Yes, the rules apply retroactively to any "actions taken by an alien before, on, or after" enactment. The only exception is if the organization was not designated a terrorist organization during the alien's activity. 8 U.S.C. § 1182 n.4.

E. Aliens and Money Laundering

§ 1.36. *What happens to aliens who launder money?*

Aliens who launder money are inadmissible. 8 U.S.C. § 1182(a)(2)(I)(i). Also, any alien "who a consular officer or the Attorney General knows is, or has been, a knowing aider, abettor, assister, conspirator, or colluder with others" in money laundering is inadmissible. 8 U.S.C. § 1182(a)(2)(I)(ii). *See generally* Eric J. Gouvin, *Bringing Out the Big Guns: The USA Patriot Act, Money Laundering, and the War on Terrorism*, 55 BAYLOR L. REV. 955 (2003); Walter Perkel, *Money Laundering and Terrorism: Informal Value Transfer Systems*, 41 AM. CRIM. L. REV. 183 (2004).

§ 1.37. *Who decides whether the alien is a money launderer?*

"[A] consular officer or the Attorney General" decides whether the alien is a money launderer, 8 U.S.C. § 1182(a)(2)(I), if he "knows or has reason to believe" that the alien "has engaged, is engaging, or seeks to enter the United States to engage" in money laundering. 8 U.S.C. § 1182(a)(2)(I)(i).

§ 1.38. *How does immigration law define money laundering?*

An alien launders money when he engages "in an offense which is described in section 1956 or 1957 of title 18, U.S. Code (relating to laundering of monetary instruments)." 8 U.S.C. § 1182(a)(2)(I)(i). 18 U.S.C. § 1956 punishes the "laundering of monetary instruments" "knowing that the property involved in a financial transaction represents the proceeds of some form of unlawful activity" and 18 U.S.C. § 1957 punishes "engaging in monetary transactions in property derived from specified unlawful activity."

§ 1.39. *What if the alien has not yet engaged in money laundering?*

An alien will be excluded if a consular officer or the Attorney General "has reason to believe" that the alien "seeks to enter the United States to engage" in money laundering. 8 U.S.C. § 1182(a)(2)(I)(i). Thus, the alien can be excluded for what someone in the government thinks he may do in the future.

§ 1.40. *How will the government identify alien money launderers?*

The Secretary of State, in conjunction with the Attorney General, the Secretary of the Treasury, and the Director of the Central Intelligence Agency establishes a "watch list" identifying known or suspected money launderers. Consular or other federal officials check the list before they issue visas or allow admission to the United States. *See* 8 U.S.C. § 1182 statutory note.

§ 1.41. *What if the alien is not convicted of money laundering?*

The government does not need a criminal conviction to justify exclusion. 8 U.S.C. § 1182(a)(2)(A)(i).

§ 1.42. *Is there any time limit?*

No. The Patriot Act applies to any alien ever suspected of money laundering and if these aliens leave the United States the government may deny their admission back into the country.

§ 1.43. *What office handles investigations of money laundering?*

The new Executive Office for Terrorist Financing and Financial Crimes (EOTF/FC) now handles money laundering investigations. This Office now leads the Justice Department's efforts to combat terrorist financing and other financial crimes, assuming many of the responsibilities once held by the Office of Enforcement.

IV. Detention of Aliens on Terrorist Allegations

§ 1.44. *Will the government release an alien terrorist suspect?*

No. The Patriot Act specifies mandatory detention of an alien the government certifies as a terrorist. 8 U.S.C. § 1226A(a). *See generally* Leslie Castro et al., Panel Discussion, *Perversities and Prospects: Immigration Enforcement and Detention in the Antiterrorism Aftermath*, 9 GEO. J. ON POVERTY L. & POL'Y 1 (2002).

For issues related to detention of citizens, see Jon Eldredge, *Detainment of United States Citizens as Enemy Combatants Under a Fourth Amendment Historical Analysis*, 6 J.L. & SOC. CHALLENGES 19 (2004).

§ 1.45. *Who "certifies" that the alien is a suspected terrorist?*

The U.S. Attorney General or Deputy Attorney General may certify that an alien is a terrorist. 8 U.S.C. § 1226A(a)(3), (4).

§ 1.46. *What is the standard for certification?*

An alien will be certified a "terrorist" if there are "reasonable grounds to believe" he is a terrorist or engaged in terrorist activity or threatens national security. 8 U.S.C. § 1226A(a)(3). This appears to be an even lower standard than that which justifies the brief investigative stop of *Terry v. Ohio*, 392 U.S. 1, 88 S. Ct. 1868 (1968). *See* Tova Indritz, *Legislation: Immigration Aspects of the USA Patriot Act*, THE CHAMPION, Apr. 2002, at 43.

§ 1.47. *Is the Secretary of State's determination reviewable?*

No. If he or she has "reasonable grounds to believe" that the organization is terrorist, the Secretary of State has unfettered power to designate any group, foreign or domestic, as a terrorist organization by publishing it in the Federal Register. *See* 8 U.S.C. § 1226A(a)(3). Indeed, it appears the government need not inform the alien of the basis of the terrorist certification or give a hearing or trial. The Attorney General need not establish even the lesser immigration standard of clear, convincing, and unequivocal evidence, much less proof beyond a reasonable doubt. As noted below, only limited habeas corpus review is available. Shirin Sinnar, *Patriotic or Unconstitutional? The Mandatory Detention of Aliens Under the USA Patriot Act*, 2003 STANFORD L. REV. 1419.

§ 1.48. *Can an alien certified as a suspected terrorist post bond?*

No, detention is mandatory. These aliens remain in custody even if the immigration judge orders their release and regardless of whether they are eligible for deportation relief. The Bush administration produced a federal regulation, 8 C.F.R. § 3.19(H)(2)(i), expanding the government's power to detain aliens. This rule allows for an alien's detention even after an immigration judge has ordered him released for lack of evidence. The Bureau of Immigration and Customs Enforcement (ICE) can set aside any immigration judge's release order whenever it believes the alien is a danger to the community or a flight risk. All ICE need do is indicate its intention to appeal to the Board of Immigration Appeals (BIA) within 10 days. If ICE then files a notice of appeal, the alien remains in detention while the BIA decides. If the BIA orders release, ICE can set aside that order under the new regulation by certifying the case to the Attorney General. 8 C.F.R. § 3.19(H)(2)(i).

§ 1.49. *How long is the detention supposed to last?*

A certified suspected terrorist can be detained for seven days without criminal or immigration charges. 8 U.S.C. § 1226A(a)(5). Aliens not charged within seven days must be released. The only review is habeas corpus. However, the government has generally used the broader "national security" provisions to mandate the continuing detention of certain aliens. The Attorney General must review this detention every six months. Continued detention is allowed if the alien cannot be removed to another country in the "reasonably foreseeable future" and the government shows that the alien's release would jeopardize national security or the safety of any individual or community.

§ 1.50. *What if the suspected alien is charged with an immigration offense?*

If the government charges the alien with any immigration violation, it will mandatorily detain him until deportation. 8 U.S.C. § 1226.

§ 1.51. *If the alien wins deportation relief, will he be released?*

No. The Patriot Act allows his detention even if the immigration judge grants him relief from deportation. 8 U.S.C. § 1226A(a)(2). The only way this person may get released is if the Attorney General decides to withdraw the terrorist certification. *Id.*

§ 1.52. *If the alien is ordered deported, will the government send him home?*

Not necessarily. The Patriot Act allows the government to continue to detain an alien who is under a final order of deportation for up to six months before the alien has a right to have his detention reviewed. 8 U.S.C. § 1226A(a)(7). The detention can extend beyond this if the government shows that "the release of the alien will threaten the national security of the United States or the safety of the community or any person." 8 U.S.C. § 1226A(a)(6).

The constitutional validity of this provision is questionable after the Supreme Court's decision in *Zadvydas v. Davis*, 533 U.S. 678, 121 S. Ct. 2491 (2001) (illegal to indefinitely detain aliens under non-executable deportation orders). *See* Laurie Joyce, *INS Detention Practices Post-*Zadvydas v. Davis, 79:22 INTERPRETER RELEASES 809 (May 24, 2002).

§ 1.53. *What about habeas corpus?*

The Patriot Act allows for habeas corpus review in the District of Columbia Circuit Court of Appeals, the United States Supreme Court or any justice of that Court, or in any district court having jurisdiction. 8 U.S.C. § 1226A(b)(1), (b)(2)(A). The alien, however, has no right to free counsel. *See* INS v. Lopez-Mendoza, 468 U.S. 1032, 104 S. Ct. 3479 (1984).

§ 1.54. *Who has been detained by the government?*

Reportedly, the government detained up to 5,000 males between the ages of 16 and 33 from Middle Eastern countries during the months following the Patriot Act's enactment. Rebecca L. Sigmund, *Chapter 8: Immigration and Border Security*, HOMELAND SECURITY

LAW HANDBOOK 216, ABS Consulting/Government Institutes (Rockville, Md. 2003).

§ 1.55. *What have been the criticisms of the alien detention provisions?*

The Department of Justice, Office of Inspector General documents that the detention of the above listed aliens has led to abusive conditions of many innocent persons who do not have even an attenuated connection to a terrorist suspect. The FBI has categorized aliens to be of "high interest" on "little or no concrete information." Department of Justice, Office of the Inspector General, *The September 11 Detainees: A Review of the Treatment of Aliens Held on Immigration Charges in Connection with the Investigation of the September 11 Attacks* 18 (Apr. 2003). Prison officials put "high interest" detainees in the most restrictive maximum-security conditions and blocked all outside communication. For weeks detainees could receive no calls or visits and were under 23-hour lockdown. *Id.* After the lockdown ended, access to visitors was still strictly limited, even access to counsel. *Id.* at 112; *Counterterrorism and Immigrant Rights Two Years Later*, 80:39 INTERPRETER RELEASES 1401, 1402 (Oct. 13, 2003).

V. How 9/11 Affected Various Types of Immigrants

§ 1.56. *What does the Patriot Act state about discrimination?*

The Patriot Act condemns discrimination against Arab Americans and Muslim Americans, stating that "[t]he concept of individual responsibility for wrongdoing is sacrosanct in American society, and applies equally to all religious, racial, and ethnic groups." Patriot Act § 102(a)(3)). This statement, however, appears as so much window dressing given the large numbers of aliens from Muslim countries singled out. Seth M. Haines, *Rounding Up the Usual Suspects: The Rights of Arab Detainees in a Post-September 11 World*, 57 ARK. L. REV. 105 (2004). Moreover, the Department of Justice's Inspector General has found "significant problems" with the treatment of these post 9/11 detainees. *DOJ's Inspector General Finds 'Significant Problems' in Treatment of Post-9/11 Detainees*, 80:23 INTERPRETER RELEASES: REPORT AND ANALYSIS OF IMMIGRATION AND NATIONALITY LAW 805 (June 9, 2003); *IG Finds Significant*

Problems with Handling of Post-September 11 Detainees, 8:13 BENDER'S IMMIGR. BULL. 1101 (July 1, 2003).

A policy of anti-discrimination conforms to a long history of tolerance toward Islam and Muslims. *See* James H. Hutson, *The Founding Fathers and Islam: Library Papers Show Early Tolerance for Muslim Faith*, LIBR. CONGRESS INFORMATION BULL. (May 2002).

A. Men from Muslim Countries: "Let's Try Racial Profiling Again"

§ 1.57. *How did 9/11 affect men from Muslim countries?*

Though the Patriot Act condemns discrimination against Arab Americans, Muslims, and South Asian Americans, government actions have specifically affected men from Muslim countries:

> The State Department announced that males between the ages of 16 to 44 from certain Muslim countries will undergo an additional 20-day security check as their applications are checked against FBI databases.
>
> The government has planned to interview 5,000 Middle Eastern men between the ages of 18 and 33 from countries linked to terrorism. While the interviews are "voluntary," and the men interviewed are not "suspected of any terrorist activity," should the interview lead to further investigation, or suspicion of criminal activity, the men may be immediately held without bond. *See generally* David A. Harris, *Racial Profiling Revisited: "Just Common Sense" in the Fight Against Terror?*, CRIM. JUST., Summer 2002, at 36; Laurie L. Levenson, Essay, *Detention, Material Witnesses & The War on Terrorism*, 35 LOY. L.A. L. REV. 1217 (2002); Jodi Wilgoren, *Prosecutors Begin Effort to Interview 5,000, but Basic Questions Remain*, N.Y. TIMES, Nov. 15, 2001, at B7.
>
> On January 8, 2002, the Justice Department prioritized the apprehension and removal from the United States of 4,000 to 6,000 men from particular countries of origin, out of more than 300,000 "absconders" whose deportability has been finalized and who have exhausted their administrative and judicial appeal rights.
>
> On November 6, 2002, the government announced that it would require special registration of male visitors to the

> United States from Iraq, Iran, Libya, Sudan, and Syria. Registration of Certain Nonimmigrant Aliens from Designated Countries, 67 Fed. Reg. 67,766 (Nov. 6, 2002). The government later expanded this to cover male visitors from another 20 countries: Afghanistan, Algeria, Bahrain, Eritrea, Lebanon, Morocco, North Korea, Oman, Qatar, Somalia, Tunisia, United Arab Emirates, Yemen, Pakistan, Saudi Arabia, Bangladesh, Egypt, Indonesia, Jordan, and Kuwait.

Richard R. Banks, *Racial Profiling and Antiterrorism Efforts*, 89 CORNELL L. REV. 1201 (2004); Jan Ting, *Immigration Law Reform After 9/11: What Has Been and What Still Needs To Be Done*, 17 TEMP. INT'L & COMP. L.J. 503 (2003).

§ 1.58. *Has the government charged these men from Muslim countries?*

No. Rather, immigration law has become a crucial component of law enforcement. The only charges brought against any of these immigrants have been minor immigration violations or ordinary offenses. Prosecution was chosen for the crimes or for immigration violations depending on which was more "efficacious." Nora V. Demleitner, *How Many Terrorists Are There? The Escalation in So-Called Terrorism Prosecutions*, 16:1 FED. SENT'G REP. 41 (Oct. 2003); Department of Justice, Office of the Inspector General, *The September 11 Detainees: A Review of the Treatment of Aliens Held on Immigration Charges in Connection with Investigation of the September 11 Attacks* 13 (Apr. 2003).

§ 1.59. *What is the historical precedent?*

On February 19, 1942, President Franklin D. Roosevelt signed Executive Order 9066 authorizing the removal of ethnic Japanese from the west coast. More than 100,000 people — men, women, and children, a great many of them U.S. citizens — were placed in concentration camps. History has not viewed these actions kindly. *See generally* GREG ROBINSON, BY ORDER OF THE PRESIDENT: FDR AND THE INTERNMENT OF JAPANESE AMERICANS (2002); Frank H. Wu, *Profiling in the Wake of September 11: The Precedent of the Japanese American Internment*, CRIM. JUST., Summer 2002, at 52. Other commentators, however, argue that the comparison is not well founded because the government now does not discriminate on appearance, skin color, race, ethnicity, or religion. Rather, the profiling is based on age, gender, and country of origin and such profiling is legal. *See* Jan Ting, *Immigration Law Reform After 9/11: What Has Been and What Still Needs To Be Done*, 17 TEMP. INT'L & COMP. L.J. 503 (2003).

B. Alien Students

§ 1.60. *Are foreign students monitored?*

Yes. In 1996, as part of IIRAIRA, Congress required the former INS to create the Coordinated Interagency Partnership for Regulating International Students (CIPRIS) system. CIPRIS was to be an electronic database for tracking foreign students and providing information to the INS of students violating their visas or committing crimes. Because of logistical problems and objections from school administrators, CIPRIS was never fully implemented. *See* Margaret D. Stock, *United States Immigration Law in a World of Terror*, 7:10 BENDER'S IMMIGR. BULL. 559 (May 15, 2002).

§ 1.61. *What is different after 9/11?*

The Patriot Act expanded student monitoring to include all educational institutions that receive foreign students. Full implementation is mandated. *See Statements of Note on Terrorist Attack: Foreign Student Monitoring After September 11*, 6:19 BENDER'S IMMIGR. BULL. 1041 (Oct. 1, 2001). This includes flight schools, language training schools, and vocational schools. The program is known as the Student and Exchange Visitor Information System (SEVIS).

The Border Security Act mandated the collection of additional data to increase student monitoring. Now, foreign students are under electronic monitoring from admittance to the United States through acceptance at school, visa issuance, a change in schools or ending their studies. Border Security Act § 501. In addition, the date of the student's entry, port of entry, date of school enrollment, date the student leaves school (e.g., graduates, quits), and the degree program or field of study is now recorded. Student visa applicants must also provide the consular officer their address, the names and addresses of relatives, and names of contacts in their residence country to verify information about the student visa applicant and previous work history, if any, including the name and addresses of employers. *See generally* Rebecca L. Sigmund, *Chapter 8: Immigration and Border Security*, HOMELAND SECURITY LAW HANDBOOK, ABS Consulting/Government Institutes (Rockville, Md. 2003); Kiera LoBreglio, *The Border Security and Immigration Im-*

provement Act: A Modern Solution to a Historic Problem?, 78 ST. JOHN'S L. REV. 933 (2004).

§ 1.62. *What does this mean for alien students?*

They must be in full compliance with their student status and have little freedom to carry less than a full class load or to leave school. Once this system is fully operational, the government will track nearly one million nonimmigrant foreign students and exchange visitors in the United States.

§ 1.63. *Does it matter that the alien student has no connection with terrorism?*

No.

§ 1.64. *What if a student does not report to school?*

Schools will now notify authorities if a student does not report to school more than 30 days after the class registration deadline.

§ 1.65. *What must schools do?*

As of January 30, 2003, all schools must now utilize SEVIS to issue a certificate of eligibility for nonimmigrant students (using the new form I-20). Schools have expressed concern regarding the technological feasibility of disseminating this information as well as regarding privacy issues.

§ 1.66. *Has SEVIS affected academic exchange regulations?*

No, SEVIS does not change the regulations governing academic exchange programs. SEVIS only gathers information and tracks academic visitors. It does not replace reporting requirements under other programs or regulations. SEVIS, for example, does not satisfy the address reporting requirements imposed by the National Security Entry-Exit Registration System (NSEERS).

C. Refugees

§ 1.67. *How has the war on terror affected refugees?*

Adversely. This is ironic given that by definition refugees have fled from violence and terror. In fiscal year 2002, the United States admitted the lowest number of refugees in 25 years, a trend that continued for fiscal year 2003. THE REFUGEE COUNCIL USA, U.S.

REFUGEE ADMISSIONS PROGRAM FOR FISCAL YEAR 2004 4 (May 2003), *reported in Counterterrorism and Immigrant Rights Two Years Later*, 80:39 INTERPRETER RELEASES 1401, 1402 (Oct. 13, 2003). Moreover, in mid-March 2003 the Department of Homeland Security announced that it would begin detaining all arriving asylum seekers from 33 countries in which al Qaeda and other terrorist groups have a presence. Department of Homeland Security, Fact Sheet, Operation Liberty Shield (March 17, 2003). This program was later suspended.

See generally Stanley Mailman & Stephen Yale-Loehr, *Detaining and Criminalizing Asylum Seekers*, 8:9 BENDER'S IMMIGR. BULL. 763 (May 1, 2003).

§ 1.68. *What other Justice Department actions adversely affected refugees?*

General policies as well as local U.S. Attorney's offices have also adversely affected asylum seekers. For example, in Miami the U.S. Attorney's office now prosecutes asylum seekers who provide false documents, effectively criminalizing migrants fleeing persecution and terror. *Counterterrorism and Immigrant Rights Two Years Later*, 80:39 INTERPRETER RELEASES 1401, 1403 (Oct. 13, 2003).

§ 1.69. *How have how these actions affected the war on terrorism?*

Commentators note that terrorists gain little advantage by entering as a refugee. Most refugees spend considerable time in refugee camps with only a remote chance of selection for U.S. resettlement. Indeed, the September 11 terrorists entered on temporary visas, not as refugees. *Counterterrorism and Immigrant Rights Two Years Later*, 80:39 INTERPRETER RELEASES 1401 (Oct. 13, 2003).

VI. Alien Terrorism Victims

§ 1.70. *What about aliens who themselves were victims of 9/11?*

The 9/11 attacks included victims from 40 counties. Rebecca L. Sigmund, *Chapter 8: Immigration and Border Security*, HOMELAND SECURITY LAW HANDBOOK, ABS Consulting/Government Institutes (Rockville, Md. 2003). The Patriot Act offers some relief if an alien or his family member was injured or killed on 9/11 or if, because of the attack, an alien was not able to meet an immigration application deadline. For example, a petition for adjustment of status will continue even if the alien sponsoring the petition was killed. Also, grandparents of any child whose parents died in the attack may qualify for special status and the public charge grounds for excluding aliens will be waived. If aliens were unable to travel because of a death or injury, various immigration requirements are waived or suspended. *See* IRA J. KURZBAN, KURZBAN'S IMMIGRATION LAW SOURCEBOOK 638–41(9th ed. 2004) (outlining petition procedures); *see generally* 8 U.S.C. § 1182(a)(4).

VII. Alien Informants

§ 1.71. *What does the Patriot Act do for informants?*

For several years there has been an "S" visa classification (a.k.a. "Snitch visa") allowing informants to receive visas. The Patriot Act expanded this program to give special immigrant status to those who provide useful and reliable information about suspected terrorists or criminal organizations. *See generally* Douglas A. Kash, *Hunting Terrorists Using Confidential Informant Reward Programs,* FBI LAW ENFORCEMENT BULL., Apr. 2002, at 2. The program is known as the Responsible Cooperators Program. The visa allows an alien to remain in the United States for three years even if in the country illegally. For those who are not eligible for the S-visa but who provide useful information, the government may consider delaying removal proceedings.

§ 1.72. *What issues remain unclear regarding the "S" visa program?*

It remains unclear how the government will determine the reliability of the informant's information. The rules provide that the Justice Department must recommend, and the Attorney General and Secretary of State must agree, that the information is useful and reliable. According to the Attorney General, the information does not have to lead to a conviction and may even appear insignificant to the informant.

VIII. Military Commissions

§ 1.73. *How were the current Military Commissions created?*

On November 13, 2001, President Bush issued a Military Order entitled The Detention, Treatment, and Trial of Certain Non-Citizens in the War Against Terrorism, 66 Fed. Reg. 57,833 (Nov. 13, 2001) (the Order) in his constitutional capacity as Commander in Chief of the Armed Forces. Christopher M. Evans, *Terrorism on Trial: The President's Constitutional Authority to Order the Prosecution of Suspected Terrorists by Military Commission*, 51:6 DUKE L.J. 1831 (2002). In response, the American Bar Association (ABA) passed a resolution in February 2002 calling for such Commissions to incorporate traditional American standards of fairness, including the presumption of innocence, proof beyond a reasonable doubt, unanimous verdicts in death penalty cases, and appeals to the Supreme Court. The ABA also called for Commission proceedings to be open to the public and press or, when necessary, to be closed except to trial observers with appropriate security clearances. The Bush Administration argued that the ABA resolution was premature because it had not yet issued any specifics for the Commissions. Charles Lane, *ABA Proposes Courts-Martial Legal Rights for Terror Suspects*, WASHINGTON POST, Feb. 5, 2002, at A2.

See generally George P. Fletcher, *On Justice and War: Contradictions in the Proposed Military Tribunals*, 25 HARV. J.L. & PUB. POL'Y 635 (2002); BrigGen Thomas L. Hemingway, *In Defense of Military Commissions*, 35 U. MEM. L. REV. 1 (2004).

§ 1.74. *Do the Commissions apply to U.S. citizens?*

No. According to the Order, "any individual who is not a United States citizen" is subject to the Order. Pres. Bush Exec. Order, Nov. 13, 2001, available at http://www.whitehouse.gov/news/releases/2001/11/20011113-27.html (last visited June 15, 2005). *See also* Department of Defense, Military Commission Order No. 1 (Mar. 21, 2002) (DOD Order). This is significant in that U.S. citizens have access to the courts — this is an open question for non-citizens.

§ 1.75. *Who traces the Commission prosecutions?*

Prosecutions of so-called "enemy combatants" do not appear in official Justice Department statistics because the Department of Defense runs the Military Commissions. Nora V. Demleitner, *How Many Terrorists Are There? The Escalation In So-Called Terrorism Prosecutions*, 16:1 FED. SENT'G REP. 38, 39 (Oct. 2003).

§ 1.76. *What are the rights of enemy combatants?*

In *Rasul v. Bush*, 542 U.S. 466, 124 S. Ct. 2686 (2004), the Supreme Court held that the federal habeas statute gave the district court jurisdiction to hear challenges of aliens held at Guantanamo Bay. In *Hamdi v. Rumsfeld*, 542 U.S. 507, 124 S. Ct. 2633 (2004), the Court held that due process required that a U.S. citizen held as an enemy combatant be given meaningful opportunity to contest the factual basis for his detention. *On remand*, 378 F.3d 426 (4th Cir. 2004). In *Padilla v. Rumsfeld*, 542 U.S. 426, 124 S. Ct. 2711 (2004), however, the Court held that the commander of a naval brig where the prisoner was detained was the only proper respondent and that the district court lacked jurisdiction.

See generally Allison Elgart, *Due Process Requires That Detainees Receive Notice and Opportunity To Contest Basis for Detention (*Hamdi v. Rumsfeld, *124 S. Ct. 2633, 2004)*, 40 HARV. C.R.-C.L. L. REV. 239 (2005); Judge Daryl L. Hecht, *Controlling the Executive's Power to Detain Aliens Offshore: What Process Is Due the Guantanamo Prisoners?*, 50 S.D. L. REV. 78 (2005); Meredith B. Osborn, *Federal Courts Have Jurisdiction over Habeas Challenges and Other Claims Brought by Guantanamo Detainees (*Rasul v. Bush, *124 S. Ct. 2686, 2004)*, 40 HARV. C.R.-C.L. L. REV. 265 (2005); Carolyn M. Zegeer, *Separation of Powers: The Judiciary's Limited Role in Reviewing the President's Detention of Enemy Combatants (*Hamdi v. Rumsfeld, *316 F.3d 450, 4th Cir. 2003)*, 16 U. FLA. J. L. & PUB. POL'Y 203 (2005).

§ 1.77. *Who can be tried by the Military Commissions?*

Any noncitizen regardless of whether he or she is inside or outside of the United States. This potentially could affect about 20 million aliens in the United States and any noncitizen anywhere in the world. Neal K. Katyal & Laurence H. Tribe, *Waging War, Deciding Guilt: Trying the Military Tribunals*, 111 YALE L.J. 1259 (2002). Also, a citizen designated as an "enemy combatant" could be tried as well. *But see* Jaykant M. Patidar, Note, *Citizenship and the Treatment of American Citizen Terrorists in the United States*, 42 BRANDEIS L.J. 805 (2004); Jesselyn A. Radack, *You Say Defendant, I Say Combatant: Opportunistic Treatment of Terrorism Suspects*

Held in the United States and the Need for Due Process, 29 N.Y.U. REV. L. & SOC. CHANGE 525 (2005); Danielle Tarin, Note, *Will an Attack on America Justify an Attack on Americans?: Congressional and Constitutional Prohibitions on the Executive's Power to Detain U.S. Citizens as Enemy Combatants*, 44 VA. J. INT'L. L. 1145 (2004).

§ 1.78. *What is the jurisdictional standard?*

An alien is subject to Commission jurisdiction if the President makes the unilateral determination that there is reason to believe that the person "has engaged in, aided or abetted, or conspired to commit, acts of international terrorism, or acts in preparation therefor, that have caused, threaten to cause, or have as their aim to cause, injury to or adverse effects on the United States, its citizens, national security, foreign policy, or economy."

Also, any alien who the President believes at any point was a member of a "named terrorist organization" is subject to Commission jurisdiction. Neal K. Katyal & Laurence H. Tribe, *Waging War, Deciding Guilt: Trying the Military Tribunals*, 111 YALE L.J. 1259 (2002). *See also* Joan Fitzpartick, *The Constitutionality and International Invalidity of Military Commissions Under the November 13, 2001 "Military Order"*, 7:1 BENDER'S IMMIGR. BULL. 7 (Jan. 1, 2002); Eric M. Freeman, *The Bush Military Tribunals: Where have we been? Where are we going?*, CRIM. JUST., Summer 2002, at 14.

§ 1.79. *Is Commission jurisdiction exclusive?*

Yes, the Order states that "military tribunals shall have exclusive jurisdiction with respect to offenses by" aliens who "shall not be privileged to seek any remedy ... in any court of the United States."

§ 1.80. *Is there any review of a Commission's decision?*

According to the Order there is no review in civilian courts. Rather, the only review of a Commission's decision will be by a three-person panel designated by the Secretary of Defense, followed by the Secretary of Defense's review, with a possible final review by the President.

§ 1.81. *When and where will the Commissions convene?*

"Any time and any place" is what the Order states. As of this writing, no Commissions are scheduled.

§ 1.82. *Who makes up a Commission?*

The Order provides for three to seven military officers appointed by the Secretary of Defense or his or her delegate. The presiding officer must be an attorney with the Judge Advocate General's Corps (JAG), the prosecutor must be a JAG or Department of Justice attorney, and defense counsel must be a JAG or a qualified civilian who is a U.S. citizen.

§ 1.83. *Does the Uniform Code of Military Justice apply?*

No, the Uniform Code of Military Justice applies only to the Army, Navy, Air Force, and Coast Guard. Thus none of its procedural protections apply such as the right to appeal all issues of fact and law and to have the strict rules of evidence apply. Christopher M. Evans, *Terrorism on Trial: The President's Constitutional Authority to Order the Prosecution of Suspected Terrorists by Military Commission*, 51:6 DUKE L.J. 1831 (2002).

§ 1.84. *What about procedural protections?*

The President's Order states that "at a minimum," the Secretary of Defense will issue regulations that "provide for ... a full and fair trial," with a Military Commission sitting as the trier of both fact and law, and "with admissibility of all evidence that has probative value to a reasonable person." Order § 4(c)(2)-(3), (6)-(7).

The Department of Defense responded with Military Commission Order No. 1, March 21, 2002. DOD Order § 6(H)(2) guarantees that upon administrative review a "not guilty" finding cannot be changed. However, the regulations still deny the judicial branch review of convictions and sentences and all legal issues are at the sole discretion of the President. Moreover, § 7(B) of the regulation provides that "[i]n the event of any inconsistency between the President's Military Order and this Order, ... the Provisions of the President's Military Order shall govern." Eric M. Freeman, *The Bush Military Tribunals: Where have we been? Where are we going?*, CRIM. JUST., Summer 2002, at 14.

§ 1.85. *What does it take for a conviction and sentence?*

The Order states that conviction and sentencing will occur "only upon the concurrence of two-thirds of the members of the commission present." Military Order § 4(c)(2)-(3), (6)-(7). However, the DOD Order apparently requires a unanimous verdict for a death sentence. *See* Neil A. Lewis, *Rules on Tribunal Require Unanimity on Death Penalty*, N.Y. TIMES, Dec. 28, 2001, at A1, *cited in* Neal K. Katyal & Laurence H. Tribe, *Waging War, Deciding Guilt: Trying the Military Tribunals*, 111 YALE L.J. 1259 n.10 (2002).

§ 1.86. *What other process will the Military Commissions provide?*

Military Commissions have guarantees for defense counsel, the right to review charges in one's native language, an interpreter, the presumption of innocence, the right to obtain witnesses and evidence, the right to remain silent, and the right to cross-examine witnesses. The Commissions, however, lack the right to appeal and the right to a jury trial. Furthermore, the trials are allowed to take place in secret and confidential evidence is allowed, which may not be accessed or contradicted by the accused person's attorney. The evidence does not have to meet the "beyond a reasonable doubt" standard but is required merely to "have probative value to a reasonable person." George P. Fletcher, *On Justice and War: Contradictions in the Proposed Military Tribunals*, 25 HARV. J.L. & PUB. POL'Y 635 (2002).

§ 1.87. *Is there legal precedent against the Order?*

Yes. In *Ex parte Milligan*, 71 U.S. 2 (1866), the Supreme Court declared that military commissions may not try civilians during an internal conflict as long as the civil courts are operating. In *Duncan v. Kahanamoku*, 327 U.S. 304, 66 S. Ct. 606 (1946), the Court extended this rule to an international armed conflict, in that case the Second World War. Moreover, the current "War on Terrorism" does not suspend international law obligations to provide due process to aliens. *See* Jordan J. Paust, *Antiterrorism Military Commissions: Courting Illegality*, 23 MICH. J. INT'L L. 1 (2001). Franklin D. Roosevelt used a military commission to try eight German spies during World War II. From a historical perspective, what happened was troubling — with serious questions remaining about the justice of the convictions and executions. *See* Gary Cohen, *The Keystone Commandoes*, ATLANTIC MONTHLY, Feb. 2002, at 46–59.

§ 1.88. *Has anybody been charged yet in a Military Commission?*

No. Military Commissions, however, might determine the fate of prisoners captured in Afghanistan and currently held at Guantanamo Bay. *See* Diane Marie Amann, *Guantanamo*, 42 COLUM. J. TRANSNAT'L L. 263 (2004).

To date, the only person charged in connection with the September 11 attacks is the French Moroccan, Zacarias Moussaoui, and this charge has not been prosecuted in a Military Commission but in federal court with six counts of conspiracy. Moussaoui was detained by INS prior to the attacks because of his suspicious behavior in a flight school in Minnesota. His continued prosecution raises many questions. *See* Seymour M. Hersh, *The Twentieth Man: Has the Justice Department Mishandled the Case Against Zacarias Moussaoui?*, THE NEW YORKER, Sept. 30, 2002, at 56.

IX. Punishing Terrorists

§ 1.89. *Do the Federal Sentencing Guidelines account for terrorist activity?*

Under the Federal Sentencing Guidelines, terrorism can be used as a sentencing enhancement under § 3(A)1.4. If a crime of terrorism was involved in the felony or if the felony was intended to promote terrorism, § 3(A)1.4 enhances the offense conduct by 12 levels. In addition, the offender's criminal history category goes to VI. In addition, upward departures may apply. *See, e.g.*, United States v. Kikumura, 918 F.2d 1084 (3d Cir. 1990) (Japanese terrorist legally received upward departure).

After the Supreme Court's decision in *United States v. Booker/United States v. Fanfan*, 125 S. Ct. 738 (2005), this Guideline, as with all the Federal Sentencing Guidelines, is now advisory. The Guidelines are now just one factor among several under 18 U.S.C. § 3553(a)(2) that sentencing courts must consider when imposing a sentence. Now, the sentence must be "sufficient but not greater than necessary" to achieve § 3553(a)(2)'s purposes.

CHAPTER 2

IMMIGRATION LAW FOR CRIMINAL LAWYERS

Other Resources:

AUSTIN T. FRAGOMEN & STEVEN C. BELL, IMMIGRATION FUNDAMENTALS: A GUIDE TO LAW AND PRACTICE (2004).

IRA J. KURZBAN, KURZBAN'S IMMIGRATION LAW SOURCEBOOK (7th ed. 2000).

NATIONAL LAWYER'S GUILD, IMMIGRATION LAW AND DEFENSE (3d ed. 1995).

Introduction

A word of warning to the criminal lawyer — immigration law can be harsh, with very few procedural protections.

§ 2.1. *What is "immigration law"?*

In the United States, the Immigration and Nationality Act (INA) is a comprehensive federal law dealing with immigration, naturalization, and exclusion of aliens, controlling both "immigration" and "emigration." "Immigration" is coming into a new country; "emigration" is leaving a former country. Look to the following sources to find immigration law:

1. The statute is 8 U.S.C. § 1101 et seq. Because this book is for the criminal lawyer, it generally uses the 8 U.S.C. citations rather than the INA citations.
2. The relevant regulations are at 8 C.F.R. § 1.1 et seq.
3. Various agency and federal court decisions interpret the statutes and regulations, including the decisions from the Board of Immigration Appeals (BIA) which are available online at www.usdoj.gov/eoir;
4. Circuit court of appeal decisions and occasional Supreme Court decisions.

See generally Daniel Kanstroom et al., Symposium, *U.S. Immigration Policy at the Millennium*, "Deportation, Social Control, and Punishment: Some Thoughts About Why Hard Laws Make Bad Cases," 113 HARV. L. REV. 1889 (2000).

§ 2.2. *What parts of the INA are relevant to the criminal lawyer?*

The following parts of the INA are relevant to the criminal lawyer:

1. Ch. 1 — Definitions — those at 8 U.S.C. § 1101(a)(15) specifying every class of immigrant;

2. Ch. 2 — System of immigration — explaining quotas, preferences, how to immigrate;
3. Title 8 U.S.C. § 1182 — listing grounds for inadmissibility;
4. Title 8 U.S.C. § 1225 — defining expedited removal of inadmissible arriving aliens;
5. Title 8 U.S.C. § 1226 — providing for apprehension and detention of aliens, including mandatory detention;
6. Title 8 U.S.C. § 1227 — listing classes of deportable aliens;
7. Title 8 U.S.C. § 1228 — defining administrative removals of aliens convicted of aggravated felonies;
8. Title 8 U.S.C. § 1229a — defining procedures for removal;
9. Title 8 U.S.C. § 1231 — listing provisions for detention and removal of aliens ordered removed;
10. Title 8 U.S.C. § 1231(a)(5) — listing provisions for reinstatement of removal order against aliens illegally reentering;
11. Title 8 U.S.C. § 1254(a) — defining temporary protected status;
12. Title 8 U.S.C. § 1255 — defining adjustment of status.

§ 2.3. *What shapes immigration policy?*

Since the first Immigration Act of 1819 and the first immigration restrictions of the Immigration Act of 1882, immigration law has become even more unforgiving, especially in 1996 with the Anti-Terrorism and Effective Death Penalty Act of 1996 (AEDPA) and the Illegal Immigration Reform and Illegal Immigrant Responsibility Act of 1996 (IIRAIRA). *See* Nancy Morawetz, *Rethinking Retroactive Deportation Laws and the Due Process Clause (Part One), in* 4:6 BENDER'S IMMIGR. BULL. 221 (Mar. 15, 1999) *and* 73 N.Y.U. L. REV. 97, 111–14 (1998) (discussing how AEDPA and IIRAIRA made it easier for the government to deport immigrants convicted of criminal conduct); Robert Pauw, *A New Look at Deportation as Punishment: Why at Least Some of the Constitution's Criminal Procedure Protections Must Apply, in* 5:11 BENDER'S IMMIGR. BULL. 475 (June 1, 2000) *and* 52 ADMIN. L. REV. 305, 334 (2000). Calls for the reform of this recent "reform" have as yet gone unheeded. *See, e.g.*, Howard F. Chang, *The Economic Effects of Immigration and the Case for Liberalizing Reforms,* 4:11 BENDER'S IMMIGR. BULL. 497 (June 1, 1999); Jason H. Ehrenberg, *A Call for Reform of Recent Immigration Legislation*, 32 U. MICH. J.L. REF. 195 (1998); Elizabeth Hull, *The Unkindest Cuts: The 1996 Welfare Reform Act's Impact on Resident Aliens*, 33 GONZAGA L. REV. 471 (1997-98); Symposium, *Understanding the Impact of the 1996 Deportation Law and the Limited Scope of Proposed Reforms*, 113 HARV. L. REV. 1936 (2000); Anthony Lewis, *The Quality of Mercy*, N.Y. TIMES, Feb 27, 1999, at A31. This situation is not terribly surprising given that much immigration policy panders to xenophobia. *See* PATRICK J. BUCHANAN, THE DEATH OF THE WEST: HOW DYING POPULATIONS AND IMMIGRANT INVASIONS IMPERIL OUR COUNTRY AND CIVILIZATION (2002). In our post-9/11 world, things are not likely to change, especially with the Patriot Act and other similar legislation dominating immigration policy. *See* **Chapter 1: Strangers in an Even Stranger Land — Aliens and Immigration Law After September 11, 2001**.

I. Whatever Happened to the INS?: Reorganization After 9/11

§ 2.4. *What was the INS?*

The Immigration and Naturalization Service (INS) was an agency within the Department of Justice (DOJ). The INS inspected aliens to determine their admissibility, adjudicated aliens' requests for benefits under the law, determined citizenship and naturalization, guarded against illegal entry into the United States, and investigated, apprehended, and removed aliens. 8 U.S.C. § 1103 (1993).

§ 2.5. *Is there still an INS?*

Nope. On March 1, 2003, the United States shifted most of the INS's functions from DOJ into the new cabinet-level Department of Homeland Security (DHS). Pub. L. No. 107-296 (2002). DHS absorbed 22 agencies and programs with combined total of 180,000 employees. *See DOJ Implements Regulatory Transfer of INS Functions to DHS*, 80:9 INTERPRETER RELEASES 305 (Mar. 3, 2003); Stanley Mailman & Stephen Yale-Loehr, *Immigration Functions in the Department of Homeland Security*, 8:8 BENDER'S IMMIGR. BULL. 663 (Apr. 15, 2003); Stanley Mailman & Stephen Yale-Loehr, *Immigration in a Homeland Security Regime*, 8:1 BENDER'S IMMIGR. BULL. 1 (Jan. 1, 2003); Rebecca L. Sigmund, *Chapter 8: Immigration and Border Security*, HOMELAND SECURITY LAW HANDBOOK, ABS Consulting/Government Institutes (Rockville, Md. 2003).

For earlier proposals of government reorganization, see generally Margaret D. Stock, *United States Immigration Law in a World of Terror*, 7:10 BENDER'S IMMIGR. BULL. 559 (May 15, 2002).

§ 2.6. *How was the INS chopped up?*

Three bureaus within DHS assumed the INS's responsibilities:

1. **CIS** (a.k.a. "**BCIS**") — Bureau of Citizenship and Immigration Services now operates the INS's former infrastructure of four service centers, three regional offices, and 33 district offices. It also took on the INS's immigration benefit services, including administering or adjudicating the following:
   - Family and employment-based petitions;
   - Employment authorization documents;
   - Asylum and refugee petitions;
   - Naturalization applications;
   - Special-status programs such as Temporary Protected Status;
   - Asylum applications;
   - Visa applications;
   - Special registration.
2. **ICE** (a.k.a. "**BICE**") — Immigration and Customs Enforcement assumed the former INS and Customs Service law enforcement functions, protecting over 8,000 federal buildings in the United States and territories. ICE includes former customs and INS agents, INS detention and deportation officers, the INS immigration litigation section, federal protective service employees, and part of INS customs. ICE also maintains the student and exchange visitor monitoring program and special registration databases. ICE's mandate is to form a "comprehensive interior enforcement strategy to systematically combat illegal immigration inside the United States by attacking its causes, not merely its symptoms." *See BICE Reorganizes*, 8:11 BENDER'S IMMIGR. BULL. 941 (June 1, 2003). (Initially ICE was named BICE for the Bureau of Immigration and Customs Enforcement, but "Bureau of" portion was dropped.)

3. **CBP** — Customs and Border Protection enforces immigration and customs laws at the borders as well as at and between the 307 ports of entry into the United States. Employees include former customs and INS inspectors, the agricultural quarantine inspection program employees, and 10,000 former border patrol agents. (Initially, CBP was named BCBP, for Bureau of Customs and Border Protection, but the "Bureau of" portion was dropped).

See Stanley Mailman & Stephen Yale-Loehr, *Immigration Functions in the Department of Homeland Security*, 8:8 BENDER'S IMMIGR. BULL. 663 (Apr. 15, 2003); Stanley Mailman & Stephen Yale-Loehr, *Immigration in a Homeland Security Regime*, 8:1 BENDER'S IMMIGR. BULL. 1 (Jan. 1, 2003); Rebecca L. Sigmund, *Chapter 8: Immigration and Border Security*, HOMELAND SECURITY LAW HANDBOOK, ABS Consulting/Government Institutes (Rockville, Md. 2003).

§ 2.7. *Where do these bureaus report?*

ICE and CBP are both under the Directorate of Border and Transportation Security while CIS reports to the Deputy Secretary of Homeland Security. The Homeland Security Act established a Director of Shared Services reporting directly to the DHS Deputy Secretary and coordinates and manages resources among all three bureaus. The Homeland Security Act also established the Bureau of Border Security to maintain the security and enforcement functions of the INS. *See also* Powers and Authority of Officers and Employees; Revisions to the Internal Review Process for Alleged Violations of the Standards for Enforcement Activities, 68 Fed. Reg. 35,273 (June 13, 2003) (promulgating rules to conform Title 8 of the Code of Federal Regulations to the governmental structures the Homeland Security Act established); *see generally* Kathleen C. Walker, *Department of Homeland Security Organization*, 8:2 BENDER'S IMMIGR. BULL. 126 (Jan. 15, 2003).

§ 2.8. *What about the immigration courts?*

The immigration courts, part of the Executive Office of Immigration Review (EOIR), are still in DOJ. EOIR is a separate agency retaining its responsibility to adjudicate immigration cases. 28 C.F.R. § 200.1 (2003) (DOJ will retain EOIR). EOIR still conducts removal (deportation) hearings and issues deportation orders. *See* **IV.B: Removal (Deportation) Hearings**, *infra*.

§ 2.9. *What about former INS policies?*

DOJ policies such as the special interest policy are valid until further notice. Press Release, U.S. Department of State, Immigration Service Transition Will Be Smooth, Agency Says: Offers Reassurances to Immigrants About Provision of Services (Feb. 26, 2003), http://usinfo.state.gov/topics/global/immigration/03022601.htm.

On February 28, 2003, the Attorney General ordered DHS to administer certain regulations formerly under DOJ's purview, without changing the scope of the regulations. Aliens and Nationality; Homeland Security, 68 Fed. Reg. 9824 (Feb. 28, 2003). This order shifted regulations formerly found in Section 3 of 8 C.F.R. to Section 1000. *Id.* For example, 8 C.F.R. § 3.27 is now 8 C.F.R. § 1003.27. Thus, for the short term, there will be no significant change to benefit administration offices and staff will remain the same. *See* Kathleen Anne Harvey, *How Does Immigration Law Today Affect Your Domestic Law Practice?*, 72 J. KAN. B.A. 16 (May, 2003).

Surveillance, investigation, detention, and deportation of aliens, however, has intensified under the new DHS.

II. Government Authority over Aliens

A. Federal Power and Jurisdiction

§ 2.10. *What is the basis of federal jurisdiction over immigration?*

One source of federal power over immigration is the Commerce Clause, article I, section 8, clause 3 of the U.S. Constitution (Congress is authorized to "regulate commerce with foreign nations and among the several states ..."). *See, e.g.*, United States v. Hernandez-Guerrero, 963 F. Supp. 933, 937 (S.D. Cal. 1997) (8 U.S.C. § 1326 held constitutional under the Commerce Clause), *aff'd*, 147 F.3d 1075 (9th Cir.), *cert. denied*, 525 U.S. 976, 119 S. Ct. 433 (1998). However, the most common constitutional sources of federal power over immigration are: the Nationalization Clause, article I, section 8, clause 4 (granting Congress the power "to establish a uniform rule of nationalization"); the Migration and Importation Clause, article I, section 9, clause 1; and the War Powers Clause, article I, section 8, clause 11. The Constitution also implies federal power over immigration incident to sovereignty, *see* The Chinese Exclusion Case [Chae Chan Pinn v. United States], 130 U.S. 581,

609, 9 S. Ct. 623 (1889), and to the power to formulate foreign policy. *See* United States v. Curtiss-Wright Export Co., 299 U.S. 304, 57 S. Ct. 216 (1936); *see generally* IRA J. KURZBAN, KURZBAN'S IMMIGRATION LAW SOURCEBOOK 19–20 (7th ed. 2000); Symposia, *Developments in the Law — Jobs and Borders: V. The Constitutionality of Immigration Federalism*, 118 HARV. L. REV. 2247 (2005).

§ 2.11. *Can states enforce immigration law?*

Immigration law has been a federal subject, despite calls to expand state and local enforcement. *See, e.g.*, Jay T. Jorgensen, *The Practical Power of State and Local Governments to Enforce Federal Immigration Laws*, 1997 BYU L. REV. 899; Hiroshi Motormura, *Federalism, International Human Rights, and Immigration Exceptionalism*, 70 COLO. L. REV. 1361 (1999). DHS, however, takes the position that states can enforce immigration law and is negotiating with "Memorandum of Understanding" to allow specially trained state officers to arrest aliens for immigration violations. IIRAIRA allowed for these agreements and they are sometimes referred to as "287(g)" programs. *Third State to Get Power to Enforce Immigration Laws*, 9:10 BENDER'S IMMIGR. BULL. 641 (May 15, 2004). As of this writing, Virginia, Florida, and Alabama have such agreements. *Id.* Considerable controversy has resulted from this action. *See* Jill Keblawi, Comment, *Immigration Arrests by Local Police: Inherent Authority or Inherently Preempted?*, 53 CATH. U. L. REV. 817 (2004); April McKenzie, Comment, *A Nation of Immigrants or a Nation of Suspects? State and Local Enforcement of Federal Immigration Laws Since 9/11*, 55 ALA. L. REV. 1149 (2004); Huyen Pham, *The Inherent Flaws in the Inherent Authority Position: Why Inviting Local Enforcement of Immigration Laws Violates the Constitution*, 31 FLA. ST. U. L. REV. 965 (2004).

§ 2.12. *What is the authority of border patrol officers?*

Traditionally, the border patrol only had the authority to enforce immigration law. Thus, agents lacked authority to make a warrantless arrest for federal drug crimes unless at the same time they were enforcing immigration law. Courts are now reading 8 U.S.C. § 1357(a)(5) as granting border patrol agents the authority to make warrantless arrests for federal crimes other than immigration violations "if ... performing duties relating to the enforcement of the immigration laws at the time of the arrest ensure[s] that INS will not be diverted from its primary duty — the administration of the immigration laws of the United States." United States v. Perkins, 166 F. Supp. 2d 1116 (W.D. Tex.), *withdrawn, reaff'd on reconsideration*, 177 F. Supp. 2d 570 (W.D. Tex. 2001). Border patrol agents still do not have the broad arrest authority that 21 U.S.C. § 878(a)(3)(B) grants to the Drug Enforcement Administration or any state or local law enforcement officer the Attorney General designates. *Id.*

B. Regulation of Aliens in the United States

§ 2.13. *Who tracks aliens in the United States?*

Today, ICE monitors aliens in the United States. ICE maintains the alien file ("A" file") on all current and former aliens.

§ 2.14. *So describe the "A" file?*

The A-file has a 9-digit file number assigned to a specific alien that follows the alien throughout his or her contact with the ICE. The A-file is self-authenticating at trial, such as in a prosecution for reentry after deportation under 8 U.S.C. § 1326. *See* **Chapter 10: Illegal Entry and Reentry — Pretrial and Trial**. Normally all relevant documents and records related to an alien are in the A-file and may include the following:

I-181: Memorandum of Creation of Lawful Permanent Residence

I-205: Warrant of Deportation (the newer I-205s not only have the alien's fingerprint but also his picture).

I-210: Notice of Action — Voluntary Departure

I-213: Record of Deportable/Inadmissible Alien

I-247: Immigration Detainer — Notice of Action

I-261: Additional Grounds of Removability

I-323: Immigration Bond Breached

I-352: Immigration Bond

I-391: Immigration Bond Canceled

I-512: Authorization for Parole of Alien in the United States.

I-551: Alien Registration Receipt Card ("Green Card")

I-586: Nonresident Alien Border Crossing Card

I-590: Registration for Classification as Refugee

I-618: Rights Advisement

I-688A and B: Employment Authorization Card

I-851: Notice of Intent to Issue Final Administrative Removal Order

I-851A: Final Administrative Removal Order

I-860: Notice/Order of Expedited Removal

§ 2.15. *What is a "work permit"?*

A work permit, formerly titled "Employment Authorization Document" (EAD), shows that the alien has an application pending with CIS for a benefit such as permanent residency, asylum, temporary work visa, Temporary Protected Status, etc. It allows an alien to work in the United States while waiting for an answer on the application. The work permit, however, does not make one a lawful permanent resident.

§ 2.16. *Who is a "lawful permanent resident"?*

Any immigrant from another country who is legally allowed to live permanently in the United States is a lawful permanent resident (LPR). For a listing of who is eligible to become an LPR and the requirements, *see* IRA J. KURZBAN, KURZBAN'S IMMIGRATION LAW SOURCEBOOK 509–90 (7th ed. 2000).

§ 2.17. *Are any noncitizens exempt from the immigration laws?*

Yes. Native Americans born in Canada can pass into the United States as long as they possess at least 50 percent blood of an American Indian tribe. 8 U.S.C. § 1359. *See* Richard Osburn, *Problems and Solutions Regarding Indigenous Peoples Split by International Borders,* 24 AM. INDIAN L. REV. 471 (2000).

§ 2.18. *Can an alien be criminally charged?*

Yes, some violations of the INA carry criminal consequences. For example, a person can be charged criminally with illegal entry in violation of 8 U.S.C. § 1325 (*see* **Chapter 11: Illegal Entry and Reentry — Pleas and Sentencing**). The first offense is a misdemeanor, but subsequent convictions are felonies. Although any alien who enters the country illegally is subject to prosecution under § 1325, the vast majority are not prosecuted.

C. "Entry" and "Admission"

§ 2.19. *What does it mean to "enter" or be "admitted" as an alien?*

When an alien comes to a port of entry, border officials perform an inspection. 8 U.S.C. § 1225(b); 8 C.F.R. § 235. "Entry" and "admission" occur upon "the lawful entry of the alien into the United States after inspection and authorization by an immigration officer." 8 U.S.C. § 1101(a)(13)(A). However, a person "present in the United States who has not been admitted or paroled, or who seeks entry at other than an open designated port of entry ... is subject to the provisions of INA § 212(a)." 8 U.S.C. § 1182(a). *See also* 8 C.F.R. § 1235.1(d)(2). Another term for "inadmissible" is "excludable."

§ 2.20. *Who is an "undocumented alien"?*

An undocumented alien is a person who has no documentation for entry or residence in the United States. Such a person has no immigration status. Undocumented aliens encounter many legal problems in the United States. For example, any alien who had been in the country illegally for more than a year who reenters or attempts to reenter the United States without being admitted is inadmissible, and is barred *for life* from immigrating to the United States. 8 U.S.C. § 1182(a)(9)(C)(i). Only after 10 years outside the country can the alien even apply for a waiver of this provision.

§ 2.21. *Who is not allowed to enter the United States?*

The government will deny an alien "admission" on any number of grounds, including health, drug abuse, criminal convictions, economic, moral, security grounds, and previous violations of immigration law.

Health — Title 8 U.S.C. § 1182(a)(1)(A)(i) precludes an alien's admission into the United States if he has a communicable disease of public health significance, including human immunodeficiency virus (HIV) infection, active tuberculosis, gonorrhea, and infectious syphilis. *See* 42 C.F.R. § 34.2(b) (2002). Also, under 8 U.S.C. § 1182(a)(1)(A)(ii), an alien seeking to become a lawful permanent resident must be vaccinated against vaccine-preventable diseases such as mumps, measles, rubella, polio, tetanus and diphtheria toxoids, pertussis, type B influenza, and hepatitis B. Title § 1182(a)(1)(C) exempts certain children adopted abroad from this requirement.) Moreover, aliens who have a physical or mental disorder that poses a threat to the property, safety or welfare of the alien or others, are inadmissible.

Waivers are available to some aliens for these health-related requirements. *See* 8 U.S.C. § 1182(g) (Supp. 2002).

Drug Abuse and Addiction — Title 8 U.S.C. § 1182(a)(1)(A)(iii) precludes admission into the United States for drug abuse defined as "[t]he non-medical use of a substance listed in section 202 of the Controlled Substances Act, as amended (21 U.S.C. [§] 802) which has not necessarily resulted in physical or psychological dependence." 42 C.F.R. § 34.2(g). "Drug addiction" is "[t]he non-medical use of a substance listed in section 202 of the Controlled Substances Act, as amended (21 U.S.C.[§] 802) which has resulted in physical or psychological dependence." 42 C.F.R. § 34.2(h).

Criminal Convictions — Title 8 U.S.C. § 1182(a)(2)(A) precludes admission into the United States for aliens who have been convicted of, or admit to committing, crimes of moral turpitude. The BIA, as well as federal district and circuit courts, have enumerated certain "moral turpitude" crimes (Crimes Involving Moral Turpitude — CIMTs). The conduct must constitute a crime under the criminal law of the jurisdiction where it occurred.

An alien trafficker in controlled substances or chemicals listed at 21 U.S.C. § 802(33)-(35) is inadmissible. Also, the trafficker's spouse or child, who has within the past five years knowingly received financial or other benefits from the trafficker, is also inadmissible. 8 U.S.C. 1182(a)(2)(C).

An alien with two or more convictions for crimes other than purely political offenses is also inadmissible. 8 U.S.C. § 1182(a)(2)(B). A "purely political offense" includes a conviction from fabricated charges or based on repression of racial, religious, or political minorities. 22 C.F.R. § 40.22(d).

The government may waive exclusion if the alien's conviction relates to a single offense of simple possession of 30 grams or less of marijuana. 8 U.S.C. § 1182(h). Also, under certain circumstances, the government will waive excludability for offenses of moral turpitude. *Id.*

See **Chapter 4: Immigration Consequences of Criminal Conviction**.

Economic Grounds — Title 8 U.S.C. § 1182(a)(4)(A)-(B) makes inadmissible those aliens who will likely become "public charges." On this question, the BCIS evaluates the alien's age, health, family status, assets, resources, financial status, education level, and skills.

If a U.S. citizen wishes to sponsor an alien spouse, a child, or fiancé(e), he or she must execute an Affidavit of Support. 8 U.S.C. § 1182(a)(4)(C). *See* U.S. Dep't of Homeland Security, Bureau of Citizenship and Immigration Services, Form I-864, Affidavit of Support Under Section 213A of the Act (May 2001), available at http://www.immigration.gov/graphics/formsfee/forms/i-864.htm. Any government entity providing the alien benefits can enforce the affidavit. 8 U.S.C. § 1183a(a)(1)(B); *see also* 8 C.F.R. § 213a.1 (definition of "means-tested public benefit"). The citizen must agree to support the alien to at least 100 percent of the federal poverty level. *See* 2003 Federal Poverty Guidelines, http://aspe.hhs.gov/poverty/03fedreg.htm; *see also* 8 U.S.C. § 1183a(a)(1)(A). The affidavit of support is effective until the alien naturalizes, departs and ends his or her LPR status, works 40 qualifying quarters, or dies. 8 U.S.C. § 1183a(3); 8 C.F.R. § 213a.2(e); *see* 42 U.S.C. § 414 (defining "quarters"). Divorce does not end the citizen's responsibility.

Security Grounds — Title 8 U.S.C. § 1182(a)(3)(A) makes inadmissible aliens engaging in any espionage, sabotage, or other unlawful activity. *See* **Chapter 1, III.A: New Grounds of Inadmissibility and Deportation** (outlining this expanded basis of excludability).

In addition, an alien is inadmissible; whose entry could have a potentially serious adverse effect on U.S. foreign policy, 8 U.S.C. § 1182(a)(3)(C)(i); who is or has been a Communist or member of another totalitarian party, 8 U.S.C. § 1182(a)(3)(D)(i) (*see also* 8 U.S.C. § 1182(a)(3)(D)(iii), (iv) and 22 C.F.R. § 40.34(d) (2002) for exceptions); who was a Nazi who persecuted any person because of race, religion, national origin, or political opinion, 8 U.S.C. § 1182(a)(3)(E)(i); or who is an alien that engaged in genocide. 8 U.S.C. § 1182(a)(3)(E)(ii).

Moreover, the President of the United States, by proclamation, can suspend the admission of persons into the United States. 8 U.S.C. § 1182(f).

Immigration Law Violations — Title 8 U.S.C. § 1182(a)(6)(A)(ii) provides that an alien in the United States who has not effected a legal entry is inadmissible. The statute excepts certain battered women and children who qualify for immigrant status as immediate relatives. *Id.*

Aliens with prior removals for misrepresenting material facts for visas, falsely claiming citizenship, or not having valid entry documents are inadmissible for five years. Aliens who have been removed two or more times, or who have been convicted of an aggravated felony, are inadmissible for 20 years. 8 U.S.C. § 1182(a)(9)(A). Other aliens who have been removed or who depart the United States while under an outstanding removal order are inadmissible for 10 years. *Id.*

Aliens unlawfully present for more than 180 days but less than one year who voluntarily depart before removal proceedings begin are inadmissible for three years. If the alien was unlawfully present for one year or more, the alien is inadmissible for 10 years. 8 U.S.C. § 1182(a)(9)(B)(i)(I), (II). *But see* 8 U.S.C. § 1182(a)(9)(B)(v) (allowing the CIS to waive inadmissibility for immigrant spouse or child of citizen or LPR if exclusion would result in extreme hardship to the citizen or LPR).

Aliens who do not attend removal hearings or who overstay their student nonimmigrant visas are inadmissible for five years after the violation. 8 U.S.C. § 1182(a)(6)(B), (G).

D. Visas

§ 2.22. *What is "immigration status"?*

Aliens admitted into the United States fall into one of two categories:

1. Nonimmigrants who wish to enter for a limited period and purpose;
2. Immigrants who want to become LPRs.

The INA classifies nonimmigrant and immigrant status for aliens who enter the United States. An alien who wishes to enter the country is presumed to be an immigrant (i.e., wishes to live in the United States permanently) and must qualify for one of the classes of immigrant visas, or else demonstrate how he or she is not an immigrant. 8 U.S.C. § 1101(a)(15). Aliens who have not yet been admitted to the country or who entered without "admission" and have been in the United States for less than two years are "applicants for admission." 8 U.S.C. § 1225(a)(1).

§ 2.23. *What exactly is a "visa"?*

A visa is the document that allows both immigrants and nonimmigrants to travel to the United States and request admission. Persons with visas are usually admitted into the United States, but this is not guaranteed by simply having been issued a visa.

§ 2.24. *Where can an alien get a visa?*

From U.S. consulates or embassies around the world. Consular officers, who are employed by the State Department, decide whether to grant visas under immigration laws as articulated in the Foreign Affairs Manual (FAM), an internal publication of the State Department. *See* David W. Merrell, *Everything You Always Wanted to Know About the FAM, but Were Too Discouraged to Dig for Yourself,* 4:11 BENDER'S IMMIGR. BULL. 540 (June 1, 1999); David W. Merrell, *The Devil's Consular Dictionary,* 5:18 BENDER'S IMMIGR. BULL. 757 (Sept. 15, 2000).

§ 2.25. *Can an alien ever legally enter the country without a visa?*

People from certain countries can enter the United States without a visa. The most common entrants without a visa are Canadians. Other countries, mostly European, fall under the visa waiver program, which permits individuals from those countries to enter without a visa.

§ 2.26. *What types of visas are available?*

There are many types of visas, lettered A through V. *See* Immigration Classifications and Visa Categories, http://uscis.gov/graphics/services/visas.htm (at CIS webpage). Aliens get visas to enter the United States at a specific time and reason and to last a specific time. The most common nonimmigrant visa is the "B" visa for temporary visits for pleasure or business. Other nonimmigrant visas include those for students and trainees, business personnel, diplomatic and international organizations, and fiancé(e)s (the K-visa) and for individuals who are in transit. *See* AUSTIN T. FRAGOMEN & STEVEN C. BELL, IMMIGRATION FUNDAMENTALS: A GUIDE TO LAW AND PRACTICE ch. 5 (2004); Stephen Yale-Loehr, Christina Sherman, Christoph Hoashi-Erhardt, & Brian Palmer, *T, U and V Visas: More*

Alphabet Soup for Immigration Practitioners, 6:3 BENDER'S IMMIGR. BULL. 113 (Feb. 1, 2001).

Some visas are subject to numerical limitations (quotas). Visas not subject to numerical limitations are granted exclusively to spouses of U.S. citizens, children of U.S. citizens younger than 21 years, and parents of children over 21 who are U.S. citizens. 8 U.S.C. § 1151(b). Visas subject to quotas are granted to people who qualify for family-sponsored, employment-related, or diversity-based immigrant visas. *See generally* DAVID WEISSBRODT, IMMIGRATION LAW AND PROCEDURE IN A NUTSHELL 102–03 (West, 4th ed. 1998).

1. Nonimmigrant Visas

§ 2.27. *What does a nonimmigrant visa do?*

A nonimmigrant visa allows an alien to travel to the United States and seek admission to the United States on a stated, temporary basis. An alien must have a nonimmigrant visa and a passport valid for six months to gain admission to the United States as a nonimmigrant. 8 C.F.R. § 212.1 (2002). Aliens admitted at ports of entry receive a form I-94, Arrival-Departure Record. U.S. Dep't of Homeland Security, Bureau of Citizenship and Immigration Services, Form I-94, Arrival-Departure Record (Aug. 1997), available at http://www.immigration.gov/graphics/formsfee/forms/i-864.htm. The form I-94 is stamped with an entry date and a date by which the alien must exit the United States.

§ 2.28. *What happens if the alien stays longer than authorized period of stay as listed on I-94?*

Staying beyond the specified period, also known as "overstaying," voids the visa. This could make the alien subsequently ineligible for readmission to the United States as a nonimmigrant. There is an exception for visas issued in a consular office of the country of nationality or if the Secretary of State finds extraordinary circumstances. 8 U.S.C. § 1202(g).

§ 2.29. *Are waivers available?*

Yes, nonimmigrant visa applicants may request a waiver of most grounds of inadmissibility. 8 U.S.C. § 1182(d) (2000 & Supp. 2002).

§ 2.30. *What is the most common kind of visa for fiancé(e)s and families?*

The "K" nonimmigrant visa is used for (1) fiancé(e)s of citizens and the children of the fiancé(e) to come to the United States for the wedding, and (2) a U.S. citizen's spouse and children to come to the United States while waiting for their immigrant visas. The citizen must file the visa petition and affidavit swearing he or she has personally met the fiancé(e) within two years of filing the petition, that he or she has a bona fide intention to marry, and that both the citizen and the fiancé(e) are legally able and willing to conclude a valid marriage within 90 days of arrival in the United States. 8 U.S.C. § 1184(d) (2002 Supp.).Those who hold K nonimmigrant visas can work for the period of authorized stay (90 days), 8 U.S.C. § 214.2(k)(9), if they are issued an employment authorization. U.S. Dep't of Homeland Security, Bureau of Citizenship and Immigration Service, Form I-765, Application for Employment Authorization (May 2002), available at http://www.immigration.gov/graphics/formsfee/forms/i-765.htm. *See* Pamela M. Stahl, *The Legal Assistance Attorney's Guide to Immigration and Naturalization*, 177 MIL. L. REV. 1, 17–19 (2003) (an informative presentation of the K-visa requirements especially as to military service personnel).

§ 2.31. *What is the appropriate visa for an LPR's spouse and children?*

The "V" nonimmigrant visa allows LPRs to bring their spouses and children to the United States while the spouses and children await receipt of an immigrant visa. The V-visa also allows the LPR to petition for visas for spouses and minor children already in the United States. *See* Pamela M. Stahl, *The Legal Assistance Attorney's Guide to Immigration and Naturalization*, 177 MIL. L. REV. 1, 20–21 (2003).

2. Immigrant Visas

§ 2.32. *What are the general requirements of immigrant visas?*

An alien who wants to live in the United States permanently as an "immigrant" must apply for an immigrant visa. *See* 8 U.S.C. § 1101(15). The aliens with the best chance of getting an immigrant visa are family-based immigrants, employment-based immigrants, and diversity-based immigrants. *See generally* 8 U.S.C. § 1151(a) (2000).

§ 2.33. *How does the visa process begin?*

The process usually begins when a citizen files a visa petition for an immigrant visa on behalf of an alien. Once the CIS approves the petition, if the alien is outside the United States, the alien then applies for an immigrant visa at the U.S. consulate-embassy in his or her home country. Upon receiving the immigrant visa, the alien can travel to the United States to be admitted as an LPR. If inside the United States, once the visa petition is approved, the alien must apply for adjustment of status to LPR at the local CIS office. For an outline of the petition process for specific aliens *see* Pamela M. Stahl, *The Legal Assistance Attorney's Guide to Immigration and Naturalization*, 177 MIL. L. REV. 1, 27–29 (2003).

§ 2.34. *What about aliens who served in the armed forces?*

Aliens that have served in the U.S. armed forces are "special immigrants" and therefore can emigrate to the United States. *See, e.g.*, U.S. Dep't of Army, Reg. 601-210, Regular Army and Army Reserve Enlistment Program ¶ 2-4a(5) (Feb. 28, 1995) (allowing citizens of the Federated States of Micronesia, Palau and the Republic of Marshall Islands to enlist in the U.S. Army). Pamela M. Stahl, *The Legal Assistance Attorney's Guide to Immigration and Naturalization*, 177 MIL. L. REV. 1, 22 (2003).

§ 2.35. *What are the family-based immigrant visas?*

Persons eligible for family-based immigrant visas are immediate relatives of U.S. citizens, including spouses, unmarried children under the age of 21 and, if the service member is at least 21 years old, the citizen's parent. For the requirements of family-based immigrant visas, see Pamela M. Stahl, *The Legal Assistance Attorney's Guide to Immigration and Naturalization*, 177 MIL. L. REV. 1, 23–24 (2003). Citizens can also apply for other relatives, but, unlike the immediate relative immigrant, there is a limit to the number of family-sponsored immigrants who may immigrate. *Id.* at 25–26 (explaining preferences under immigration law). *See generally* 8 U.S.C. § 1151(c).

§ 2.36. *What about visas for battered spouses and children?*

Immigration law protects battered spouses and children, allowing the alien to "self-petition" as an immediate relative if the alien married or intended to marry the citizen in good faith and during the marriage or relationship the citizen battered or subjected the spouse or child to extreme cruelty. 8 U.S.C. § 1154(a)(1)(A)(iii)(I). Also, if the battering spouse loses his or her immigration status because of a domestic violence conviction, the alien-victim can maintain his or her status. 8 U.S.C. § 1154(a)(1)(A)(iii)(II)(aa)(CC)(bbb), (ccc). *See also* 8 U.S.C. § 1154a(1)(vi) (allowing battered alien to apply for LPR status).

§ 2.37. *What are diversity-based immigrant visas?*

Each fiscal year, the United States allows 55,000 aliens from around the world to emigrate to the United States under this program. 8 U.S.C. § 1151(e). The aliens must have the equivalent of a high school education, or at least two years of work experience in an occupation that requires at least two years of training or experience within five years of the date of application. The diversity-based immigrant visas are awarded through an annual lottery conducted by the Department of State's National Visa Center, which chooses winners randomly from qualified applicants. 22 C.F.R. § 42.33(c). For other requirements *see* Pamela M. Stahl, *The Legal Assistance Attorney's Guide to Immigration and Naturalization*, 177 MIL. L. REV. 1, 26–27 (2003).

III. Citizenship and Naturalization

§ 2.38. *Who is "a citizen"?*

A citizen is someone who was born on U.S. soil (*jus soli*), born to parents or a parent with citizenship (*jus sanguinis*), or who has naturalized to become a citizen. *See* 8 U.S.C. § 1401. *Jus soli* citizenship in the United States is part of our common law heritage from England. *See* United States v. Wong Kim Ark, 169 U.S. 649, 18 S. Ct. 456 (1898). *Jus sanguinis* citizenship is conferred by virtue of the blood or citizenship of one's parents. 8 U.S.C. § 1401(c). *See* John W. Guendelsberger, *Access to Citizenship for Children Born Within the State to Foreign Parents*, 40 AM. J. COMP. L. 379 note (1992). The Fourteenth Amendment grants citizenship to all persons born or naturalized in the United States. *See generally* Stanley

Mailman & Ted J. Chiappari, *Some Recent Developments in the Law of U.S. Nationality*, 4:13 BENDER'S IMMIGR. BULL. 684 (July 1, 1999); Robert A. Mautino, *Acquisition of United States Citizenship*, 6:1 BENDER'S IMMIGR. BULL. 3 (Jan. 1, 2001).

Citizenship is a status that an alien does not relinquish by simply failing to assert. *See, e.g.*, Rivera v. Ashcroft, 394 F.3d 1129 (9th Cir. 2005) (petitioner's deportation under false name did not relinquish citizenship).

§ 2.39. *Who exactly is "an alien"?*

An alien is any person who is not a national or citizen of the United States. 8 U.S.C. § 1101(a)(3).

§ 2.40. *Who is "a national" of the United States?*

A national is a person owing permanent allegiance to the United States, even though not a citizen. 8 U.S.C. § 1101(a)(21), (22). Traditionally, only persons living in territories acquired by the United States were noncitizen nationals. Perdomo-Padilla v. Ashcroft, 333 F.3d 964 (9th Cir. 2003), *cert. denied*, 540 U.S. 1104, 124 S. Ct. 1041 (2004). Today, Congress has conferred citizenship on those born in most U.S. territories including Puerto Rico, the U.S. Virgin Islands, Guam, and the Northern Mariana Islands. American Samoans, however, continue to be nationals whom the government cannot deport. *See generally* Julie A. Hammersmith, Note, *Disregarding A Definition In* Perdomo-Padilla v. Ashcroft*: Making the INA Definition of a "National" Mean What it Does Not Say* (Perdomo-Padilla v. Ashcroft, *333 F.3d 964, 9th Cir. 2003,* cert. denied, *124 S. Ct. 1041, 2004)*, 73 U. CIN. L. REV. 235 (2004).

An alien cannot become a national by lengthy residence in the United States. *Id. See also* Oliver v. INS, 517 F.2d 426 (2d Cir. 1975), *cert. denied*, 423 U.S. 1056, 96 S. Ct. 789 (1976); Lory Diana Rosenberg, *Identity Crisis: What Does "National" Mean?*, 8:17 BENDER'S IMMIGR. BULL. 1423 (Sept. 1, 2003). Merely taking an oath such as a military service oath is not enough to make an alien a national. Reyes-Alcaraz v. Ashcroft, 363 F.3d 937 (9th Cir. 2004).

§ 2.41. *How does one apply to have the government recognize citizenship?*

Either fill out a copy of form N-600, Application for Certificate of Citizenship, with DHS or apply for a passport with the State Department.

§ 2.42. *Which children born in the United States do not become citizens?*

Children of foreign diplomats become LPRs and are not U.S. citizens at birth. 8 C.F.R. § 1101.3(a) (2002).

§ 2.43. *Which children born outside the United States become citizens?*

A child of a citizen may be a citizen by derivation. Determining whether a given person has a claim to derivative citizenship can be very complicated and depends on the immigration law in effect at the time the person was born, whether the parents where married, whether the mother or father legitimized the child, and other factors.

§ 2.44. *Is there an equal protection problem for requiring more difficult proof requirements for citizen fathers than for citizen mothers?*

No. In *Tuan Anh Nguyen v. INS*, 533 U.S. 53, 58–59, 121 S. Ct. 2053 (2001), the Supreme Court held that the different statutory requirements for a child's acquisition of citizenship dependant on whether the citizen parent is a mother or father was consistent with the Equal Protection Clause. *See* Jacqueline Barrett, Note, *Are Sex-Based Classifications in Citizenship Laws Really Constitutional? (*Nguyen v. INS, *121 S. Ct. 2053, 2001)*, 16 TEMP. INT'L & COMP. L.J. 391 (2002); Norman T. Deutsch, Nguyen v. INS *and the Application of Intermediate Security to Gender Classifications: Theory, Practice, and Reality*, 30 PEPP. L. REV. 185 (2003); Melanie L. Shender, Nguyen v. INS*: No, Your Honor, Men Are Not from Mars*, 36 U.C. DAVIS L. REV. 1023 (2003).

§ 2.45. *What are the recent changes to derivative citizenship law?*

In 2000, Congress amended 8 U.S.C. § 1431 (2001) to expand the standards for acquiring U.S. citizenship through derivation.

§ 2.46. *What other ways can a person become a citizen?*

Naturalization. If you are not lucky enough to be born a citizen, acquire, or derive U.S. citizenship, the only other way is naturalization. Any sovereign nation has the power to grant citizenship. *See* Nishimura Ekiu v. United States, 142 U.S. 651, 659, 12 S. Ct. 336 (1892); *see also* Fong Yue Ting v. United States, 149 U.S. 698, 711, 13 S. Ct. 1016 (1893); The Chinese Exclusion Case [Chae Chan Pinn v. United States], 130 U.S. 581, 609, 9 S. Ct. 623 (1889). The U.S. Constitution authorizes Congress to "establish a uniform rule of naturalization." U.S. CONST. art. 1, § 8, cl. 4. *See* Pamela M. Stahl, *The Legal Assistance Attorney's Guide to Immigration and Naturalization*, 177 MIL. L. REV. 1, 33–49 (2003) (outlining steps for naturalization).

IV. Immigration Court and Proceedings

A. Immigration Detention

§ 2.47. *Can ICE detain a person suspected of being an alien?*

Yes. Service offices have the statutory authority to interrogate aliens and to make warrantless arrests of aliens who they believe are illegally in the United States. 8 U.S.C. § 1226(c). *See* United States v. Drummond, 240 F.3d 1333 (11th Cir. 2001) (INS detentions are civil and do not trigger Speedy Trial Act). This includes juveniles. *See* Areti Georgopoulos, *Beyond the Reach of Juvenile Justice: The Crisis of Unaccompanied Immigrant Children Detained by the United States*, 23 LAW & INEQ. 117 (2005).

After 9/11, the former INS and then ICE detained a great number of aliens with no ties to even a notion of terrorist activity, all this at an astronomic cost to the American taxpayer. The Supreme Court, in *Demore v. Hyung Joon Kim*, 538 U.S. 510, 123 S. Ct. 1708 (2003), *rev'g* 276 F.3d 523 (9th Cir. 2002), has made it more likely that the government will detain even LPRs. *See generally* Lory Diana Rosenberg, *Gonna Need Somebody on Your Bond — Pre-Removal Detention under the INA*, 8:17 BENDER'S IMMIGR. BULL. 1409 (Sept. 1, 2003) (outlining the detention provisions for various types of LPRs); Beth Roberto, *Constitutional Law — Mandatory Detention of Lawful Permanent Residents Without Individualized Hearing Not Violative of Due Process (*Demore v. Kim*, 538 U.S. 510 (2003)*, 28 SUFFOLK TRANSNAT'L L. REV. 163 (2004); Brian Smith, *Another Step Away from Full Due Process Protections*

(Charles Demore v. Hyung Joon Kim, *538 U.S. 510, 2003)*, 38 AKRON L. REV. 207 (2005).

§ 2.48. *Can the alien get out of ICE detention?*

Often this can be done by posting a bond or by other detention challenges. *See* Donald Kerwin & Charles Wheeler, *All Locked Up and Nowhere to Go: Challenges to INS Detention*, 5:1 BENDER'S IMMIGR. BULL. 3 (Jan. 1, 2000).

An immigration judge can allow release upon posting of a bond of at least $1,500 and other requirements, or release on conditional parole. 8 U.S.C. § 1226(a). Release on bond uses Immigration form I-352 and it usually includes a rider (I-351) with a condition prohibiting the alien from unauthorized employment. 8 U.S.C. § 1226(c); 8 C.F.R. § 103.6(a).

The immigration judge can redetermine the bond in an informal hearing — even by telephone. 8 C.F.R. §§ 3.14(a), 3.25(c), 236.1(d). Some immigration courts will provide bond redetermination worksheets (form I-771).

§ 2.49. *What factors are considered in setting a bond?*

An immigration judge will consider stable employment, length of residence, family ties, appearance at prior court or administrative proceedings, and previous criminal immigration violations. *See, e.g., In re* Andrade, 19 I&N Dec. 488 (BIA 1987). An alien may appeal an immigration judge's bond determination or revocation to the BIA within 30 days, without a fee. 8 C.F.R. § 3.1(b)(7), 3.19(f).

§ 2.50. *Can aliens convicted of a crime get a bond?*

Some can, but most criminal aliens cannot, regardless of whether they are sentenced to probation or released on parole for the conviction. 8 U.S.C. § 1226(c). Check with local immigration practitioners for current detention policies regarding specific convictions.

§ 2.51. *Can aggravated felons get bond?*

Generally not, if the alien's aggravated felony conviction is recent. However, an aggravated felony *in the past* might not preclude release on bond, unless the alien was just released from custody *for that crime. See* Pastor-Camarena v. Smith, 977 F. Supp. 1415, 1417 (W.D. Wash. 1997) (statute precluding release of aggravated felons by INS "applies immediately after release from incarceration, not to aliens released many years earlier"). Title 8 U.S.C. § 1101(a)(43) lists aggravated felonies. *But see* Alice E. Loughran, *Congress, Categories, and the Constitution — Whether Mandatory Detention of Criminal Aliens Violates Due Process*, 18 GEO. IMMIGR. L.J. 681 (2004).

§ 2.52. *Is there judicial review of the immigration judge's bond decision?*

No, there is no judicial review of ICE's decisions on arrest, detention, and release. 8 U.S.C. § 1226(e). All the alien can do is administratively appeal to the BIA. 8 C.F.R. § 236.1(d)(3). Arguably, however, an alien may file a habeas corpus petition for release. *Compare* current 8 U.S.C. § 1252 (limiting judicial review) *with* Argiz v. INS, 704 F.2d 384 (7th Cir. 1983) (related to former 8 U.S.C. 1252(a)).

§ 2.53. *What about aliens who cannot be sent back to their countries?*

Presently, ICE has 90 days to remove a person. Otherwise, the detainee is entitled to have an individual review of the situation to determine if he is a danger to others or to property or is a flight risk. If the detainee is neither a danger nor a flight risk, the individual is supposed to be released with work authorization and a requirement to check in with ICE on a specific schedule. Some criminal aliens with convictions for drugs, firearms, or violent offenses have remained in ICE custody indefinitely, despite having been ordered deported, because their countries of origin will not take them back. In *Zadvydas v. Davis*, 533 U.S. 678, 121 S. Ct. 2491 (2001), the Supreme Court held that 8 U.S.C. § 1231(a)(6) has an implicit time limitation necessary to bring about the alien's deportation but that it "does not permit indefinite detention." *Zadvydas*, 533 U.S. at 689. To read the statute otherwise would "raise a serious constitutional problem" under the Fifth Amendment's Due Process Clause. *Zadvydas*, 533 U.S. at 690. Thus, if "there is no significant likelihood of removal in the reasonably foreseeable future," the alien's continued detention must end. *Zadvydas*, 533 U.S. at 701. *See generally* Rachel Canty, *The New World of Immigration Custody Determinations after* Zadvydas v. Davis, 18 GEO. IMMIGR. L.J. 467 (2004). In these cases, one option for relief might be to file a habeas corpus action under 28 U.S.C. § 2241.

Countries that do not take their citizens back include Cambodia, Vietnam, Cuba, and Laos. *See* http://www.cis.org/articles/2001/crime/law.html#59 (last visited June 15, 2005); http://www.usdoj.gov/oig/reports/INS/a0241/findings2.htm (last visited June 15, 2005). Other countries that do not take their citizens back for different political reasons are countries of the former Soviet Union and Somalia. http://seattlepi.nwsource.com/local/ins061.shtml (last visited June 15, 2005).

B. Removal (Deportation) Hearings

§ 2.54. *What was the first deportation in this country?*

The first American deportation was of Thomas Morton of the Massachusetts Bay Colony for various infractions including free-living, encouraging conviviality and merriment, writing bawdy verse, ridiculing the Puritans, selling firearms to Indians, and erecting a Maypole. In 1627 the Pilgrims cut down the pole, arrested Morton, and exiled him to the Isle of Shoals. He escaped to England but reentered this country in 1630, only to have his property confiscated and be exiled to England. He reentered again, in 1634, and was imprisoned, fined, and exiled to Maine. (This is not atypical of what one sees today in federal court.)

Other notable deportations in American history include Roger Williams from the Massachusetts Bay Colony on September 13, 1635 (for criticizing the Massachusetts Bay Company charter and advocating separation of church and state), Anne Hutchinson from the Massachusetts Bay Colony on March 22, 1638 (for being a religious dissident who stressed the individual's intuition over institutionalized beliefs), and Ann Austin and Mary Fisher on July 11, 1656 (for being Quakers — they were the first of that religion to arrive in America).

§ 2.55. *What is a "removal"?*

A removal is the alien's departure following a final order of removal. 8 U.S.C. § 1231(a)(1)(A). This is the same as a "deportation."

§ 2.56. *What is a "removal hearing"?*

A removal hearing is an adversarial administrative proceeding before an immigration judge to determine either admissibility (formerly "excludability") or removability (formerly "deportability"). 8 U.S.C. § 1229a. Before 1996, 8 U.S.C. § 1226 covered exclusion proceedings, and 8 U.S.C. § 1252 covered deportation proceedings. *See generally* Charles H. Kuck, *Window or Aisle: Removal and Expedited Removal Process and Proceedings, in* 2 1997-98 IMMIGRATION & NATIONALITY LAW HANDBOOK 225 (American Immigration Lawyers Ass'n 1997).

§ 2.57. *Do all aliens get removal hearings?*

No. Under 8 U.S.C. § 1228(b), an immigration enforcement officer can, without a hearing, order the alien's "expedited removal" if the alien is not a lawful permanent resident (LPR) and has an aggravated felony conviction. *See* **Chapter 5: Aggravated Felonies**. In this situation, the alien has no chance to ask for relief. 8 U.S.C. § 1228(b)(5).

§ 2.58. *Must ICE seek the removal of everyone it can?*

Not under the INS, but this is unclear under the ICE. In a memorandum, former INS Commissioner Doris Meissner advised that "INS officers may decline to prosecute a legally sufficient immigration case if the Federal immigration enforcement interest that would be served by prosecution is not substantial." *See also* Paul W. Virtue, *Restoring Fairness: A Look at Prosecutorial Discretion,* 5:12 BENDER'S IMMIGR. BULL. 555 (June 15, 2000) (citing Hotel & Rest. Employees Union v. Attorney General, 594 F. Supp. 502, 505 (D.D.C. 1984)). Commissioner Meissner's Memorandum responded to many well-publicized cases of aliens deported for minor infractions after a lifetime in the United States.).

§ 2.59. *Who else can conduct a removal hearing?*

Federal district court judges can remove aliens under certain circumstances. *See* 8 U.S.C. § 1252a(c). A federal judge cannot, however, order as a condition of supervised release under 18 U.S.C. § 3583(d) an alien's deportation without a deportation hearing. United States v. Tinoso, 327 F.3d 864 (9th Cir. 2003).

1. Immigration Court

§ 2.60. *What is "immigration court"?*

The immigration courts and their appellate division, the BIA, are independent from DHS and still under DOJ. *See* 28 C.F.R. § 200.1 (2003) (DOJ will retain EOIR). Together, they constitute the Executive Office of Immigration Review (EOIR). *See* www.usdoj.gov/eoir (for a complete listing of immigration courts). The EOIR is an administrative body, not a court under Article III of the Constitution. Immigration judges are also not administrative law judges as defined under 5 U.S.C. § 3105. Generally, the immigration courts conduct removal hearings brought by the ICE against aliens and the BIA reviews the immigration court's determinations.

§ 2.61. *How are immigration courts organized?*

Immigration courts are, in essence, trial courts. The BIA is the body that reviews immigration court decisions. These courts conduct what used to be called "deportation" and "exclusion" hearings but are now referred to as "removal hearings" or "admissibility" hearings.

§ 2.62. *Are immigration judges Article III judges or are they administrative law judges?*

Neither. An immigration judge is an attorney "whom the Attorney General appoints as an administrative judge within the Executive Office of Immigration Review qualified to conduct specified classes of proceedings." 8 U.S.C. § 1101(b)(4) (1996). The immigration judge can serve as both judge and prosecutor at the deportation hearing. La Tourneur v. INS, 538 F.2d 1368, 1370 (9th Cir. 1976) (approving the dual role of the immigration judge is consistent with due process), *cert. denied*, 429 U.S. 1044, 97 S. Ct. 748 (1977). *But cf.* Flores by Galvez-Maldonado v. Meese, 942 F.2d 1352, 1368 (9th Cir. 1991) (under the Constitution, "combining the roles of prosecutor and adjudicator in a single entity is a recipe for fundamentally unfair and erroneous decision making"), *rev'd on other grounds*, Reno v. Flores, 507 U.S. 292, 113 S. Ct. 1439 (1993).

§ 2.63. *How can you find out about an immigration case?*

The EOIR has a toll-free number to get information on any immigration court case: 1-800-898-7180. All one needs is the alien's 9-digit "A" number.

2. Removal Hearing Procedures

§ 2.64. *What terms are used at a removal hearing?*

The alien is called the respondent, and the charging document is called the notice to appear (NTA). The case in immigration court begins by service of this document. 8 U.S.C. § 1229(a). The NTA (form I-862) is the equivalent of an indictment/information /complaint in a criminal case.

a. Noticing The Respondent

§ 2.65. *How does the deportation hearing begin?*

When ICE files the NTA (form I-862), the removal proceeding begins. 8 U.S.C. § 1229. *See also* 8 C.F.R. §§ 3.13, 3.14. Only specific agents within ICE can issue an NTA and, if this is not done, the immigration judge lacks jurisdiction. *See* 8 C.F.R. § 239.1; *see generally* John J. Dvorske, *Commencement of Deportation Proceedings Under Antiterrorism and Effective Death Penalty Act (AEDPA) and Illegal Immigration Reform and Immigrant Responsibility Act (IIRIRA)*, 185 A.L.R. FED. 221 (2004).

For deportation hearings before April 1, 1997, the charging document was an Order to Show Cause (OSC), form I-221. Before February 6, 1956, an arrest warrant began the deportation proceedings.

§ 2.66. *What must the NTA list?*

In addition to being written in English, the NTA must specify the items and facts listed at 8 U.S.C. § 1229:

- The nature of the proceedings against the alien;
- The legal authority under which the government is conducting the proceedings;
- The alleged illegal conduct;
- The charges and statutes the respondent allegedly violated;

- The respondent's right to counsel at no expense to the government;
- The notice that the respondent must give his address and telephone number;
- The time and place of the hearing and consequences of failing to appear, except for exceptional circumstances.

§ 2.67. *How must the government serve the NTA?*

Either in person or, if not practicable, through service by mail to the alien or counsel. 8 U.S.C. § 1229(a)(1); 8 C.F.R. § 3.13. Certified mail is not required.

If service on the respondent is not proper, the immigration court lacks jurisdiction. 8 C.F.R. § 3.14.

§ 2.68. *Can ICE later lodge additional charges in the NTA?*

Yes, but the charges must be in writing and must be read in open court just like a superceding indictment. 8 C.F.R. § 3.30.

§ 2.69. *What if the respondent is a minor or incompetent?*

Special rules apply. In the case of an incompetent respondent, the government must serve the NTA by following 8 C.F.R. § 1240.4 (serving an incompetent respondent) and/or 8 C.F.R. § 103.5a(c)(2)(ii) (2002) (serving minors and incompetents). If the service regulations are not followed, the immigration court lacks jurisdiction. *See In re* Mejia-Andino, 23 I&N Dec. 533 (BIA 2002) (en banc) (BIA affirmed immigration judge's determination that INS violated 8 C.F.R. § 103.5a(c)(2)(ii) and thus failed to give jurisdiction to immigration judge).

For a generalized discussion of juveniles in immigration court *see* Stephen Yale-Loehr, *Special Juvenile Immigrants*, 6:13 BENDER'S IMMIGR. BULL. 658 (July 1, 2001).

b. Hearings Before the Immigration Judge

§ 2.70. *How is a removal hearing conducted?*

A removal hearing has two parts:

The first determines removability or, in the case of an alien not admitted to LPR status, admissibility. This is like the guilt or innocence phase of a criminal trial. The alien pleads to the charges on the charging document or NTA. If the alien denies any charge, a hearing is conducted to determine whether the respondent is either inadmissible or removable. If either inadmissibility or removability is based upon a criminal conviction, acceptable documentary evidence of the conviction submitted by ICE is usually all that is needed to establish removability at the evidentiary "hearing."

Second, if the respondent is inadmissible or removable, the immigration judge determines whether the respondent has some form of relief. This is analogous to the punishment phase of a criminal trial. If the INA does not allow for any relief, both parts of the proceedings tend to be handled very quickly.

§ 2.71. *Where is venue?*

Venue is where the government files the NTA, 8 C.F.R. § 3.20, but the respondent can request a change of venue under 8 C.F.R. § 3.20(b) for good cause, including the following: administrative convenience, expeditious resolution of the case, witness location, transportation costs, or location of counsel.

§ 2.72. *What if the respondent does not speak English?*

The immigration judge must ensure that an interpreter is available, in particular when the immigration judge determines that the respondent cannot speak and understand English well enough to help in his own defense.

§ 2.73. *Are the immigration courts "of record"?*

Yes, usually by tape recording. The immigration court that last had control of the case will have the Record of Proceedings (ROP), including the following:

- OSC or NTA;
- Tape of the hearing or a transcript of the tape;
- Exhibits;
- Immigration judge's oral decision (see 8 C.F.R. § 3.37);
- Immigration judge's written decision (if it exists);
- Parties' briefs and motions;
- Other forms.

§ 2.74. *Are removal hearings criminal proceedings?*

No. Removal hearings are civil, despite the fact that the Supreme Court recognizes that they may result "in loss of both property and life; or of all that makes life worth living." Ng Fung Ho v. White, 259 U.S. 276, 284, 42 S. Ct. 492 (1922).

The basis for removal, however, may be a criminal conviction such as an aggravated felony. *See* 8 U.S.C. § 1101(a)(43); *see also* **Chapter 4: Immigration Consequences of Criminal Convictions** *and* **Chapter 5: Aggravated Felonies**. In such cases the removal is often impossible for the alien to fight. *But see* Manuel D. Vargas, *Removal Defense Checklist*, 4:12 BENDER'S IMMIGR. BULL. 592 (June 15, 1999) (a good article on defending against removal of a convicted alien).

§ 2.75. *Are removal hearings conducted like criminal proceedings?*

Yes and no. Immigration judges conduct hearings that are similar to criminal prosecutions but lack the procedural protections one would expect from a criminal proceeding — for example, application of the *ex post facto* clause, Mahler v. Eby, 264 U.S. 32, 38, 44 S. Ct. 283 (1924); also, *Miranda* warnings are not required in a deportation hearing. United States v. Arroyos-Serna, 17 Fed. Appx. 844 (10th Cir. 2001). There is no jury and the immigration judge is empowered to make both findings of fact and conclusions of law. The rules of evidence do not apply, and hearsay is routinely admitted. *But see* Robert Pauw, *A New Look at Deportations as Punishment: Why at Least Some of the Constitution's Procedure Protections Must Apply*, *in* 5:11 BENDER'S IMMIGR. BULL. 475 (June 1, 2000) *and* 52 ADMIN. L. REV. 305, 334 (2000).

In general, however, "[t]he Due Process Clause requires that aliens 'threatened with deportation' are provided with the right to 'a full and fair hearing.'" Sanchez-Cruz v. INS, 255 F.3d 775, 779 (9th Cir. 2001) (quoting Getachew v. INS, 25 F.3d 841, 845 (9th Cir. 1994)).

§ 2.76. *What if the immigration judge is biased?*

This violates due process and invalidates the removal order. *See, e.g.*, Reyes-Melendez v. INS, 342 F.3d 1001 (9th Cir. 2003) (immigration judge's moral judgments about respondent's many sexual relationships that produced numerous children took over role of prosecuting agency and denied due process). "A neutral judge is one of the most basic due process protections." Castro-Cortez v. INS, 239 F.3d 1037, 1049 (9th Cir. 2001).

§ 2.77. *What if the respondent is a minor or incompetent?*

Special rules apply outlining the immigration judge's conduct. If the immigration judge fails to designate the respondent as incompetent, he improperly accepts a concession of deportability, violating 8 C.F.R. § 1240.1(c) (2002). If the respondent's concession of deportability, in for instance an I-213 Record of Deportable Alien Form, is the only evidence in the record the removal is illegal. Moreover, the error is not harmless because it is arguably the result of unfairness in ICE's actions. *See In re* Amaya-Castro, 21 I&N Dec. 583 (BIA 1996) (en banc) (terminating case against minor under regulation governing concession of deportability); Stephen Yale-Loehr, *Special Juvenile Immigrants*, 6:13 BENDER'S IMMIGR. BULL. 658 (July 1, 2001).

§ 2.78. *What about removal proceedings from an unconstitutional search?*

An alien usually does not have the right to have illegally obtained evidence excluded from the deportation proceeding. *See* INS v. Lopez-Mendoza, 468 U.S. 1032, 1051, 104 S. Ct. 3479 (1984); Mitchell V. Daris & Kathleen B. Simon, *The Exclusionary Rule in INS Deportation Hearings: A New Look at the* Lopez-Mendoza *Cost Benefit Analysis after the 1986 Immigration Reform and Control Act*, 23 LAND & WATER L. REV. 537 note (1988). In the Ninth Circuit, however, an unconstitutional search is an invalid basis to begin a removal proceeding. For example, a stop based solely on the Hispanic appearance of a person is an egregious constitutional violation warranting suppression in the deportation proceeding. *See* Gonzalez-Rivera v. INS, 22 F.3d 1441, 1444 (9th Cir. 1994).

§ 2.79. *Does the respondent have the right to a lawyer?*

Yes, but not gratis. The person facing a removal hearing has no right to free counsel. 8 U.S.C. § 1252(b)(2) ("the alien shall have the privilege of being represented [at no expense to the government] by such counsel, authorized to practice in such proceedings, as he shall choose"). Title 8 U.S.C. § 1229(b)(1) gives the alien at least 10 days to get a lawyer. Title 8 U.S.C. § 1229(b)(2) provides that ICE must give the alien a list, updated not less than quarterly, of people and agencies willing to represent the alien *pro bono*. *See* Gregory G. Sarno, Annotation, *Adequacy of Counsel's Representation of Alien in Deportation Proceedings*, 91 A.L.R. FED. 394 (1989 & 2004 Supp.); Lory Diana Rosenberg, *Separate Opinion — It's*

Alive: A Noncitizen's Right to Competent Counsel Before the EOIR and BCIS After Matter of Assaad *(23 I&N Dec. 553 (BIA 2003)),* 8:11 BENDER'S IMMIGR. BULL. 943 (June 1, 2003); David R. Robertson, Note, *An Opportunity To Be Heard: The Right to Counsel in a Deportation Hearing,* 63 WASH. L. REV. 997 (1988).

The right to a lawyer is all part of the respondent's right to a full and fair hearing giving the respondent a "reasonable opportunity to present evidence on his behalf." Colmenar v. INS, 210 F.3d 967, 971 (9th Cir. 2000).

§ 2.80. *How does a lawyer appear?*

He must submit a form EOIR-28 with the immigration court and must serve a copy on the ICE chief counsel (formerly on the immigration service).

§ 2.81. *Can the immigration judge conduct the removal hearing without counsel?*

No, after the lawyer submits the EOIR-28 the immigration judge may not conduct the removal hearing absent counsel without a clear showing of the respondent's waiver. *See* Montilla v. INS, 926 F.2d 162 (2d Cir. 1991). Moreover, the immigration judge must grant the respondent's request for continuance to get a lawyer. *See* Rios-Berrios v. INS, 776 F.2d 859 (9th Cir. 1985).

§ 2.82. *What is the "master calendar hearing"?*

The master calendar hearing is akin to an initial appearance in criminal court, except that the immigration judge will often decide the merits of the case. The immigration judge must advise the respondent of the following rights:

- To counsel;
- To a list of free legal services;
- To present evidence;
- To cross-examine witnesses;
- To appeal.

At the master calendar hearing, the immigration judge interrogates a group of aliens, determines who qualifies for an individualized merits hearing, and generally deports the rest. The number of respondents varies according to courtroom size, availability of agents, and the judge's own predilection and sense of due process; it can be as large as 20 or more. However, the hearing to determine whether the alien is deserving of relief (the Merits Hearing) is individual.

§ 2.83. *How does an immigration judge determine whether an alien is removable?*

The immigration judge looks at the charges in the NTA, such as whether the alien has a criminal conviction, and determines, as a matter of law, whether the facts charged are reasonable, substantial, and probative. The standard for such a determination is clear and convincing evidence.

To determine whether the individual is an alien, the immigration judge may simply ask the respondent for his or her place of birth and information about his or her entry into the United States. The judge also inquires as to family status. If an alien admits to being born outside the United States and the judge is satisfied that no issues of law or fact remain, the judge may determine that the alien is removable.

§ 2.84. *What happens if the alien stays silent during the removal hearing?*

The immigration judge can draw a negative inference from the alien's silence or refusal to testify at a removal hearing. *See* Daniel Kanstroom, *Hello Darkness: Involuntary Testimony and Silence as Evidence in Deportation Proceedings*, 4 GEO. IMMIGR. L.J. 599 (1990).

§ 2.85. *Who must prove alienage?*

ICE must prove by clear, convincing, and unequivocal evidence that the respondent is an alien. Often, though, the alien admits to this. A person born in another country is presumed an alien. If the respondent admits to being foreign-born, then the burden of proof of legal presence in the United States shifts to the alien.

§ 2.86. *Can an immigration hearing be held in the absence of the alien?*

Yes, pursuant to 8 U.S.C. § 1252(b). Even if the alien is not present, he can be ordered removed if ICE establishes deportability by clear, convincing, and unequivocal evidence and shows that it provided written notice. 8 U.S.C. § 1230(b)(5); 8 C.F.R. § 3.26(c). ICE need only show that the written notice was sent to the alien's most recent address. 8 U.S.C. § 1230(b)(5)(A). *See also* 8 U.S.C.

§ 1229a(b)(5)(A) (alien can be removed *in absentia* once clear and convincing evidence establishes that alien or counsel received written notice).

Once presented with the NTA, the alien must file, in writing and within five days, any change of address or telephone on form EOIR-33. 8 C.F.R. § 3.15. *See also* 8 U.S.C. § 1229(a)(b)(5)(B) (government need not give written notice of removal proceedings to alien who fails to give address); Manjiyani v. INS, 343 F.3d 1018 (9th Cir. 2003) (*in absentia* deportation upheld for failure to notify immigration court of address change despite fact that respondent had notified ICE of address with application for permanent residency, employment authorization, and excludability waiver).

§ 2.87. *What happens to an alien deported in absentia?*

An alien who fails to appear is ineligible for relief from removal for 10 years. 8 U.S.C. § 1230(b)(7). The alien can move to reopen the *in absentia* order within 90 days upon "exceptional circumstances" as defined at 8 U.S.C. § 1230(e)(1). *See* Lopez v. INS, 184 F.3d 1097 (9th Cir. 1999) (*in absentia* deportation reopened for fraud and ineffectiveness of prior attorney and possibility of voluntary departure relief for alien); *see also* Iris Gomez, *The Consequences of Nonappearance: Interpreting New Section 242B of the Immigration and Nationality Act*, 30 SAN DIEGO L. REV. 75 (1993).

§ 2.88. *After a removal, when can the alien legally return?*

An alien who is formally removed is barred from legally returning to the United States for five years, absent a special permission from the Attorney General. 8 U.S.C. § 1182(a)(9)(A)(i). If the alien returns to the United States within the five-year period, but without such special permission, he or she is barred for 10 years and is subject to prosecution for the crime of reentry after deportation in violation of 8 U.S.C. § 1326. *See* **Chapter 10: Illegal Entry and Reentry — Pretrial and Trial**.

A person deported for a felony conviction cannot reenter for 10 years; if the person is deported on the basis of an aggravated felony, the prohibition is for life unless special permission to reenter is authorized by the Attorney General. 8 U.S.C. § 1182(a)(9)(A)(i). An alien who comes back and is caught faces severe penalties under 8 U.S.C. § 1326(b)(2), with a statutory maximum of 20 years and a correspondingly high Federal Sentencing Guideline calculation. U.S. SENTENCING GUIDELINES MANUAL

§ 2L2.2 (2004). *See* **Chapter 11: Illegal Entry and Reentry — Pleas and Sentencing**.

§ 2.89. *What if the government cannot remove the alien to his country?*

Generally, if a country will not accept an alien or if a government does not exist, the alien stays in the United States under a form of parole with incarceration as an option. The U.S. government at this point may be changing its policy. *Acceptance by a Country and Existence of a Government Not Required for Removal, DHS/DOJ Propose*, 81:28 INTERPRETER RELEASES 925 (July 19, 2004). *See contra* David Cheng, *Émigrés of the Killing Fields: The Deportation of Cambodian Refugees as a Violation of International Human Rights*, 25 B.C. THIRD WORLD L.J. 221 (2005).

c. Determining Relief

§ 2.90. *How must the immigration judge handle possible removal relief?*

The immigration judge must advise the alien of all possible relief from deportation and "apparent eligibility." 8 C.F.R. §§ 240.11(a)(2), 242.17; Moran-Enriquez v. INS, 884 F.2d 420, 422 (9th Cir. 1989). If eligible, the immigration judge must give the alien the chance to apply for that relief, including adjustment of status with waivers, registry, cancellation of removal, withholding of removal, suspension of deportation (before April 1, 1997), and asylum. *See* **V. Deportation Relief**, *infra*.

§ 2.91. *Who has the burden on the question of relief?*

The alien must, through application, prove to the judge that he merits a favorable act of discretion. 8 C.F.R. § 240.11. *See also* IRA J. KURZBAN, KURZBAN'S IMMIGRATION LAW SOURCEBOOK 201 (7th ed. 2000).

3. BIA Appeals

§ 2.92. *Can the alien appeal the immigration judge's decision?*

The immigration law judge is supposed to advise each alien of the right of appeal to the BIA within 30 days and if the respondent does not waive his right to appeal will provide the respondent a form EOIR-26, *see* 8 C.F.R. §§ 3.3, 3.38, 240.15, 240.53, as well as a Notice of Appeal form I-290(a). The 30 day period starts from the mailing of the immigration judge's written order or date of oral decision.

§ 2.93. *What effect does BIA review have?*

The BIA reviews both the legal and factual determinations made by the immigration judge. The order of the BIA is administratively final. Once the order of removal becomes final, review must go to the federal court of appeals or, for criminal aliens, is contingent upon habeas corpus review.

§ 2.94. *Are BIA decisions precedent?*

The BIA designates which of its decisions are precedent. 8 C.F.R. § 3.1(g). The INS was bound to follow BIA precedent and presumably the agencies in DHS doing the work of the former INS will as well. The circuit courts generally still recognize the nonprecedent decisions as expressing the BIA's position. *See* Davila-Bardales v. INS, 27 F.3d 1 (1st Cir. 1994); *but see* Guillen-Garcia v. INS, 60 F.3d 340 (7th Cir. 1995) (nonprecedential decisions have no precedential value), *cert. denied,* 516 U.S. 1073, 116 S. Ct. 775 (1996).

4. Judicial Review of ICE and EOIR

§ 2.95. *Can the alien appeal beyond the BIA?*

This depends on the basis of the removal. Usually, an alien has the right to appeal the BIA's decision to the federal circuit court that has venue. 8 U.S.C. § 1252(b)(1); United States v. Mendoza-Lopez, 481 U.S. 828, 107 S. Ct. 2148 (1987). However, under IIRAIRA several categories of aliens — including those deported on the basis of an aggravated felony or other crime — have no right to seek statutory judicial review of their removal. 8 U.S.C. § 1252(a)(2)(C). *See* Peter Hill, *Did Congress Eliminate All Judicial Review of Orders of Deportation, Exclusion, and Removal for Criminal Aliens?,* 2:10 BENDER'S IMMIGR. BULL. 345 (May 15, 1997); David B. Pakula & Lawrence P. Lataif, *Judicial Review of BICS Decisions: Will There Be Any?,* 80:19 INTERPRETER'S RELEASES 677 (May 12, 2003).

In 2001, however, the Supreme Court undermined the effect of the statute. In *INS v. St. Cyr,* 533 U.S. 289, 121 S. Ct. 2271 (2001) and *Calcano-Martinez v. INS*, 533 U.S. 348, 121 S. Ct. 2268 (2001), the Court held that noncitizens subject to final orders of removal based upon criminal convictions can still go to federal court to raise questions of law challenging the order of removal. Thus, aliens can legally challenge their final orders of removal by habeas corpus in federal district court under 28 U.S.C. § 2241. Also, the two cases held that people who pleaded guilty to deportable offense at the time when they may have been eligible for INA § 212(c) relief would still have this relief available to them. *See also* Restrepo v. McElroy, 369 F.3d 627 (2d Cir. 2004), *on remand, writ of habeas corpus denied,* 354 F. Supp. 2d 254 (E.D.N.Y. 2005).

§ 2.96. *What if the respondent is deported on the basis of drug trafficking?*

Under IIRAIRA there is no right to appeal from this ground of removal. This is true even if the respondent does not have a conviction. Alarcon-Serrano v. INS, 220 F.3d 1116 (9th Cir. 2000). *See also* Olivera-Garcia v. INS, 328 F.3d 1083 (9th Cir. 2003) (deportation for accessory after the fact of aggravated felony conviction unreviewable under IIRAIRA).

§ 2.97. *What if the alien absconds while appeal is pending?*

The fugitive disentitlement doctrine bars judicial review of a removal order against an alien who disappears while his appeal is pending. Antonio-Martinez v. INS, 317 F.3d 1089 (9th Cir. 2003).

5. Removals Without Hearings

§ 2.98. *Can an alien be removed without a removal hearing?*

Yes. IIRAIRA created removal proceedings for aliens convicted of aggravated felonies. *See* 8 U.S.C. § 1228.

§ 2.99. *What is "expedited removal"?*

This is a new concept in immigration law that encompasses the process formerly known as "summary exclusion." Congress created the procedure in 1996 to streamline the removal of certain classes of aliens who illegally entered the United States with an aggravated felony conviction. The statute also allowed for the "reinstatement" without a hearing or a prior order of removal or deportation. 8

U.S.C. § 1231. (For the definition of "aggravated felony" see 8 U.S.C. § 1101(a)(43)). The aliens are removed without a formal deportation hearing, and the process has great potential for abuse and mistakes. *See, e.g.*, Diaz v. Reno, 40 F. Supp. 2d 984 (N.D. Ill. 1999) (U.S. citizen deported through expedited removal proceeding remained in Mexico for three weeks before resolution); *see also* Nicholas Merlin, Comment, *Immigration Policy and the Expedited Removal Rule: "Equity for Some, Justice for None,"* 16 ST. THOMAS L. REV. 163 (2003).

§ 2.100. *What is the legal status of this procedure?*

The Ninth Circuit has ruled that the reinstatement procedure done without an immigration judge is invalid because INA § 240(a) states that an immigration judge shall conduct all proceedings on admissibility or deportability. Morales-Izquierdo v. Ashcroft, 388 F.3d 1299 (9th Cir. 2004), *vacated for reh'g en banc*, Morales-Izquierdo v. Gonzales, 2005 U.S. App. LEXIS 19582 (9th Cir. Sept. 12, 2005). Although the case applied to reinstated deportations, the reasoning would also apply to any expedited removal without an immigration judge.

V. Deportation Relief

§ 2.101. *What relief can the judge grant?*

The main forms of relief an immigration judge can grant include the following:

- Voluntary departure, 8 U.S.C. § 1229c;
- Adjustment of status, 8 U.S.C. § 1255;
- Cancellation of removal, 8 U.S.C. § 1229b;
- Asylum and withholding of removal, 8 U.S.C. §§ 1158, 1253;
- Temporary protected status, 8 U.S.C. § 1254a (available to those under Temporary Protective Status, such as Salvadorans, Guatemalans, Hondurans, Nicaraguans, Liberians);
- Various waivers of inadmissibility.

There may be other options as a basis for relief from removal, such as the United Nations Convention against Torture. *See* Marissa Maurer & Morton Sklar, *Guidelines for Filing Conventions Against Torture Motions*, 4:9 BENDER'S IMMIGR. BULL. 381 (May 1, 1999); Kristen B. Rosati, *Article 3 of the UN Convention Against Torture: A Powerful Tool to Prevent Removal Just Became More Powerful,*

4:4 BENDER'S IMMIGR. BULL. 137 (Feb. 15, 1999). Moreover, if the alien has a pre-1996 case there may be other types of relief from deportation and *ex post facto* issues. *See* Judge Lupe S. Salinas, *Deportations, Removals and the 1996 Immigration Acts: A Modern Look a the Ex Post Facto Clause*, 22 B.U. INT'L L.J. 245 (2004).

A. Voluntary Departure

§ 2.102. *What is a "voluntary departure"?*

A voluntary departure allows the alien to leave the United States independently if he can pay for the trip. 8 U.S.C. § 1229(c); Diric v. INS, 400 F.2d 658 (9th Cir.), *cert. denied*, 394 U.S. 1015, 89 S. Ct. 1633 (1969). The alien can then immediately return to the United States if there is a legal way to do so. In addition, because a voluntary departure is not a deportation, an alien cannot be prosecuted for reentry after deportation if he comes back to the country illegally. 8 U.S.C. § 1326.

§ 2.103. *What are some of the requirements for voluntary departure?*

The alien must prove he has been of "good moral character" for the last five years and be able to pay the travel expenses. There is a limit of 120 days for prehearing voluntary departure and 60 days for post-hearing voluntary departure. 8 U.S.C. § 1229(c). Failure to depart after the alien has received a voluntary departure from ICE renders the alien ineligible, for 10 years, for relief from another voluntary departure, cancellation of removal, adjustment of status, change of status, or registry. 8 U.S.C. § 1230B(d). The alien also becomes subject to a mandatory $1,000 to $5,000 civil penalty. *Id.*; Nadine Wettstein, *Voluntary Departure under IIRAIRA*, 2:13 5 BENDER'S IMMIGR. BULL. 15 (July 1, 1997). *See also* 8 U.S.C. § 1230(B)(a).

§ 2.104. *When can voluntary departure be granted?*

ICE can grant a voluntary departure in the following circumstances: (1) before the deportation hearing if the alien pays his own way out of the country; (2) after immigration proceedings have begun at or just before a master calendar hearing; or (3) after a complete merit hearing.

§ 2.105. *How soon must the alien leave after receiving voluntary departure?*

An immigration judge can grant only 60 days, but ICE can extend this to 120 days.

B. Adjusting Status

§ 2.106. *What is "adjustment of status"?*

Adjustment of status occurs when a nonpermanent resident becomes an LPR. 8 U.S.C. § 1255(a). There are several ways for an alien to do this, such as marrying a U.S. citizen. 8 U.S.C. § 1255(d). Usually, ICE decides whether to grant adjustment of status, although an immigration judge can also grant this relief during a removal hearing. 8 C.F.R. § 245.2(a)(1). Under certain circumstances, a judge can grant adjustment of status even if ICE has denied the adjustment. 8 U.S.C. § 1255; 8 C.F.R. § 242.17(a). *See generally* Romualdo P. Eclavea, Annotation, *Suspension of Deportation and Adjustment of Status for Permanent Residence of Alien Under § 244(a)(1) of Immigration and Nationality Act (8 U.S.C. § 1254(a)(1)(A))*, 45 A.L.R. FED. 185 (1979 & 2004 Supp.).

Adjustment of status is now available to spouses or children whom a citizen or legal permanent resident has battered. *See* Cyrus D. Mehta, *Procedural and Tactical Considerations in Representing Battered Immigrants*, 4:14 BENDER'S IMMIGR. BULL. 759 (July 15, 1999). Adjusting status can also be a basis for relief from removal (deportation). 8 U.S.C. § 1255.

C. Cancellation of Removal

§ 2.107. *What is "cancellation of removal"?*

This is a remedy that has replaced the former "suspension of deportation," INA § 212(c), and "waivers of deportation." *See* former 8 U.S.C. § 1182(c). The eligibility criteria vary for LPRs and non-LPRs.

Requirements for legal permanent residents include the following:

1. Five years as a legal permanent resident;

2. Physical presence in the United States for seven years after admission in any status,
3. No aggravated felony convictions.

See 8 U.S.C. § 1229b(a).

Requirements for persons who are not permanent residents are more strict:

1. No aggravated felony convictions;
2. A person of good moral character;
3. No CIMTs;
4. No drug convictions;
5. The alien must be admissible;
6. Physical presence in the United States for 10 years without absences of more than 180 days;
7. Exceptional and extremely unusual hardship to the alien's immediate relatives (citizens or legal permanent relatives).

See 8 U.S.C. § 1229(b); Maureen O'Sullivan, *The Cancellation of Deportation and Exclusion Jurisprudence: What Can We Expect from Removal Proceedings?*, 2 1997-98 IMMIGRATION & NATIONALITY LAW HANDBOOK 259 (American Immigration Lawyers Ass'n 1997); Kurtis A. Kemper, Annotation, *Validity, Construction and Application for Cancellation of Removal of Alien Under 8 U.S.C. § 1229b(b)(1)(D), Including Jurisdictional Issues*, 196 A.L.R. FED. 337 (2004); *see also* 8 U.S.C. § 1229a.

D. Asylum

§ 2.108. *When are asylum and withholding of removal appropriate?*

Persons fleeing persecution may seek entry to the United States or remain if they are already here. Asylum is an option for aliens "physically present in the United States or at a land border or port of entry, irrespective of such alien's status." 8 U.S.C. § 1158(a). If ICE does not grant asylum or withholding of removal, then immigration judges have exclusive jurisdiction to grant either. Asylum is not available to aggravated felons, but withholding can be an option. 8 U.S.C. § 1158.

See generally Bill Frelick, *U.S. Detention of Asylum Seekers: What's the Solution*, 10:7 BENDER'S IMMIGR. BULL. 564 (April 1, 2005).

E. Suspension of Deportation

§ 2.109. *What is "suspension of deportation"?*

This relief is generally an option only for aliens in proceedings before April 1, 1997. 8 U.S.C. § 1254(a). For a description of eligibility, *see* IRA J. KURZBAN, KURZBAN'S IMMIGRATION LAW SOURCEBOOK, 578–80 (7th ed. 2000); *see also* Romualdo P. Eclavea, Annotation, *Suspension of Deportation and Adjustment of Status for Permanent Residence of Alien Under § 244(a)(1) of Immigration and Nationality Act (8 U.S.C. § 1254(a)(1)(A))*, 45 A.L.R. FED. 185 (1979 & 2004 Supp.).

§ 2.110. *What are "waivers of inadmissibility"?*

Immigration statutes allow ICE to waive inadmissibility on several grounds; these waivers are available during the removal hearing. *See* Charles H. Kuck, *Window or Aisle: Removal and Expedited Removal Process and Proceedings*, 2 1997-98 IMMIGRATION & NATIONALITY LAW HANDBOOK 244 (American Immigration Lawyers Ass'n 1997).

F. Waiver

§ 2.111. *Can the government still allow the deported alien to return?*

Yes, an alien with certain convictions can apply for a waiver to return under 8 U.S.C. § 1182(h). This does not apply to a drug conviction unless it was for a first possession of 30 grams or less of marijuana. The alien must have applied for permanent residency and do any one of the following:

- Show hardship to a citizen or LPR relative;
- Apply under the Violence Against Women Act as an abused spouse or child of a citizen or LPR;
- Only be inadmissible for prostitution;
- Have 15 years pass since becoming inadmissible.

LPRs must have had seven years pass between becoming an LPR and the Notice to Appear for their removal hearing and not have an aggravated felony conviction. Oddly enough, a non-LPR alien with an aggravated felony conviction that does not involve drugs can apply for this waiver.

G. Private Immigration Bills

§ 2.112. *Can Congress intervene for an individual alien?*

Yes. The procedure is somewhat rare and, for the poor, not always a ready option. But, if a Congressman or Congresswoman or a Senator can get a bill passed for an individual alien it serves to circumvent the normal immigration process. *See* Ryan Quinn & Stephen Yale-Loehr, *Private Immigration Bills: An Overview*, 9:19 BENDER'S IMMIGR. BULL. 1147 (Oct. 1, 2004).

CHAPTER 3
BORDER STOPS

Other Resources:

WILLIAM W. GREENHALGH, THE FOURTH AMENDMENT HANDBOOK: A CHRONOLOGICAL SURVEY OF SUPREME COURT DECISIONS (Criminal Justice Section: American Bar Ass'n, 2nd. ed. 2003).

Jon Adams, *Rights at United States Borders,* 19 BYU J. PUB. L. 353 (2005).

Introduction

This chapter treats border searches of both aliens and citizens. The Fourth Amendment works differently at the border (some say not at all) and this distinction has become especially significant in the aftermath of 9/11. Media reports incorrectly indicated that the hijackers illegally entered the United States across the border, which prompted calls to severely restrict movement across the borders.

United States v. Arvizu, 534 U.S. 266, 122 S. Ct. 744 (2002), was the first Supreme Court case involving a roving border patrol seizure after 9/11. *See* **VII. Roving Border Patrols,** *infra. Arvizu* does not mention the 9/11 attacks but the heightened border security and the legal standards applied to border seizures post-September 11 are closely related to the issues in *Arvizu.*

One can only surmise how 9/11 will affect border law in the coming years. *See, e.g.*, Lauren Bercuson, *Picture Perfect? X-Ray Searches at the United States Border Require Guidance*, 35 U. MIAMI INTER-AM. L. REV. 577 (2004); Kiera LoBreglio, *The Border Security and Immigration Improvement Act: A Modern Solution to a Historic Problem?*, 78 ST. JOHN'S L. REV. 933 (2004).

§ 3.1. *How does the Fourth Amendment apply to aliens in general?*

This is something of an open question. Aliens lawfully present in the United States have standing to raise Fourth Amendment defenses and even aliens unlawfully in the country had this right. *See, e.g.*, United States v. Montoya de Hernandez, 473 U.S. 531, 105 S. Ct. 3304 (1985). However, in *United States v. Verdugo-Urquidez*, 494 U.S. 259, 110 S. Ct. 1056, *reh'g denied*, 494 U.S. 1092, 110 S. Ct. 1839 (1990), the Supreme Court questioned whether unlawful aliens have Fourth Amendment standing. The analysis may involve whether the unlawful alien has a "substantial connection" with the United States. *See* Gavin Skok, *Protecting the Right of Aliens Unlawfully Present in the United States to Raise Fourth Amendment Defenses in Criminal Prosecutions*, 3:12 BENDER'S IMMIGR. BULL. 604 (June 15, 1998).

I. Border Searches and the Fourth Amendment

§ 3.2. *How is the Fourth Amendment different at the border?*

Under the Fourth Amendment, there must be a warrant or individualized suspicion before police can search a person. At the border, however, officials can search all persons and property without probable cause, individualized suspicion, or warrant as long as the searches are "routine." Notions of national security control these questions. United States v. Montoya de Hernandez, 473 U.S. 531, 538, 105 S. Ct. 3304 (1985); Carroll v. United States, 267 U.S. 132, 45 S. Ct. 280 (1925). Even first-class mail can be opened without a warrant or on less than probable cause.

However, "proximity to the frontier does not automatically place a 100-mile strip of citizenry within a deconstitutionalized zone, with its attendant de-escalation of Fourth Amendment requirements." United States v. McDaniel, 463 F.2d 129, 132–33 (5th Cir. 1972), *cert. denied*, 413 U.S. 919, 93 S. Ct. 3046 (1973).

§ 3.3. *So, is a border search an exception to the Fourth Amendment?*

Yes. This exception is nearly as old as the Fourth Amendment, in existence since 1789. Act of July 31, 1789, chap. 5, 1 stat. 29, 43 (1789). *See* United States v. Ramsey, 431 U.S. 606, 619, 97 S. Ct. 1972 (1977) ("border searches ... have been considered to be 'reasonable' by the single fact that the person or item in question had entered into our country from outside.... This longstanding recognition that searches at our borders without probable cause and without a warrant are nonetheless 'reasonable' has a history as old as the Fourth Amendment itself"); *see also* United States v. Cardenas, 9 F.3d 1139, 1147 (5th Cir. 1993), *reh'g denied*, 15 F.3d 1081 (5th Cir. Tex.), *cert. denied*, 511 U.S. 1134, 114 S. Ct. 2150 (1994).

Although a border search is an exception to the Fourth Amendment, it is limited to the immediate vicinity of the border or its "functional equivalent." Almeda-Sanchez v. United States, 413 U.S. 266, 272–73, 93 S. Ct. 2535 (1973). For example, border officials on roving patrols away from the border must have a reasonable suspicion before stopping a motor vehicle. United States v. Brignoni-Ponce, 422 U.S. 873, 95 S. Ct. 2574 (1975).

§ 3.4. *What then is a "routine search"?*

Any general nonintrusive search of people or items along the border or a point of entry is "routine." "Intrusive" searches such as body cavity, x-rays of a person, or strip searches require reasonable suspicion.

§ 3.5. *What about when the search is of a vehicle?*

As to vehicles, the Supreme Court holds the definition of "routine" is much broader. Thus, a border search involving disassembly of a vehicle's gas tank does not require reasonable suspicion and "[c]omplex balancing tests to determine what is a 'routine' search of a vehicle, as opposed to a more 'intrusive' search of a person, have no place in border searches of vehicles." United States v. Flores-Montano, 541 U.S. 149, 152, 124 S. Ct. 1582 (2004). This "leav[es] open the question of 'whether, and under what circumstances, a border search might be deemed "unreasonable" because of the particularly offensive manner it is carried out'." *Flores-Montano* at 541 U.S. at 155 (quoting United States v. Ramsey, 431 U.S. 606, 618, n.13, 97 S. Ct. 1972 (1977)).

The Court specifically rejected the Ninth Circuit's balancing approach requiring reasonable suspicion for "non-routine" searches of vehicles looking to such factors as the use of tools, whether the search threatened safety and health, and the degree of psychological intrusion. United States v. Molina-Tarazon, 279 F.3d 709 (9th Cir. 2002) (removal of a gas tank was non-routine because tools had to be used with concern that the tank could be damaged; reasonable suspicion found on other grounds).

§ 3.6. *What about when the border search targets a specific person?*

Targeting a specific person makes the search "non-routine," meaning that there must be reasonable suspicion before the search is lawful. Several factors influence this determination such as the force used to effect the search. *See* United States v. Tsai, 282 F.3d 690 (9th Cir. 2002) (defendant "under suspicion" before landing justifying non-routine search); United States v. Robles, 45 F.3d 1, 5 (1st Cir.), *cert. denied*, 514 U.S. 1043, 115 S. Ct. 1416 (1995).

§ 3.7. *What about when ethnicity is the basis of the border search?*

Usually, a stop based on ethnicity is contrary to the Fourth Amendment, but the Constitution allows such "routine" stops at the border because the person or item enters from outside the country. Thus, even if a search is based largely on the basis of race or ethnicity, it is not a constitutional violation. *See* United States v. Ojebode, 957 F.2d 1218, 1223 (5th Cir. 1992) ("even if such stops are made largely on the basis of ethnicity, there is no constitutional violation"), *cert. denied*, 507 U.S. 923, 113 S. Ct. 1291 (1993). However, if the search is "non-routine" it must be based on reasonable suspicion, which in turn cannot be based on "broad profiles which cast suspicion on entire categories of people." United States v. Jimenez-Medina, 173 F.3d 752, 754 (9th Cir. 1999). Ethnicity can only be a factor in determining reasonable suspicion.

§ 3.8. *What about a person who leaves instead of enters the country?*

It does not matter. The Fourth Amendment does not apply when a person exits the United States. United States v. Oriakhi, 57 F.3d 1290, 1296 (4th Cir.) ("The rationale for exempting border searches from the Fourth Amendment's probable cause and warrant requirements rests on fundamental principles of national sovereignty, which applies equally to exit and entry searches."), *cert. denied*, 516 U.S. 952, 116 S. Ct. 400 (1995), *writ of habeas corpus dismissed*, 187 F.3d 632 (4th Cir. 1999); United States v. Berisha, 925 F.2d 791, 795 (5th Cir.) ("[g]iven the substantial national interest in regulating the exportation of domestic currency at the border and similar features of incoming and outgoing border crossing searches for fourth amendment purposes, we hold that in the context of a routine stop and search for currency, the rationale applied to border searches under the Fourth Amendment encompasses persons exiting as well as entering our borders"), *reh'g en banc denied*, 930 F.2d 914 (5th Cir. 1991).

§ 3.9. *Can all government agents conduct border searches?*

No. Only agents with specific statutory authorization, namely Immigration and Customs Enforcement (ICE) agents and the Coast Guard, can conduct a border search. *See* United States v. Whiting, 781 F.2d 692, 696–98 (9th Cir. 1986) (border exception not applicable to Commerce agent's search).

§ 3.10. *Are there limitations to the border patrol officer's powers?*

Yes, 8 U.S.C. § 1357 defines a border patrol agent's powers as follows:

> Any officer employed with the Service authorized under regulations prescribed by the Attorney General shall have power without warrant (1) to interrogate any alien or person believed to be an alien as to his right to be or to remain in the United States; (2) to arrest any alien who in his presence or view is entering or attempting to enter the United States in violation of any law or regulation made ... (3) within a reasonable distance from any external boundary of the United States to board and search for aliens any vessels within the territorial waters of the United States and any railway car, aircraft, conveyance, or vehicle, and within a distance of 25 miles from any such external boundary to have access to private lands, but not dwellings, for the purpose of patrolling the border to prevent the illegal entry of aliens into the United States.

See United States v. Romero-Bustamente, 337 F.3d 1104 (9th Cir. 2003) (8 U.S.C. § 1357 allows border patrol access without warrant to private lands but not dwellings within 25 miles of border — "dwelling" includes backyard sheds and other curtilage); United States v. Garcia-Acuna, 175 F.3d 1143 (9th Cir.) (border patrol has no jurisdiction to enforce traffic laws but could use traffic violation as evidence of reasonable suspicion of federal criminal law violation), *amended by* 1999 U.S. App. LEXIS 16535 (9th Cir. July 19, 1999), *cert. denied*, 528 U.S. 1030, 120 S. Ct. 550 (1999).

§ 3.11. *Does the border patrol have authority to make Terry stops for narcotics?*

It depends on the circuit. The Fifth Circuit holds that they do, United States v. Perkins, 352 F.3d 198 (5th Cir. 2003), *cert. denied*, 541 U.S. 980, 124 S. Ct. 1894 (2004), and the Ninth Circuit holds that they do not. United States v. Santa-Maria, 15 F.3d 879 (9th Cir. 1994).

§ 3.12. *What are ideas for suppression hearings?*

Motions could include preserving recordings of agent's audio transmissions, requests for vehicle sensor information, or for records of citizen complaints against agents as well as statistics of the agents' seizures. Testimony could be from local residents or about road and weather conditions or the border patrol's conduct during stops. Counsel should also consider visiting the site of the stop.

II. *Miranda* and Border Stops

§ 3.13. *Does Miranda apply at the border?*

As part of the same idea of constitutional exception, government officials at the border can initially question a person and even conduct a secondary interview. *Miranda* warnings are not required. United States v. Moya, 74 F.3d 1117, 1120 (11th Cir. 1996) ("a secondary interview is part of the border routine and does not require *Miranda* warning"). Further interrogation, however, usually requires *Miranda* warnings. *But see* United States v. Galindo-Gallegos, 244 F.3d 728 (9th Cir.) (citing Berkemer v. McCarty, 468 U.S. 420, 104 S. Ct. 3138 (1984)) (questioning several detained aliens "in a circle" did not violate *Miranda* given that questioning was in public view with witnesses), *amended by* 255 F.3d 1154 (9th Cir. 2001).

§ 3.14. *Is the defendant's language relevant?*

It may be. Courts have invalidated *Miranda* waivers because the waiver and interrogation were in English when the defendant's primary language was Spanish. *See, e.g.*, United States v. Garibay, 143 F.3d 534 (9th Cir. 1998).

III. Detention and Arrest at the Border

§ 3.15. *Can border officials detain a person during a search?*

Yes. Moreover, the detention can be quite long because the Fourth Amendment balance leans heavily in the government's favor. United States v. Montoya de Hernandez, 473 U.S. 531, 544, 105 S. Ct. 3304 (1985) (upholding detention of suspected alimentary canal smugglers for 16 hours); United States v. Gonzalez-Rincon, 36 F.3d 859, 864 (9th Cir. 1994) ("[A]t the border one's expectation of privacy is less than in the interior and the Fourth Amendment balance between the government's interest and the traveler's privacy rights is struck more favorably to the government.... Such searches are deemed reasonable under the Fourth Amendment by the single fact that the person or item in question has entered into our country from outside"), *cert. denied*, 514 U.S. 1008, 115 S. Ct. 1323 (1995) (internal quotations and citations omitted).

§ 3.16. *Does a border search have to occur right after entry?*

Not necessarily. For example, one court found a valid "border search" even though the passenger had left customs, gone to baggage claim, moved about the airport for 30 minutes, and checked into an adjacent hotel. United States v. Hill, 939 F.2d 934, 937 (11th Cir. 1991).

§ 3.17. *When arresting a border suspect, must the agents have probable cause?*

Although an agent does not need probable cause to search at the border, the Constitution requires probable cause to arrest. United States v. Buckner, 179 F.3d 834 (9th Cir. 1999), *cert. denied*, 528 U.S. 1094, 120 S. Ct. 831 (2000).

IV. Searches of Bags, Persons, and Body Cavities

§ 3.18. *Can border officials search all baggage?*

Yes. Border officials, be they customs agents or border patrol, *see* **Chapter 2, I: Whatever Happened to the INS? — Reorganization After 9/11**), may search all the baggage of anybody entering the United States. Torres v. Puerto Rico, 442 U.S. 465, 472–73, 99 S. Ct. 2425 (1979) ("The authority ... to search [the luggage of] arriving international travelers is based on its inherent sovereign authority to protect its territorial integrity").

§ 3.19. *Can border officials strip search people?*

Yes. However, the officials must have real or reasonable suspicion of criminal activity, because strip searches are "non-routine" searches. The suspicion of illegal concealment must be based upon something more than the border crossing and substantial enough to make the search a reasonable exercise of authority. United States v. Gonzalez-Rincon, 36 F.3d 859, 864 (9th Cir. 1994), *cert. denied*, 514 U.S. 1008, 115 S. Ct. 1323 (1995); United States v. Asbury, 586 F.2d 973, 975–76 (2d Cir. 1978). The analysis looks to the degree of intrusiveness and the type of search. For example, border searches involving the removal of shoes are less intrusive and more routine than strip and body cavity searches. United States v. Ramos-Saenz, 36 F.3d 59, 61–62 (9th Cir.), *amended by* 881 P.2d 298 (Cal. 1994). *See also* United States v. Reyes, 821 F.2d 168, 170 (2d Cir. 1987), *cert. denied*, 484 U.S. 1068, 108 S. Ct. 1032 (1988); United States v. Henao-Castano, 729 F.2d 1364, 1366 (11th Cir. 1984), *cert. denied*, 473 U.S. 923, 105 S. Ct. 3552 (1985).

§ 3.20. *What about body cavity searches?*

Body cavity searches at the border require an even higher standard of suspicion than strip searches. Generally, a body cavity search requires a clear indication that the suspect is carrying contraband in a body cavity. The greater the intrusion, the greater the standard of required suspicion. United States v. Afanador, 567 F.2d 1325, 1328 (5th Cir. 1978).

§ 3.21. *What about alimentary canal searches?*

Once a reasonable suspicion exists that a person is an alimentary canal smuggler, the government may detain the traveler for sufficient time to allow the contents of the suspect's stomach to void. United States v. Rodriguez, 74 F.3d 1164, 1164–65 (11th Cir.), *cert. denied*, 518 U.S. 1025, 116 S. Ct. 2565 (1996). The government may even give him laxatives. For longer detentions, however, the agents must obtain a judicial determination of the reasonableness of the extended detention. Generally, failure to obtain such a judicial determination within 48 hours shifts the burden to the government to demonstrate a bona fide emergency or extraordinary circumstances justifying the lengthy delay. United States v. Adekunle, 2 F.3d 559, 562 (5th Cir. 1993).

V. "Border Searches" Not at the Border: Functional Equivalent and Extended Border Searches

§ 3.22. *Can officials conduct "border searches" away from the border?*

Yes, if the site is the "functional equivalent" of the border. The "functional equivalent of the border" is generally thought of as the first point where an entrant may practically be detained. United States v. Cardenas, 9 F.3d 1139, 1147–48 (5th Cir. 1993), *reh'g denied*, 15 F.3d 1081 (5th Cir. Tex.), *cert. denied*, 511 U.S. 1134, 114 S. Ct. 2150 (1994). Thus, searches at an established station near the border or at a point marking the confluence of two or more roads extending from the border might be the "functional equivalents of border searches." Almeda-Sanchez v. United States, 413 U.S. 266, 272–73, 93 S. Ct. 2535 (1973).

§ 3.23. *What is the legal test for "functional equivalent of the border"?*

The courts have applied a three-pronged test: (1) reasonable certainty that the border was crossed; (2) no opportunity for the object of the search to have changed materially since the crossing; and (3) the search must have occurred at the earliest practical point after the border was crossed. United States v. Hill, 939 F.2d 934, 937 (11th Cir. 1991).

§ 3.24. *Are airports — even well within the United States — "borders"?*

Yes. Airports are the "functional equivalent" of a border. Almeda-Sanchez v. United States, 413 U.S. 266, 273, 93 S. Ct. 2535 (1973). For an easy to understand chart of the law of airport stops and searches, *see* Jon M. Sands & Robyn Greenberg Varcoe, *Buying the Reasonable Suspicion Ticket at Airports*, THE CHAMPION, Dec. 1998, at 20–21.

§ 3.25. *What is an "extended border" search?*

Courts have used the extended border search analysis to allow certain searches to occur long before or after the person or item crossed the actual border. United States v. Whiting, 781 F.2d 692, 695 (9th Cir. 1986) (search allowed 15 hours and 20 miles from the border); United States v. Cardona, 769 F.2d 625, 628–29 (9th Cir. 1985) (where condition of the Federal Express package bound for Colombia but opened in California was "all but certain to remain unchanged" until crossing out of the United States); Castillo-Garcia v. United States, 424 F.2d 482 (9th Cir. 1970) (even 24 hours before the anticipated crossing and 3,000 miles from the border); Rodriguez-Gonzalez v. United States, 378 F.2d 256 (9th Cir. 1967) (seven hours and 100 miles from the border).

§ 3.26. *How does the "functional equivalent" compare to an extended border search?*

Unlike a functional equivalent border search, an extended border search takes place after the first practical point where the entering person or package may be stopped. United States v. Cardenas, 9 F.3d 1139, 1148 (5th Cir. 1993), *reh'g denied*, 15 F.3d 1081 (5th Cir. Tex.), *cert. denied*, 511 U.S. 1134, 114 S. Ct. 2150 (1994). Because extended border searches involve a higher degree of intrusion upon an individual's expectation of privacy than searches at the border, some circuit courts have held that only "reasonable suspicion" may justify them. United States v. Cardona, 769 F.2d 625, 628–29 (9th Cir. 1985). Moreover, there must be a reasonable certainty that a border was crossed. *Cardenas*, 9 F.3d at 1150; United States v. Perez, 644 F.2d 1299, 1302 (9th Cir. 1981). For automobiles, there must be a reasonable certainty that any contraband was in the vehicle at the crossing. *Id.*

VI. Border Checkpoints

§ 3.27. *What about checkpoint stops away from the border?*

Border officials may stop vehicles routinely and question passengers at traffic or airport checkpoints. Random stops, however, are not allowed. Thus, the border patrol may maintain permanent checkpoints at intersections of roads leading away from the border and stop vehicles to question the occupants briefly, even though the agents have no reason to believe that a particular vehicle contains contraband or illegal aliens. United States v. Villamonte-Marquez, 462 U.S. 579, 587, 103 S. Ct. 2573 (1983) (citing United States v. Martinez-Fuerte, 428 U.S. 543, 545, 96 S. Ct. 3074 (1976)); *Martinez-Fuerte*, 428 U.S. at 562 ("stops and questioning at issue may be made in the absence of any individualized suspicion at reasonably located checkpoints"). Courts review stops at non-check points with more scrutiny. United States v. Ellis, 330 F.3d 677 (5th Cir. 2003) (immigration checkpoint stop of commercial bus at non-border checkpoint resulting in seizure of passenger illegal); United States v. Portillo-Aguirre, 311 F.3d 647 (5th Cir. 2002) (immigration checkpoint stop of commercial bus at non-border checkpoint resulting in seizure of passenger illegal), *reh'g en banc denied*, 336 F.3d 345 (5th Cir. 2003).

Because it is a border checkpoint, even though away from the border, this is different than what the Fourth Amendment normally allows. *See, e.g.*, Illinois v. Lidster, 540 U.S. 419, 124 S. Ct. 885 (2004) (Fourth Amendment normally bars police from making suspicionless stops of motorists at checkpoints for general "crime control").

§ 3.28. *Can border officials do more at checkpoints?*

No. At traffic checkpoints, border officials may direct a vehicle to the side and conduct a search only if they have probable cause or a valid consent. United States v. Martinez-Fuerte, 428 U.S. 543, 566–67, 96 S. Ct. 3074 (1976) ("checkpoint searches are constitutional only if justified by consent or probable cause to search"); United States v. Ortiz, 422 U.S. 891, 896–97, 95 S. Ct. 2585 (1975) ("[a]t traffic checkpoints removed from the border and its functional equivalents, officers may not search private vehicles without consent or probable cause"); United States v. Inocencio, 40 F.3d 716, 723 (5th Cir. 1994) ("Although only reasonable suspicion is needed to stop a vehicle for an immigration check, probable cause or consent is necessary in order to search a vehicle"), *reh'g denied sub nom.* United States v. Hinojosa, 1995 U.S. App. LEXIS 3437 (5th Cir. Jan. 30, 1995), *supplemented,* 48 F.3d 163 (5th Cir. Tex. 1995); United States v. Pinedo-Montoya, 966 F.2d 591, 594 (10th Cir. 1992) ("officers may not selectively search vehicles at a border unless they have probable cause or consent to justify the search").

VII. Roving Border Patrols

§ 3.29. *Has the Supreme Court articulated a new standard?*

United States v. Arvizu, 534 U.S. 266, 122 S. Ct. 744 (2002) was the first Supreme Court case involving a roving border patrol seizure following 9/11. The Court held that a "formalistic approach" individually rejecting several factors did not adhere to the "totality of the circumstances" standard for determining whether reasonable suspicion supported the stop.

§ 3.30. *Did Arvizu change the legal standard?*

This is an open question. *United States v. Arvizu,* 534 U.S. 266, 122 S. Ct. 744 (2002), may not have changed the standard and instead reaffirmed the "totality of the circumstances" approach. The case then can be interpreted as a message that appellate courts should not disturb the district court's factual findings under such a totality standard.

§ 3.31. *How is the agent's experience evaluated in such a totality analysis?*

An agent's experience can certainly be considered, but under *United States v. Arvizu,* 534 U.S. 266, 122 S. Ct. 744 (2002), general claims of experience cannot substitute for objective and observed facts. If the "totality of the circumstances" is the standard, then the focus should be the objective facts (i.e., circumstances), not the experience of the agent observer. The Supreme Court, in *Arvizu,* did reaffirmed that the courts, and not law enforcement, are the final judges of reasonable suspicion.

§ 3.32. *What about roving patrols away from a border?*

The Fourth Amendment may apply here in full. For example, a roving patrol conducted 20 miles from the border must conform to the

Fourth Amendment. United States v. Venzor-Castillo, 991 F.2d 634, 637 (10th Cir. 1993) ("because that stop was not a functional equivalent of the border, the court applied Fourth Amendment considerations and determined it was unreasonable"). Although border officials still have a lot of power here, courts "are not prepared to approve the wholesale seizure of miscellaneous persons, citizens or non-citizens in the absence of well-founded suspicion based on particular, individualized, and objectively observable factors which indicate that the person is engaged in criminal activity." United States v. Garcia-Camacho, 53 F.3d 244, 249 (9th Cir. 1995) (internal quotations omitted).

§ 3.33. *What standards must the officials follow during roving patrols?*

"Except at the border and its functional equivalents, officers on roving patrol may stop vehicles only if they are aware of specific articulable facts, together with rational inferences from those facts, that reasonably warrant suspicion that the vehicles contain aliens who may be illegally in the country." United States v. Brignoni-Ponce, 422 U.S. 873, 884, 95 S. Ct. 2574 (1975). "[T]he test is ... whether, based upon the whole picture, they, as experienced Border Patrol officers, could reasonably surmise that the particular vehicle they stopped was engaged in criminal activity". United States v. Cortez, 449 U.S. 411, 421, 101 S. Ct. 690 (1981).

§ 3.34. *Is race a factor on a roving patrol?*

Yes. Under *United States v. Brignoni-Ponce,* 422 U.S. 873, 95 S. Ct. 2574 (1975), Mexican appearance is a relevant factor when the stop occurs near the U.S./Mexico border. United States v. Lopez-Martinez, 25 F.3d 1481, 1487 (10th Cir. 1994). However, it cannot be the only factor. The fact that a passenger appears to be Hispanic is not alone sufficient to create a reasonable suspicion to conduct a roving border stop. "[T]ested by any objective standard there is nothing suspicious about six persons riding in a sedan. The conduct does not become suspicious simply because the skins of the occupants are nonwhite or because they sit up straight or because they do not look at a passing police car." Gonzalez-Rivera v. INS, 22 F.3d 1441, 1446 (9th Cir. 1994) (quoting United States v. Mallides, 473 F.2d 859, 861 (9th Cir. 1973)).

The Ninth Circuit has further held that race or ethnicity cannot be a factor in determining reasonable suspicion, finding language to that effect in *Brignoni-Ponce* dictum. United States v. Montero-Camargo, 208 F.3d 1122 (9th Cir.), *cert. denied*, 531 U.S. 889, 121 S. Ct. 211 (2000). This is due to the changing ethnic composition in the Southwest, where Hispanic heritage is no longer so out of the norm to justify it as a factor of reasonable suspicion. *Id.*

§ 3.35. *What about searching a car during a roving patrol?*

Border officials on roving patrol need probable cause or a valid consent to search a stopped vehicle. United States v. Brignoni-Ponce, 422 U.S. 873, 881–82, 95 S. Ct. 2574 (1975); Almeda-Sanchez v. United States, 413 U.S. 266, 273, 93 S. Ct. 2535 (1973) ("[t]he search of the [defendant's] automobile by a roving patrol ... [i]n the absence of probable cause or consent ... violated the ... Fourth Amendment right to be free of 'unreasonable searches and seizures'").

VIII. Mail Searches

§ 3.36. *Can agents search foreign mail?*

Yes. Under the rationale justifying border searches, officials may search mail arriving from foreign countries without regard to the Fourth Amendment. United States v. Ramsey, 431 U.S. 606, 620, 97 S. Ct. 1972 (1977) ("no different constitutional standards should apply simply because the envelopes were mailed, not carried"); United States v. Richards, 638 F.2d 765, 772 (5th Cir.) ("[a]ffixing a postage stamp to a parcel should not grant it immunity that would not be accorded a package carried by a traveler"), *reh'g denied*, 646 F.2d 962 (5th Cir.), *cert. denied*, 454 U.S. 1097, 102 S. Ct. 669 (1981), *post-conviction proceeding*, 837 F.2d 965 (11th Cir. 1988).

§ 3.37. *Are there limitations to the search of international mail?*

Border or customs officials need to have "reasonable cause," a lower standard than probable cause or reasonable suspicion. "Reasonable cause" exists when officials are aware of specific articulated facts and rational inferences that reasonably warrant a suspicion that the package contains illegal materials. United States v. Taghizadeh, 87 F.3d 287, 289 (9th Cir.) ("the reasons for the application of such a mild standard are clear — border searches of international mail intrude on neither a constitutional nor a statutory expectation of privacy"), *amended by* 1996 U.S. App. LEXIS 20316 (9th Cir. Aug. 14, 1996).

§ 3.38. *Can officials make "controlled deliveries" of mail?*

Yes. When law enforcement agents lawfully learn that there is contraband in a container they can open it to check for contraband and then reseal and deliver it to the intended recipient. Illinois v. Andreas, 463 U.S. 765, 769, 103 S. Ct. 3319 (1983).

IX. Searching for Aliens

§ 3.39. *What about seizure of suspected aliens?*

A border patrol agent may seize a person to investigate whether he is an illegal alien. To justify the seizure, however, the agent must articulate objective facts that provide a reasonable suspicion that the person (in this case, the subject of the seizure) was an illegal alien. The agent must have a rational basis for separating illegal aliens from American citizens and legal aliens; the sole basis for the seizure cannot be simply the defendant's racial background or national origin. Orhorhaghe v. INS, 38 F.3d 488, 497 (9th Cir. 1994).

For issues related to smuggling of aliens, see **Chapter 8: Alien Smuggling and Hostage Taking**.

§ 3.40. *What about searching private property for aliens?*

The Fourth Amendment requires a warrant to search private buildings for illegal aliens. The Fourth Amendment requires strict probable cause standards in criminal cases but not in civil deportation proceedings. Blackie's House of Beef v. Castillo, 659 F.2d 1211, 1222, 1225 (D.C. Cir. 1981), *cert. denied*, 455 U.S. 940, 102 S. Ct. 1432 (1982).

§ 3.41. *Can illegally seized evidence be admitted in deportation hearings?*

Yes. Although such evidence would be suppressed in the criminal case, the evidence can be admitted in deportation proceedings, which are civil. INS v. Lopez-Mendoza, 468 U.S. 1032, 1051, 104 S. Ct. 3479 (1984). *See* **Chapter 2: Immigration Law for Criminal Lawyers**.

X. "Blind Mule" (Border Drug) Cases

§ 3.42. *What is a "blind mule"?*

A blind mule is a person who is used without his knowledge to transport narcotics. *See* United States v. Son Anh Chu, 988 F.2d 981, 983 (9th Cir. 1993). Most cases arise from the border circuits, the Fifth, Ninth, and Tenth. The cases involve many similar traits — for example, the client is a Mexican national, is poor, speaks little or no English, denies knowing of the drugs, and generally has no significant criminal record.

§ 3.43. *Can the government offer expert testimony in blind mule cases?*

Agents have testified, as "experts," that drug smugglers do not entrust large quantities to unknowing dupes. *See* United States v. Cordoba, 104 F.3d 225, 229 (9th Cir. 1997) (agent testimony that sophisticated drug organizations do not entrust 300 kilograms of cocaine to someone who does not know what he is transporting); *see also* United States v. Hooks, 780 F.2d 1526, 1532 (10th Cir.) (agent testimony that drugs worth $10,000 demonstrate that the accused had knowledge), *cert. denied*, 475 U.S. 1128, 106 S. Ct. 1657 (1986); *but see* United States v. Litterell, 574 F.2d 828, 833 (5th Cir. 1978) ("[I]t might be an asset for ... courier to be uninformed about the nature of his delivery, since he would have no reason to be nervous or apprehensive about a task he believed to be perfectly legitimate."). Some courts have limited such testimony to specific situations such as conspiracy cases. *See, e.g.*, United States v. McGowan, 274 F.3d 1251 (9th Cir. 2001) (agent testimony on modus operandi of drug trafficking organizations inadmissible when defendant not charge with conspiracy), *cert. denied*, 537 U.S. 1050, 123 S. Ct. 619, *cert. denied, motion granted by* 537 U.S. 1066, 123 S. Ct. 661 (2002); United States v. Vallejo, 237 F.3d 1008 (9th Cir.), *amended, reh'g en banc denied*, 246 F.3d 1150 (9th Cir. 2001) (same); *see also* United States v. Varela-Rivera, 279 F.3d 1174 (9th Cir. 2002).

§ 3.44. *Is such "expert" testimony subject to a pretrial hearing?*

Under the Supreme Court's holding in *Kumho Tire Co. v. Carmichael*, 526 U.S. 137, 119 S. Ct. 1167 (1999), it should be. Trial courts must ensure that all expert testimony, not just scientific expert testimony, is relevant and reliable. Moreover, recently amended Federal Rule of Evidence 702, incorporating *Kumho*, indicates this as well. At the present time, however, courts seem to be allowing this type of agent testimony. *See* United States v. Hankey, 203 F.3d 1160, 1169 (9th Cir.) (trial court's admission of testimony by a police gang expert allowed because testimony is based "on the knowledge and experience of the expert, rather than the methodology or theory behind it"), *cert. denied*, 530 U.S. 1268, 120 S. Ct. 2733 (2000). This issue undoubtedly will continue to play out in the courts.

§ 3.45. *Is sufficiency of evidence an issue?*

Courts have reversed blind mule convictions for lack of sufficient evidence. United States v. Reveles, 190 F.3d 678 (5th Cir. 1999) (drug possession convictions reversed because circumstantial evidence was insufficient to prove defendant's knowledge); United States v. Reyna, 148 F.3d 540 (5th Cir. 1998) (same). With this in mind, defense counsel should be prepared to make, and prosecutors to defend against, Federal Rule of Criminal Procedure Rule 29 motions for judgments of acquittal. Also, failure to renew a motion for judgment of acquittal at the end of evidence may result in review for plain error instead of *de novo* review. United States v. Carpenter, 95 F.3d 773, 775 (9th Cir. 1996), *cert. denied*, 519 U.S. 1155, 117 S. Ct. 1094 (1997); United States v. Johnson, 87 F.3d 133, 136 (9th Cir.), *reh'g denied*, 96 F.3d 1447 (5th Cir. 1996), *cert. denied*, 520 U.S. 1192, 117 S. Ct. 1482 (1997).

§ 3.46. *Are there language issues in blind mule cases?*

Most certainly — they include not only translations of the defendant's interrogation but also mistaken translations during trial. As the Ninth Circuit ruled, "an incorrect or incomplete translation is the functional equivalent of no translation." Perez-Lastor v. INS, 208 F.3d 773, 778 (9th Cir. 2000). Thus, when court interpreters mistranslate statements for the court or the jury, the mistake should be corrected immediately. Mistranslations include the subtleties of regional dialects; for example, on the border someone may say that he met with an *amigo*, normally translated into English as "friend." In northern Mexico and in some areas of the border, however, the term *amigo* more often denotes an acquaintance or someone just met. People from this region generally use a term like *compadre* to denote a "friend." This has great relevance if a defendant states that a "friend" provided him a truck that was later found to contain drugs.

PART II

ALIENS AND CRIMINAL CONVICTIONS

CHAPTER 4

IMMIGRATION CONSEQUENCES OF CRIMINAL CONVICTIONS

Other Resources:

NATIONAL LAWYER'S GUILD, IMMIGRATION LAW AND DEFENSE (3d ed. 1995).

NORTON TOOBY, CRIMINAL DEFENSE OF IMMIGRANTS vols. I & II (2003).

The basis of this chapter includes the following two articles:

Robert J. McWhirter, *Hell Just Got Hotter: The Rings of Immigration Hell Revisited*, 5:6 CRIM. PRAC. L. REP. 1 (July 1997).

Robert J. McWhirter, *Hell Just Got Hotter: The Rings of Immigration Hell and the Immigration Consequences to Aliens Convicted of Crimes Revisited*, 11 GEO. IMMIGR. L.J. 507 (1996).

Other articles of use include the following:

Tova Indritz, *Puzzling Consequences of Criminal Immigration Cases: Part I*, THE CHAMPION, Jan./Feb. 2002, at 12.

Tova Indritz, *Puzzling Out the Immigration Consequences of Various Criminal Convictions: Part II*, THE CHAMPION, Mar. 2002, at 20.

Tova Indritz, *Puzzling Out the Immigration Consequences of Various Criminal Convictions: Part III*, THE CHAMPION, Jan./Feb. 2002, at 22.

William R. Maynard, *Deportation: An Immigration Law Primer for the Criminal Defense Lawyer*, THE CHAMPION, June 1999, at 12.

Lory Diana Rosenberg & Nelson Vargas-Padilla, *An Odyssey of Immigration Consequences of Crime: The BIA's 2001 Interpretations*, 78 INTERPRETER RELEASES 909 (June 4, 2001).

Richard L. Prinz, *Criminal Aliens under IIRAIRA*, 2:3 BENDER'S IMMIGR. BULL. 79 (Feb. 1, 1997).

Introduction

A deportation may result "in loss of both property and life; or of all that makes life worth living." Ng Fung Ho v. White, 259 U.S. 276, 284, 42 S. Ct. 492 (1922). Indeed, "[o]ur immigration statute exhibits an unyielding, unforgiving and vengeful attitude toward those who have sinned and been rehabilitated. It likewise is relentless in its mandate to deport for minor infractions of the law." Jack Wasserman, *Grounds and Procedures Relating to Deportation*, 13 SAN DIEGO L. REV. 125, 128 (1975). For many aliens, a criminal conviction pales in comparison with the risk of deportation.

I. Telling Aliens of Immigration Consequences

§ 4.1. *Must lawyers and judges tell aliens of immigration consequences?*

Although a deportation may result "in loss of both property and life; or of all that makes life worth living," Ng Fung Ho v. White, 259 U.S. 276, 284, 42 S. Ct. 492 (1922), most cases generally do not hold judges, prosecutors, or defense attorneys accountable for failing to advise aliens of the immigration consequences of criminal convictions. Several state statutes, however, require it and cases recognize that effective lawyers and judges attend to collateral consequences of criminal convictions. See the American Bar Association *Standards for Criminal Justice*:

> To the extent possible, defense counsel should determine and advise the defendant sufficiently in advance of the entry of any plea, as to the possible collateral consequences that might ensue from entry of the contemplated plea.

Pleas of Guilty, Responsibilities of Defense Counsel, ABA STANDARDS FOR CRIMINAL JUSTICE 14-3.2(f) (1999). This standard has provided authority to find counsel ineffective for failing to advise of immigration consequences. *See, e.g.*, People v. Garcia, 799 P.2d

413, 415 (Colo. Ct. App. 1990) (citing to former 3 ABA STANDARDS FOR CRIMINAL JUSTICE 14-3.2(b) (2d ed. 1980) (commentary at 14-75)), *aff'd*, 815 P.2d 937 (Colo. 1991). The Ninth Circuit has recently relied heavily on the ABA standard in finding that an attorney's misadvising a client that there were no immigration consequences to a plea was ineffective assistance of counsel. United States v. Kwan, 407 F.3d 1005 (9th Cir.) (noting that Supreme Court recognizes ABA standards as useful guide to reasonable attorney performance), *amended by* 2005 U.S. App. LEXIS 14813 (9th Cir. July 21, 2005).

A. Duty of Trial Court

§ 4.2. *Must a federal court advise of immigration consequences?*

Currently, the Due Process Clause requires a federal trial court to explain only the direct consequences of conviction. Brady v. United States, 397 U.S. 742, 755, 90 S. Ct. 1463 (1970). Although immigration consequences may follow by operation of law, immigration proceedings are not "direct consequences" as they are civil, Harisiades v. Shaughnessy, 342 U.S. 580, 594, 72 S. Ct. 512, *reh'g denied*, 343 U.S. 936, 72 S. Ct. 767 (1952), and deportation is not punishment for crime. Galvan v. Press, 347 U.S. 522, 531, 74 S. Ct. 737, *reh'g denied*, 348 U.S. 852, 75 S. Ct. 17 (1954). *See generally* Gabriel J. Chin & Richard W. Holms, Jr., *Effective Assistance of Counsel and the Consequences of Guilty Pleas*, 87 CORNELL L. REV. 697 (Mar. 2002).

§ 4.3. *Must state courts advise of immigration consequences?*

This depends on the state. Several states do not require such advice. *See, e.g.*, State v. Rodriguez, 17 Ariz. App. 553, 554–55, 499 P.2d 167, 168–69 (1972); State v. Vera, 159 Ariz. 237, 239, 766 P.2d 110, 112 (Ct. App. 1988). However, as many as 18 state statutes require that trial judges advise defendants of immigration consequences. *See* INS v. St. Cyr, 533 U.S. 289, 322 n.48 (2001); *see also* Gabriel J. Chin & Richard W. Holmes, Jr., *Effective Assistance of Counsel and the Consequences of Guilty Pleas*, 87 CORNELL L. REV. 697, 706–08 nn.66–114 (2002).

§ 4.4. *Is the law changing?*

Yes. The legal fiction that all civil consequences of criminal convictions are not "direct" is hard to maintain. *See, e.g.*, United States v. Littlejohn, 224 F.3d 960 (9th Cir. 2000) (guilty plea rendering defendant ineligible for food stamps and Social Security benefits, though "civil," is a direct consequence of which effective counsel must advise). So far, however, courts have not extended this analysis to the immigration context. *See* United States v. Amador-Leal, 276 F.3d 511 (9th Cir.) (trial court need not inform defendant of immigration consequences because of fiction that immigration law did not guarantee defendant's deportation), *cert. denied*, 535 U.S. 1070, 122 S. Ct. 1946 (2002).

B. Duty of Counsel

§ 4.5. *Must an attorney advise aliens of immigration consequences?*

As with judges, an attorney only has the duty to warn an alien of the direct consequences of a conviction. "The only consequences considered direct are the maximum prison term and the fine for the offense charged." United States v. Salmon, 944 F.2d 1106, 1130 (3d Cir. 1991) (citing United States v. Pearson, 910 F.2d 221, 223 (5th Cir. 1990), *cert. denied*, 498 U.S. 1093, 111 S. Ct. 977 (1991)), *cert. denied*, 502 U.S. 1110, 112 S. Ct. 1213 (1992). *See also* United States v. Parrino, 212 F.2d 919, 921 (2d Cir.) (deportation is a collateral consequence of conviction), *cert. denied*, 348 U.S. 840, 75 S. Ct. 46 (1954). However, "[t]he distinction between a collateral and direct consequence of a criminal conviction, like many of the lines drawn in legal analysis, is obvious at the extremes and often subtle at the margin." United States v. Russell, 686 F.2d 35, 38 (D.C. Cir. 1982). *But see* United States v. Del Rosario, 902 F.2d 55, 59 (D.C. Cir.) (failure to advise of immigration consequences merely collateral), *cert. denied*, 498 U.S. 942, 111 S. Ct. 352 (1990).

See generally Gregory G. Sarno, Annotation, *Ineffective Assistance of Counsel: Misrepresentation, or Failure To Advise, of Immigration Consequences of Guilty Plea — Federal Cases*, 90 A.L.R. FED. 748 (1988); Gregory G. Sarno, Annotation, *Ineffective Assistance of Counsel: Misrepresentation, or Failure To Advise, of Immigration Consequences of Guilty Plea — State Cases*, 65 A.L.R. 4TH 719 (1988 & 2004 Supp.); Gregory G. Sarno, Annotation, *Ineffec-*

tive Assistance of Counsel: Misrepresentation, or Failure To Advise, of Immigration Consequences of Waiver of Jury Trial, 103 A.L.R. FED. 867 (1991 & 2004 Supp.); John J. Francis, *Failure to Advise Non-Citizens of Immigration Consequences of Criminal Convictions: Should This Be Grounds to Withdraw a Guilty Plea?*, 36 U. MICH. J.L. REF. 691 (2003); Rob A. Justman, *The Effects of AEDPA and IIRIRA on Ineffective Assistance of Counsel Claims for Failure to Advise Alien Defendant's of Deportation Consequences of Pleading Guilty to an "Aggravated Felony,"* 2004 UTAH L. REV. 701.

§ 4.6. *How have promulgated standards dealt with this issue?*

The rule exonerating counsel and courts for any responsibility in failing to advise defendants, especially alien defendants, of the collateral consequences of a criminal conviction is at odds with what most attorneys and judges consider the standards for effective representation. *See, e.g.*, Pleas of Guilty, Responsibilities of Defense Counsel, STANDARDS FOR CRIMINAL JUSTICE 14-3.2(f) (2000). Many commentators argue that the "collateral consequences rule" is inconsistent with the Supreme Court's decision in *Strickland v. Washington*, 466 U.S. 668, 104 S. Ct. 2052 (1984). *See* Gabriel J. Chin & Richard W. Holmes, Jr., *Effective Assistance of Counsel and the Consequences of Guilty Pleas*, 87 CORNELL L. REV. 697, 718 (Mar. 2002) ("lawyers who ignore collateral consequences of legal actions are, to that extent, bad lawyers"). *See also* Lory Diana Rosenberg, *Indigent Defense: Preventive Lawyering: How Defense Counsel Can Defend Immigrant's Rights*, THE CHAMPION, Mar. 2003, at 43; Guy Cohen, Note, *Weakness of the Collateral Consequences Doctrine: Counsel's Duty to Inform Aliens of the Deportation Consequences of Guilty Pleas*, 16 FORDHAM INT'L L.J. 1094 (1992-93); Jamie Ostroff, Comment, *Are Immigration Consequences of a Criminal Conviction Still Collateral? How the California Supreme Court's Decision in IN RE: Resendiz Leaves This Question Unanswered.* (IN RE: Resendiz, *19 P.3d 1171, Cal. 2000*) 32 SW. U.L. REV. 359–82 (2003).

§ 4.7. *What does the Supreme Court say?*

In *INS v. St. Cyr*, 533 U.S. 289, 121 S. Ct. 2271 (2001), the Supreme Court recognized that "[t]here can be little doubt, as a general matter, alien defendants considering whether to enter into a plea agreement are acutely aware of the immigration consequences of their conviction." *St. Cyr,* 121 S. Ct. at 2291. Relying on the ABA Standards, *id.* at 2291 n.48 (quoting Pleas of Guilty, Responsibilities of Defense Counsel, STANDARDS FOR CRIMINAL JUSTICE 14-3.2 cmt. at 14-75 (1980)). Moreover, "[e]ven if the defendant were not initially aware of § 212(c), competent defense counsel, following the advice of numerous practice guides, would have advised him concerning the provision's importance." *St. Cyr,* 121 S. Ct. at 2291 n.50 (citing brief for National Association of Criminal Defense Lawyers et al. as *amicus curiae* 6–8). Indeed, "preserving the client's right to remain in the United States may be more important to the client than any potential jail sentence." *Id.* (quoting BENDER, CRIMINAL DEFENSE TECHNIQUES §§ 60A.01, 60A.02[2] (1999)).

§ 4.8. *How have the federal circuit courts treated St. Cyr?*

Despite the statement in *INS v. St. Cyr,* 533 U.S. 289, 121 S. Ct. 2271 (2001), that competent lawyering includes advice on collateral consequences such as deportation, the courts have distinguished the case. For example, in *United States v. Fry,* 322 F.3d 1198 (9th Cir. 2003), *remanded by post-conviction proceeding,* Unites States v. Moore, 87 Fed. Appx. 668 (9th Cir. 2004), the alien petitioner claimed that his counsel was ineffective for failing to inform him of the immigration consequences of a fraud conviction. Indeed, turning *St. Cyr* around, the Ninth Circuit noted that such advice on immigration consequences is not necessary because the Supreme Court had observed "that, as a general matter, alien defendants considering whether to enter into a plea agreement are acutely aware of immigration consequences." *St. Cyr,* 533 U.S. at 322. *See also* United States v. Gonzalez, 202 F.3d 20, 25 (1st Cir. 2000); United States v. Banda, 1 F.3d 354, 356 (5th Cir. 1993); Varela v. Kaiser, 976 F.2d 1357, 1358 (10th Cir. 1992), *cert. denied,* 507 U.S. 1039, 113 S. Ct. 1869 (1993); United States v. Del Rosario, 902 F.2d 55, 59 (D.C. Cir.), *cert. denied,* 498 U.S. 942, 111 S. Ct. 352 (1990); Santos v. Kolb, 880 F.2d 941, 945 (7th Cir. 1989), *cert. denied,* 493 U.S. 1059, 110 S. Ct. 873 (1990); United States v. Yearwood, 863 F.2d 6, 7–8 (4th Cir. 1988); United States v. Campbell, 778 F.2d 764, 769 (11th Cir. 1985); United States v. Santelises, 476 F.2d 787 (2d Cir. 1973), 509 F.2d 703, 704 (2d Cir. 1975) (per curiam).

§ 4.9. *What do state courts require?*

Several state courts hold that state law requires lawyers to advise aliens about potential deportation.

See, e.g., Williams v. State, 641 N.E.2d 44, 49 (Ind. Ct. App. 1994) (state constitution requires advice about deportation); State v. Arvanitis, 522 N.E.2d 1089, 1094–95 (Ohio Ct. App. 1986); Lyons v. Pearce, 694 P.2d 969, 971 n.2, 974–77 (Ore. 1985) (en banc). A growing number of states require advice about deportation by statute or court rule. *See, e.g.*, INS v. St. Cyr, 533 U.S. 289, 121 S. Ct. 2271, 2291 n.48 (2001) (listing rules and statutes); Christina La Brie, *Lack of Uniformity in Deportation of Criminal Aliens*, 25 N.Y.U. REV. L. & SOC. CHANGE 357, 373, 393 (1999) (listing state statutes). California rejected the bright line rule prohibiting claims regarding ineffectiveness assistance of counsel for failure to advise on deportation consequences. *In re* Resendiz, 19 P.3d 1171 (Cal. 2000), *reh'g denied*, 2001 Cal. LEXIS 3812 (Cal. June 13, 2001). *Cf.* People v. Correa, 108 Ill.2d 541, 485 N.E. 2d 307, 312 (1985) (deportation was collateral consequence, but erroneous and misleading advice defendant was given fell below required range of competence); *see also* United States v. Russell, 686 F.2d 35, 41–42 (D.C. Cir. 1982) (allowing defendant to withdraw guilty plea pursuant to former Federal Rule of Criminal Procedure 32(d) because the government incorrectly informed defendant that conviction would not subject him to deportation); People v. Soriano, 194 Cal. App. 3d 1470, 1480, 240 Cal. Rptr. 328, 235–36 (1987) ("What is uncontested is that counsel, knowing defendant was an alien ..., did not make it her business to discover what impact his negotiated sentence would have on his deportability."); People v. Pozo, 746 P.2d 523, 527 (Col. 1987) (en banc) (counsel must investigate relevant immigration law when counsel is aware defendant is a noncitizen); Ghanavati v. State, 820 So. 2d 989 (Fla. 2002); *Correa*, 485 N.E.2d at 309–12 (counsel ineffective for giving erroneous advice in response to the defendant's specific questions about deportation); Segura v. State, 749 N.E.2d 496, 500, 507 (Ind. 2001) (counsel's failure to advise of immigration consequences may constitute deficient performance, depending on counsel's knowledge of defendant's status, familiarity with consequences, and other evidence establishing a reasonable probability that defendant would not have pled guilty); Aldus v. State, 748 A.2d 463 (Me. 2000) (counsel's failure to explain that noncitizen defendant wanted to defer proceedings or to inquire if defendant wished to obtain information as to why INS was interested in her before entering her plea was ineffective assistance); State v. Viera, 760 A.2d 840 (N.J. Super. Ct. 2000) (counsel ineffectively represented the interest of the defendant by circling "N/A" regarding deportation on the plea form without further inquiry, where she knew defendant had difficulty reading and writing English); State v. Garcia, 727 A.2d 97 (N.J. Super. Ct. 1999) (ordering a hearing to determine whether counsel provided misinformation about deportation and, if so, whether counsel's conduct "was within the range of competence demanded of attorneys in criminal cases.").

§ 4.10. *What then should a defense attorney tell an alien client?*

Obviously, the attorney needs to give the alien defendant some indication of what will happen in immigration court. Moreover, the defense attorney should warn the alien defendant not to admit to criminal charges if immigration authorities ask him. Even when the conviction is vacated, the defendant may still have admitted sufficient facts to warrant deportation under the different immigration court standards. *See generally* Jennifer Welch, *Defending Against Deportation: Equipping Public Defenders to Represent Non-citizens Effectively*, 92 CAL. L. REV. 541 (2004).

Also, counsel should advise convicted aliens of opportunities to avoid deportation. For example, if the alien is eligible for cancellation of removal under 8 U.S.C. § 1229(b), he should begin while incarcerated to establish the equities involved.

II. Aliens and Crime

A. Deportation and Exclusion

§ 4.11. *How can a criminal conviction hurt an alien's immigration status?*

Criminal convictions can get the alien expelled from the United States in two ways:

- Deportation/Removal — Title 8 U.S.C. § 1227 provides the basis for deportation and affects the alien's chance to get relief from deportation such as asylum, withholding, adjustment of status, or cancellation of removal;

- Exclusion/Inadmissibility — Title 8 U.S.C. § 1182 affects the alien after the fact from renewing or changing immigration status.

Counsel should readily refer to 8 U.S.C. § 1227, 8 U.S.C. § 1182, and 8 U.S.C. § 1101(a)(43) defining aggravated felonies.

§ 4.12. *What are the criminal grounds for deportation and exclusion?*

Under 8 U.S.C. § 1227(a)(2) the government can deport an alien for committing the following crimes:

- Any offense "relating to" controlled substances;
- Either two Crimes Involving Moral Turpitude (CIMT) or one felony CIMT committed within five years of the alien's entry;
- Any aggravated felony;
- Any firearms offense;
- A domestic violence offense, stalking, child abuse, child abandonment or neglect, civil or criminal violation of a protective order;
- Managing a prostitution business;
- Being a drug addict/abuser.

Under 8 U.S.C. § 1182(a)(2) and (a)(1) the government can exclude an alien for committing the following crimes:

- Any offense "relating to" controlled substances;
- A CIMT unless the offense is excepted as follows: (1) a petty offense where the potential sentence is a year or less and the alien received a sentence of six months or less, (2) the offense was by a youthful offender where the alien was under 18 and five years have passed since the conviction or release from imprisonment;
- Formal admission of a controlled substance offense or CIMT (no conviction necessary);
- Being a drug addict/abuser;
- Dealing drugs, where the government has "reason to believe" the alien has been or helped a drug dealer;
- Prostitution;
- Two or more crimes where the total sentence was five years or more.

As this listing demonstrates, deportability and excludability are not always the same. If an alien is excludable but not deportable, counsel should advise the alien not to leave the United States because the government will not allow him back in.

§ 4.13. *So what is the difference for an alien?*

It depends on the alien's status and ultimate wishes. An alien that is a legal permanent resident (LPR) or with other immigration status (e.g., a refugee, visa holder, under Temporary Protected Status) does not want to lose that status with a deportation based on a criminal conviction. His or her priority would be to avoid the following convictions in order:

1. An aggravated felony;
2. A drug conviction;
3. A felony conviction for a crime involving moral turpitude (CIMT);
4. Other crimes and criminal conduct.

Conversely, an undocumented alien is already deportable for entering or staying illegally. This alien may have a greater interest in avoiding a finding of inadmissibility to leave open the chance of coming back to the United States legally.

§ 4.14. *But how can the government "exclude" an alien already here?*

It is an after-the-fact order. If the immigration judge or other immigration officials (*see* **Chapter 2: Immigration Law for Criminal Lawyers** outlining the transfer of responsibilities from the former INS) finds the alien *excludable/inadmissible*, the government will not let him back in the United States. But, the government will not deport the alien from the United States unless he is also *deportable/removable*. Often the alien is both *excludable* and *removable*. At times, however, the lists are different. Thus, the oddity of an alien that is inadmissible but not deportable. This alien should not leave the United States because the government will not let him back in.

If counsel can begin to understand this contrivance of immigration law the rest may start to become clear.

§ 4.15. *Can a deported alien ever legally come back?*

Not for a long time:

- If the alien is inadmissible he is ineligible to return for five years (8 U.S.C. § 1182(a)(9)(A)(i));
- If this is the alien's second removal he is ineligible to return for 20 years (*id.*);
- If the alien departed under an outstanding removal order he is ineligible to return for 10 years or 20 years if it is the second time (8 U.S.C. § 1182(a)(9)(A)(ii));
- If the alien is removed for a felony he is ineligible to return for 10 years (*id.*);
- If the alien is removed for an aggravated felony he is ineligible to return for 20 years (*id.*).

§ 4.16. *Can the government still allow the alien to return?*

Yes, an alien with certain convictions can apply for a waiver to return under 8 U.S.C. § 1182(h). This does not apply to a drug conviction unless it was for a first possession of 30 grams or less of marijuana or hashish. The alien must have applied for permanent residency and do any one of the following:

- Show hardship to a citizen or LPR relative;
- Apply under the Violence Against Women Act as an abused spouse or child of a citizen or LPR;
- Only be inadmissible for prostitution;
- Have 15 years pass since becoming inadmissible.

LPRs must have seven years between becoming an LPR and the Notice to Appear for their removal hearing and not have an aggravated felony conviction. Oddly enough, a non-LPR alien with an aggravated felony conviction that does not involve drugs can apply for this waiver.

§ 4.17. *Do all aliens with criminal convictions get a deportation hearing?*

No. Under 8 U.S.C. § 1228(b), an immigration enforcement officer can, without a hearing, order the alien's "expedited removal" if the alien is not an LPR and has an aggravated felony conviction. *See* **Chapter 5: Aggravated Felonies**. In this situation, the alien has no chance to ask for relief. 8 U.S.C. § 1228(b)(5).

§ 4.18. *What happens if the alien does come back illegally?*

If he gets caught, the government can charge him with illegal entry under 8 U.S.C. § 1325, or reentry after deportation under 8 U.S.C.

§ 1326 with enhanced penalties for felony or aggravated felony removals. *See* **Chapter 10: Illegal Entry and Reentry — Pretrial and Trial** *and* **Chapter 11: Illegal Entry and Reentry — Pleas and Sentencing**.

The government can reinstate the original removal order without a new hearing. 8 U.S.C. § 1231(a)(5).

B. Citizenship

§ 4.19. *What does citizenship have to do with criminal consequences?*

Citizens cannot be deported — everyone else can. Don't make the mistake of thinking that the label "legal permanent resident" (LPR) means permanent no matter what. Although LPRs enjoy more defenses to deportation than other aliens, conviction for any number of crimes can result in deportation. *See* 8 U.S.C. § 1227 (allowing for deportation of legal permanent residents); B. John Ovink, *Why a Plea Bargain May No Longer Be a Bargain for Legal Permanent Resident Aliens*, FED. LAW., May 1999, at 49.

§ 4.20. *How do you know whether someone is a citizen?*

Questions of citizenship are not always simple. As discussed in **Chapter 2, III: Citizenship and Naturalization**, U.S. citizenship is conferred by blood or by place of birth. 8 U.S.C. § 1401 (1994). (*See also* **Chapter 2, II.B, § 2.17**, regarding American Indian tribes.) If by blood, the citizenship is "derivative" — a person can be a citizen if a parent was or became one, regardless of where the child was born. Derivative citizenship depends on a number of confusing factors, including whether the citizen parent was the mother or father, the immigration laws in effect at the time of the parents' and/or defendant's birth, and the parents' marital status. *See* NATIONAL LAWYER'S GUILD, IMMIGRATION LAW AND DEFENSE (3d ed. 1995); Daniel Levy, *Children Born Out of Wedlock after the 1995 Amendment to the Definition of Child for Immigration Purposes*, 3:19 BENDER'S IMMIGR. BULL. 1 (Oct. 1, 1998).

§ 4.21. *What if my client is not a citizen?*

If your client lacks citizenship, determine his immigration status. Aliens are generally divided into two groups: those with legal status and those without. Those entitled to reside and work here permanently are called "lawful permanent residents" (LPRs), "permanent residents," "immigrants," or "resident aliens." The card that evidences permanent resident status is commonly called a "green card," although it has not been green for over 30 years. After residing in the United States for a period of time (usually five years after receiving LPR status), an otherwise eligible immigrant may apply to become a United States citizen through a process called "naturalization."

See generally Teresa A. Miller, *Citizenship & Severity: Recent Immigration Reforms and the New Penology*, 17 GEO. IMMIGR. L.J. 611 (2003).

§ 4.22. *What are the types of alien immigrants?*

Aliens who are not LPRs may be in the United States legally in a temporary or "nonimmigrant" visa status with tourist visas and border crossing cards, student visas, and several types of temporary worker visas. The various types of legal, nonimmigrant visas are listed in § 101(a)(15) of the Immigration and Nationality Act. 8 U.S.C. § 1101(a)(15). Many aliens, especially in the border areas, are here illegally without any status.

C. Cultural Concerns

§ 4.23. *Are there unique cultural issues in these cases?*

Aliens often come from unique cultures with different expectations about the criminal justice system. Language barriers can also affect the alien's decisions. *See* CULTURAL ISSUES IN CRIMINAL DEFENSE (James G. Connell, III, & Rene L. Valladares, eds. 2003); IMMIGRANTS IN COURTS (Joanne Moore, ed. 1999); Flo Messier, *Alien Defendants in Criminal Proceedings: Justice Shrugs*, 36 AM. CRIM. L. REV. 1395 (1999). Failing to present relevant cultural differences that affect the case's outcome is ineffective assistance of counsel. Kwan Fai Mak v. Blodgett, 970 F.2d 614 (9th Cir. 1992), *cert. denied*, 507 U.S. 951, 113 S. Ct. 1363 (1993).

D. Cooperating Aliens

§ 4.24. *What benefits are there for aliens cooperating with authorities?*

If the alien is willing to work as a police informant and his testimony substantially contributes to the success of an investigation or prosecution, he might avoid deportation by obtaining a "snitch" or "S" visa. *See* 8 U.S.C. § 1101(a)(15)(S) (1994) (providing for avoidance of deportation for persons giving assistance to police).

E. Immigration Detention for Convictions

§ 4.25. *How does a criminal conviction affect immigration detention?*

Most aliens facing removal hearings can post a bond and secure release or even be released on their own recognizance. But, if the alien has a criminal conviction it may mean detention while his or her immigration case is pending.

§ 4.26. *Can aliens convicted of a crime get a bond?*

Some can, but most criminal aliens cannot, regardless of whether they are sentenced to probation or released on parole for the conviction. Title 8 U.S.C. § 1226(c) mandates detention of noncitizens removable on certain criminal grounds even if the alien is eligible for relief from deportation. The Supreme Court has found this constitutional even with respect to lawful permanent residents. Demore v. Hyung Joon Kim, 538 U.S. 510, 123 S. Ct. 1708 (2003), *rev'g* 276 F.3d 523 (9th Cir. 2002). This applies to convictions or release from custody after October 8, 1998.

§ 4.27. *Can aggravated felons get bond?*

Generally not, if the alien's aggravated felony conviction is recent. However, an aggravated felony *in the past* might not preclude release on bond, unless the alien was just released from custody *for that crime. See* Pastor-Camarena v. Smith, 977 F. Supp. 1415, 1417 (W.D. Wash. 1997) (statute precluding release of aggravated felons by INS "applies immediately after release from incarceration, not to aliens released many years earlier"). Title 8 U.S.C. § 1101(a)(43) lists aggravated felonies.

§ 4.28. *What other convictions mandate immigration detention?*

Immigration law mandates detention for aliens with the following convictions or engaged in the following activities:

- Drug Crimes (exception: if person has been "lawfully admitted" and has one conviction only for simple possession for personal use of less than 30 grams of marijuana, with no other drug convictions);
- Firearm Offenses;
- Prostitution or procuring (or attempting to procure) a prostitute;
- CIMT committed within five years of admission with an actual sentence of at least one year that does not fit under the petty offense exception;
- Two CIMT convictions;
- More than one crime for which the aggregate sentences to confinement were at least five years (unless "lawfully admitted");
- Participation in human trafficking;
- Money laundering.

III. Immigration Law and Convictions

A. "Conviction" and "Sentencing" Under Immigration Law

§ 4.29. *What constitutes a "conviction" for immigration purposes?*

The term conviction means the following:

> (i) a judge or jury has found the alien guilty or the alien has entered a plea of guilty or *nolo contendere* or has admitted sufficient facts to warrant a finding of guilt, and
>
> (ii) the judge has ordered some form of punishment, penalty, or restraint on the alien's liberty to be imposed.

8 U.S.C. § 1101(a)(48). The second prong can be satisfied by imposed jail time (whether or not suspended), probation, participation in rehabilitative programs, community service, and payment of fines.

§ 4.30. *What is a "sentence" under immigration law?*

A sentence under immigration law includes "the period of incarceration or confinement ordered by a court of law regardless of any suspension of the imposition or execution of that imprisonment or sentence in whole or in part." 8 U.S.C. § 1101(a)(48).

§ 4.31. *How does this definition affect deportability?*

A sentence to less than one year will prevent the following convictions from being classified as aggravated felony offenses for immigration purposes.

- Crime of violence under 18 U.S.C. § 16;
- Theft including receipt of stolen property;
- Burglary;
- Bribery of a witness;
- Commercial bribery;
- Counterfeiting;
- Forgery;
- Trafficking in vehicles with altered VIN numbers;
- Obstruction of justice;
- Perjury and subornation of perjury;
- Falsifying documents or trafficking in false documents.

See 8 U.S.C. § 1101(a)(43)(F), (G), (S). Even if a conviction for one of the above offenses is a misdemeanor with a suspended sentence of one year or more, the conviction is an aggravated felony. Thus, if counsel representing the alien can get a sentence of 364 days or less these crimes are not aggravated felonies. *See* 8 U.S.C. § 1101(a)(48)(B).

§ 4.32. *Does federal or state law control the definition of conviction?*

Federal law controls. A disposition that is not a "conviction" under state law may still be a "conviction" for immigration purposes. *In re* Salazar-Regino, 23 I&N Dec. 223, 231 (BIA 2002) (en banc).

B. Immigration Courts, Prior Convictions, and Categorical Approach

§ 4.33. *How will an immigration judge interpret a record of conviction?*

The immigration judge will use a "modified categorical approach" when looking at the alien's conviction to see if it is a deportable conviction.

First, the immigration judge will look to see if the statute of conviction categorically establishes a deportable felony. United States v. Tighe, 266 F.3d 1187, 1196 (9th Cir. 2001); United States v. Bonat, 106 F.3d 1472 (9th Cir.), *cert. denied*, 522 U.S. 874, 118 S. Ct. 192 (1997); *In re* Danesh, 19 I&N Dec. 669, 670 (BIA 1988) ("[I]n deportation proceedings the immigration judge cannot go beyond the judicial record to determine the guilt or innocence of an alien.") (citing *In re* Khalik, 17 I&N Dec. 518 (BIA 1980)); *In re* Roberts, 20 I&N Dec. 294 (BIA 1991). Thus, the elements of an underlying criminal offense must correspond to those in a federal immigration statute for a conviction of that offense to support a removal order or other immigration consequences. *See, e.g., In re* Martin, 23 I&N Dec. 491, 505 (BIA 2002) (en banc) (J. Rosenberg, dissenting) (citing *In re* Espinoza-Gonzalez, 22 I&N Dec. 889, 891 (BIA 1999) (en banc)); Lory Diana Rosenberg, *Separate Opinion — The Immigration Consequences of a "Crime as Defined": How to Analyze and Assess a Criminal Conviction*, 8:5 BENDER'S IMMIGR. BULL. 373 (Mar. 1, 2003).

Second, only if the statute is unclear will the immigration judge "modify" the categorical approach and look to the judicially-noticeable documents. United States v. Sandoval-Venegas, 292 F.3d 1101 (9th Cir. 2002); United States v. Rivera-Sanchez, 247 F.3d 905, 909 (9th Cir. 2001) (en banc); United States v. Palmer, 68 F.3d 52, 55–56 (2d Cir. 1995) ("'if the statutory description ... blankets both violent and non-violent crimes, the court may peek beneath the coverlet'") (quoting United States v. Winter, 22 F.3d 15, 18 (1st Cir. 1994)).

§ 4.34. *What are "judicially noticeable" documents?*

These include "the indictment, the judgment of conviction, jury instructions, a signed guilty plea, or the transcript from the plea proceedings." United States v. Casarez-Bravo, 181 F.3d 1074, 1077 (9th Cir. 1999). This does not include the California Abstract of

Judgment. United States v. Navidad-Marcos, 367 F.3d 903 (9th Cir. 2004).

C. Immigration Law and Criminal Dispositions

1. Probation

§ 4.35. *How does probation count under immigration law?*

Probation does not constitute part of the "term of a sentence" because it does not include incarceration but it does indicate that a conviction exists. 8 U.S.C. § 1101(a)(48). The only situation where "probation" would not necessarily indicate the existence of a conviction would be if there was no finding of guilt, no plea of guilty, or *nolo contendere*, and no admission of sufficient facts. In the federal system, this would be pretrial diversion.

When probation is imposed together with a suspended sentence, the suspended sentence constitutes a "sentence" because the statute states specifically that a period of incarceration or confinement amounts to a sentence "regardless of suspension of that imposition or execution of that imprisonment or sentence in whole or in part." 8 U.S.C. § 1101(a)(48)(B).

2. Deferred Adjudications and Diversion Agreements

§ 4.36. *Are diversion agreements convictions?*

Yes, if they involve a finding of guilt. *In re* Roldan-Santoyo, 22 I&N Dec. 512 (BIA 1999) (en banc), *rev'd sub nom.* Lujan-Armendariz v. INS, 222 F.3d 728 (9th Cir. 2000); *In re* Punu, 22 I&N Dec. 224 (BIA 1998).

§ 4.37. *What if the adjudication of guilt has been deferred?*

For immigration purposes, a "conviction" exists even if adjudication of guilt has been deferred, so long as the alien has entered a plea of guilty, or *nolo contendere*, or has admitted sufficient facts to warrant the finding of guilt, and the judge has ordered some form of punishment, penalty, or restraint of the alien's liberty. 8 U.S.C. § 1101(a)(48)(A). *See also In re* Punu, 22 I&N Dec. 224 (BIA 1998); *but see* Martinez-Montoya v. INS, 904 F.2d 1018 (5th Cir.

1990) (Texas deferred adjudication not a conviction for immigration purposes); *In re* Roldan-Santoyo, 22 I&N Dec. 512 (BIA 1999) (en banc), *rev'd sub nom.* Lujan-Armendariz v. INS, 222 F.3d 728 (9th Cir. 2000). With drug convictions, ICE can use deferred convictions for deportation when the following three elements are present: (1) the criminal court's finding of guilt or the alien's admission of facts establishing guilt; (2) the imposition of some form of punishment, penalty, or restraint on the defendant's liberty; and (3) the ability to enter a conviction without further proceedings if the defendant violates the terms of probation or fails to comply with the court's conditions. *In re* Ozkok, 19 I&N Dec. 546 (BIA 1988). *See also* Garberding v. INS, 30 F.3d 1187 (9th Cir. 1994); Chong v. INS, 890 F.2d 284 (11th Cir. 1989); Gregory G. Sarno, Annotation, *Effect of Expungement of Conviction on § 241(a)(4), (11) of Immigration and Nationality Act of 1952 (8 U.S.C. § 1251(a)(4), (11)), Making Aliens Deportable for Crimes Involving Moral Turpitude or Drugs*, 98 A.L.R. FED. 750 (1990 & 2004 Supp.).

3. Expunged Convictions

§ 4.38. *Does expunging a conviction protect the alien's immigration status?*

Usually not, because an expungement still involves a finding of guilt only overturned for equitable reasons. Doe v. INS, 120 F.3d 200, 203 (9th Cir. 1997); United States v. Johnson, 962 F.2d 579, 582 (7th Cir. 1992). *See also* Beltran-Leon v. INS, 134 F.3d 1379 (9th Cir. 1998). Moreover, relying on 8 U.S.C. § 1101(a)(48)(A), the BIA gives no effect to a state action that expunges, dismisses, cancels, vacates, discharges, or otherwise removes a guilty plea or verdict. *In re* Luviano, 23 I&N Dec. 718 (BIA 2005) (expunged state firearm convictions still "convictions" for immigration purposes); *In re* Marroquin-Garcia, 23 I&N Dec. 705 (BIA 2005) (same); *In re* Roldan-Santoyo, 22 I&N Dec. 512 (BIA 1999) (en banc), *rev'd sub nom.* Lujan-Armendariz v. INS, 222 F.3d 728 (9th Cir. 2000).

See generally Gregory G. Sarno, *Effect of Expungement of Conviction on § 241(a)(4), (11) of Immigration and Nationality Act of 1952 (8 U.S.C. § 1251(a)(4), (11)), Making Aliens Deportable for Crimes Involving Moral Turpitude or Drugs*, 98 A.L.R. FED. 750 (1990 & 2004 Supp.); Tova Indritz, *INS Considers State Expungements, Set Asides, Dismissals as "Convictions,"* THE CHAMPION, May 1999, at 10; James A. R. Nafziger & Michael

Yimesgen, *The Effect of Expungement on Removability of Non-Citizens*, 36 U. MICH. J.L. REF. 915 (2003).

§ 4.39. *What about expungements under the federal First Offender Act?*

This depends on the circuit in which the alien defendant finds himself. In the Ninth Circuit an expungement under the federal First Offender Act, 18 U.S.C. § 3607, for first time simple possession drug offenses results in protection against deportation. Lujan-Armendariz v. INS, 222 F.3d 728 (9th Cir. 2000) (vacating first-time drug possession conviction under ARIZ. REV. STAT. § 13-907(A) eliminates conviction for immigration purposes). The Seventh and Eighth Circuits, however, disagree. Gill v. Ashcroft, 335 F.3d 574 (7th Cir. 2003); Vasquez-Velezmoro v. INS, 281 F.3d 693 (8th Cir. 2002).

§ 4.40. *What about state rehabilitative expungements?*

Again, it depends on the circuit. Under *Lujan-Armendariz v. INS*, 222 F.3d 728 (9th Cir. 2000), a dismissal or expungement under a state counterpart to the federal First Offender Act, 18 U.S.C. § 3607, which applies only to drug offenses, is not a conviction for immigration purposes. In the other circuits, the BIA applies *In re Roldan-Santoyo*, 22 I&N Dec. 512 (BIA 1999) (en banc) (dispositions under state counterparts to the federal First Offender Act are convictions for immigration purposes), *rev'd sub nom.* Lujan-Armendariz v. INS, 222 F.3d 728 (9th Cir. 2000). *See In re* Salazar-Regino, 23 I&N Dec. 223, 231 (BIA 2002) (en banc).

§ 4.41. *What about state expungements under non-rehabilitative statutes?*

A conviction that has been expunged under state law continues to constitute a conviction for immigration purposes. Murillo-Espinoza v. INS, 261 F.3d 771, 774 (9th Cir. 2001) (theft conviction that was expunged under ARS § 13-907 supported removal). *See also* Ramirez-Castro v. INS, 287 F.3d 1172 (9th Cir. 2002) (misdemeanor firearms conviction expunged under California law remains a conviction under immigration law).

4. Suspended Sentences

§ 4.42. *What about a suspended sentence?*

A suspended sentence of incarceration is still a sentence to imprisonment under immigration laws. 8 U.S.C. § 1101(a)(48)(B). The suspended time counts whenever immigration consequences result from the length of a sentence. For example, a sentence of imprisonment of at least one year following a conviction for a burglary or theft offense, or a "crime of violence," renders any of these crimes an aggravated felony. *See* 8 U.S.C. § 1101(a)(43)(G) and (F); United States v. Hernandez-Valdovinos, 352 F.3d 1243 (9th Cir. 2003); United States v. Echavarria-Escobar, 270 F.3d 1265 (9th Cir. 2001), *cert. denied*, 535 U.S. 1069, 122 S. Ct. 1943 (2002).

5. Modified Sentences

§ 4.43. *What about modified sentences?*

The modification of a sentence, even after the sentence has been served, may avoid immigration consequences. *In re* Song, 23 I&N Dec. 173 (BIA 2001). Thus, a one-day sentence reduction — from 365 days to 364 days imprisonment — will prevent many offenses from constituting aggravated felonies.

6. Vacated Sentences and Cases On or After Appeal

§ 4.44. *What about when an appellate court has vacated a judgment?*

A conviction that a trial or appeals court vacates because it is legally defective is not a conviction for immigration purposes. *In re* Rodriguez-Ruiz, 22 I&N Dec. 1378 (BIA 2000); *In re* Sirhan, 13 I&N Dec. 592 (BIA 1970). In *In re Rodriguez-Ruiz*, the Board of Immigration Appeals held that a conviction that has been vacated under a state law provision (specifically New York Criminal Procedure Law Article 440) does not constitute a conviction for immigration purposes within the meaning of 8 U.S.C. § 1101(a)(48)(A). The Board distinguishes its decision in *In re Roldan-Santoyo*, 22 I&N Dec. 512 (BIA 1999) (en banc), *rev'd sub nom.* Lujan-Armendariz v. INS, 222 F.3d 728 (9th Cir. 2000), by noting that the respondent's conviction was not expunged as was the case in *Roldan-Santoyo*. Instead the record revealed that the respondent's conviction had been vacated. *See BIA Speaks on Criminal Convictions, Aggravated Felonies, Other Issues*, 76 INTERPRETER RELEASES 518, 519 (Apr. 2, 1999) (summary of *In re Roldan-Santoyo*); *Ninth Circuit Overturns BIA on the Meaning of "Conviction" for Immigration Purposes*, 77 INTERPRETER RELEASES 1117 (Aug. 7, 2000) (discussion of *Lujan-Armendariz*); Lory Diana Rosenberg & Nelson Vargas-Padilla, *An Odyssey of Immigration Consequences of Crime: The BIA's 2001 Interpretations*, 78 INTERPRETER RELEASES 909, 911 (June 4, 2001).

§ 4.45. *What about when the trial court vacates a conviction on equitable grounds?*

A conviction that a trial court vacates for equitable reasons remains a conviction for immigration purposes. A state court writ of *audita querela* will be honored only if there is "'a legal defect in the conviction, or in the sentence which taints the conviction. Equities or gross injustice, in themselves, will not satisfy the legal objection requirement and will not provide a basis for relief.'" Doe v. INS, 120 F.3d 200, 203 (9th Cir. 1997) (quoting United States v. Johnson, 962 F.2d 579, 582 (7th Cir. 1992)). *See also* Beltran-Leon v. INS, 134 F.3d 1379 (9th Cir. 1998).

7. Pre-Plea or Pretrial Diversions

§ 4.46. *Does pretrial diversion count as a conviction?*

No. A disposition under a pre-plea diversion statute is not a conviction. *In re* Grullon, 20 I&N Dec. 12 (BIA 1989). Unlike an adjudication that is withheld after a plea or admission, no plea is taken.

8. Juvenile Adjudications

§ 4.47. *Do juvenile adjudications make an alien deportable?*

No. A juvenile court disposition of delinquency is not a conviction for immigration purposes. *In re* Ramirez-Rivero, 18 I&N Dec. 135 (BIA 1981). Moreover a youthful offender disposition under a statute comparable to the federal Juvenile Delinquency Act is not a conviction. *In re* Devison-Charles, 22 I&N Dec. 1362 (BIA 2000) (en banc).

§ 4.48. *What about juvenile criminal acts not resulting in conviction?*

Some criminal acts are grounds for deportation even without a conviction, such as drug addiction or abuse, alien smuggling, document fraud, and — after September 30, 1996 — false claim to U.S. citizenship, and illegal voting. These could apply to juveniles. Also, if the youth violated a restraining or protective order it can trigger deportation under 8 U.S.C. § 1227(a)(2)(E)(ii) for "violation of a family protective order." Moreover, a juvenile disposition for delivery of a controlled substance will likely fall under 8 U.S.C. § 1182(a)(2)(C) requiring only "reason to believe" the noncitizen is a drug trafficker making the juvenile inadmissible. Moreover, making a false claim to U.S. citizenship renders even a child inadmissible, with no waiver available. 8 U.S.C. § 1182(a)(6)(C)(ii). *Cf.* 8 U.S.C. § 1227(a)(3)(D)(i).

9. Undesignated Offenses

§ 4.49. *How does an offense later designated a misdemeanor count?*

Usually as a misdemeanor, qualifying the alien for an exception to the CIMT finding for a petty offenses where "the maximum penalty possible for the crime of which the alien was convicted ... did not exceed imprisonment of one year and ... the alien was not sentenced to a term of imprisonment in excess of six months." 8 U.S.C. § 1182(a)(2)(A)(ii)(II). Undesignated sentences are akin to an indeterminate sentence where the BIA looks to the maximum sentence possible for the offense to determine whether the offense qualifies under the petty offense exception. *See In re* D-, 20 I&N Dec. 827, 829 (BIA 1994); *see also* Garcia-Lopez v. Ashcroft, 334 F.3d 840 (9th Cir. 2003) (BIA must treat California "wobbler" designated to misdemeanor as a misdemeanor); LaFarga v. INS, 170 F.3d 1213, 1215 (9th Cir.) (Arizona "Class 6 undesignated" offense that is "open-ended" allows for relief from deportation), *amended by* 99 Cal. Daily Op. Service 2484 (9th Cir. Apr. 5, 1999); Scott A. Kozlov, *Deportation as a Collateral Consequence of a Guilty Plea: Why the Federal Precedent Should Be Re-Evaluated*, 26 VAL. U.L. REV. 895 (1992).

10. Pardoned Offenses

§ 4.50. *Can the government deport an alien for a pardoned offense?*

Yes. On deciding "whether a full and unconditional presidential or gubernatorial pardon could implicitly remove the immigration consequences of a crime," the BIA held that the pardon would not help the alien. *In re* Jung Tae Suh, 23 I&N Dec. 626 (BIA 2003). Thus, a presidential or gubernatorial pardon waives only the grounds of removal specifically set forth at 8 U.S.C. § 1227(a)(2)(A)(v) (2000) and the BIA would read no implicit waivers into the statute.

11. Cases On or After Appeal

§ 4.51. *Are cases on direct appeal "convictions" for deportation hearings?*

Before 1996, the conviction was not "final" when the case was on direct appeal and deportation proceedings would not begin. *In re* L-R-, 8 I&N Dec. 269, 270 (BIA 1959), *overruled in part, In re* Ozkok, 19 I&N Dec. 546 (BIA 1988). IIRAIRA changed this. *See* 8 U.S.C. § 1101(a)(48). Now, the conviction is final as soon as a defendant alien is sentenced.

D. Old Convictions and *Ex Post Facto* Issues

§ 4.52. *Aliens with old convictions shouldn't have to worry, right?*

Wrong! As of 1996, deportation for an aggravated felony is applied retroactively. 8 U.S.C. § 1101(a)(43). Title 8 U.S.C. § 1101(a)(43) came into being with the Anti-Drug Abuse Act of 1988. Even an alien convicted long before 1988 for a crime now defined as an aggravated felony will be removed as an "aggravated felon." *But see* Nancy Morawetz, *Rethinking Retroactive Deportation Laws and the Due Process Clause (Part One), in* 73 N.Y.U. L. REV. 97 (1998) *and* 4:6 BENDER'S IMMIGR. BULL. 221 (Mar. 15, 1999).

§ 4.53. *Are there exceptions?*

Perhaps. The Ninth Circuit held that a retroactive application of the deportation statute to aggravated felons with pre-1996 convictions is not permissible if the alien entered a guilty plea "in reliance upon the relief afforded by INA § 212(c) [8 U.S.C. § 1182(c)]." United States v. Magana-Pizano, 200 F.3d 603, 614 (9th Cir. 1999). *See also* Kathleen M. Sullivan, *Commentary on* Magana-Pizano, 5:2 BENDER'S IMMIGR. BULL. 75 (Jan. 15, 2000).

IV. Criminal Acts and Immigration Law

§ 4.54. *What happens to aliens convicted of crime?*

It depends on the conviction and comes down to three questions:

1. Does the conviction make the alien "removable"?
2. Does the alien have any discretionary relief from removal?
3. Does the alien have a chance to get discretionary relief from the immigration judge?

See **Chapter 2: Immigration Law for Criminal Lawyers.**

§ 4.55. *What criminal acts make the alien removable?*

Counsel must look to 8 U.S.C. § 1101(a)(43) (listing aggravated felonies), 8 U.S.C. § 1227(a)(2) (listing other criminal grounds for removal), and 8 U.S.C. § 1182 (listing basis for inadmissibility). These statutes are the first and best source for an answer to whether a convicted alien will be removed. As William Maynard wrote in an excellent article "[t]here is no shortcut to understanding them. Counsel must simply study and apply §§ 1101(a)(43) and 1227(a)(2) one case at a time." William R. Maynard, *Deportation: An Immigration Law Primer for the Criminal Defense Lawyer*, THE CHAMPION, June 1999, at 12, 14.

Generally, the following types of criminal conduct and convictions can get the alien removed:

A. Certain criminal acts not resulting in conviction;
B. Aggravated felonies as defined at 8 U.S.C. § 1101(a)(43);
C. Drug convictions;
D. Moral turpitude misdemeanors and felonies;
E. Specific deportable offenses including firearms, domestic violence, alien smuggling, document fraud, and alien voting offenses.

These categories overlap considerably but will be treated in succession in **IV.A** through **IV.E**, *infra*.

§ 4.56. *How do you know if the alien has relief from removal?*

This can be complicated. *See* **Chapter 2: Immigration Law for Criminal Lawyers**. For aggravated felons the answer is easy — in most cases, there is no relief. An alien can apply for adjustment of status even with a conviction for some aggravated felonies; withholding of deportation is available but this is not likely — most defendants do not qualify. *But see* Brian K. Bates, *"Guerilla Lawyers": Survival and Resistance against Government Forces (Part 1)*, 4:18 BENDER'S IMMIGR. BULL. 909 (Sept. 15, 1999); Brian K. Bates, *"Guerilla Lawyers:" Survival and Resistance Against Government Forces (Part 2)*, 4:19 BENDER'S IMMIGR. BULL. 951 (Oct. 1, 1999) (excellent two-part article on defending aggravated felons in immigration court).

§ 4.57. *How can one determine discretionary relief?*

The immigration judge will do this based on factors such as the alien's contacts with this country (e.g., family, work, community involvement), among other things. *See* **Chapter 2: Immigration Law for Criminal Lawyers**.

A. Criminal Acts Not Resulting in Conviction

§ 4.58. *If the alien avoids conviction, does that end his immigration problems?*

Not necessarily. Under 8 U.S.C. § 1101(f), immigration consequences are possible even without a conviction. Moreover, 8 U.S.C. § 1227(a) defines several criminal conduct grounds for removal that do not require convictions, such as alien smuggling, criminal acts relating to national security, violations of a domestic protective order, and drug abuse or addiction.

Also, aliens who have not shown "good moral character" can be denied naturalization, voluntary departure from the United States, or discretionary relief from removal even if they are statutorily eligible for such relief. Under 8 U.S.C. § 1101(f), an immigration judge will not find "good moral character" for various aliens including habitual drunkards and drug addicts, professional gamblers, prostitutes, or polygamists. An alien cannot be deported for being any of these but still may suffer consequences if trying to naturalize, voluntarily depart, or apply for other forms of relief from deportation. 8 U.S.C. § 1227(a)(2)(B)(ii). *See* Gregory G. Sarno, Annotation, *Effect of Expungement of Conviction on § 241(a)(4), (11) of Immigration and Nationality Act of 1952 (8 U.S.C. § 1251(a)(4), (11)), Making Aliens Deportable for Crimes Involving Moral Turpitude or Drugs*, 98 A.L.R. FED. 750 (1990 & 2004 Supp.).

B. Aggravated Felonies

This category is the broadest and most frequently expanded basis for criminal deportation. Any alien convicted of an aggravated felony at any time after admission is deportable. 8 U.S.C. § 1227(a)(2)(A)(iii). Title 8 U.S.C. § 1101(a)(43) lists "aggravated felonies." Because of the increased complexity of aggravated felony law, this edition devotes a new chapter to the subject. *See* **Chapter 5: Aggravated Felonies.**

C. Drug Convictions

§ 4.59. *What about convictions for drug crimes?*

Drug trafficking under 8 U.S.C. § 1101(a)(43)(B) is an aggravated felony. This includes any second conviction for simple drug possession. United States v. Garcia-Olemdo, 112 F.3d 399, 400–01 (9th Cir. 1997). Even if not an aggravated felony, any controlled substance offense (defined in the federal Controlled Substance Act) with the exception of 30 grams or less of marijuana renders the alien deportable. 8 U.S.C. § 1227(a)(2)(B)(i). It makes no difference whether the offense is a felony or misdemeanor, nor does the amount of the controlled substance matter. *See generally* Lory Diana Rosenberg, *Which Controlled Substance Convictions?*, 9:7 BENDER'S IMMIGR. BULL. 406 (April 1, 2004).

Even proof of addiction is ground for deportation or exclusion. 8 U.S.C. §§ 1227(a)(2)(B)(ii), 1182(a)(1)(A)(iv).

§ 4.60. *What about when a drug offense has been expunged?*

Expungement of a first conviction of simple possession has been used to eliminate the ground for deportability and removal. Garberding v. INS, 30 F.3d 1187 (9th Cir. 1994); *In re* Manrique, Int.

Dec. 3250 (BIA 1995) (en banc). This is probably not true today under 8 U.S.C. § 1101(a)(48) and *In re Roldan-Santoyo*, 22 I&N Dec. 512 (BIA 1999) (en banc), *rev'd sub nom.* Lujan-Armendariz v. INS, 222 F.3d 728 (9th Cir. 2000).

§ 4.61. *What about accessory after the fact or misprision of a drug felony?*

Neither conviction of accessory after the fact nor misprision of felony is a drug offense even if the principal offense involved drugs. *In re* Batista-Hernandez, 21 I&N Dec. 955 (BIA 1997) (en banc). However, the BIA has held that accessory after the fact constitutes obstruction of justice, and this is an aggravated felony under 8 U.S.C. § 1101(a)(43) if a one-year sentence is imposed. *Id.*

§ 4.62. *What if the conviction does not identify the drug involved?*

A conviction that does not identify the drug involved cannot establish a federally listed controlled substance and thus is not a controlled substance drug offense under immigration law. *In re* Paulus, 11 I&N Dec. 274 (BIA 1965).

§ 4.63. *Are there any exceptions to deportation for a drug conviction?*

One — a person who has one conviction for simple possession of 30 grams or less of marijuana for one's own use may have a claim to relief from deportation. 8 U.S.C. § 1182(h); 8 U.S.C. § 1227(a)(2)(B)(i).

§ 4.64. *Is Cancellation of Removal Available to Drug Offenders?*

Yes, if the underlying drug conviction does not constitute an aggravated felony and the alien meets the statutory requirements set forth in 8 U.S.C. § 1229b(a) or 8 U.S.C. § 1229b(b). However, because the term "aggravated felony" is so broadly defined, a drug conviction will rarely fall outside its scope. *See* Lopez v. Gonzales, 417 F.3d 934, 936 (8th Cir. 2005) (stating that "any drug conviction that would qualify as a felony under either state or federal law is an aggravated felony"). An example of a non-aggravated felony drug offense is the Arizona state crime of first-time simple possession. In Arizona, this offense does not constitute an "aggravated felony" because it is punishable only by probation and is not a trafficking offense. *See* United States v. Robles-Rodriguez, 281 F.3d 900, 905–06 (9th Cir. 2002); *compare* United States v. Arellano-Torres, 303 F.3d 1173, 1180 (9th Cir. 2002) (holding that the crime of first-time simple drug possession in Nevada constitutes an "aggravated felony"), *cert. denied*, 538 U.S. 915, 123 S. Ct. 1502 (2003).

D. Moral Turpitude Misdemeanors and Felonies

1. Moral Turpitude Misdemeanors

§ 4.65. *Can a defendant be deported on a misdemeanor conviction?*

Yes, under 8 U.S.C. § 1227(a)(2)(A)(ii). Deportation for misdemeanor convictions can occur when the alien is the following:

1. "Convicted";
2. Of two or more "moral turpitude" crimes;
3. Not from a "single scheme of criminal misconduct."

Because nothing is ever simple with immigration law, the terms "conviction," "moral turpitude," and "single scheme of criminal misconduct" are terms of art.

§ 4.66. *What does it mean to have a "conviction"?*

See **III.A: "Conviction" and "Sentencing" Under Immigration Law**, *supra*.

§ 4.67. *What is a Crime Involving Moral Turpitude (CIMT)?*

Although the term "moral turpitude" evades precise definition, Jordan v. De George, 341 U.S. 223, 229, 71 S. Ct. 703, *reh'g denied*, 341 U.S. 956, 71 S. Ct. 1011 (1951), "moral turpitude refers generally to conduct that is inherently base, vile, or depraved, and contrary to the accepted rules of morality and the duties between persons or to society in general." *In re* L-V-C-, 22 I&N Dec. 594, 603 (BIA 1999) (en banc). *See also In re* Tran, 21 I&N Dec. 291 (BIA 1996); *In re* Danesh, 19 I&N Dec. 669 (BIA 1988). A CIMT is an intrinsically wrong act or *mala en se* regardless of the statutory prohibition. *In re* P-, 6 I&N Dec. 795, 798 (BIA 1955). Among the tests employed to determine a CIMT is whether the act is accompanied by vicious motive or a corrupt mind. *See In re* Perez-

Contreras, 20 I&N Dec. 615, 618 (BIA 1992); *In re* Serna, 20 I&N Dec. 579, 581 (BIA 1992). Generally, crimes of moral turpitude have an intent element demonstrating moral laxity, bad character, or violence.

§ 4.68. *Does a moral turpitude crime require an element of intent?*

Moral turpitude crimes usually, but not always, require proof of criminal intent but not necessarily specific intent. INA § 237(a)(2)(A)(1). *See also In re* Torres-Varela, 23 I&N Dec. 78, 83–84 (BIA 2001) (en banc); *In re* Tran, 21 I&N Dec. 291 (BIA 1996); *In re* Danesh, 19 I&N Dec. 669 (BIA 1988). Repeated violations of a statute with no mental state as an element does not turn an offense into one involving moral turpitude. *In re* Torres-Valera, 23 I&N Dec. at 86. Where the minimal mental state for the offense is "criminal negligence," the crime is not a CIMT. *See In re* Perez-Contreras, 20 I&N Dec. 615, 618 (BIA 1992) (negligent assault). Where the *mens rea* is recklessness, the crime *may* be a CIMT. Some crimes with no mental state are CIMT. *In re* Dingena, 11 I&N Dec. 723 (BIA 1966) (statutory rape is a CIMT despite lack of intent element in statute).

§ 4.69. *Is it the statute or the conduct that defines a CIMT?*

The statute. The defendant's underlying conduct does not control whether the crime is one of moral turpitude. *In re* Short, 20 I&N Dec. 136, 137 (BIA 1989); *In re* B-, 6 I&N Dec. 98, 106 (BIA 1954) ("It is well settled that the presence or absence of moral turpitude must be determined, in the first instance, *from a consideration of the crime as defined by the statute*; that we cannot go behind the judgment of conviction to determine the precise circumstances surrounding the crime") (emphasis in original). Only if moral turpitude "necessarily inheres" in the offense as defined by statute is the crime a CIMT. *In re* Khourn, 21 I&N Dec. 1041 (BIA 1997).

§ 4.70. *What is "a single scheme of criminal misconduct"?*

To deport an alien for misdemeanor convictions, the government must prove two separate misdemeanor crimes that did not arise from the same temporally connected event. Pacheco v. INS, 546 F.2d 448, 452 (1st Cir. 1976) ("single scheme" is determined by a "temporally integrated episode of continuous activity" without interruption that might allow the alien to consider his conduct), *cert.*

denied, 430 U.S. 985, 97 S. Ct. 1683 (1977); Nason v. INS, 394 F.2d 223, 227 (2d Cir.) ("Congress meant to give the alien a second chance, not to spare the recidivist."), *cert. denied*, 393 U.S. 830, 89 S. Ct. 98 (1968). All doubts on this issue resolve in favor of the noncitizen. Costello v. INS, 376 U.S. 120, 128, 84 S. Ct. 580 (1964); Fong Haw Tan v. Phelan, 333 U.S. 6, 68 S. Ct. 374 (1948).

§ 4.71. *What are possible resolutions to avoid a CIMT finding?*

Prosecutors and defense attorneys should consider pleas to deferred prosecution, pretrial diversion, or a crime not involving moral turpitude. Often, alien defendants will agree to more jail or prison time for such a plea. Remember, the alien must have two or more separate misdemeanor convictions to be deportable. One tactic is to suggest that the court find guilt on the "same course of criminal conduct," despite the allegation of two crimes.

2. Moral Turpitude Felonies

§ 4.72. *What moral turpitude felonies can get an alien deported?*

An alien is now deportable if the following occurs:

- He is convicted;
- Of a crime involving moral turpitude;
- Committed within five years after "entry";
- A sentence of one year or longer may be imposed."

See 8 U.S.C. § 1227(a)(2)(A)(i)(II).

§ 4.73. *What does "entry" mean?*

When an alien comes to a port of entry, border officials perform an inspection. 8 U.S.C. § 1225(b), 8 C.F.R. § 235. "Entry" and "admission" occurs upon "the lawful entry of the alien into the United States after inspection and authorization by an immigration officer." 18 U.S.C. § 1101(a)(13)(A). However, a person "present in the United States who has not been admitted or paroled, or who seeks entry at other than an open designated port of entry ... is subject to the provisions of INA § 212(a)." (8 U.S.C. § 1182(a)). *See also* 8 C.F.R. § 1235.1(d)(2). Another term for "inadmissible" is "excludable." *See* **Chapter 2: Immigration Law for Criminal Lawyers**.

§ 4.74. *What does entry have to do with deportation for CIMT?*

Before an alien is deportable for a moral turpitude felony under 8 U.S.C. § 1227(a)(2)(A)(i)(I), the Bureau of Immigration and Customs Enforcement (ICE) must establish that the alien committed the crime within five years of the alien's "entry" into the United States. Thus, if the alien has been living in the United States for longer than five years since his last entry, he cannot be deported for one moral turpitude felony, so long as it is not an aggravated felony under 8 U.S.C. § 1101(a)(43). Except for legal permanent resident aliens, any alien who crosses a border to leave the United States must begin the five-year period again upon returning to this country. For legal permanent resident aliens, ICE must show that the alien actually intended to interrupt residency by leaving the United States. Brief, casual, and innocent departures do not count against legal, permanent resident aliens. Rosenberg v. Fleuti, 374 U.S. 449, 462, 83 S. Ct. 1804 (1963). Thus, the LPR who takes brief trips to his country of origin will not restart the "entry" calculation.

§ 4.75. *What is the definition of "sentenced to confinement or confined"?*

This means *an actual* sentence of confinement in a correctional institution for at least one year. Thus, suspending the imposition of a sentence used to negate this element and prevented deportation. Okoroha v. INS, 715 F.2d 380 (8th Cir. 1983); Petsche v. Clingan, 273 F.2d 688 (10th Cir. 1960). Now, however, the alien is deportable whenever a sentence of "one year or longer may be imposed." 8 U.S.C. § 1227(a)(2)(A)(i)(II). Neither suspending nor receiving less than a year matters.

3. Specific Moral Turpitude Offenses

Several publications have good lists of crimes the BIA and courts have determined to be CIMTs. DAN KESSELBRENNER & LORY D. ROSENBERG, IMMIGRATION LAW AND CRIME app. E (1995); NORTON TOOBY, CRIMES INVOLVING MORAL TURPITUDE (2004); NORTON TOOBY, CRIMINAL DEFENSE OF IMMIGRANTS vols. I & II (2003); Hilary Hochman, *Special Considerations in Representing the Noncitizen Defendant*, in DEFENDING A FEDERAL CRIMINAL CASE 842–43 (1995 ed.).

The following is a brief list of common offenses:

Passing Bad Checks — Writing bad checks may or may not be a CIMT. *Compare In re* Balao, 20 I&N Dec. 440 (BIA 1992) (passing bad checks involves moral turpitude because fraud was an element of offense) *with In re* Bart, 20 I&N Dec. 436 (BIA 1992) (offense of passing bad checks does not involve moral turpitude because fraud was not an element of the offense).

Assault — Simple assault does not involve moral turpitude. *In re* Short, 20 I&N Dec. 136 (BIA 1989). An assault offense that requires a mental state of criminal recklessness does not involve moral turpitude unless the statute also requires that the assault was with intent to commit serious bodily injury. *In re* Fualaau, 21 I&N Dec. 475 (BIA 1996) (en banc). Reckless assault causing bodily injury is not a CIMT. *Id.* Other assault offenses that have an intent element that itself constitutes a CIMT are CIMTs. *See, e.g.*, United States *ex rel.* Rizzio v. Kenney, 50 F.2d 418 (2d Cir. 1931) (intent to rob); *In re* Quadara, 11 I&N Dec. 457 (BIA 1966) (same); *In re* Beato, 10 I&N Dec. 730 (BIA 1964) (intent to rape).

Aggravated Assaults — Aggravated assaults can be CIMTs where there is a sufficient aggravating factor. Although the "aggravated assault" label is not dispositive, *In re* G-R-, 2 I&N Dec. 733, 747 (BIA 1946), it does indicate the willfulness of the act. *Cf.* Guerrcro de Nodahl v. INS, 407 F.2d 1405 (9th Cir. 1969) (willful infliction on child of cruel or inhuman corporal punishment or injury resulting in a traumatic condition involves intent to commit a CIMT); *In re* Tran, 21 I&N Dec. 291 (BIA 1996) (willfully inflicting corporal injury resulting in a traumatic condition on spouse); Grageda v. INS, 12 F.3d 919 (9th Cir. 1993) (same); *In re* Danesh, 19 I&N Dec. 669 (BIA 1988) (knowing injury of a peace officer is CIMT); *In re* Logan, 17 I&N Dec. 367 (BIA 1980) (assault with a deadly weapon is a CIMT). Thus, reckless assault coupled with an element of injury, but not serious injury, is probably not a CIMT.

Fraud — A conviction for an offense in which fraud is an essential element of the crime always involves moral turpitude. Jordan v. De George, 341 U.S. 223, 71 S. Ct. 703, *reh'g denied*, 341 U.S. 956, 71 S. Ct. 1011 (1951).

Theft — A theft offense that includes a knowledge element that the items were stolen or the intent to deprive the rightful owner permanently of his or her property involves moral turpitude. *Compare In re* De La Nues, 18 I&N Dec. 140 (BIA 1981) (theft is a CIMT) *and* Wadman v. INS, 329 F.2d 812, 814 (9th Cir. 1964) (knowledge that items were stolen was sufficient to render offense turpitudinous) *with In re* M-, 2 I&N Dec. 686 (BIA 1946) (joyriding does not involve moral turpitude because statute included temporary taking of a motor vehicle). Possession of stolen property involves moral turpitude without regard to the triviality of the offense. Michel v. INS, 206 F.3d 253 (2d Cir.), *adopted, writ of habeas corpus denied*, 119 F. Supp. 2d 485 (M.D. Pa. 2000).

Burglary — Burglary is generally a CIMT based on the intent to commit a crime and generally possession of burglary tools is a CIMT because it includes intent to use or permit the use of the tool to commit a burglary. *See In re* Serna, 20 I&N Dec. 579 (BIA 1992).

Criminal Trespass — Criminal trespass is not a CIMT unless there is an intent to commit a CIMT while trespassing. *See In re* Esfandiary, 16 I&N Dec. 659, 661 (BIA 1979) (conviction for malicious trespass was a CIMT because it included specific intent to commit petit larceny).

DUI — Misdemeanor DUI is not a CIMT because most misdemeanor DUI statutes do not require a specific mental state beyond negligence. As outlined above, CIMTs usually generally require at least a reckless *mens rea*. *See* United States v. Portillo-Mendoza, 273 F.3d 1224, 1228 (9th Cir.) (analyzing California's DUI statute), *remanded by* 25 Fed. Appx. 543 (9th Cir. 2001); United States v. Trinidad-Aquino, 259 F.3d 1140, 1145 (9th Cir. 2001). If the DUI results in an injury, however, any assault charge can have a reckless *mens rea* and be a CIMT or a crime of violence/aggravated felony. *See* United States v. Ceron-Sanchez, 222 F.3d 1169, 1172–73 (9th Cir. 2000) (aggravated assault with a dangerous instrument (automobile) is aggravated felony). Also, driving under the influence with knowledge that one's license had been suspended or revoked has a knowledge element and therefore is a CIMT. *In re* Lopez-Meza, 22 I&N Dec. 1188 (BIA 1999) (en banc). Conversely, multiple DUI convictions making it an "aggravated" DUI under many state statutes, *see, e.g.*, ARS § 28-1383.A.2, are not CIMT because nothing changes the original *mens rea*. Also, if the record of conviction establishes or leaves open the possibility that the defendant was only in "actual physical control" of a vehicle and not "driving" *per se*, it is not a CIMT. *See* Hernandez-Martinez v. Ashcroft, 343 F.3d. 1075 (9th Cir. 2003) (former ARS § 28-697A is "divisible"); *In re* Torres-Varela, 23 I&N Dec. 78 (BIA 2001) (en banc); Chuck Roth, *Moral Turpitude in the DWI Context,* 4:22 BENDER'S IMMIGR. BULL. 1067 (Nov. 15, 1999).

Endangerment — If there is no element of actual injury, the endangerment offense may not be a CIMT. *Cf. In re* Fualaau, 21 I&N Dec. 475 (BIA 1996) (en banc) (reckless assault causing bodily injury is not a CIMT; reckless assault with an element of serious bodily injury would be).

Child Abuse — Whether such a conviction involves moral turpitude may depend on the subsection under which the individual is convicted. Child abuse done with criminal negligence probably is not a CIMT. It is, however, a specific deportable offense outlined in the next section at **IV.E.2: Domestic Violence and Child Abuse**.

Prostitution — This is a CIMT. "Engaging in" prostitution makes the alien inadmissible under 8 U.S.C. § 1182(a)(2)(D). Alien customers of prostitutes (i.e., "Johns"), however, have no immigration consequences. Pimping, pandering or "running" prostitution is an aggravated felony under 8 U.S.C. § 1101(a)(43)(I) & (K).

Aliens smuggled for prostitution, however, can get a "T" or "U" visa under 8 U.S.C. § 1101(a)(15)(T), (U) if among other factors they can show they will suffer "extreme hardship involving unusual and severe harm" if deported. *See generally* Dina Francesca Haynes, *Used, Abused, Arrested and Deported: Extending Immigration Benefits to Protect the Victims of Trafficking and to Secure the Prosecution of Traffickers,* 26 HUM. RTS. Q. 221 (2004). Also, if the witnesses was otherwise a victim of crime he may have the right to ask for a U-visa. *See generally* Lory Diana Rosenberg, *Consideration of (Not So) New "T" and "U" Visas and How They Work,* 8:20 BENDER'S IMMIGR. BULL. 1628 (Oct. 15, 2003); Greta D. Stoltz, *The U Visa: Another Remedy for Battered Immigrant Women,* 7 SCHOLAR 127 (2004).

E. Specific Deportable Offenses

Several of the following categories are independent grounds for deportation even though some are also aggravated felonies or CIMTs or both.

1. Weapons Offenses

§ 4.76. *What about convictions for weapons offenses?*

Title 8 U.S.C. § 1227(a)(2)(C) governs deportability for weapons offenses and applies to an alien convicted of felony possession of firearms or ammunition, 18 U.S.C. § 922(g)(1); possession of a firearm or ammunition by an illegal alien, 18 U.S.C. § 922(g)(5); or possession of a stolen firearm or ammunition, 18 U.S.C. § 922(j).

Any conviction for trafficking in weapons is an aggravated felony under 8 U.S.C. § 1101(a)(43)(C). *See* **Chapter 5: Aggravated Felonies.**

§ 4.77. *What about discharging a firearm in a grossly negligent manner?*

Willfully discharging a gun in a grossly negligent manner in violation of state statutes could make the alien deportable. In *Valerio-Ochoa v. INS*, 241 F.3d 1092 (9th Cir.), *amended by* 2001 U.S. App. LEXIS 7508 (9th Cir. Feb. 15, 2001), 2001 Cal. Daily Op. Service 3262, 2001 D.A.R. 4036 (9th Cir. Apr. 25, 2001), *cert. denied*, 534 U.S. 821, 122 S. Ct. 55 (2001), the court dismissed the petition the alien filed after the INS ordered him deported. The court found that California Penal Code 246.3 holding that the willfully discharging a gun in a grossly negligent manner falls within the "use" of 8 U.S.C. § 1227(a)(2)(C) regarding firearms violations and as such was a deportable offense.

2. Domestic Violence and Child Abuse

§ 4.78. *What about domestic violence offenses?*

The 1996 Immigration Act made convictions for domestic violence, stalking, child abuse, child neglect, or child abandonment deportable offenses. 8 U.S.C. § 1127(a)(2)(E). Violation of a protective order is also a ground for deportation for convictions since September 30, 1996. The language of this subsection is broad and probably includes almost any type of conviction or violation of a protective order.

§ 4.79. *How is "domestic violence" defined?*

A "crime of domestic violence" is defined as

> Any crime of violence (as defined in section 16 of Title 18) against a person committed by a current or former spouse of the person, by an individual with whom the person shares a child in common, by an individual who is cohabiting with or has cohabited with the person as a spouse, by an individual similarly situated to a spouse of the person under the domestic or family violence laws of the jurisdiction where the offense occurs, or by any other individual against a person who is protected from that individual's acts under the domestic or family violence laws of the United States or any State, Indian tribal government, or unit of local government.

8 U.S.C. § 1227(a)(2)(C). Both misdemeanors and felonies appear to fall under this statute but the language is broad and at many points undefined.

§ 4.80. *Can an alien be deported for committing a crime of domestic violence or stalking?*

Yes. Although the INA states expressly that a "crime of stalking" constitutes an immigration violation under INA § 237(a)(2)(E)(I), no reported cases have construed what constitutes a "crime of stalking" for immigration purposes. Federal courts have rejected simply following "state labels" in determining the existence of a particular crime for dispositional purposes. *See, e.g.*, United States v. Taylor, 495 U.S. 575, 591–92, 110 S. Ct. 2143 (1990) (citing United States v. Nardello, 393 U.S. 286, 293–94, 89 S. Ct. 534 (1969)).

§ 4.81. *Can an alien be deported for child abuse?*

Yes. An alien can be deported for child abuse, child neglect, and/or child abandonment. 8 U.S.C. § 1227(a)(2)(E)(i).

§ 4.82. *What about when an alien has violated a court order?*

In 1996 IIRAIRA added INA § 237(a)(2)(E)(I) to make it an immigration offense if the alien has "convictions, or violations of court orders, occurring after [September 30, 1996]." *In re* Ajami, 22 I&N Dec. 949 (BIA 1999) (citing § 350(b), 110 Stat. at 3009-640). The section requires a court's determination that the defendant has "engaged in conduct that violates the portion of a protection order that involves protection against credible threats of violence, repeated harassment, or bodily injury to the person or persons for whom the protection order was issued." If the order is broader than this and the court's determination is not specific, the person is not deportable for the violation.

3. Alien Smuggling

§ 4.83. *What about convictions for smuggling aliens?*

A noncitizen that "knowingly" aids, abets, or assists in the smuggling of aliens within five years after entry is subject to exclusion and deportation. 8 U.S.C. §§ 1182(a)(6)(E)(i), 1227(a)(1)(E)(i). Pleading an alien to misdemeanor aiding and abetting the illegal entry of another under 18 U.S.C. § 2 (1994) and 8 U.S.C. § 1325 (1994), to avoid the felony alien smuggling charge under 8 U.S.C. § 1324 (1994), does not avoid exclusion or deportation.

Counsel's best option is to look to one of the statutorily enumerated exceptions under 8 U.S.C. §§ 1182(a)(6)(E)(ii) and 1227(a)(1)(E)(ii), relating to helping family members enter illegally, or to plead the client to "accessory after the fact" of the illegal entry of another.

In certain circumstances, alien smuggling is an aggravated felony. *See* 8 U.S.C. § 1101(a)(43)(N); Stephen Yale-Loehr, *New Developments to Combat Alien Smuggling and Document Fraud,* 2:1 BENDER'S IMMIGR. BULL. 3 (Jan. 1, 1997) (details grounds for deportation and relief).

4. Document Fraud and False Social Security Cards

§ 4.84. *Can the government deport an alien for false statements?*

Yes. An alien is deportable for violating the civil document fraud statute. 8 U.S.C. § 1324(c). *See* **Chapter 9: Immigration Document Fraud and False Statements**.

Immigration document fraud has complicated immigration consequences. Title 8 U.S.C. § 1101(a)(43)(P) makes it an aggravated felony for anyone to alter a passport or other immigration document in violation of 18 U.S.C. § 1543. The act also expanded the definition of aggravated felon to someone who commits an offense described in 18 U.S.C. § 1546, the criminal document fraud provision. Thus under 8 U.S.C. §§ 1251 to 1260 a violation of § 1546 can constitute a basis of deportation. Specifically an alien can be deported under 8 U.S.C. § 1227. Qureshi v. INS, 519 F.2d 1174 (5th Cir. 1975) (violation of this section constituted "conviction" under 8 U.S.C. § 1251(a)(5) authorizing deportation even though conviction resulted from *nolo contendere* plea). Moreover, any alien who falsely represents, or has falsely represented, himself or herself to be a citizen of the United States for any purpose or benefit under the INA, including 8 U.S.C. § 1324a, dealing with the unlawful employment of aliens, or any other federal or state law is inadmissible. This provision applies to representations made on or after September 30, 1996. Pichardo v. INS, 216 F.3d 1198 (9th Cir. 2000) (alien inadmissible after guilty plea to making false claim of United States citizenship and his admission to using false birth certificate when trying to enter United States).

§ 4.85. *How will deportation for false statements affect the alien's chance to come back to the United States?*

ICE provides the State Department the names of aliens with final orders of deportation under INA § 274C by entering the names in the Department's automated visa lookout system (AVLOS). *See* State Department Cable No. 91-State-170273 (May 23, 1991).

§ 4.86. *Does the alien have any relief from deportation on this basis?*

Maybe. Legislation establishes a waiver for this ground of inadmissibility under INA § 212(a)(6)(F) for the following: (1) lawful permanent residents who temporarily left the country voluntarily and are otherwise admissible; and (2) aliens seeking admission or adjustment based on immediate relative or family preference petitions. *See* INA § 212(d)(12). Only aliens who have not previously been fined under INA § 274C and whose offense was committed solely to assist, aid, or support the alien's spouse or child are eligible for the waiver. This family relationship must have existed at the time of the civil document fraud offense. A similar waiver of the ground of deportation under INA § 237(a)(3)(C).

§ 4.87. *What about aliens that help others commit document fraud?*

Document fraud liability extends to those who engage in document fraud to help others obtain any immigration benefit, even simply helping an alien with false papers. *See* Stephen Yale-Loehr,

New Developments to Combat Alien Smuggling and Document Fraud, 2:1 BENDER'S IMMIGR. BULL. 3 (Jan. 1, 1997).

§ 4.88. *What happens to a person who becomes a citizen though fraud?*

The government will prosecute the alien under 18 U.S.C. § 1425(b) and the district court will revoke citizenship under 8 U.S.C. § 1451(e). United States v. Inocencio, 328 F.3d 1207 (9th Cir.) (failure to revoke naturalization after fraud is ministerial error correctable after five years), *cert. denied*, 540 U.S. 926, 124 S. Ct. 334 (2003).

§ 4.89. *What about false use of a Social Security number?*

Congress has never included use of a false Social Security number as a ground for deportation. A false Social Security number is not evidence per se of bad moral character and if the immigration judge takes it as a negative factor, the alien can show evidence of "reforming" by current use of a valid number. *See* Charles Wheeler, *The Immigration Consequences of Using a False Social Security Number*, 8:11 BENDER'S IMMIGR. BULL. 952 (June 1, 2003).

Prosecutors and defense attorneys can have the defendant plead to possession of false Social Security cards, 18 U.S.C. § 1228(a)(6), instead of false immigration documents, to avoid the basis for deportation. Often, the alien is caught with both types of documents, and the penalty for both is the same under Federal Sentencing Guideline § 2L2.2 or § 2F2.1. In certain circumstances, this crime is an aggravated felony. *See* 8 U.S.C. § 1101(a)(43)(P).

5. Alien Voting

§ 4.90. *What about a conviction as an "alien voter"?*

Under IIRAIRA, an alien is excludable or deportable for voting in violation of federal, state, or local constitutional provisions, laws, or regulations. 18 U.S.C. § 611.

6. DUI Convictions

§ 4.91. *Is felony driving under the influence a crime of violence?*

No. The Supreme Court has recently held that diving under the influence is not a crime of violence under 18 U.S.C. § 16 (defining crimes of violence) and thus not an aggravated felony under 8 U.S.C. § 1101(a)(43)(F). Leocal v. Ashcroft, 125 S. Ct. 377 (2004). Proof on culpability, (i.e., intent) that is no more than negligent, the mental state for a DUI conviction, cannot constitute a crime of violence.

Leocal resolved a split in the circuits. *Compare* Montiel-Barraza v. INS, 275 F.3d 1178 (9th Cir. 2002) (per curiam) (multiple DUI priors not crime of violence); United States v. Trinidad-Aquino, 259 F.3d 1140 (9th Cir. 2001) (DUI with injury to another not crime of violence); United States v. Chapa-Garza, 243 F.3d 921 (5th Cir. 2001) (overturning United States v. Camacho-Marroquin, 188 F.3d 649 (5th Cir. 1999), *on rehearing, opinion withdrawn, petition dismissed, stay lifted, motion granted by* 222 F.3d 1040 (5th Cir. 2000)), *with* Tapia-Garcia v. INS, 237 F.3d 1216 (10th Cir. 2001); Le v. Attorney General, 196 F.3d 1352 (11th Cir. 1999).

Leocal also overrules the BIA's interpretation that DUIs were crimes of violence. *See In re* Puente-Salazar, Int. Dec. 3412 (BIA 1999) (en banc) (BIA held that a felony DUI is a crime of violence under 18 U.S.C. § 16(b) making the alien deportable under 8 U.S.C. § 1227(a)(2)(A)(3)); *In re* Magallanes-Garcia, Int. Dec. 3341 (BIA 1998). *Leocal* conformed to commentators that evaluated the BIA's ruling and determined that Congress never intended DUIs to be a "crime of violence" resulting in deportation. *See, e.g.*, Karen Crawford & Thomas Hutchins, *Ignoring Congress: The BIA and Crimes of Violence in* Puente *and* Magallanes, 6:2 BENDER'S IMMIGR. BULL. 67 (Jan. 15 2001).

§ 4.92. *Even if a DUI offense is not a "crime of violence" or CIMT, are there immigration consequences?*

Possibly. One or more offenses for simple driving under the influence, which may not be either a CIMT or a "crime of violence" under the immigration laws, *In re* Ramos, 23 I&N Dec. 336 (BIA 2002) (en banc); *In re* Torres-Varela, 23 I&N Dec. 78 (BIA 2001) (en banc), still may result in immigration consequences if the defendant was confined to a penal institution for 180 days or more. 8 U.S.C. § 1101(f)(7).

V. Aliens in Prison

§ 4.93. *Do federal prisons treat aliens more harshly?*

Yes. Several cases recognize that the Federal Bureau of Prisons does not allow aliens to spend the last six months of their sentences in halfway houses, to get high-paying prison jobs, to qualify for prison drug treatment programs with sentencing reductions, and to qualify for "low" security classification. *See, e.g.*, United States v. Farouil, 124 F.3d 838, 845–47 (7th Cir. 1997); United States v. Charry-Cubillos, 91 F.3d 1342, 1343–45 (9th Cir. 1996); United States v. Smith, 27 F.3d 649, 650–56 (D.C. Cir. 1994); *see also* United States v. Gonzalez-Portillo, 121 F.3d 1122, 1123–25 (7th Cir. 1997), *cert. denied*, 522 U.S. 1061, 118 S. Ct. 720 (1998); United States v. Veloza, 83 F.3d 380, 382 (11th Cir. 1996); United States v. Ebolum, 72 F.3d 35, 38–39 (6th Cir. 1995); United States v. Restrepo, 999 F.2d 640, 645–47 (2d Cir.), *cert. denied*, 510 U.S. 954, 114 S. Ct. 405 (1993).

§ 4.94. *Is there any benefit to being an alien in prison?*

Possibly. One of the consequences of being an alien serving in federal and state prisons is that the alien can receive a reduction of up to 50% of his sentence by being deported. 8 U.S.C. § 1231(a)(4)(B). The Immigration and Nationality Act provides for early release of nonviolent offenders for deportation. For state prisoners to receive this, there must be enacting legislation. *See, e.g.*, ARS § 41-1604.14, Release of Prisoners with Detainers; Eligibility; Revocation of Release. Generally, the Immigration Act limits its availability to nonviolent offenders and the states can also add other requirements. Often aliens in state custody will be eligible for an Institutional Hearing Program (IHP) where they will actually get their deportation hearing in the state prison.

VI. Consequences of Returning After Deportation

One consequence of a deportation based on a felony or aggravated felony conviction is that the alien cannot legally return to the United States for 15 years (felony) or life (aggravated felony) without securing advance permission from the Attorney General to reapply for admission. Given that many aliens may attempt to return anyway, counsel should seriously consider advising the alien of the penalties for this crime.

§ 4.95. *What happens to the alien deported for a criminal conviction who comes back to the United States?*

Aliens who return illegally after deportation can be charged with the crime of reentry after deportation, in violation of 8 U.S.C. § 1326(b)(1) or (2). *See* **Chapter 10: Illegal Entry and Reentry — Pretrial and Trial** *and* **Chapter 11: Illegal Entry and Reentry — Pleas and Sentencing**.

§ 4.96. *What happens to the aggravated felon who returns to the United States?*

Aggravated felons who return are severely punished under 8 U.S.C. § 1326(b)(2). This statute provides for a maximum penalty of 20 years and carries an offense level of 24 under Federal Sentencing Guideline § 2L1.2 — roughly equivalent to committing voluntary manslaughter.

§ 4.97. *What about non-aggravated felons who return illegally?*

Non-aggravated felons who reenter face up to 10 years in prison under 8 U.S.C. § 1326(b)(1). This carries a base offense level of 12 under Federal Sentencing Guideline § 2L1.2. Even three misdemeanor convictions for drug crimes or crimes against a person count as a felony under 8 U.S.C. § 1326(b)(1).

CHAPTER 5

AGGRAVATED FELONIES

Introduction

I. Aggravated Felonies in General

II. Convictions Defined

- **A. "Convictions," Expungements, Suspended Sentences, Youth Offenders**
- **B. Categorical Approach**

III. *Ex Post Facto* and Retroactive Effect of Statute

IV. Immigration Consequences and Deportation Relief

V. Types of Aggravated Felonies

- **A. Generally**
- **B. Drug Offenses**
- **C. Murder, Rape, and Sexual Abuse**
- **D. Crimes of Violence**
- **E. Theft and Burglary**
  - **1. Generally**
  - **2. Theft**
  - **3. Burglary**
- **F. Fraud Offenses**
- **G. Firearms Offenses**
- **H. Alien Smuggling**
- **I. DUI Convictions**

Other Resources:

NORTON TOOBY, AGGRAVATED FELONIES: INSTANT ACCESS TO ALL CASES DEFINING AGGRAVATED FELONIES (2nd ed. 2003).

NORTON TOOBY, CRIMINAL DEFENSE OF IMMIGRANTS vols. I & II (2003).

Kurtis A. Kemper, Annotation, *What Constitutes "Aggravated Felony" for Which Alien Can Be Deported or Removed Under § 237(a)(2)(A)(iii) of Immigration and Nationality Act (8 U.S.C. § 1227(a))*, 168 A.L.R. FED. 575 (2001 & 2005 Supp.).

Introduction

Aggravated felonies are the immigration equivalent of the death penalty. This category is the broadest and most frequently expanded basis for criminal deportation. They need be neither felonies nor "aggravated." Convictions for relatively minor offenses can cause an end to a legal life in the United States or any chance of getting one. Any alien convicted of an aggravated felony at any time after admission is deportable. 8 U.S.C. § 1227(a)(2)(A)(iii).

This chapter overlaps **Chapter 4, IV.B: Aggravated Felonies** concerning the consequences of aggravated felony convictions and **Chapter 10: Illegal Entry and Reentry — Pretrial and Trial** and **Chapter 11: Illegal Entry and Reentry — Pleas and Sentencing** concerning reentry after deportation cases.

I. Aggravated Felonies in General

§ 5.1. *What are "aggravated felonies"?*

Title 8 U.S.C. § 1101(a)(43) lists aggravated felonies. Whenever an alien is charged with a crime, *look at this statute*!

This chapter will not cover every possible part of this statute, only the highlights. Several subsections are clear or, indeed, outright superfluous. *See, e.g.*, 8 U.S.C. § 1101(a)(43)(O) defining prior illegal reentry after an aggravated felony as an aggravated felony); *In re* Alvarado-Alvino, 22 I&N Dec. 718 (BIA 1999) (simple reentry conviction under 8 U.S.C. § 1325 was not an aggravated felony since noncitizen was not deported on the basis of having committed a criminal offense defined in § 1101(a)(43)).

§ 5.2. *Is the aggravated felony list at 8 U.S.C. § 1101(a)(43) clear?*

With several categories, no. For instance, the term "aggravated felonies" can include misdemeanors. Making this even more difficult is that several agencies and courts interpret the statute including the following:

- ICE interpretations;
- Board of Immigration Appeals (BIA) case law, *see generally* Brian K. Bates, *"Guerrilla Lawyers:" Survival And Resistance Against Government Forces*, 4:18 BENDER'S IMMIGR. BULL. 909

(Sept. 15, 1999) (defending against aggravated felonies in immigration court).

- Circuit court appeals from BIA decisions, *compare* United States v. Ibarra-Galindo, 206 F.3d 1337 (9th Cir. 2000) (BIA interpretation of aggravated felony statute entitled to "no deference"), *cert. denied*, 531 U.S. 1102, 121 S. Ct. 837 (2001), *with* United States v. Mead Corp., 533 U.S. 218, 121 S. Ct. 2164 (courts "obligated" to give agency some deference), *on remand appeal reinstated*, 18 Fed. Appx. 851 (2001) *and* INS v. Aguirre-Aguirre, 526 U.S. 415, 119 S. Ct. 1439 (1999) (BIA has express delegation of interpretive authority).
- District and circuit cases from prosecutions for 8 U.S.C. § 1326, *see* **Chapter 10: Illegal Entry and Reentry — Pretrial and Trial**;
- District and circuit cases interpreting Federal Sentencing Guideline § 2L1.2 on punishment for reentry after deportation subsequent to an aggravated felony conviction, *see* **Chapter 11: Illegal Entry and Reentry — Pleas and Sentencing**.

§ 5.3. *How did the "aggravated felony" concept come into immigration law?*

The "aggravated felony" came into being in immigration and federal criminal law with the Anti-Drug Abuse Act of 1988. 8 U.S.C. § 1101(a)(43). Originally, 8 U.S.C. § 1101(a)(43) listed a rather modest number of "aggravated felonies" including drug trafficking, arms trafficking, murder, and conspiracy to commit those acts. United States v. Andrino-Carillo, 63 F.3d 922, 925 (9th Cir. 1995), *cert. denied*, 516 U.S. 1064, 116 S. Ct. 746 (1996).

The Immigration Act of 1990 added more aggravated felonies, including "illicit trafficking" in a controlled substance, money laundering, and crimes of violence for which the term of imprisonment imposed was at least five years.

The Violent Crime Control and Law Enforcement Act of 1994, the Immigration and Nationality Technical Corrections Act of 1994, and § 440(e) of the Antiterrorism and Effective Death Penalty Act of 1996 added new crimes.

IIRAIRA again expanded the list of "aggravated felonies." *See, e.g.*, United States v. Velasco-Medina, 305 F.3d 839, 843 (9th Cir. 2002), *cert. denied*, 540 U.S. 1210, 124 S. Ct. 1488 (2004) (noting that "IIRIRA expanded the definition of 'aggravated felony' by [inter alia] reducing the prison sentence required to trigger 'aggravated felony' status for burglary from five years to one year."); United States v. Corona-Sanchez, 234 F.3d 449, 454 (9th Cir. 2000) (IIRAIRA added new offenses and "'dramatically broadened the definition's reach by expanding the terms of many offenses already denominated aggravated felonies.'") (quoting Maria v. McElroy, 68 F. Supp. 2d 206, 210 (E.D.N.Y. 1999)), *on rehearing, rev'd and remanded by* 291 F.3d 1201 (9th Cir. 2002); *see also* 8 U.S.C.§ 1101(a)(43) (definition of aggravated felony); INS v. St. Cyr, 533 U.S. 289, 296 n.4, 121 S. Ct. 2271 (2001).

Title 8 U.S.C. § 1101(a)(43) now numbers 21 subsections with sub-sub-sections listing over 50 different crimes as "aggravated felonies."

§ 5.4. *What about foreign convictions?*

Under 8 U.S.C. § 1101(a)(43), foreign convictions for aggravated felonies count if the defendant completed his sentence within the last 15 years. This 15-year limitation, however, only applies to foreign convictions. United States v. Gonzalez-Mendez, 150 F.3d 1058 (9th Cir.), *cert. denied*, 525 U.S. 1010, 119 S. Ct. 528 (1998).

II. Convictions Defined and Categorical Approach

A. "Convictions," Expungements, Suspended Sentences, Youth Offenders

§ 5.5. *What is a "conviction" for defining an aggravated felony?*

Title 8 U.S.C. § 1101(a)(48) defines convictions under immigration law as follows:

> (i) a judge or jury has found the alien guilty or the alien has entered a plea of guilty or *nolo contendere* or has admitted sufficient facts to warrant a finding of guilt, and
>
> (ii) the judge has ordered some form of punishment, penalty, or restraint on the alien's liberty to be imposed.

The second prong can be satisfied by imposed jail time (whether or not suspended), probation, participation in rehabilitative programs, community service, and payment of fines. *See* **Chapter 4: Immigration Consequences of Criminal Convictions**.

§ 5.6. *Do expunged convictions count?*

No. Murillo-Espinoza v. INS, 261 F.3d 771 (9th Cir. 2001) (INA definition of conviction precludes giving effect to Arizona expungement statute); Lujan-Armendariz v. INS, 222 F.3d 728 (9th Cir. 2000) (expunged convictions under federal First Time Offender Act, 18 U.S.C. § 3607, not convictions under 8 U.S.C. § 1101(a)(48)). However, if the defendant made no formal admission of guilt in the first place, it is not a conviction. *In re* Rodriguez-Ruiz, 22 I&N Dec. 1378 (BIA 2000) (convictions vacated on grounds not related to a rehabilitative or expungement statute cannot support removal); *In re* Grullon, 20 I&N Dec. 12 (BIA 1989) (Florida deferred adjudication disposition not a conviction, no formal admission of guilt). *See* **Chapter 4, III.C.3: Expunged Convictions**.

If the alien's conviction only *might* be expunged under a given statute, even if nearly assured, the government can order the alien's removal. Chavez-Perez v. Ashcroft, 386 F.3d 1284 (9th Cir. 2004).

§ 5.7. *What about a suspended sentence?*

A suspended sentence of incarceration is still a sentence to imprisonment under immigration laws. 8 U.S.C. § 1101(a)(48)(B). The suspended time counts whenever immigration consequences result from the length of a sentence. For example, a sentence of imprisonment of at least one year following a conviction for a burglary or theft offense or a "crime of violence" renders any of these crimes an aggravated felony. *See* 8 U.S.C. § 1101(a)(43)(G), (F); United States v. Hernandez-Valdovinos, 352 F.3d 1243 (9th Cir. 2003); United States v. Echavarria-Escobar, 270 F.3d 1265 (9th Cir. 2001), *cert. denied*, 535 U.S. 1069, 122 S. Ct. 1943 (2002).

§ 5.8. *What about convictions under Youth Offender Acts?*

These are not "convictions." Dillingham v. INS, 267 F.3d 996 (9th Cir. 2001) (foreign drug possession convictions that qualify under the federal first time offender expungement provisions (18 U.S.C. § 3607) not convictions for immigration purposes); Paredes-Urrestarazu v. INS, 36 F.3d 801 (9th Cir. 1994) (federal Youth Corrections Act convictions cannot serve as the basis for a deportation); *In re* Devison-Charles, 22 I&N Dec. 1362 (BIA 2000) (en banc) (New York juvenile corrections act conviction not a conviction for 8 U.S.C. § 1101(a)(48)(A) purposes).

B. Categorical Approach

§ 5.9. *When does a given statute define an aggravated felony?*

Courts use a "modified" categorical approach to decide whether a prior conviction is an aggravated felony for deportation purposes. The alien's actual conduct is not really the issue, but whether the underlying statute of conviction presents an aggravated felony.

First, the reviewing court will only compare the conviction's statutory definition with 8 U.S.C. § 1101(a)(43). If the statute only defines an aggravated felony and is not "divisible" (i.e., with subsections that proscribe conduct that is not an aggravated felony), the conviction is an aggravated felony under immigration law. *See, e.g.*, United States v. Pallares-Galan, 359 F.3d 1088 (9th Cir. 2004); United States v. Perez-Corona, 295 F.3d 996 (9th Cir. 2002) (Arizona joyriding not categorically an aggravated felony); United States v. Rivera-Sanchez, 247 F.3d 905 (9th Cir. 2001) (en banc) (California drug statute, which proscribes, *inter alia*, transporting narcotics for personal use, too broad to constitute aggravated felony without engaging in modified categorical analysis); United States v. Lomas, 30 F.3d 1191 (9th Cir. 1994) (use of a categorical approach to determine if a prior drug conviction is an aggravated felony), *cert. denied*, 513 U.S. 1176, 115 S. Ct. 1158 (1995).

Second, if the statute of conviction is "divisible" the reviewing court will look to "judicially noticeable" documents to decide whether the alien's conduct fits under the part of the statute constituting an aggravated felony. *E.g.*, Martinez-Perez v. Ashcroft, 393 F.3d 1018 (9th Cir. 2004) (charging papers and judgment showed defendant violated part of statute constituting an aggravated felony for grand theft) *opinion withdrawn and amended*, 417 F.3d 1022 (9th Cir. 2005); United States v. Contreras-Salas, 387 F.3d 1095 (9th Cir. 2004) (pleadings and presentence report failed to clarify that defendant violated part of statute that was an aggravated felony).

§ 5.10. *What are "judicially noticeable" documents?*

Judicially noticeable documents include judgments, indictments, and plea documents, but not abstracts of judgments. United States v. Navidad-Marcos, 367 F.3d 903 (9th Cir. 2004) ("abstract of judgment" is not a judicially noticeable document); United States v. Franklin, 235 F.3d 1165 (9th Cir. 2000) (judgment of conviction and citation to statute of conviction needed to conduct a proper categorical analysis).

§ 5.11. *Which party has the burden under the categorical approach?*

The government has the burden to satisfy the modified categorical approach. United States v. Navidad-Marcos, 367 F.3d 903 (9th Cir. 2004); United States v. Franklin, 235 F.3d 1165 (9th Cir. 2000).

III. *Ex Post Facto* and Retroactive Effect of Statute

§ 5.12. *How does the ex post facto clause affect the aggravated felony definitions?*

It apparently does not. United States v. Lazo-Ortiz, 136 F.3d 1282 (11th Cir.), *cert. denied*, 525 U.S. 853, 119 S. Ct. 131 (1998); United States v. Guzman-Bruno, 27 F.3d 420 (9th Cir.) (being deported alien is continuing offense for determining which version of the Federal Sentencing Guidelines to apply), *cert. denied*, 513 U.S. 975, 115 S. Ct. 451 (1994); United States v. Arzate-Nunez, 18 F.3d 730 (9th Cir. 1994) (operative date for evaluating *ex post facto* issues is date of violation of the INA, not date of prior offense).

§ 5.13. *Are the added definitions retroactive?*

Yes. The expanded definitions of aggravated felonies apply "retroactively to all defined offenses whenever committed, and ... make aliens so convicted eligible for deportation notwithstanding the passage of time between the crime and the removal order." Aragon-Ayon v. INS, 206 F.3d 847, 852–53 (9th Cir. 2000) (new definition applies to all "actions taken" by the Attorney General on or after September 30, 1996, regardless of the date of conviction) (citing Valderrama-Fonseca v. INS, 116 F.3d 853 (9th Cir. 1997)). *See also* Seale v. INS, 323 F.3d 150 (1st Cir. 2003); *but cf.* INS v. St. Cyr, 533 U.S. 289, 121 S. Ct. 2271 (2001) (eliminating discretionary relief based on the expanded aggravated felony definition had an impermissible retroactive effect on certain aliens); *see generally* Ron Wada, *An Argument Against Deportability Based on a Retroactively Defined Aggravated Felony*, 3:20 BENDER'S IMMIGR. BULL. 1035 (Oct. 15, 1998); Bruce Robert Marley, *Exiling the New Felons: The Consequences of the Retroactive Application of Aggra-*

vated Felony Convictions to Lawful Permanent Residents, 35 SAN DIEGO L. REV. 855 (1998); *see also* Restrepo v. McElroy, 369 F.3d 627 (2d Cir. 2004), *on remand, writ of habeas corpus denied,* 354 F. Supp. 2d 254 (E.D.N.Y. 2005); United States v. Leon-Paz, 340 F.3d 1003 (9th Cir. 2003).

§ 5.14. *What about old criminal convictions and retroactive effect?*

According to the definition of aggravated felony at 8 U.S.C. § 1101(a)(43), it does not matter when the person committed what is now an aggravated felony; he or she will be deported as an aggravated felon. *But see* Nancy Morawetz, *Rethinking Retroactive Deportation Laws and the Due Process Clause (Part One), in* 4:6 BENDER'S IMMIGR. BULL. 221 (Mar. 15, 1999) *and* 73 N.Y.U. L. REV. 97 (1998); Morawetz (Part Two), 4:7 BENDER'S IMMIGR. BULL. 275 (Apr. 1, 1999); Morawetz (Part Three), 4:8 BENDER'S IMMIGR. BULL. 311 (Apr. 15, 1999); Morawetz (Part Four), 4:9 BENDER'S IMMIGR. BULL. 367 (May 1, 1999); Ron Wada, *An Argument Against Deportability Based on a Retroactively Defined Aggravated Felony,* 3:20 BENDER'S IMMIGR. BULL. 1035 (Oct. 15, 1998).

An alien with a pre-April 24 1996 conviction, however, may have some relief from deportation. *See* **IV: Immigration Consequences and Deportation Relief**, *infra*.

IV. Immigration Consequences and Deportation Relief

See **Chapter 4: Immigration Consequences of Criminal Convictions** for a more detailed discussion of immigration consequences.

§ 5.15. *What do ICE and immigration court do to aggravated felons?*

Remove them. An "aggravated felon" is almost guaranteed deportation. 8 U.S.C. §§ 1229b(a)(3), 1229c(a)(1). (*See* **Chapter 2: Immigration Law for Criminal Lawyers.**) *See, e.g.,* Ocampo-Duran v. Ashcroft, 254 F.3d 1133 (9th Cir. 2001) (aggravated felony causes the alien's deportation or removal at any time after admission); *but see* Brian K. Bates, *"Guerrilla Lawyers:" Survival and Resistance Against Government Forces,* 4:18 BENDER'S IMMIGR. BULL. 909 (Sept. 15, 1999) (defending against aggravated felonies in immigration court).

§ 5.16. *Does the alien have any deportation relief?*

Basically, no. An aggravated felon alien will be ineligible for almost all deportation relief:

- Voluntary departure under 8 U.S.C. § 1254(e)(2) = **no.**
- Cancellation of removal = **no**. *See* United States v. Corona-Sanchez, 291 F.3d 1201, 1210 n.8 (9th Cir. 2002) (en banc).
- Waiver of deportation = **no**, 8 U.S.C. § 1182 (1994).
- Adjustment of status with a waiver = **almost always no**. In rare cases because of the quirk in the statute a non-Legal Permanent Resident (LPR) at the time of conviction with a non-drug aggravated felony conviction *may* adjust status through a close U.S. citizen or LPR family member with a waiver under 8 U.S.C. § 1182(h).
- Political asylum or withholding = **no**. But, if the aggravated felon has the equivalent of a very strong asylum claim he can apply to stop the deportation under 8 U.S.C. § 1231(b)(3) and the United Nations Convention Against Torture. *See* Evangeline G. Abriel, *Presumed Ineligible: The Effect of Criminal Convictions on Application for Asylum, and Withholding of Deportation Under Section 515 of the Immigration Act of 1990*, 6 GEO. IMMIGR. L.J. 27 (1992).
- Visas = **no**. But, "T" or "U" visas for aggravated felons cooperating with authorities who are victims of alien smuggling or a serious crime may be available. *See* 8 U.S.C. § 1101(a)(15)(T) and (U).

See generally IRA J. KURZBAN, KURZBAN'S IMMIGRATION LAW SOURCEBOOK (7th ed. 2000); Jeffery B. Fawell & Robert S. White, *Effects of Recent Immigration Legislation on Criminal Aliens and Defense Practitioners*, THE CHAMPION, Sept./Oct. 1995, at 10; Valerie Neal, Note, *Slings And Arrows of Outrageous Fortune: The Deportation of "Aggravated Felons,"* 36 VAND. J. TRANSNAT'L L. 1619–55 (2003).

§ 5.17. *What about aliens with convictions before April 24, 1996?*

LPRs who plead guilty to a non-firearms aggravated felony could have had a waiver under former 8 U.S.C. § 1182(c). Thus, their reliance on that waiver may hold despite the changes in the immigration statute eliminating the waiver. INS v. St. Cyr, 533 U.S. 289, 121 S. Ct. 2271 (2001) (eliminating discretionary relief based on the expanded aggravated felony definition had an impermissible retroactive effect on certain aliens). *See also* Practice Guides at www.ailf.org.

The Ninth Circuit specifically held that a retroactive application of the deportation statute to aggravated felons with pre-1996 convictions may not be permissible if the alien entered a guilty plea "in reliance upon the relief afforded by INA § 212(c) [8 U.S.C. § 1182(c)]." United States v. Magana-Pizano, 200 F.3d 603, 613–14 (9th Cir. 1999). *See also* Kathleen M. Sullivan, *Commentary on* Magana-Pizano, 5:2 BENDER'S IMMIGR. BULL. 75 (Jan. 15, 2000). To be eligible for relief under *Magana-Pizano*, the alien must (1) be a lawful permanent resident; (2) have lived legally in the United States for at least seven years on the date of deportation; (3) not have served a sentence of more than five years; (4) have been convicted on or before April 24, 1996, or pled guilty on or before April 24, 1996, believing that the plea would not be the basis for deportation; and (5) have a final order of deportation.

§ 5.18. *What are the effects of aggravated felony deportation?*

After removal for an aggravated felony under 8 U.S.C. § 1227(a), the alien is denied admission to the United States for 20 years (8 U.S.C. § 1182(a)), placed in expedited removal proceedings (8 U.S.C. § 1228), and arrested and detained pending a decision on removal from the United States (8 U.S.C. § 1226(c)). The alien is also ineligible for relief from removal and barred from relief from inadmissibility under 8 U.S.C. § 1182(h).

§ 5.19. *Do all convicted aliens get a deportation hearing?*

No. Under 8 U.S.C. § 1228(b), an immigration enforcement officer can, without a hearing, order the alien's "expedited removal" if the alien is not an LPR and has an aggravated felony conviction. *See* **Chapter 5: Aggravated Felonies**. In this situation, the alien has no chance to ask for relief. 8 U.S.C. § 1228(b)(5).

§ 5.20. *Can aggravated felons get judicial review?*

No. Aggravated felons have no direct judicial review from a final order of removal or deportation. *See* Aragon-Ayon v. INS, 206 F.3d 847, 850 (9th Cir. 2000).

§ 5.21. *Can aggravated felons get bond in immigration court?*

No. Convictions for aggravated felonies trigger mandatory detention without bond. *See* Demore v. Hyung Joon Kim, 538 U.S. 510, 123 S. Ct. 1708 (2003), *rev'g* 276 F.3d 523 (9th Cir. 2002); *see also* Deborah F. Buckman, Annotation, *Validity, Construction, and Application of Mandatory Predeportation Detention Provision of Immigration and Nationality Act (8 U.S.C. § 1226(c)) as Amended,* 187 A.L.R. FED. 325 (2003 & 2004 Supp.).

§ 5.22. *What happens to aggravated felons caught returning?*

Bad things. A conviction for reentry after deportation under 8 U.S.C. § 1326(b)(2) will carry a significantly higher federal prison term if the defendant was previously convicted of an aggravated felony. *See* 8 U.S.C. § 1326(b)(2); Federal Sentencing Guideline § 2L1.2; **Chapter 11: Illegal Entry and Reentry — Pleas and Sentencing.**

V. Types of Aggravated Felonies

A. Generally

§ 5.23. *Where should counsel first look?*

As stated, go to 8 U.S.C. § 1101(a)(43) and see if the statute lists the given crime. This section will provide some highlights of specific subsections of § 1101(a)(43) as to various crimes. This statute has 21 subsections identifying particular crimes that are within the definition. Courts have found aliens subject to deportation or removable under 8 U.S.C. § 1227(a) where their crimes constitute the following:

- trafficking in controlled substances, 8 U.S.C. § 1101(a);
- a crime of violence, § 1101(a)(43(F);
- a theft or burglary offense, § 1101(a)(43)(G);
- an offense relating to alien smuggling, § 1101(a)(43)(N);
- crimes of murder, rape, or sexual abuse of a minor, § 1101(a)(43)(A);
- an offense relating to fraud or deceit, § 1101(a)(43)(M);
- an offense relating to bribery, counterfeiting, forgery, or trafficking in vehicles with altered identification numbers, § 1101(a)(43)(R);

- an offense relating to obstruction of justice, perjury, or bribery of a witness within the meaning of § 1101(a)(43)(S).

§ 5.24. *Can misdemeanors be "aggravated felonies"?*

Yes, a misdemeanor, either federal or state, can be an "aggravated felony." The definition of the crime under federal law controls. *E.g.*, United States v. Gonzalez-Tamariz, 310 F.3d 1168 (9th Cir.) (state court misdemeanor punishable up to one year is aggravated felony), *amended by* 2002 U.S. App. LEXIS 27927 (9th Cir. Nov. 18, 2002), *amended and rehearing en banc denied*, 2003 U.S. App. LEXIS 386 (9th Cir. Jan. 13, 2003), *cert. denied*, 538 U.S. 1008, 123 S. Ct. 1921 (2003); United States v. Pacheco, 225 F.3d 148 (2d Cir. 2000) (same), *cert. denied*, 533 U.S. 904, 121 S. Ct. 2246 (2001); Wireko v. Reno, 211 F.3d 833 (4th Cir. 2000) (state misdemeanor for sexual battery was crime of violence and therefore aggravated felony subjecting alien to deportation under 8 U.S.C. § 1227(a)(2)(A)(iii)); United States v. Ibarra-Galindo, 206 F.3d 1337, 1339 (9th Cir. 2000) ("[W]e agree with the six other circuits that have addressed this issue that the term 'felony' as used within § 924(c)(2) refers to crimes denominated as felonies under *either* federal or state law.") (emphasis in original), *cert. denied*, 531 U.S. 1102, 121 S. Ct. 837 (2001); *see also* Joseph Justin Rollin, *Humpty Dumpty Logic: Arguing Against the "Aggravated Misdemeanor" in Immigration Law*, 6:10 BENDER'S IMMIGR. BULL. 445 (May 15, 2001).

Generally, any offense, whether misdemeanor or felony, can qualify as an aggravated felony if it fits under 8 U.S.C. § 1101(a)(43)'s definition. United States v. Alvarez-Gutierrez, 394 F.3d 1241 (9th Cir. 2005). *See also United States v. Gonzalez-Tamariz* (finding misdemeanor battery convictions with one-year suspended sentence qualified as aggravated felony); United States v. Graham, 169 F.3d 787 (3d Cir.) (petty larceny conviction where one year sentence imposed constitutes aggravated felony), *cert. denied*, 528 U.S. 845, 120 S. Ct. 116 (1999).

§ 5.25. *What about a misdemeanor under federal law?*

This may not be an aggravated felony. Cazarez-Gutierrez v. Ashcroft, 356 F.3d 1015 (9th Cir.) (Arizona felony conviction of possession of methamphetamine would have been misdemeanor under federal law and thus did not qualify as "aggravated felony"), *opinion withdrawn*, 366 F.3d 736 (9th Cir.), *reh'g*, 382 F.3d 905

(9th Cir. 2004), *on rehearing, judgment entered (case transferred to district court for consideration as petition for habeas corpus). But see* Jenkins v. INS, 32 F.3d 11 (2d Cir. 1994) (attempted possession of a controlled substance, a felony under state law but a misdemeanor under federal law, is aggravated felony).

§ 5.26. *Does the term include state convictions?*

Yes. To determine whether an alien's state conviction is an "aggravated felony," the court looks only at the state's statutory definition of the offense, not the underlying factual circumstances of the crime or the name of the offense. United States v. Baron-Medina, 187 F.3d 1144 (9th Cir. 1999), *cert. denied*, 531 U.S. 1167, 121 S. Ct. 1130 (2001); United States v. Lomas, 30 F.3d 1191 (9th Cir. 1994), *cert. denied*, 513 U.S. 1176, 115 S. Ct. 1158 (1995). If all the elements of the state offense are in a federal offense listed at 8 U.S.C. § 1101(a)(43), the state offense counts. *See, e.g.*, United States v. Castillo-Rivera, 244 F.3d 1020 (9th Cir.) (California Penal Code § 12021(a)(1) analogues 18 U.S.C. § 922(b)(1)), *cert. denied*, 534 U.S. 931, 122 S. Ct. 294 (2001).

The federal jurisdictional element is irrelevant. *In re* Vasquez-Muniz, 23 I&N Dec. 207 (BIA 2002) (en banc) (a state or foreign crime can be aggravated felony if "described in" federal statute even if lacking jurisdictional element). *See* Cazarez-Gutierrez v. Ashcroft, 356 F.3d 1015 (9th Cir.), *opinion withdrawn*, 366 F.3d 736 (9th Cir.), *reh'g*, 382 F.3d 905 (9th Cir. 2004) (an offense is only an aggravated felony if it is a felony under federal law or trafficking component exists), *on rehearing, judgment entered (case transferred to district court for consideration as petition for habeas corpus)*; Gerbier v. Holmes, 280 F.3d 297 (3d Cir. 2002) (same); Aguirre v. INS, 79 F.3d 315 (2d Cir. 1996) (same); *see also* United States v. Hernandez-Avalos, 251 F.3d 505 (5th Cir.) (state felony offense though punishable under the enumerated federal laws as a misdemeanor is an aggravated felony for immigration purposes), *cert. denied*, 534 U.S. 935, 122 S. Ct. 305 (2001).

§ 5.27. *Does the sentence the alien received on his prior matter?*

A sentence to less than one year will prevent the following convictions from being classified as aggravated felony offenses for immigration purposes.

- Crime of violence under 18 U.S.C. § 16;
- Theft including receipt of stolen property;
- Burglary;
- Bribery of a witness;
- Commercial bribery;
- Counterfeiting;
- Forgery;
- Trafficking in vehicles with altered VIN numbers;
- Obstruction of Justice;
- Perjury and subornation of perjury;
- Falsifying documents or trafficking in false documents.

See 8 U.S.C. § 1101(a)(43)(F), (G), (S). Even if a conviction for one of the above offenses is a misdemeanor with a suspended sentence of one year or more, the conviction is an aggravated felony. Thus, if counsel representing the alien can get a sentence of 364 days or less, these crimes are not aggravated felonies. *See* definition of "term of imprisonment" at 8 U.S.C. § 1101(a)(48)(B); **Chapter 4, III.A: "Conviction" and "Sentencing" Under Immigration Law.**

Remember, even if the sentence is suspended, it counts as part of the one year. United States v. Hernandez-Valdovinos, 352 F.3d 1243 (9th Cir. 2003); United States v. Echavarria-Escobar, 270 F.3d 1265 (9th Cir. 2001), *cert. denied*, 535 U.S. 1069, 122 S. Ct. 1943 (2002).

§ 5.28. *What about common law crimes?*

When 8 U.S.C. § 1101(a)(43) lists common law crimes — theft, burglary, sexual abuse of a minor — without a cite to a statute, the courts create a standard "generic" definition setting out the elements of the crime. Courts will then use this to determine if the given state or federal crime is an aggravated felony. *See* Sareang Ye v. INS, 214 F.3d 1128 (9th Cir. 2000) (applying Taylor v. United States, 495 U.S. 575, 110 S. Ct. 2143 (1990)).

§ 5.29. *What about accessory after the fact or misprision of a felony?*

Misprision of a felony is not an aggravated felony under 8 U.S.C. § 1101(a)(43)(S), but the INS interpreted accessory after the fact an obstruction related offense and therefore an aggravated felony. United States v. Innie, 7 F.3d 840 (9th Cir. 1993) (accessory after the fact to murder does not qualify as a crime of violence), *cert. denied*, 511 U.S. 1042, 114 S. Ct. 1567 (1994), *remanded after appeal*, 77 F.3d 1207 (9th Cir. 1996); *In re* Espinoza-Gonzalez, 22 I&N Dec. 889 (BIA 1999) (en banc) (misprision not an aggravated felony when compared to federal obstruction offenses (see 18 U.S.C. §§ 1501–1518)). *But see In re* Batista-Hernandez, 21 I&N Dec. 955 (BIA 1997) (en banc) (accessory after the fact convictions can be deemed obstruction-related offenses and therefore aggravated felonies pursuant to 8 U.S.C. § 1101(a)(43)(S)).

§ 5.30. *Are convictions for conspiracy and attempts aggravated felonies?*

Yes, under 8 U.S.C. § 1101(A)(43)(U) a conviction of conspiracy or attempt of any of the other aggravated felonies is an aggravated felony.

B. Drug Offenses

§ 5.31. *Is drug trafficking an aggravated felony?*

Yes, under 8 U.S.C. § 1101(a)(43)(B). Drug trafficking offenses have been aggravated felonies since the Anti-Drug Abuse Act of 1988, the inception of 8 U.S.C. § 1101(a)(43). *See* Russell J. Davis, Annotation, *Construction and Application of § 212(a)(23) of Immigration and Nationality Act (8 U.S.C. § 1182(a)), Excluding Aliens Who Are Drug "Traffickers" or Who Have Been Convicted of Violating Narcotics or Marijuana Laws*, 32 A.L.R. FED. 538 (1977 & 2004 Supp.).

§ 5.32. *How does the statute define "drug trafficking"?*

The definition of aggravated felony includes "illicit trafficking in a controlled substance (as defined in section 802 of Title 21), including a drug trafficking crime (as defined in section 924(c) of Title 18.)" 8 U.S.C. § 1101(a)(43)(B). Title 18 U.S.C. § 924(c) defines a "drug trafficking crime" as including "any felony" punishable under the Controlled Substances Act (21 U.S.C. § 801 et seq.), the Controlled Substances Import and Export Act (21 U.S.C. § 951 et seq.), or the Maritime Drug Law Enforcement Act (46 U.S.C. App. § 1901 et seq.). Gerbier v. Holmes, 280 F.3d 297 (3d Cir. 2002) (rejecting characterization of defendant's conviction for trafficking in cocaine as an aggravated felony where state conviction did not require proof of intent to distribute).

§ 5.33. *Does this include state drug offenses?*

Yes, "[t]he Controlled Substances Act defines 'felony' as 'any Federal or State offense *classified* by applicable Federal or State law as a felony.'" United States v. Robles-Rodriguez, 281 F.3d 900, 903–04 (9th Cir. 2002) (citing 21 U.S.C. § 802(13)) (emphasis added). Put another way, state drug convictions count if the statutory elements would constitute a felony under U.S.C. Title 21.

§ 5.34. *Does this include misdemeanor drug trafficking offenses?*

Yes, as stated *supra*, even a misdemeanor under federal law can be an aggravated felony. *See* United States v. Ibarra-Galindo, 206 F.3d 1337, 1339 (9th Cir. 2000) ("[W]e agree with the six other circuits that have addressed this issue that the term 'felony' as used within § 924(c)(2) refers to crimes denominated as felonies under *either* federal or state law.") (emphasis in original), *cert. denied*, 531 U.S. 1102, 121 S. Ct. 837 (2001); *see, e.g.*, Jenkins v. INS, 32 F.3d 11 (2d Cir. 1994) (attempted possession of a controlled substance, a felony under state law but a misdemeanor under federal law, is aggravated felony); *see also* Joseph Justin Rollin, *Humpty Dumpty Logic: Arguing Against the "Aggravated Misdemeanor" in Immigration Law*, 6:10 BENDER'S IMMIGR. BULL. 445 (May 15, 2001).

§ 5.35. *Does simple possession count as an aggravated felony?*

Yes, at least in the Ninth Circuit. The Ninth Circuit has ruled that that two prior misdemeanor drug possession convictions constitute an "aggravated felony" because the first misdemeanor possession makes the second a felony under federal drug statutes. United States v. Zarate-Martinez, 133 F.3d 1194 (9th Cir.), *cert. denied*, 525 U.S. 849, 119 S. Ct. 123 (1998); United States v. Garcia-Olmedo, 112 F.3d 399 (9th Cir. 1997). Following this, the Ninth Circuit then ruled that one single conviction for drug possession can constitute an "aggravated felony." United States v. Ibarra-Galindo, 206 F.3d 1337 (9th Cir. 2000), *cert. denied*, 531 U.S. 1102, 121 S. Ct. 837 (2001). *See generally* Katherine Brady, *Commentary on* United States v. Ibarra-Galindo — *Is First Offense Simple Possession an Aggravated Felony?*, 5:7 BENDER'S IMMIGR. BULL. 303 (Apr. 1, 2000); *but see In re* K-V-D-, Int. Dec. 3422 (BIA 2000) (BIA ruling that state felony conviction for simple possession punished only as a misdemeanor under federal law is not aggravated felony), *overruled by In re* Yanez-Garcia, 23 I&N Dec. 390 (BIA 2002); *but compare* United States v. Robles-Rodriguez, 281 F.3d 900 (9th Cir. 2002) (Arizona conviction for drug possession not aggravated felony because under Arizona Proposition 200, incarceration was not authorized) *with* United States v. Arellano-Torres, 303 F.3d 1173 (9th Cir. 2002) (under Nevada Proposition 36, conviction for first possession was an aggravated felony for sentencing purposes), *cert. denied,* 538 U.S. 915, 123 S. Ct. 1502 (2003). The specific reasoning is that the conviction is an "aggravated felony" if it satisfies the two-pronged definition because the offense (1) is punishable under the Controlled Substances Act, and (2) qualifies as a "felony" because it is punishable by imprisonment exceeding one year. *See, e.g.,* United States v. Rios-Beltran, 361 F.3d 1204, 1207 (9th Cir. 2004); United States v. Ballesteros-Ruiz, 319 F.3d 1101, 1103 (9th Cir. 2003).

Adding to the confusion, however, is that the Ninth Circuit has conflicting opinions depending on the context on whether simple drug possession constitutes an aggravated felony under 8 U.S.C. § 1101(a)(43). *Compare* Cazarez-Gutierrez v. Ashcroft, 356 F.3d 1015 (9th Cir.), *opinion withdrawn,* 366 F.3d 736 (9th Cir.), *reh'g,* 382 F.3d 905 (9th Cir. 2004) (simple drug possession is not an aggravated felony under § 1101(a)(43) for immigration purposes), *on rehearing, judgment entered (case transferred to district court for consideration as petition for habeas corpus), with United States v. Ibarra-Galindo* (simple drug possession is an aggravated felony under § 1101(a)(43) for sentencing purposes).

§ 5.36. *What other types of drug crimes are aggravated felonies?*

Aggravated felonies include attempted possession, United States v. Lugo, 170 F.3d 996 (10th Cir. 1999); aiding and abetting cocaine possession with intent to distribute, United States v. Baca-Valenzuela, 118 F.3d 1223 (8th Cir. 1997); and felony sale of a controlled substance, Nakhleh v. INS, 38 F.3d 829 (6th Cir. 1994).

§ 5.37. *What about accessory after the fact?*

Conviction under the federal accessory after the fact statute is probably not an aggravated felony, but a conviction for accessory after the fact to the manufacture of methamphetamine is an aggravated felony. *See* Olivera-Garcia v. INS, 328 F.3d 1083 (9th Cir. 2003) (leaving open whether a conviction solely under the federal accessory after the fact statute would be a violation of law relating to a controlled substance).

§ 5.38. *What about misprision of a felony?*

Misprision of felony is not a drug offense even if the principal offense involved drugs. *In re* Batista-Hernandez, 21 I&N Dec. 955 (BIA 1997) (en banc). Also, misprision of a felony may not be an aggravated felony because it does not appear to be in the language of 8 U.S.C. § 1101(a)(43).

§ 5.39. *What if the conviction does not identify the drug involved?*

A conviction that does not identify the drug involved cannot establish a federally listed controlled substance and thus is not a controlled substance drug offense under immigration law. *In re* Paulus, 11 I&N Dec. 274 (BIA 1965).

§ 5.40. *What about conspiracy or attempt to commit drug trafficking?*

These are aggravated felonies under 8 U.S.C. § 1101(a)(43). Coronado-Durazo v. INS, 123 F.3d 1322 (9th Cir. 1997).

§ 5.41. *What about solicitation offenses?*

Solicitation is not a drug-trafficking offense because a generic solicitation offense is not an offense related to a controlled substance and therefore not an aggravated felony. *See* United States v. Rivera-Sanchez, 247 F.3d 905 (9th Cir. 2001) (en banc) (California conviction for transporting marijuana was not an aggravated felony on its face because the statute punishes solicitation); Leyva-Licea v. INS, 187 F.3d 1147 (9th Cir. 1999) (Arizona conviction for solicitation to possess marijuana for sale is not a violation of a law relating to a controlled substance and was therefore not a deportable offense); Coronado-Durazo v. INS, 123 F.3d 1322 (9th Cir. 1997) (Arizona conviction for solicitation to possess cocaine is not a violation of a law relating to a controlled substance and is therefore not a deportable offense).

C. Murder, Rape, And Sexual Abuse

§ 5.42. *Are murder, rape or sexual abuse aggravated felonies?*

Yes, they are specifically listed at 8 U.S.C. § 1101(a)(43)(A). Cedano-Viera v. Ashcroft, 324 F.3d 1062 (9th Cir. 2003) (Nevada conviction for lewdness with a child under 14 constitutes sexual abuse of a minor); United States v. Marin-Navarette, 244 F.3d 1284 (11th Cir.) (Washington conviction for third-degree attempted child molestation was an aggravated felony), *cert. denied*, 534 U.S. 941, 122 S. Ct. 317 (2001); Castro-Baez v. Reno, 217 F.3d 1057 (9th Cir. 2000) (rape is an aggravated felony); United States v. Baron-Medina, 187 F.3d 1144 (9th Cir. 1999) (California conviction for lewd conduct with a child under 14 is an aggravated felony), *cert. denied*, 531 U.S. 1167, 121 S. Ct. 1130 (2001).

§ 5.43. *Is there anything special about the definitions of rape and murder?*

For the aggravated felony statute, no. The traditional murder and rape definitions control under 8 U.S.C. § 1101(a)(43)(A). United States v. Padilla-Reyes, 247 F.3d 1158 (11th Cir.) (violation of Florida lewd assault statute § 800.04, constitutes sexual abuse of a minor since under common usage, physical or nonphysical abuse is covered), *cert. denied*, 534 U.S. 913, 122 S. Ct. 256 (2001); Castro-Baez v. Reno, 217 F.3d 1057, 1059 (9th Cir. 2000) ("ordinary, contemporary, and common meaning" used to find that conviction under California Penal Code § 261(a)(3) is "rape"; citation to *Black's Law Dictionary* defining rape as "'act of sexual intercourse committed by a man with a woman not his wife and without her consent [statutory rape excluded], committed when the woman's resistance is overcome by force or fear, or under other prohibitive conditions'"); United States v. Baron-Medina, 187 F.3d 1144, 1147 (9th Cir. 1999) ("common, everyday meanings" of "sexual" and "minor" used to find that conviction under California Penal Code § 288(a) is "sexual abuse of a minor"; citations to *Black's Law Dictionary* and *Webster's Third New International Dictionary* for definition of abuse), *cert. denied*, 531 U.S. 1167, 121 S. Ct. 1130 (2001); *In re* Rodriguez-Rodriguez, 22 I&N Dec. 991 (BIA 1999) (en banc) (looking to the definition of sexual abuse of a minor contained within 18 U.S.C. § 3509(a)(8) to create a uniform federal definition).

§ 5.44. *For statutory rape, could there be a constitutional challenge?*

Possibly. The difference in state substantive law regarding statutory rape may enable a successful equal protection challenge. United States v. Shannon, 110 F.3d 382 (7th Cir.) (providing detailed analysis of statutory rape age differences between states), *reh'g denied*, 1997 U.S. App. LEXIS 13070 (7th Cir. May 23, 1997), *cert. denied*, 522 U.S. 888, 118 S. Ct. 223 (1997); Yeung v. INS, 76 F.3d 337 (11th Cir. 1996) (applying rational basis review for equal protection violation in INS interpretation treating similarly situated noncitizens in a disparate manner).

D. Crimes of Violence

§ 5.45. *What is a "crime of violence"?*

Title 18 U.S.C. § 16 defines a crime of violence, which constitutes an aggravated felony if the sentence was at least one year. 8 U.S.C. § 1101(a)(43)(F); Sareang Ye v. INS, 214 F.3d 1128 (9th Cir. 2000). Thus, "[s]ection 16 of Title 18, in turn, provides that 'crime of violence' means: (a) an offense that has as an element the use, attempted use, or threatened use of physical force against the person or property of another, or (b) any other offense that is a felony and that, by its nature, involves a substantial risk that physical force against the person or property of another may be used in the course of committing the offense." *Sareang Ye*, 214 F.3d at 1133 (quoting 8 U.S.C. § 16). *See* Katherine Brady & Erica Tomlinson, *Intent Requirement of the Aggravated Felony "Crime of Violence,"* 4:10 BENDER'S IMMIGR. BULL. 420 (May 15, 1999); Cecelia M. Espenoza, *Crimes of Violence by Non-Citizens and the Immigration Consequences*, 26 COLO. LAW. 89 (1997).

§ 5.46. *Are there exceptions?*

There is an exception for purely political offenses. 8 U.S.C. § 1101(a)(43)(F).

§ 5.47. *What are crimes of violence?*

- Unauthorized use of a motor vehicle, United States v. Galvan-Rodriguez, 169 F.3d 217 (5th Cir.), *cert. denied*, 528 U.S. 837, 120 S. Ct. 100 (1999);

- Indecency with a child, United States v. Velazquez-Overa, 100 F.3d 418 (5th Cir. 1996), *cert. denied*, 520 U.S. 1133, 117 S. Ct. 1283 (1997), as well as child sexual abuse, United States v. Lopez-Patino, 391 F.3d 1034 (9th Cir. 2004);
- Burglary of a habitation, United States v. Guadardo, 40 F.3d 102 (5th Cir. 1994);
- Attempted sexual abuse of a child, United States v. Reyes-Castro, 13 F.3d 377 (10th Cir. 1993);
- Assisting or instigating escape or attempted escape of a prisoner, United States v. Aragon, 983 F.2d 1306 (4th Cir.), *amended by* LEXIS Slip Op. (4th Cir. S.C. Jan. 25, 1993);
- Armed bank robbery, United States v. Maddalena, 893 F.2d 815 (6th Cir. 1989), *reh'g denied*, 1990 U.S. App. LEXIS 4830 (6th Cir. Feb. 28, 1990);
- Unarmed bank robbery, Sousa v. INS, 226 F.3d 28 (1st Cir. 2000), *dismissed in part, writ of habeas corpus granted in part*, 135 F. Supp. 2d 75 (D. Mass. 2001);
- Attempted lewd assault, Ramsey v. INS, 55 F.3d 580 (11th Cir. 1995);
- Statutory rape, *In re* B-, Int. Dec. 3270 (BIA 1996);
- Misdemeanor sexual battery, Wireko v. Reno, 211 F.3d 833 (4th Cir. 2000);
- Terrorism, *In re* S-S-, Int. Dec. 3317 (BIA 1997);
- Washington conviction for indecent liberties with minor, United States v. Wood, 52 F.3d 272, 275 (9th Cir.), *cert. denied*, 516 U.S. 881, 116 S. Ct. 217 (1995);
- Nevada conviction for battery causing substantial bodily harm, which was classified as a gross misdemeanor under state law, United States v. Gonzalez-Tamariz, 310 F.3d 1168 (9th Cir.), *amended by* 2002 U.S. App. LEXIS 27927 (9th Cir. Nov. 18, 2002), *amended and rehearing en banc denied*, 2003 U.S. App. LEXIS 386 (9th Cir. Jan. 13, 2003), *cert. denied*, 538 U.S. 1008, 123 S. Ct. 1921 (2003);
- Convictions for assaulting wife and children, Matsuk v. INS, 247 F.3d 999 (9th Cir. 2001);
- Voluntary manslaughter, United States v. Trinidad-Aquino, 259 F.3d 1140, 1146 (9th Cir. 2001); Eun Kyung Park v. INS, 252 F.3d 1018 (9th Cir. 2001);
- Possession of a short-barreled shotgun, United States v. Rivas-Palacios, 244 F.3d 396 (5th Cir. 2001).

§ 5.48. *What are not crimes of violence?*

- Arizona conviction for felony child endangerment, United States v. Hernandez-Castellanos, 287 F.3d 876 (9th Cir. 2002);
- Conviction for entry into a locked vehicle, Sareang Ye v. INS, 214 F.3d 1128 (9th Cir. 2000);
- Accessory after the fact to murder for hire, United States v. Innie, 7 F.3d 840, 848–52 (9th Cir. 1993), *cert. denied*, 511 U.S. 1042, 114 S. Ct. 1567 (1994), *remanded after appeal*, 77 F.3d 1207 (9th Cir. 1996);
- Drug trafficking, United States v. Arrellano-Rios, 799 F.2d 520, 523 (9th Cir. 1986);
- Second-degree manslaughter with recklessness *mens rea*, Jobson v. Ashcroft, 326 F.3d 367 (2d Cir. 2003).
- Connecticut third-degree assault with no intent to cause physical injury, Chrzanoski v. Ashcroft, 327 F.3d 188 (2d Cir. 2003); Milbin v. Ashcroft, 293 F. Supp. 2d 158 (D. Conn. 2003);
- Consensual sex between 18-year-old and 15-year-old girlfriend, Chue Xiong v. INS, 173 F.3d 601 (7th Cir. 1999), *overruled in part by amendment to INA*;
- Entering a motor vehicle without authority with intent to commit theft, Solorzano-Patlan v. INS, 207 F.3d 869 (7th Cir. 2000);
- Vehicle burglary in violation of state law, Sareang Ye v. INS, 214 F.3d 1128 (9th Cir. 2000);
- Driving vehicle under influence of alcohol, Leon v. INS, 27 Fed. Appx. 868 (9th Cir. 2001);
- New York second-degree assault, Persaud v. McElroy, 225 F. Supp. 2d 420 (S.D.N.Y. 2002), *stay denied*, 2003 U.S. Dist. LEXIS 618 (S.D.N.Y. Jan. 13, 2003);
- Pennsylvania conviction for vehicular homicide, Francis v. Reno, 269 F.3d 162 (3d Cir. 2001);
- Sexual abuse of a minor, Chue Xiong v. INS, 173 F.3d 601 (7th Cir. 1999), *overruled in part by amendment to INA. Cf. In re* Sweetser, Int. Dec. 3390 (BIA 1999) (en banc) (using categorical approach to determine a conviction for negligent child abuse resulting in death was not a crime of violence);
- Unlawfully carrying a firearm in a place licensed to sell alcoholic beverages, United States v. Hernandez-Neave, 291 F.3d 296 (5th Cir. 2001);

- Arizona conviction for felony endangerment, United States v. Hernandez-Castellanos, 287 F.3d 876 (9th Cir. 2002);
- California conviction for gross vehicular manslaughter while intoxicated, Lara-Cazares v. Gonzales, 408 F.3d 1217 (9th Cir. 2005).

§ 5.49. *Is felon in possession of a firearm a crime of violence?*

Being a felon in possession of a firearm is not a crime of violence. *See, e.g.*, United States v. Garcia-Cruz, 40 F.3d 986 (9th Cir. 1994) (possession of firearm is not a crime of violence for career offender status); *see also* United States v. Canon, 993 F.2d 1439, 1441 (9th Cir. 1993) (possession of firearm is not a crime of violence under 18 U.S.C. § 924(c)); United States v. Sahakian, 965 F.2d 740 (9th Cir. 1992) (possession of firearm is not a crime of violence for career offender status); *cf.* United States v. Hayes, 7 F.3d 144 (9th Cir. 1993) (possession of unregistered sawed-off shotgun is crime of violence for career offender status).

However, being a felon in possession of a firearm qualifies as an aggravated felony under 8 U.S.C. 1101(a)(43)(E). United States v. Castillo-Rivera, 244 F.3d 1020 (9th Cir.) (California conviction for being a felon in possession of a firearm qualifies as aggravated felony), *cert. denied*, 534 U.S. 931, 122 S. Ct. 294 (2001). *See* **V.G: Firearms Offenses**, *infra*.

§ 5.50. *What about attempted crimes of violence?*

Only convictions for an attempt that involves serious risk of physical injury to another is a crime of violence and thus an aggravated felony. United States v. Riley, 183 F.3d 1155 (9th Cir. 1999), *cert. denied*, 528 U.S. 1174, 120 S. Ct. 1204 (2000); United States v. Weekley, 24 F.3d 1125, 1125 (9th Cir. 1994) ("A risk is a risk. But a risk of a risk is not enough of a risk."); *accord* United States v. Sparks, 87 F.3d 276 (9th Cir. 1996) (attempted home invasion not "crime of violence").

E. Theft and Burglary

1. Generally

§ 5.51. *When is a theft or burglary offense an aggravated felony?*

A theft or burglary offense is an aggravated felony under 8 U.S.C. § 1101(a)(43)(G) if the term of imprisonment is at least one year. Sat Jagroop Singh Randhawa v. Ashcroft, 298 F.3d 1148, 1152 (9th Cir. 2002), *motion granted, remanded by* 114 Fed. Appx. 828 (9th Cir. 2004); Sareang Ye v. INS, 214 F.3d 1128 (9th Cir. 2000).

§ 5.52. *How does the length of sentence affect the definition?*

The sentence imposed is key to meeting the "at least one year" requirement. Matsuk v. INS, 247 F.3d 999 (9th Cir. 2001) (sentence of 365 days qualifies as a year for aggravated felony purposes). Even though the conviction may be for a state misdemeanor, a sentence imposed for a year or more is an aggravated felony. *See* United States v. Corona-Sanchez, 291 F.3d 1201 (9th Cir. 2002) (en banc) (a sentence imposed under a recidivist statute does not meet the one-year sentence requirement for a theft-related aggravated felony); United States v. Graham, 169 F.3d 787 (3d Cir.) (conviction for petit larceny misdemeanor still "aggravated felony"), *cert. denied*, 528 U.S. 845, 120 S. Ct. 116 (1999).

§ 5.53. *What about suspended sentences?*

If the sentence is a year or more it is an aggravated felony regardless whether the sentence was suspended. United States v. Christopher, 239 F.3d 1191 (11th Cir.) (shoplifting conviction where 12-month suspended sentence imposed constituted aggravated felony), *reh'g en banc denied*, 252 F.3d 444 (11th Cir.), *cert. denied*, 534 U.S. 877, 122 S. Ct. 178 (2001); United States v. Pacheco, 225 F.3d 148 (2d Cir. 2000) (one-year suspended sentences enough to qualify misdemeanor offense as aggravated felony), *cert. denied*, 533 U.S. 904, 121 S. Ct. 2246 (2001); United States v. Tejeda-Perez, 199 F.3d 981 (8th Cir. 1999) (suspended sentence of one to fifteen years satisfies one year requirement for theft offense).

2. Theft

§ 5.54. *How is "theft" defined?*

Although theft may be broadly defined, it should have some reference to the "generic" definition. *See* United States v. Taylor, 495 U.S. 575, 110 S. Ct. 2143 (1990); United States v. Corona-Sanchez, 291 F.3d 1201 (9th Cir. 2002) (en banc) (California statute for conviction for petty theft with a prior not an aggravated felony because the statute was over-inclusive); Sareang Ye v. INS, 214 F.3d 1128 (9th Cir. 2000). The *Corona-Sanchez* court adopted the following generic definition of theft offense:

> "[A] taking of property or an exercise of control over property without consent with the criminal intent to deprive the owner of rights and benefits of ownership, even if such deprivation is less than total or permanent."

Corona-Sanchez, 291 F.3d at 1205 (quoting Hernandez-Mancilla v. INS, 246 F.3d 1002, 1009 (7th Cir. 2001)). *See also* Nevarez-Martinez v. INS, 326 F.3d 1053 (9th Cir. 2003) (critical aspect of the generic definition of theft is "the criminal intent to deprive the owner"); Huerta-Guevara v. Ashcroft, 321 F.3d 883 (9th Cir. 2003) (Arizona conviction for possession of a stolen vehicle does not facially qualify as a theft offense that amounts to an aggravated felony); United States v. Perez-Corona, 295 F.3d 996 (9th Cir. 2002) (Arizona conviction for unlawful use of means of transportation not a theft offense for sentencing enhancement); *cf.* Martinez-Perez v. Ashcroft, 393 F.3d 1018 (9th Cir. 2004) (grand theft), *opinion withdrawn and amended*, 417 F.3d 1022 (9th Cir. 2005); Sat Jagroop Singh Randhawa v. Ashcroft, 298 F.3d 1148, 1152 (9th Cir. 2002) (federal conviction for possession of stolen mail is a theft offense amounting to an aggravated felony), *motion granted, remanded by* 114 Fed. Appx. 828 (9th Cir. 2004).

§ 5.55. *How does aiding and abetting theft count?*

Aiding and abetting theft does not constitute theft for the aggravated felony definition. United States v. Corona-Sanchez, 291 F.3d 1201, 1207–08 (9th Cir. 2002) (en banc) (noting that "[u]nder California law, aiding and abetting liability is quite broad, extending even to promotion and instigation.").

§ 5.56. *Does it matter if the alien pleaded nolo contendere?*

No. Rodas v. Ashcroft, 84 Fed. Appx. 872 (9th Cir. 2003) (*nolo contendere* to California grand theft was aggravated felony).

3. Burglary

§ 5.57. *Is burglary an aggravated felony?*

It depends. Burglaries with a sentence of a year or more are aggravated felonies. 8 U.S.C. § 1101(a)(43)(G). A burglary conviction does not qualify, however, unless the offense conduct meets the definition of burglary in *Taylor v. United States*, 495 U.S. 575, 110 S. Ct. 2143 (1990). *See* Sareang Ye v. INS, 214 F.3d 1128, 1132 (9th Cir. 2000) (a burglary offense is "the unlawful or unprivileged entry into, or remaining in, a building or structure, with intent to commit a crime"), *citing* Lopez-Elias v. Reno, 209 F.3d 788 (5th Cir. 2000), *cert. denied*, 531 U.S. 1069, 121 S. Ct. 757 (2001), *and* Solorzano-Patlan v. INS, 207 F.3d 869, 874 (7th Cir. 2000) (alien's "burglary" under state law does not necessarily fit definition of "aggravated felony" under § 1101(a)(43)(G)); *see also* Lory Diana Rosenberg, *"Tayloring" the Interpretation of Burglary Offenses*, 8:14 BENDER'S IMMIGR. BULL. 1212 (July 15, 2003).

§ 5.58. *Is burglary of a car an aggravated felony?*

Generally not. Huerta-Guevara v. Ashcroft, 321 F.3d 883 (9th Cir. 2003) (determining Arizona possession of a stolen motor vehicle conviction did not qualify as a theft-related aggravated felony); Sareang Ye v. INS, 214 F.3d 1128 (9th Cir. 2000) (prior conviction under California Penal Code § 459 for vehicular burglary is not an aggravated felony); Solorzano-Patlan v. INS, 207 F.3d 869 (7th Cir. 2000) (vehicular burglary neither a crime of violence nor burglary offense and therefore is not an aggravated felony); *In re* Perez, 22 I&N Dec. 1325 (BIA 2000) (en banc) (vehicular burglary does not qualify as a burglary-related aggravated felony).

F. Fraud Offenses

§ 5.59. *Which frauds are aggravated felonies?*

Under 18 U.S.C. § 1101(a)(43)(M), fraud and tax crimes involving a loss of over $10,000 are aggravated felonies. Thus, aliens who enter a plea of guilty to an amount less than $10,000, regardless of the punishment, are not aggravated felons. *See* Evangelista v. Ashcroft, 359 F.3d 145 (2d Cir. 2004) (offense of attempting to evade or defeat tax was "related to tax evasion" and therefore aggravated felony because government's loss exceeded $10,000), *cert. denied*, 125 S. Ct. 1293 (2005); Chang v. INS, 307 F.3d 1185 (9th Cir. 2002); Abreu-Reyes v. INS, 292 F.3d 1029 (9th Cir. 2002) (convictions for bribery and subscribing to a false tax return involved fraud or deceit and loss over $10,000), *reh'g granted, prior opinion withdrawn*, 350 F.3d 966 (9th Cir. 2003) ("The prior opinion issued in this case, published at 292 F.3d 1029 (9th Cir. 2002), is inconsistent with United States v. Corona-Sanchez, 291 F.3d 1201, 1211–12 (9th Cir. 2002) (en banc) (discussing use of presentence reports for determining whether an alien is removable for having committed an aggravated felony), which was issued four days before the prior opinion. Because the en banc court's opinion in Corona-Sanchez takes precedence, the prior opinion in this case published at 292 F.3d 1029 (9th Cir. 2002) is WITHDRAWN."); Chowdhury v. INS, 249 F.3d 970, 975 (9th Cir. 2001) (money laundering not aggravated felony since indictment alleged less than $10,000 in laundering); *see also* Valansi v. Ashcroft, 278 F.3d 203 (3d Cir. 2002) (convictions involving fraud must have involved intent to defraud).

§ 5.60. *What about when the alien has an old fraud conviction?*

It does not matter that the alien received his conviction when the requisite loss was more, only that now the requisite loss is $10,000. Bazuaye v. INS, No. 97 Civ. 1280 (S.D.N.Y. Mar. 18, 1997) (conviction on 1992 counterfeiting charges with losses of $15,000 aggravated felony because Act changed the definition of "aggravated felony" by decreasing the requisite loss amount from $200,000 to $10,000). *But cf.* INS v. St. Cyr, 533 U.S. 289, 121 S. Ct. 2271 (2001) (eliminating discretionary relief based on the expanded aggravated felony definition had an impermissible retroactive effect on certain aliens).

§ 5.61. *Is it the loss or restitution that controls?*

The amount of loss, not the amount of restitution, controls whether an alien's fraud conviction is an aggravated felony under 8 U.S.C. § 1101(a)(43)(M)(i). Munroe v. Ashcroft, 353 F.3d 225 (3d Cir. 2003). *Cf.* Chang v. INS, 307 F.3d 1185 (9th Cir. 2002) (restitution order over $10,000 did not convert bank fraud conviction predicated on a $605.30 check into an aggravated felony); Chowdhury v. INS, 249 F.3d 970 (9th Cir. 2001) (money laundering not aggravated felony since indictment alleged less than $10,000 in laundering).

§ 5.62. *What document controls on the finding of loss amount?*

Usually the plea agreement. Chang v. INS, 307 F.3d 1185 (9th Cir. 2002) (federal bank fraud conviction for $605.30 not an aggravated felony under either a categorical or modified categorical approach where parties specified in plea agreement that loss was exactly $605.30). *Cf.* Ferreira v. Ashcroft, 390 F.3d 1091 (9th Cir. 2004) (loss of more than $10,000 determined by restitution in plea agreement of $22,000).

§ 5.63. *Is counterfeiting an aggravated felony?*

Yes. A federal conviction for possession of counterfeit obligations is an aggravated felony under 8 U.S.C. 1101(a)(43)(R). Albillo-Figueroa v. INS, 221 F.3d 1070 (9th Cir. 2000).

G. Firearms Offenses

§ 5.64. *What firearms offenses count as aggravated felonies?*

Title 8 U.S.C. § 1101(a)(43)(C) states the following is an aggravated felony:

> Illicit trafficking in firearms or destructive devices (as defined in section 921 of Title 18) or in explosive materials (as defined in section 841(c) of that title).

Also, 8 U.S.C. § 1101(a)(43)(E) states that the following is an aggravated felony:

> (E) an offense described in —
>
> (i) section 842(h) or (i) of Title 18, or section 844(d), (e), (f), (g), (h), or (i) of that title (relating to explosive materials offenses);
>
> (ii) section 922(g)(1), (2), (3), (4), or (5), (j), (n), (o), (p), or (r) or 924(b) or (h) of Title 18 (relating to firearms offenses); or

(iii) section 5861 of Title 26 (relating to firearms offenses);

See United States v. Mendoza-Reyes, 331 F.3d 1119 (9th Cir.) (Washington conviction for first-degree unlawful possession of a firearm is aggravated felony under 8 U.S.C. § 1101(a)(43)(E)(ii)), *cert. denied*, 540 U.S. 925, 124 S. Ct. 332 (2003).

§ 5.65. *Is felon in possession of a firearm an aggravated felony?*

Yes. *See* United States v. Castillo-Rivera, 244 F.3d 1020 (9th Cir.) (California conviction for being a felon in possession of a firearm qualifies as an aggravated felony under 8 U.S.C. 1101(a)(43)(E)), *cert. denied*, 534 U.S. 931, 122 S. Ct. 294 (2001).

§ 5.66. *What about when a non-felon alien possesses a firearm?*

This is not an aggravated felony. United States v. Sandoval-Barajas, 206 F.3d 853 (9th Cir. 2000) (Washington conviction for possession of firearm by noncitizen not aggravated felony).

§ 5.67. *What if the alien has a state firearms conviction?*

Counsel must compare the state conviction to the federal firearm statutes. The language of 8 U.S.C. § 1101(a)(43)(E) invites an inquiry into differences between the state statute and its federal analogue. United States v. Castillo-Rivera, 244 F.3d 1020 (9th Cir.) (absence of interstate commerce requirement in state felon in possession statute does not render the statute dissimilar enough to disqualify offense as an aggravated felony), *cert. denied*, 534 U.S. 931, 122 S. Ct. 294 (2001); United States v. Sandoval-Barajas, 206 F.3d 853 (9th Cir. 2000) (state statute proscribing aliens from possessing firearms not similar enough to 18 U.S.C. § 922(g)(5) to constitute aggravated felony); United States v. Villanueva-Gaxiola, 119 F. Supp. 2d 1185 (D. Kan. 2000) (California conviction for possession of short-barreled shotgun not aggravated felony); *In re* Vasquez-Muniz, 23 I&N Dec. 207 (BIA 2002) (en banc) (adopting Ninth Circuit's analysis in *Castillo-Rivera* and overruling previous BIA decision).

H. Alien Smuggling

§ 5.68. *Is alien smuggling an aggravated felony?*

Yes, 8 U.S.C. § 1101(a)(43)(N) states as follows:

> (N) an offense described in paragraph (1)(A) or (2) of section 1324(a) of this title (relating to alien smuggling), except in the case of a first offense for which the alien has affirmatively shown that the alien committed the offense for the purpose of assisting, abetting, or aiding only the alien's spouse, child, or parent (and no other individual) to violate a provision of this chapter.

§ 5.69. *What does "relating to alien smuggling" mean?*

Courts hold that the "relating to alien smuggling" parenthetical is a descriptive, rather than a limiting, phrase. Thus, harboring and transporting aliens, both part of 8 U.S.C. § 1324, are aggravated felonies. Castro-Espinosa v. Ashcroft, 257 F.3d 1130 (9th Cir. 2001); United States v. Galindo-Gallegos, 244 F.3d 728 (9th Cir.) (transportation conviction aggravated felony because parenthetical language a mere helpful descriptive aid), *amended by* 255 F.3d 1154 (9th Cir. 2001); United States v. Salas-Mendoza, 237 F.3d 1246 (10th Cir. 2001) (transporting illegal aliens within U.S. boundaries clearly "related to" alien smuggling for purposes of 8 U.S.C. § 1101(a)(43)(N)); Ruiz-Romero v. Reno, 205 F.3d 837 (5th Cir. 2000) (parenthetical comment in subsection referring to alien smuggling merely descriptive as opposed to restrictive). *But see* Gavilan-Cuate v. Yetter, 94 F. Supp. 2d 1039 (D. Minn. 2000) (conspiracy to transport and harbor illegal aliens under 8 U.S.C. § 1324(a) not an "aggravated felony" because not related to alien smuggling), *rev'd and remanded*, 276 F.3d 418 (8th Cir. 2002).

§ 5.70. *Is aiding and abetting illegal entry an aggravated felony?*

So far, no. The scope of subsection 8 U.S.C. § 1101(a)(43)(N) is "explicitly confined" to 8 U.S.C. § 1324 convictions. Thus, an aiding and abetting conviction under 8 U.S.C. § 1325(a) is not an aggravated felony. Rivera-Sanchez v. Reno, 198 F.3d 545 (5th Cir. 1999).

I. DUI Convictions

§ 5.71. *Is felony driving under the influence a crime of violence?*

No. The Supreme Court has recently held that driving under the influence is not a crime of violence under 18 U.S.C. § 16 (defining crimes of violence) and thus not an aggravated felony under 8 U.S.C. § 1101(a)(43)(F). Leocal v. Ashcroft, 125 S. Ct. 377 (2004). Proof on culpability, (i.e., intent) that is no more than negligent, the mental state for a DUI conviction, cannot constitute a crime of violence.

Leocal resolved a split in the circuits. *Compare* Montiel-Barraza v. INS, 275 F.3d 1178 (9th Cir. 2002) (per curiam) (multiple DUI priors not crime of violence); United States v. Trinidad-Aquino, 259 F.3d 1140 (9th Cir. 2001) (DUI with injury to another not crime of violence); United States v. Chapa-Garza, 243 F.3d 921 (5th Cir. 2001) (overturning United States v. Camacho-Marroquin, 188 F.3d 649 (5th Cir. 1999), *on rehearing, opinion withdrawn, petition dismissed, stay lifted, motion granted by* 222 F.3d 1040 (5th Cir. 2000)), *with* Tapia-Garcia v. INS, 237 F.3d 1216 (10th Cir. 2001); Le v. Attorney General, 196 F.3d 1352 (11th Cir. 1999).

PART III
IMMIGRATION CRIMES

CHAPTER 6

ALIEN EMPLOYMENT CRIMES

Other Resources:

AUSTIN T. FRAGOMEN, JR., & STEVEN C. BELL, IMMIGRATION EMPLOYMENT COMPLIANCE HANDBOOK (2005 ed.) (an extensive examination of relevant statutes and regulations affecting employers who hire aliens including pertinent forms, including the Handbook for Employers (form M-274, Instructions for completing form I-9, the employment eligibility verification form).

Robert F. Koets, Annotation, *Validity, Construction, and Application of § 274a of Immigration and Nationality Act (8 U.S.C. § 1324a), Involving Unlawful Employment of Aliens*, 130 A.L.R. FED. 381 (1996).

Stanley Mailman & Stephen Yale-Loehr, *The Intersection of Immigration and Employment Law*, 4:17 BENDER'S IMMIGR. BULL. 873 (Sept. 1, 1999).

Maria Isabel Medina, *The Criminalization of Immigration: Employer Sanctions and Marriage Fraud*, 5 GEO. MASON L. REV. 669 (1997).

Symposia, *Developments in the Law — Jobs and Borders*, 118 HARV. L. REV. 2171 (2005).

Introduction

§ 6.1. *Can employers get prosecuted for hiring unauthorized aliens?*

Yes. However, compared to the overwhelming numbers of unauthorized aliens hired in this country the prosecutions are rare. Few reported decisions exist and law review commentaries are sparse.

§ 6.2. *How can an employer avoid liability?*

Follow the Bureau of Citizenship and Immigration Services (CIS) rules for hiring or verifying an employee's immigration status.

- Do not hire anyone who cannot present adequate documentation, regardless of whether the person is a citizen;
- Do not accept fraudulent documents;
- Do not complete an I-9 form using false statements;
- Audit I-9 forms at least once a year, identify those that need to be retained, and correct any problems to avoid fines and other liability;
- Use the same verification process for citizens and noncitizens of any race.

See AUSTIN T. FRAGOMEN, JR., & STEVEN C. BELL, IMMIGRATION EMPLOYMENT COMPLIANCE HANDBOOK (2005 ed.).

I. Immigration Employment Law History

§ 6.3. *When did the United States start restricting immigrant labor?*

The United States traditionally had a policy of allowing all aliens in the country to encourage the free flow of labor. Over time and starting in the 1920s, this policy changed:

- **1920s:**

  Immigration Act of 1921 — annual limit of 375,000 — the "Red Scare"

  Immigration Act of 1924 — national quota system to save the "national character."

- **1942 — Bracero Treaty:**

  Responding to World War II labor shortages, the Bracero Treaty with Mexico allowed for temporary visas for short-term workers. Under this treaty, 4.6 million Mexican workers came to the United States. The treaty was renewed but both sides complained of a "leak out" problem with workers working for less than "Bracero" contact wages and staying illegally in the United States.

- **1952:**

  Mexicans try to negotiate for employer sanctions to stem the lower-than-contract wage problem. The United States responded with the "Texas Proviso," making it illegal to harbor aliens but not illegal to employ an alien.

- **1954:**

  "Operation Wetback" launched with the INS arresting over 1 million workers and deporting many with their U.S. born children.

- **1960-70:**

  The Mexican government lobbies for legal temporary worker programs without success.

- **1965:**

  Congress passes the Immigration and Naturalization Act of 1965 limiting visas but making a preference in the visa system for skilled labor. Congress amended this Act in 1976, 1978, and 1980 to further restrict Mexican migration.

- **1986:**

  President Ronald Reagan declared illegal immigration a "threat to national security." In response, Congress passed the Immigration Reform and Control Act of 1986. This provided amnesty for 2.3 million Mexicans and for the first time employer sanctions for those who knowingly hire unauthorized workers.

- **1994-95:**

  The North American Free Trade Agreement (NAFTA) accepted but it does not deal with immigration labor issues with one exception — NAFTA provides for a small number of high-level intra-country executives to receive U.S. visas.

- **1994:**

  California passes Proposition 187 barring illegal immigrants from nonemergency health care and public schools. The courts later find this measure unconstitutional.

- **1996:**

  Congress passes the Illegal Immigration Reform and Immigrant Responsibility Act of 1996 increasing the penalties on unauthorized migrants. The Mexican government vigorously protested this Act.

  Congress passes the Welfare Act denying even legal immigrants unemployment or health benefits. The main effect is that the INS becomes overwhelmed with citizenship applications.

- **2000-01:**

  President Fox of Mexico proposes "NAFTA-Plus" suggesting a "guest worker" program for Mexican laborers. President Bush expresses agreement with the proposal. After the terrorist attacks of September 11, 2001 this ideas gets left behind.

- **2005:**

  Congress passes the Real ID Act making asylum claims more difficult and allowing for the construction of an even larger border fence. The Act also prohibits undocumented workers from having driver's licenses.

See James T. Kimer, *Landmarks in U.S. Immigration Policy*, 39:1 NACLA: REPORT ON THE AMERICAS 34 (July/Aug. 2005).

II. Intent of the Statute

§ 6.4. *Why did Congress hold employers criminally liable?*

Congress passed 8 U.S.C. § 1324a as part of the Immigration Reform and Control Act of 1986 (IRCA) to stem the tide of illegal immigration by removing the incentive of economic benefit for coming to the United States. Etuk v. Slattery, 936 F.2d 1433 (2d Cir. 1991); Steiben v. INS, 932 F.2d 1225 (8th Cir. 1991); Nat'l Ctr. for Immigrants' Rights v. INS, 913 F.2d 1350 (9th Cir. 1990), *cert. granted in part*, 499 U.S. 946, 111 S. Ct. 1412, *rev'd on other grounds*, 502 U.S. 183, 112 S. Ct. 551 (1991); Patel v. Quality Inn South, 846 F.2d 700 (11th Cir. 1988), *cert. denied*, 489 U.S. 1011, 109 S. Ct. 1120 (1989); United States v. Jackson, 825 F.2d 853 (5th Cir. 1987), *cert. denied*, 484 U.S. 1011, 108 S Ct 711, 484 U.S.

1019, 108 S. Ct. 730 (1988); EEOC v. Tortilleria "La Mejor," 758 F. Supp. 585 (E.D. Cal. 1991). The statute was supposed to make combating the employment of illegal aliens a central policy of immigration law. Hoffman Plastic Compounds, Inc. v. NLRB, 535 U.S. 137, 122 S. Ct. 1275 (2002).

The statute was also meant to preserve legal immigration, create criminal liability for violation of the law, and preserve jobs for authorized workers by reducing the number of unauthorized workers. United States v. Van, 931 F.2d 384 (6th Cir. 1991); United States v. Todd Corp., 900 F.2d 164 (9th Cir.), *amended, reh'g denied*, 1990 U.S. App. LEXIS 7226 (9th Cir. May 4, 1990).

At the same time, the statute was meant to minimize the burden on employers. Collins Foods Int'l, Inc. v. INS, 948 F.2d 549 (9th Cir. 1991) ("reasonable man" standard applied under the statute).

§ 6.5. *How did Congress attempt to achieve its end?*

The statute sought to establish an "employment verification system" to deny employment to aliens not authorized to work in the United States. As of 1986, an employer commits a crime by knowingly hiring an undocumented alien. *See generally* Lawrence A. Kobrin & Richard L. Reinhold, *Domestic Employment Checklist*, 63 N.Y. St. B.J. 28 (July/Aug. 1992); Ira Kurzban, *Employer Sanctions*, 61 Fla. B.J. 25 (June 1987); Nancy-Jo Merritt, *The Immigration Reform and Control Act of 1986: What Employers Need To Know*, 22 Ariz. B.J. 6 (April/May 1987); Michael D. Patrick, *Employer Sanctions — 10 Key I-9 Issues*, 212 N.Y.L.J. 3 (Dec. 15, 1994); Mary L. Sfasciotti, *Employer Sanctions Under the Immigration Reform and Control Act of 1986*, 76 Ill. B.J. 384 (1988); Nicolas J. Watkins & Joel Stewart, *Employer Sanctions and the Employer's Response*, 66 Fla. B.J. 60 (May 1992).

§ 6.6. *Does the statute have retroactive effect?*

No. IRCA, including the employer sanctions at 8 U.S.C. § 1324a, does not have retroactive effect. Rios v. Enterprise Ass'n Steamfitters Local Union 638, 860 F.2d 1168 (2d Cir. 1988). *Cf.* Maka v. INS, 904 F.2d 1351 (9th Cir. 1990), *amended on other grounds*, 932 F.2d 1352 (9th Cir. 1991) (employer still liable who hired unauthorized alien before Act but knew that the alien quit and was rehired after November 6, 1986).

III. The Crime of Employing Aliens

A. Hiring and Authorization

§ 6.7. *What does 8 U.S.C. § 1324a proscribe?*

IRCA at 8 U.S.C. § 1324a makes it illegal for an employer to hire, recruit, or refer for a fee an employee not authorized to work. *See* Robert C. Rice, *Alien Employment Control and Employer Compliance Under the Immigration Reform and Control Act of 1986*, 29 S. TEX. L. REV. 313 (1988). If an employer unknowingly hires an unauthorized alien, or if the alien becomes unauthorized while employed, the employer must fire the alien when the employer finds out. Hoffman Plastic Compounds, Inc. v. NLRB, 535 U.S. 137, 122 S. Ct. 1275 (2002).

§ 6.8. *Who is authorized to work?*

Citizens and legal permanent residents (LPRs) are automatically authorized to work as well as other aliens CIS has authorized. *See* 8 U.S.C. §§ 1255a, 1324a, 1324b.

§ 6.9. *What can happen to employers with unauthorized employees?*

Employers who violate § 1324a are subject to civil fines and criminal penalties. There are two types of offenses: (1) hiring an alien knowing that the alien was illegally in the country; and (2) failure to comply with the employment document verification process, including inaccurately recording required form I-9 information.

§ 6.10. *When must an employer fire an alien?*

An employer must fire an unauthorized alien within a reasonable time of learning of the alien's status. There is no statutory or regulatory guidance as to the number of days. 8 U.S.C. § 1324a(a)(2); New El Rey Sausage Co. v. INS, 925 F.2d 1153 (9th Cir. 1991) (no blanket rule regarding days to fire unauthorized employee); Mester Mfg. Co. v. INS, 879 F.2d 561 (9th Cir. 1989) (two-week delay in firing alien after receiving INS notice violated IRCA).

§ 6.11. *Are corporations liable?*

Yes. *See, e.g.*, Furr's/Bishop's Cafeterias, L.P. v. INS, 976 F.2d 1366 (10th Cir. 1992) (restaurant chain subject to civil penalties as second-time offender, even though it was the first time the specific restaurant caught hiring unauthorized alien).

§ 6.12. *Can an individual within a corporation be liable?*

Yes. Liability is upon the "person or other entity" who knowingly hires an unauthorized alien or who hires an individual without complying with the statute's verification requirements. Steiben v. INS, 932 F.2d 1225 (8th Cir. 1991) (rejecting argument that 8 U.S.C. § 1324a imposed liability only on the corporation).

B. "Employees" and "Hiring" Defined

§ 6.13. *Who is an "employee"?*

An employee is "an individual who provides services or labor for an employer for wages or other remuneration." 8 C.F.R. § 274a.1(f). This includes remuneration outside the United States. This definition of employment includes persons under contract, subcontract, or labor exchange. 8 C.F.R. §§ 274a.1(c), 274a.5.

§ 6.14. *When is an employee "hired" for verification purposes?*

Generally, "hiring" is when employment begins for "wages or other remuneration." 8 C.F.R. § 274a.1(c). *See* Jenkins v. INS, 108 F.3d 195 (9th Cir. 1997) (property owner had already "hired" alien worker when workers were clearing brush in owner's yard, owner's admission to agent that he hired workers, and worker's identification of owner as employer). "Hiring" also includes "referring or recruiting for a fee." 8 C.F.R. § 274a.1(d).

§ 6.15. *Are independent contractors "employees"?*

Generally not, but the regulations prohibit an employer from using a contractor to avoid complying with the verification requirements. 8 C.F.R. § 274a.5. There are several factors that determine whether an individual is an independent contractor, including the following:

- The status of the employee/contractor under Internal Revenue Service rules;
- The amount of control the employer exercises over the employee/contractor;

- The financial control the employer exercises over the employee/contractor, and
- The relationship of the parties.

See generally 8 C.F.R. § 274a.1(j).

§ 6.16. *Does a person hiring domestic workers have to verify?*

Probably not, but this is an open question. If a private person hires somebody simply to work in the yard, he or she probably does not have to fill out form I-9 and other employment verification requirements. 8 C.F.R. § 274a.1(h) exempts domestic employment from the employment eligibility verification requirements. The statute, however, does not mention this exemption. 8 U.S.C. § 1324a. *See* Jenkins v. INS, 108 F.3d 195 (9th Cir. 1997).

IV. Investigations of Employers

A. Investigations

§ 6.17. *How does the Bureau of Immigration and Customs Enforcement (ICE) investigate employers?*

Immigration officers can subpoena employers for copies of form I-9 forms before ICE fills out a criminal complaint and can issue subpoenas for testimony or to enforce the Immigration Nationality Act. 8 U.S.C. § 1225. Also, 8 U.S.C. § 1324a(e) now allows ICE to issue subpoenas in sanction cases. Steiben v. INS, 932 F.2d 1225 (8th Cir. 1991) (INS within authority to issue regulation imposing sanctions on agents hiring aliens, as well as employers). The Attorney General designates who can issue subpoenas.

§ 6.18. *What decides between a civil and criminal case?*

Generally, ICE refers a case to the U.S. Attorney's office when it appears the employer engaged in criminal behavior. This behavior includes knowingly accepting fraudulent documents, falsely completing forms such as I-9s, or knowingly hiring 10 illegal aliens within a year. It also includes referrals when ICE believes the employer has committed alien harboring under 8 U.S.C. § 1324.

B. An Employer's Verification Requirements

§ 6.19. *What must be verified?*

Under 8 U.S.C. § 1324a, employers must verify the employment eligibility of all employees hired after November 6, 1986 by checking workers' citizenship status and work authorizations. All new hires must show the same documents, even if born in the United States.

§ 6.20. *How is the verification done?*

The prospective employee and employer must fill out form I-9.

Section One of form I-9 requires the prospective employee to give his name and indicate citizenship or alien status by checking a box. The employee must sign the form under penalty of perjury.

Section Two requires the employer to verify the identity and employment eligibility of the employee, as well as the date of employment. To do this, the employer must physically examine the employee's documents to ensure they "appear to be genuine and related to the individual," and attest to this examination. The employer cannot be "in substantial compliance" of the verification section if he fails to sign or date the certification portion of Section Two. If necessary, the employer must also complete Section Three, verifying employment eligibility.

§ 6.21. *Is a "green card" enough for an employer to verify?*

Yes. Under 8 U.S.C. § 1324a(b)(1)(C), (D), presentation of an alien registration card ("green card") is one way an LPR can establish work eligibility. Etuk v. Slattery, 936 F.2d 1433 (2d Cir. 1991) (INS "Form I-94 Arrival Record" to LPRs whose green cards had been lost or stolen provided adequate temporary proof of LPR status and work authorization).

§ 6.22. *Is the green card the only way to show work authorization?*

No, a combination of other documents can also establish a prospective employee's identity and employment eligibility, though a green card is often a prerequisite for documents such as a driver's license or a Social Security card. Employers must examine a combination of the following: Social Security card plus a driver's license or resident alien card; or a passport or alien registration card and immigration service documents. Documents like birth certificates, voter registration cards, school IDs and report cards, and military registration cards are not acceptable.

Although the employer must examine the alien's documents, the employer does not have to compare documents with examples in the CIS handbook. Collins Foods Int'l, Inc. v. INS, 948 F.2d 549 (9th Cir. 1991).

§ 6.23. *Who in a company must verify authorization?*

Under 8 U.S.C. § 1324a(b), all employees have the burden of verifying an employee's work authorization. Tovar v. United States Postal Serv., 3 F.3d 1271 (9th Cir. 1993).

§ 6.24. *What is the knowledge requirement?*

If an employer "knows" the alien has no authorization to work it is illegal to hire the alien. 8 U.S.C. § 1324a(a)(1)(A). This includes constructive knowledge. *See* New El Rey Sausage Co. v. INS, 925 F.2d 1153 (9th Cir. 1991) (INS's giving employer notice of suspected unauthorized employees was constructive knowledge); Mester Mfg. Co. v. INS, 879 F.2d 561 (9th Cir. 1989) (employer had constructive knowledge of unauthorized worker, even if no employee had actual specific knowledge); Etuk v. Slattery, 803 F. Supp. 644 (E.D.N.Y. 1992); *cf.* Collins Foods Int'l, Inc. v. INS, 948 F.2d 549 (9th Cir. 1991) (employer who telephonically offered alien job without seeing documentation did not have "constructive knowledge" that alien was unauthorized).

§ 6.25. *In what form must the employer's knowledge come?*

Title 8 U.S.C. § 1324a does not require that the employer's knowledge come in any specific way. CIS and ICE action, however, can put an employer on notice that it should check the green card numbers of named employees and fire them if they are unauthorized. Mester Mfg. Co. v. INS, 879 F.2d 561 (9th Cir. 1989).

§ 6.26. *What are the penalties for failing to verify?*

The statute provides for civil administrative proceedings for violations involving most offenses, with penalties from a minimum of $250 to a maximum of $10,000 per employed alien. 8 U.S.C. § 1324a(e)(4). The statute also provides criminal misdemeanor penalties for pattern and practice violations and fines of not more than $3,000 per alien and imprisonment for not more than six months, or both. 8 U.S.C. § 1324a(f)(1).

§ 6.27. *What are the penalties for paperwork violations?*

An employer may have to pay not less than $100 or more than $1,000 for each alien for whom there is a paperwork violation. ICE guidelines provide that the penalty for a first-time violator should be the statutory minimum. It will be increased based on several aggravating factors, for example, if significant time passed between the date of hire and the date form I-9 form was completed.

§ 6.28. *Does an employer have a continuing duty to verify forms?*

Yes. An employer has a continuing duty under 8 U.S.C. § 1324a to prepare and make available for inspection I-9 verification forms. Big Bear Super Market No. 3 v. INS, 913 F.2d 754 (9th Cir. 1990).

C. False Verification Documents

§ 6.29. *What about employers who manufacture hiring documents?*

An employer who "with knowledge or reckless disregard of the fact" falsely makes documents such as an I-9 form or an application for a labor certificate commits a crime. Among other things, it is unlawful for an employer to "knowingly prepare, file, or assist an alien in any application for benefits under [the Act]" with such knowledge or reckless disregard. 8 U.S.C. § 1324c(a)(5). "Falsely makes" includes putting material misrepresentations in a document.

§ 6.30. *Does the statute also penalize material omissions?*

Yes. A person can be charged with making a false document if he fails to state a material fact. 8 U.S.C. § 1324c(f).

§ 6.31. *What other false document charges exist?*

Title 18 U.S.C. § 1546 parallels 8 U.S.C. § 1324c and penalizes the use or possession of immigration documents such as visas, permits, or border crossing cards as evidence of authorized stay or employment. To be guilty, a person must know that the document is forged, counterfeited, or obtained by fraudulent or unlawful means. Thus, because § 1546 penalizes false attestations, both the alien and the employer can be charged for making a false representation on an I-9 form. 18 U.S.C. § 1546.

§ 6.32. *Must an employer disclose his role in preparing documents?*

Yes. Under 8 U.S.C. § 1324c(e), a person can be charged for not disclosing that he prepared a false document. The penalty is a fine and/or imprisonment of not more than five years. In addition, the person is prohibited from preparing or assisting in preparing future applications. A second offender will be fined, imprisoned for not more than 15 years, or both.

V. Harboring Aliens

§ 6.33. *What is "harboring" an alien?*

The alien harboring statute, 8 U.S.C. § 1324, is part of the alien smuggling statute the government uses to punish alien smugglers ("coyotes"). *See* **Chapter 8: Alien Smuggling and Hostage Taking**. The statute punishes persons who harbor or conceal aliens, usually as part of alien smuggling operations. The government used this statute to punish members of the Sanctuary Movement who helped Salvadoran and Guatemalan refugees escape death squads in their home countries. United States v. Aguilar, 883 F.2d 662 (9th Cir. 1989), *cert. denied*, 498 U.S. 1046, 111 S. Ct. 751 (1991), *overturned (superceded by statute as stated in)*, United States v. Gonzalez-Torres, 273 F.3d 1181 (9th Cir. 2001); United States v. Merkt, 764 F.2d 266 (5th Cir.), *reh'g denied en banc*, 772 F.2d 904 (5th Cir. 1985). At that time, however, the statute did not apply to a person merely employing an alien.

§ 6.34. *So, does employment now violate the harboring statute?*

Yes, 8 U.S.C. § 1324 now applies to an employer even though other statutes with lesser penalties also proscribe unlawful employment of aliens. United States v. Myung Ho Kim, 193 F.3d 567 (2d Cir. 1999) (Congress specifically amended harboring statute to apply to employers).

§ 6.35. *When is hiring someone "harboring"?*

An employer is an "alien harborer" if he knowingly hires at least 10 aliens during any 12-month period, "with actual knowledge" that the aliens are undocumented or otherwise unauthorized to work. Activities that can get an employer in trouble include: continuing to knowingly employ illegal aliens; failing to complete forms for unauthorized workers; refusing admittance to ICE agents without warrants; or aiding aliens to leave the workplace without detection.

§ 6.36. *What are the penalties for harboring an alien?*

Under 8 U.S.C. § 1324(a)(1)(B)(ii), an employer can receive a fine and/or imprisonment of not more than five years. Federal Sentencing Guideline § 2L1.1 would control the actual sentence

§ 6.37. *What is the mens rea for harboring an alien?*

To prove harboring, the government must prove that the employer had actual knowledge that the aliens were unauthorized at the time of hire. The *mens rea* for the other crimes mentioned in this chapter only require the government to establish a "pattern or practice" of hiring illegal aliens.

§ 6.38. *What about repeatedly hiring undocumented aliens?*

Title 8 U.S.C. § 1324a provides for misdemeanor criminal penalties for employers who have a "pattern or practice" of hiring aliens. The federal regulations define "pattern or practice" as a regular, repeated, or intentional activity excluding isolated, sporadic, or accidental acts. 8 C.F.R. § 274a.1(k). The law also punishes second and third violations of this offense.

VI. Defenses

A. Constitutional Defenses

§ 6.39. *What are some of the constitutional issues?*

The recordkeeping provisions of IRCA are not void for vagueness and the statute's penalties are not so harsh, oppressive, and fundamentally unfair so as to deny due process. Big Bear Super Market No. 3 v. INS, 913 F.2d 754 (9th Cir. 1990) (statutes create clear obligation to maintain records for INS inspection). Courts have also found the statute legally enacted. Maka v. INS, 904 F.2d 1351 (9th Cir. 1990), *amended on other grounds*, 932 F.2d 1352 (9th Cir. 1991) (notice of fine given to employer's mother, wife, and attorney, rather than employer did not violate employer's due process rights); Mester Mfg. Co. v. INS, 879 F.2d 561 (9th Cir. 1989) (8 U.S.C. § 1324a not void as unconstitutionally passed simply because it was presented to the President for his signature after the Congress had adjourned *sine die*).

§ 6.40. *What about the employer's Fourth Amendment rights?*

Presently, an employer could have a privacy interest in form I-9 under the Fourth Amendment. The form I-9, however, is a government form and generally government records enjoy no expectation of privacy. *See* Shapiro v. United States, 335 U.S. 1, 68 S. Ct. 1375 (1948); Katharine Lorr, *Employer Sanctions and the Fourth Amendment: Lessons from OSHA for the Immigration Bar*, 4 GEO. IMMIGR. L.J. 1 (1990).

§ 6.41. *What about the employee's Fourth Amendment rights?*

The question is open whether illegal aliens have any Fourth Amendment rights. *See* Gavin Skok, *Protecting the Rights of Aliens Unlawfully Present in the United States to Raise Fourth Amendment Defenses in Criminal Prosecutions*, 3:12 BENDER'S IMMIGR. BULL. 604 (June 15, 1998). Moreover, there is no definitive answer as to when an employee has privacy rights on an employer's premises. Lisa DiPoala, *Immigration Reform and Control Act of 1986: A License For Warrantless Searches*, 40 SYRACUSE L. REV. 817 (1989).

§ 6.42. *Would the exclusionary rule apply?*

"As a general rule, the exclusionary rule does not attach to civil or administrative proceedings." *In re* Establishment of Hern Ironworks, 881 F.2d 722, 729 (9th Cir. 1989) (citing INS v. Lopez-Mendoza, 468 U.S. 1032, 104 S. Ct. 3479 (1984)). Some courts, however, applied the exclusionary rule in civil administrative proceedings. *See generally* United States v. Janis, 428 U.S. 433, 96 S. Ct. 3021 (1976). For an "egregious" Fourth Amendment violation, the exclusionary rule may apply even in immigration court proceedings. *See* Gonzalez-Rivera v. INS, 22 F.3d 1411 (9th Cir. 1994).

§ 6.43. *What about freedom of religion defenses?*

Courts have held that 8 U.S.C. § 1324a does not violate the First Amendment's free exercise or establishment clauses. American Friends Service Committee v. Thornburgh, 941 F.2d 808 (9th Cir. 1991), *amended by* 961 F.2d 1405 (9th Cir. 1992); Intercommunity Ctr. for Justice and Peace v. INS, 910 F.2d 42 (2d Cir. 1990). Both cases, however, treat the issues in a cursory fashion.

B. Good Faith Defense

§ 6.44. *What if the employer acted in good faith?*

Title 8 U.S.C. § 1324a(a)(3) provides an affirmative defense for allegations of knowingly hiring unauthorized aliens where the employer made a good faith effort to comply with the verification process. Mester Mfg. Co. v. INS, 879 F.2d 561 (9th Cir. 1989). *Cf.* Maka v. INS, 904 F.2d 1351 (9th Cir. 1990) (good faith defense not available to employer who did not complete verification form for unauthorized alien — fine of $3,000 upheld), *amended on other grounds*, 932 F.2d 1352 (9th Cir. 1991). Also, 8 U.S.C. § 1324a(e)(5) states that "good faith" is a mitigating factor when determining an employer's penalties for violating the verification process. Big Bear Super Market No. 3 v. INS, 913 F.2d 754 (9th Cir. 1990) (ALJ can reduce INS fine for paperwork violations for employer's substantial good faith throughout the investigation). Moreover, under 8 U.S.C. § 1324a(B)(6) good faith is a defense for an employer's paperwork violations if the violations were "technical and procedural failures."

C. Compliance Defenses

§ 6.45. *What about if the employer does not know the requirements?*

The employer's claimed ignorance of the statutory requirements will not insulate against penalty under 8 U.S.C. § 1324a(a)(2) for the continued employment of an unauthorized alien. This is because the statute imposes a continuing duty on the employer to prepare, and make available for inspection, verification forms (I-9 forms) for all of its employees. Big Bear Super Market No. 3 v. INS, 913 F.2d 754 (9th Cir. 1990) (unintentional oversight of employees regarding forms' preparation only served to mitigate penalty).

§ 6.46. *Is it a defense if CIS erred?*

No. Mere reliance on an assumption that CIS had erred is not sufficient to satisfy 8 U.S.C. § 1324a(a)(2)'s prohibition against employing a person knowing them to be unauthorized to work in the United States. New El Rey Sausage Co. v. INS, 925 F.2d 1153 (9th Cir. 1991).

§ 6.47. *What about when the employer is merely driving the alien?*

Generally, the mere transportation of an alien to a place of employment will not establish the element of willful transportation "in furtherance of" the alien's violation of law under 8 U.S.C. § 1324a. United States v. Moreno-Duque, 718 F. Supp. 254 (D. Vt. 1989) (Congress intended to create criminal liability for knowing employment of illegal aliens).

VII. Discrimination Issues

§ 6.48. *Does the law have anti-discrimination provisions?*

IRCA prohibits employers from discriminating on the basis of national origin. Also, an employer must now verify eligibility of employees fairly, without violating 8 U.S.C. § 1324b, which prohibits an employer from committing an unfair employment-related act, including citizenship discrimination and document abuse. Andrew P. Karabetsos, *Immigration-Related Employment Discrimination Under IRCA*, 82 ILL. B.J. 32 (1994); Michael A. Scaperlanda, *Paradox of a Title: Discrimination Within the Anti-Discrimination Provisions of the Immigration Reform and Control Act of 1986*, 1988 WIS. L. REV. 1043; Kiren Dosanjh Zucker, *From* Hoffman Plastic *To The After-Acquired Evidence Doctrine: Protecting Undocumented Workers' Rights Under Federal Anti-Discrimination Statutes*, 26 WHITTIER L. REV. 601 (2004) (*see* Hoffman Plastic Compounds, Inc. v. NLRB, 535 U.S. 137, 122 S. Ct. 1275 (2002)).

§ 6.49. *What is the required mental state for an employer?*

Only those employment practices "made for the purpose or with the intent of discriminating against an individual" are illegal. 8 U.S.C. § 1324b(a)(6). Commentators warn that employers will now fear the penalties for hiring illegal aliens more than the anti-discrimination provisions causing more discrimination. *See* Maria

Isabella-Medina, *The Criminalization of Immigration Law: Employer Sanctions and Marriage Fraud*, 5 GEO. MASON L. REV. 669, 694 (1997).

§ 6.50. *Who has the evidentiary burden?*

The plaintiff. Aliens who are authorized to work and nonaliens who seek a remedy under the anti-discrimination provisions must show that prospective employers have intentionally discriminated against them because of national origin.

§ 6.51. *Do employment laws protect a foreign national overseas?*

No. A foreign national hired overseas does not qualify for employment in the United States, and thus Title VII or ADEA does not allow him to challenge the employer's failure to transfer him to United States. Chaudhry v. Mobil Oil Corp., 186 F.3d 502 (4th Cir. 1999).

§ 6.52. *Does an undocumented alien have a right to unionize?*

Yes. Undocumented alien workers are not excluded from NLRA's definition of "employees" eligible to vote in union elections. NLRB v. Kolkka, 170 F.3d 937 (9th Cir. 1999) (unionizing legal where employer hired workers with questionable documentation and none of the election participants had certain termination date).

§ 6.53. *Can an unauthorized alien claim disability?*

Probably not. Manis Constr. Co. v. Arellano, 411 S.E.2d 233 (Va. Ct. App. 1991) (illegal alien's pursuit of unlawful employment not acceptable means of marketing his residual work capacity for entitlement to compensation for partial disability), *reh'g en banc denied*, 1992 Va. App. LEXIS 70 (Va. Ct. App. Mar. 2, 1992).

§ 6.54. *Can an unauthorized alien claim back pay?*

No. IRCA foreclosed the National Labor Relations Board (NLRB) from awarding back pay to an alien unauthorized to work in the United States. Hoffman Plastic Compounds, Inc. v. NLRB, 535 U.S. 137, 122 S. Ct. 1275 (2002) (alien engaged in union-organizing activities laid off not entitled to remedy of back pay). *See also* Sure-Tan, Inc. v. NLRB, 467 U.S. 883, 104 S. Ct. 2803 (1984) (NLRA applied to undocumented workers, but back pay due under the

NLRA should be tolled for any period during which a worker was not lawfully employed); Del Rey Tortilleria, Inc. v. NLRB, 976 F.2d 1115 (7th Cir. 1992) (NLRB barred from ordering back pay to undocumented aliens wrongfully discharged); *contra* Jennifer Berman, *The Needle and the Damage Done: How* Hoffman Plastics [*sic*] *Promotes Sweatshops and Illegal Immigration and What to Do About It*, 13 KAN. J.L. & PUB. POL'Y 585 (2004); Christine Dana Smith, *Give Us Your Tired, Your Poor:* Hoffman *and the Future of Immigrants' Workplace Rights*, 72 U. CIN. L. REV. 363 (2003); Beth L. Throne, Hoffman Plastic Compounds, Inc. v. NLRB*: Empowering the Unscrupulous Employer and Stigmatizing the Undocumented Worker*, 2003 TEMPLE INT'L & COMP. L.J. 595.

§ 6.55. *Is an alien entitled to worker's compensation?*

There is a split in the courts as to whether an illegal alien is an employee for worker's compensation rights with some courts holding that even an illegal alien is an "employee" under such statutes. Marjorie A. Shields, Annotation, *Application of Workers' Compensation Laws to Illegal Aliens*, 121 A.L.R. 5TH 523 (2004); Jason Schumann, *Working in the Shadows: Illegal Aliens' Entitlement to State Worker' Compensation*, 89 IOWA L. REV. 709 (2004).

CHAPTER 7
MARRIAGE FRAUD

Other Resources:

Eric C. Surette, *Validity, Construction, and Application of 8 U.S.C. § 1325(c), Prohibiting Knowingly Entering Into Marriage To Avoid Immigration Laws*, 159 A.L.R. FED. 497 (2000 & 2004 Supp.).

Vonnell C. Tingle, Note, *Immigration Marriage Fraud Amendments of 1986: Locking In by Locking Out?*, 27 J. FAM. L. 733 (1988-1989).

Related resources:

Suzanne H. Jackson, *To Honor and Obey: Trafficking in "Mail-Order Brides,"* 2002 GEO. WASH. L. REV. 475 (describing the legal system facing trafficked immigrant women).

Introduction

§ 7.1. *What immigration benefit does marriage provide?*

Spouses of United States citizens and legal permanent residents (LPRs) have priority to enter the United States as permanent residents. 8 U.S.C. §§ 1151(a), 1151(b)(2), 1152(a)(4), 1153(a), 1154(a). Marrying a U.S. citizen is the easiest way to get immigration status because such aliens are "immediate relatives" and admitted without reference to the numerical quotas for other immigrants. 8 U.S.C. § 1151(b) (1982). Also, in three years the alien spouse can become a United States citizen, in contrast to the five years for other immigrants. 8 U.S.C. § 1430.

Immigration law has long reflected this family reunification policy. *See, e.g.*, Immigration Act of May 26, 1924, 43 Stat. 153 (1924); War Brides Act of Dec. 28, 1945, Pub. L. No. 271, ch. 591, 59 Stat. 659 (1945); Immigration and Nationality Act of June 27, 1952, Pub. L. No. 414, 616 Stat. 163 (1952); Immigration and Nationality Act Amendments of October 3, 1965, Pub. L. 89-236, 79 Stat. 911 (1965).

The problem, of course, is when parties enter into "sham" marriages to circumvent the normal immigration process. "Immigration marriage fraud is certainly not a victimless crime.' Those who engage in it unfairly cut in front of those aliens lawfully waiting in line to emigrate here. This kind of marriage fraud undermines the sovereign power of the Unites States to control who may be allowed resident status." Azizi v. Thornburgh, 908 F.2d 1130, 1141 (2d Cir. 1990).

I. The Statutes

§ 7.2. *What statutes prevent sham marriages?*

Congress enacted the Immigration Marriage Fraud Amendments of 1986 against sham marriages. Pub. L. No. 99-639, 100 Stat. 3537 (§ 2(d), codified at 8 U.S.C. § 1325(c)). These amendments allow the ICE (former the INS — *see* **Chapter 2, I: Whatever Happened to the INS? — Reorganization After 9/11**) to review marriages and decide whether a marriage is a sham, regardless of the marriage's validity under state law. Like employer crimes (*see* **Chapter 6: Alien Employment Crimes**), the marriage fraud statute at 8 U.S.C. § 1325 creates criminal sanctions for an activity society normally encourages — marriage. *See* Maria Isabel Medina, *The Criminalization of Immigration: Employer Sanctions and Marriage Fraud*, 5 GEO. MASON L. REV. 669 (1997). This criminalization of immigration-related activities appears part of a general trend. *See, e.g.*, **Chapter 5: Aggravated Felonies**.

§ 7.3. *How else did Congress deter sham marriages?*

Congress also established the following:

- A five-year waiting period for an LPR who entered as a spouse of a citizen but is now seeking entry of a second alien spouse, 8 U.S.C. § 1154(a); 8 C.F.R. § 204.1(a)(2);
- The automatic denial of a petition for an alien who attempted to fraudulently get the immigration marriage benefit, 8 U.S.C. § 1154(c); 8 C.F.R. § 204.1(d);
- The requirement that an alien who marries a citizen during deportation proceedings must live outside the United States for two years before applying for permanent resident status, 8 U.S.C. § 1154(h; 8 C.F.R. § 204.1(a)(2)(iii);
- For fiancé(e)s, the requirement that the parties must have previously met in person within two years before filing the petition, 8 U.S.C. § 1184(d); 8 C.F.R. § 214.2(k);
- Denying discretion to approve an alien spouse application for adjustment of status before the two-year period ends, 8 U.S.C. § 1255(d).

§ 7.4. *What is the criminal statute for marriage fraud?*

The marriage fraud criminal statute is 8 U.S.C. § 1324(c):

> Any individual who knowingly enters into a marriage for the purpose of evading any provision of the immigration laws shall be imprisoned for not more than 5 years, or fined not more than $250,000, or both.

The predecessor statute at 8 U.S.C. § 1325(b) was redesignated to (c) without substantive change by Pub. L. 104-208, § 105(a), 110 Stat. 3009-556. *See* United States v. Vickerage, 921 F.2d 143 (8th Cir. 1990), *reh'g en banc denied,* 1991 U.S. App. LEXIS 555 (8th Cir. Jan. 14, 1991); United States v. Mercedes-Mercedes, 851 F.2d 529 (1st Cir. 1988).

§ 7.5. *To whom does the statute apply?*

The statute applies to the U.S. citizen or permanent resident alien (LPR) and also to the nonresident alien involved in the fraudulent marriage.

§ 7.6. *Can the government charge the "spouses" with other crimes?*

Yes, false statements under 18 U.S.C. § 1001. Any false or fraudulent misrepresentation regarding the actual purpose of a marriage may violate 18 U.S.C. § 1001. United States v. Zalman, 870 F.2d 1047, 1054–55 (6th Cir.), *cert. denied*, 492 U.S. 921, 109 S. Ct. 3248 (1989). This includes an exculpatory denial during the course of questioning. Brogan v. United States, 522 U.S. 398, 118 S. Ct. 805 (1998) (rejected "exculpatory no" doctrine).

II. The Petition Process

§ 7.7. *What is the petition?*

Changing the status of the alien spouse begins with filing a petition. The petition is form I-751, Joint Petition to Remove the Conditional Basis of Alien's Permanent Resident Status. The spouses must file this with the director of the regional service center having jurisdiction over the alien's residence. 8 C.F.R. § 216.4(a). The alien must be in the United States when the petition is filed. 8 C.F.R. § 216.4(a)(4).

§ 7.8. *What is the status of alien spouses?*

Congress established a two-year conditional status for the alien spouse after the citizen spouse files the petition for immediate relative classification. 8 U.S.C. § 1186a(a)(1). To change this and become a permanent resident the spouses must petition the Bureau of Citizenship and Immigration Services (CIS) and appear for a personal interview within 90 days before the end of the two years. 8 U.S.C. § 1186a(c). If the parties do not do this the alien's status ends and a deportation proceeding will start. 8 U.S.C. § 1186a(c)(2).

§ 7.9. *Who files the petition?*

The citizen spouse files the petition. 8 U.S.C. § 1154(a) (1982); 8 C.F.R. § 204.1(1) (1986). At the same time, the alien spouse applies to adjust his or her status to LPR.

§ 7.10. *What must the petition contain?*

The petition must contain the following statements:

1. The marriage is valid under state or other jurisdiction law;
2. The marriage has not been "judicially annulled or terminated";
3. The marriage was not only for immigration benefit, 8 C.F.R. § 216.4(a)(5) (evidence may include documents showing joint ownership of property, joint tenancy, commingling of financial resources, children's birth certificates, and affidavits of third parties);
4. The parties paid nothing except attorney's fees for the petition. 8 U.S.C. § 1186a(d)(1)(A); 8 C.F.R. § 216.4(a).

The petition also lists the addresses and names of employers for each spouse since two years before the original filing date. 8 U.S.C. § 1186a(d)(1)(B). At the same time, the parties must file proof of marriage and, if applicable, proof of dissolution of any prior marriages. 8 C.F.R. § 204.2(2) (1986).

§ 7.11. *What will CIS do after getting the petition?*

Within 90 days of the interview, CIS will decide the marriage's validity. 8 U.S.C. § 1186a(c)(3)(A); 8 C.F.R. § 216.4(c). The regional director can decide not to interview the parties if the petition demonstrates "the marriage was not for the purpose of evading the immigration laws." 8 C.F.R. § 216.4(b). Otherwise, the director shall adjudicate the petition within 90 days, 8 C.F.R. § 216.4(c), and decide whether to grant LPR status. 8 U.S.C. § 1186a(c)(3)(B); 8 C.F.R. § 216.4(d). Concurrently, CIS also decides whether to grant permanent residency to the alien spouse. 8 U.S.C. § 1255(a) (1982); 8 C.F.R. § 204.1(2) (1986).

§ 7.12. *What if the citizen spouse does not file the petition?*

CIS can grant a hardship waiver if the citizen spouse did not file a timely petition. 8 U.S.C. § 1186a(c)(4); 8 C.F.R. § 216.5). The alien spouse must prove (1) extreme hardship would result if deported, or (2) "the qualifying marriage was entered into in good faith by the alien spouse, but the qualifying marriage has been terminated ... by the alien spouse for good cause and the alien was not at fault in failing to meet the requirements ...." 8 U.S.C. § 1186a(c)(4); 8 C.F.R. § 216.5(a). The alien can apply for a waiver where the joint petition cannot be filed because the marriage was terminated by annulment, divorce, or death of the petitioning spouse, or refusal of petitioning spouse to file the joint petition. 8 C.F.R. § 216.4(a).

III. "Marriages" and "Sham Marriages" Under Immigration Law

§ 7.13. *How is the marriage valid for the ICE?*

ICE will look to the following to decide a marriage's validity:

1. Whether the marriage is valid under the law where it was entered. *See* United States v. Sacco, 428 F.2d 264 (9th Cir.), *cert. denied*, 400 U.S. 903, 91 S. Ct. 141 (1970), *reh'g denied*, 401 U.S. 926, 91 S. Ct. 864 (1971).
2. Whether the marriage is valid under immigration law, i.e., the parties must intend to establish a life together. United States v. Lutwak, 195 F.2d 748 (7th Cir. 1952), *cert. granted*, 344 U.S. 809, 73 S. Ct. 13, *aff'd*, 344 U.S. 604, 611–12, 73 S. Ct. 481, *reh'g denied*, 345 U.S. 919, 73 S. Ct. 726 (1953); *Adams*, 673 F.2d at 1039–40.

See In re Lew, 11 I&N Dec. 148 (1965); *see generally* Rachel Blitzer, *The Kiss of Death for "Living In Marital Union": Strict Judicial Scrutiny of Department of Homeland Security Marital Fraud Procedures*, 2004 U. CHI. LEGAL F. 495; Nancy K. Richins, Comment, *The Marriage Viability Requirement: Is It Viable?*, 18 SAN DIEGO L. REV. 89 (1980).

§ 7.14. *Does immigration law define "marriage"?*

No. Immigration law does not define marriage and relies instead on state law. *See In re* Burrus, 136 U.S. 586, 593–94, 10 S. Ct. 850 (1890) ("The whole subject of the domestic relations of husband and wife, parent and child, belongs to the laws of the States, and not to the laws of the United States."). The only guidance for Immigration officials is the Supreme Court's statement that "[t]he common understanding of a marriage, which Congress must have had in mind when it made provision for 'alien spouses' in the War Brides Act, is that the two parties have undertaken to establish a life together and assume certain duties and obligations." United States v. Lutwak, 195 F.2d 748 (7th Cir. 1952), *cert. granted*, 344 U.S. 809, 73 S. Ct. 13, *aff'd*, 344 U.S. 604, 611, 73 S. Ct. 481, *reh'g denied*, 345 U.S. 919, 73 S. Ct. 726 (1953).

§ 7.15. *What is a "sham marriage"?*

A "sham marriage" is one entered into only to evade the numerical restrictions limiting immigration. *See* United States v. Lutwak, 195 F.2d 748 (7th Cir. 1952), *cert. granted*, 344 U.S. 809, 73 S. Ct. 13, *aff'd*, 344 U.S. 604, 611, 73 S. Ct. 481 ("Congress did not intend to provide aliens with an easy means of circumventing the quota system by fake marriages in which neither of the parties ever intended to enter into the marital relationship ...."), *reh'g denied*, 345 U.S. 919, 73 S. Ct. 726 (1953). If the marriage is for "the purpose of evading immigration laws" the immigration benefit is not available. 8 U.S.C. §§ 1154(c), 1186b(b)(1)(A). *See* Johl v. United States, 370 F.2d 174 (9th Cir. 1966) (marriage ceremony solely to obtain LPR status with the understanding that he and his purported spouse would not live together as man and wife violated the law); United States v. Rubenstein, 151 F.2d 915 (2d Cir.) (alien marriage to citizen only to obtain visa with no intention of consummation and an agreement to divorce within six months was not valid marriage and no right to visa), *cert. denied*, 326 U.S. 766, 66 S. Ct. 168 (1945). More specifically, a "sham marriage" occurs "if the bride and groom did not intend to establish a life together at the time they were married." United States v. Hose, 163 F.3d 608 (9th Cir. 1998) (quoting Bark v. INS, 511 F.2d 1200, 1201 (9th Cir. 1975)).

§ 7.16. *What are the types of sham marriages?*

Generally sham marriages come in two forms:

1. A citizen marries an alien in a collusive contract usually involving a fee with the understanding that the marriage will be dissolved after the alien becomes an LPR. This type of crime can involve larger marriage fraud conspiracies or "rings."
2. A unilateral or "one-sided"' marriage where the alien deludes a citizen into the marriage and abandons the citizen after getting permanent resident status.

See United States v. Tagalicud, 84 F.3d 1180, 1185 (9th Cir. 1996) ("[M]arriage fraud may be committed by one party to the marriage, or a person who arranged the marriage, yet the other spouse may genuinely intend to marry.").

§ 7.17. *What is a "spouse" under immigration law?*

Although the Immigration Act, 8 U.S.C. §§ 1101–1557, does not define marriage, it does define "spouse" at 8 U.S.C. § 1101(a)(35):

The term "spouse," "wife," or "husband" do not include a spouse, wife, or husband by reason of any marriage ceremony where the contracting parties thereto are not physically present in the presence of each other, unless the marriage shall have been consummated.

§ 7.18. *Can both spouses be charged with marriage fraud?*

Yes. Both spouses can be criminally charged with marriage fraud. The key is whether they both intended the marriage to be "real" or "sham." Pena-Urrutia v. INS, 640 F.2d 242 (9th Cir. 1981); Garcia-Jaramillo v. INS, 604 F.2d 1236 (9th Cir. 1979), *cert. denied*, 449 U.S. 828, 101 S. Ct. 94 (1980). The citizen is often not charged. *See* United States v. Silien, 825 F.2d 320 (11th Cir. 1987) (selective prosecution claim for failure to prosecute citizen spouses rejected). Also, the alien is often not prosecuted because the most common response from ICE to a fraudulent marriage is deportation and subsequent denial of an entry visa.

§ 7.19. *What effect does divorce have on the alien spouse's status?*

Divorce, or "judicial termination" of a marriage, does not automatically result in loss of immigration status if the marriage was in "good faith." If divorce occurs within the two years the petition is pending, the alien spouse loses status and subjects the alien to deportation. 8 U.S.C. §§ 1186a(b)(1), 1251(a)(9)(B); 8 C.F.R. § 216.3. *See generally* Dan Danilov & Mark Nerheim, *Marriage, Divorce, Legal Separation and the Alien*, 18 INT'L LAW. 675 (1984). An exception exists if the alien spouse can prove abuse. ICE interviews both spouses before removing status.

§ 7.20. *What effect does legal separation have?*

A legal separation might qualify as a "judicially terminated" marriage. *See In re* Lew, 11 I&N Dec. 148 (1965) (separation showed "bona fide husband and wife relationship" did not exist). Generally however, legal separation is not a dissolution of the marriage. 24 AM. JUR. 2D Divorce § 440 (1983) ("A limited divorce does not put an end to the marriage relation or destroy the relation of husband and wife, but merely suspends certain of the mutual rights and obligations ...."). *See* Dabaghian v. Civiletti, 607 F.2d 868 (9th Cir. 1979); Bark v. INS, 511 F.2d 1200, 1201–02 (9th Cir. 1975) (evidence of separation insufficient to prove that a marriage was not bona fide when entered as "[a]liens cannot be required to have more conventional or more successful marriages than citizens.... Conduct of the parties after marriage is relevant only to the extent that it bears upon their subjective state of mind at the time they were married."); Chan v. Bell, 464 F. Supp. 125, 128–30 (D.D.C. 1978) (INS's only role is to prove lack of parties' intent to make a life together at the time of the marriage); *In re* McKee, 17 I&N Dec. 332, 333 (BIA 1980) (INS could not deny the benefit solely because the parties were living apart).

Whether a separation is a divorce may depend on the wording of the separation agreement. *See In re* Lenning, 17 I&N Dec. 476 (1980) (legal separation was a "conversion divorce" with a written separation agreement convertible without further judicial action into an absolute divorce).

§ 7.21. *Does wanting status automatically make a sham marriage?*

No. If an alien marries a citizen so that he or she can get a green card it does not automatically make the marriage a sham but is evidence of a possible sham marriage. *See* United States v. Orellana-Blanco, 294 F.3d 1143 (9th Cir. 2002).

IV. Investigating Marriages

§ 7.22. *How does the ICE begin a marriage investigation?*

After reviewing the petition, ICE most often interviews each spouse to find if the marriage is a sham. 8 U.S.C. § 1154(b) (1982); 8 C.F.R. § 103.2(b)(1) (1986). Any marriage within two years of the petition is statutorily presumed fraudulent if the marriage has been judicially annulled or terminated. 8 U.S.C. § 1251(c) (1982). From the petition and interview, the CIS investigator decides whether the petition is true, 8 U.S.C. § 1154(b) (1982), and whether to approve the alien spouse's permanent residency. 8 U.S.C. § 1154(b); 8 C.F.R. § 204.4 (1986). If the petition is approved, the alien spouse is granted LPR status and the coveted green card. 8 U.S.C. § 1154(b) (1982).

§ 7.23. *How does CIS determine marriage validity?*

CIS determines the marriage validity by determining: whether the couple has joint ownership of property, whether they share a residence, whether they commingle financial resources, and whether they have children. The validity of the marriage under state law is immaterial to the charge. Johl v. United States, 370 F.2d 174 (9th Cir. 1966). CIS routinely interrogates spouses about intimate aspects of their marital relationship while separating the spouses and asking for details. *See, e.g.*, *Green Card* (Paramount Pictures 1990); *but see* Stokes v. INS, 393 F. Supp. 24 (S.D.N.Y. 1975).

§ 7.24. *What effect does the spouses living together have?*

This is evidence of a real marriage. *See* United States v. Bartle, 835 F.2d 646 (6th Cir. 1987), *cert. denied*, 485 U.S. 969, 108 S. Ct. 1245 (1988); United States v. Al-Kurna, 808 F.2d 1072 (5th Cir.) (marriage fraud charge possible where alien falsely stated that he and wife were living together), *cert. denied*, 481 U.S. 1023, 107 S. Ct. 1909 (1987); *but see* United States v. Qaisi, 779 F.2d 346 (6th Cir. 1985) (immaterial that parties not living together).

§ 7.25. *What effect does consummating the marriage have?*

The parties must have intended to consummate the marriage. United States v. Lutwak, 195 F.2d 748 (7th Cir. 1952), *cert. granted*, 344 U.S. 809, 73 S. Ct. 13, *aff'd*, 344 U.S. 604, 73 S. Ct. 481, *reh'g denied*, 345 U.S. 919, 73 S. Ct. 726 (1953); United States v. Lozano, 511 F.2d 1 (7th Cir.) (no consummation shows sham marriage), *cert. denied*, 423 U.S. 850, 96 S. Ct. 94 (1975). However, having sex one time does not necessarily show the intent to consummate a marriage. *See* United States v. Kone, 307 F.3d 430 (6th Cir. 2002) (marriage sham even though defendant once had sexual relations with "wife" where woman was recruited and promised $1,000 to marry defendant, she spent less than one hour with him before wedding, she was dropped off at her house and spent her wedding night alone, and they never lived together).

§ 7.26. *How do most cases dealing with marriage fraud arise?*

If CIS refuses the petition because the marriage was fraudulent, the alien spouse may be subject to deportation. 8 U.S.C. § 1251(a)(9) (1982). In fact, most marriage fraud cases arise in the context of challenges to a deportation order. *See, e.g.*, Salas-Velazquez v. INS, 34 F.3d 705 (8th Cir. 1994). If a sham marriage is not discovered at the initial petition and interview, there is usually no subsequent investigation of the marriage to uncover the fraud unless a spouse or party reports it.

V. Constitutional Issues

§ 7.27. *What rights does the marriage fraud statute affect?*

Marriage is a "fundamental right," and to criminalize a fundamental right is at odds with constitutional analysis. *See* United States v. Lutwak, 195 F.2d 748 (7th Cir. 1952), *cert. granted,* 344 U.S. 809, 73 S. Ct. 13, *aff'd,* 344 U.S. 604, 73 S. Ct. 481, *reh'g denied,* 345 U.S. 919, 73 S. Ct. 726 (1953). Questions also exist regarding state recognition of the validity of "sham" marriages for limited purposes. For example, states have accepted marriages solely for the purpose of legitimizing a child. *See, e.g.,* Erickson v. Erickson, 48 N.Y.S.2d 588 (Sup. Ct. 1944); *see generally* John H. Wade, *Limited Purposes Marriages,* 45 MOD. L. REV. 159 (1982).

The Supreme Court has recognized a core area of marital intimacy that is constitutionally protected from government intrusion. *See* Planned Parenthood v. Casey, 505 U.S. 833, 112 S. Ct. 2791 (1992) (striking down state requirement that wives notify husbands before undergoing abortions). However, though a U.S. citizen has a fundamental right to marry, Zablocki v. Redhail, 434 U.S. 374, 98 S. Ct. 673 (1978), "no constitutional right of a citizen spouse is violated by deportation of his or her alien spouse." Burrafato v. United States Dep't of State, 523 F.2d 554, 555 (2d Cir. 1975), *cert. denied,* 424 U.S. 910, 96 S. Ct. 1105 (1976).

§ 7.28. *What constitutional problems exist with the interview process?*

The spouses' interview may raise Fifth Amendment issues because the alien or citizen could face criminal charges. These marriage interviews and investigations have been the subject of much criticism on constitutional grounds as invasions of privacy. *See* David Moyce, Comment, *Petitioning on Behalf of an Alien Spouse: Due Process Under the Immigration Laws,* 74 CAL. L. REV. 1747 (1986); Note, *The Constitutionality of the INS Sham Marriage Investigation Policy,* 99 HARV. L. REV. 1238 (1986).

§ 7.29. *Have courts upheld the statute's constitutionality?*

So far, yes. Courts have determined that the statute as applied and on its face is not unconstitutionally vague. United States v. Solomon, 1996 WL 399814 (S.D.N.Y. 1996) (ruling on former 8 U.S.C. § 1325(b), court noted that statute did not "trap the innocent" or chill innocent behavior and does not threaten arbitrary or discriminatory enforcement). Moreover, the statute does not involve First Amendment freedoms and is not overbroad because it does not reach constitutionally protected conduct.

§ 7.30. *What is the extent of judicial review?*

Limited. The Supreme Court generally defers to the congressional plenary power to supervise aliens. However, lower federal courts restrained the former INS in marriage fraud investigations requiring greater due process and mandating that the INS avoid questions regarding intimate details of the marriage. *See* Stokes v. INS, 393 F. Supp. 24 (S.D.N.Y. 1975).

§ 7.31. *What about § 5 of the statute?*

Section 5 of the Immigration Marriage Fraud Amendments states that an alien who marries a U.S. citizen or permanent resident while involved in deportation or exclusion hearings cannot present evidence that the marriage is bona fide and the alien cannot adjust status. 8 U.S.C. § 1255(e). The section also prevents the alien from receiving the status of immediate relative or second preference until he has completed a two-year foreign residency requirement, i.e., he must reside outside the United States for a two-year period after the marriage. 8 U.S.C. § 1154. Accordingly, because this provision allows no opportunity for the alien to prove the bona fides of the marriage, it establishes a presumption of marriage fraud. *See also In re* Egbunine, Int. Dec. 3034 (BIA 1987); *Recent Developments, Immigration Marriage Fraud Amendments of 1986: The Overlooked Immigration Bill*, 10 HARV. WOMEN'S L.J. 319, 322, 325 (1987). Commentators argue that § 5 violates the alien's procedural due process rights by depriving aliens who marry during deportation hearings of the opportunity to present evidence and to apply for adjustment of status. Jesse I. Santana, *The Proverbial Catch-22: The Unconstitutionality of Section Five of the Immigration Marriage Fraud Amendments of 1986*, 25 CAL. W. L. REV. (1988/1989).

VI. Trial Issues

A. Criminal Intent

§ 7.32. *What criminal intent must the government prove?*

Marriage fraud is not a specific intent crime. The government need not prove that the defendant knew the specific law violated, only that he acted with knowledge that his conduct violated some immigration law. The standard is whether the defendant "knew or had reason to know of the immigration laws." United States v. Chowdhury, 169 F.3d 402 (6th Cir. 1999); United States v. Vickerage, 921 F.2d 143 (8th Cir. 1990), *reh'g en banc denied,* 1991 U.S. App. LEXIS 555 (8th Cir. Jan. 14, 1991).

§ 7.33. *What can the alien show to defend against the charge?*

Evidence would include anything about the intent of the parties to enter a real marriage, including the intent of the defendant to live with the spouse "until death do us part." United States v. Hose, 163 F.3d 608 (9th Cir. 1998) (uncontradicted evidence that wife married husband for love and intended to live with him "until death do us part").

B. Motions

§ 7.34. *What about a motion to sever?*

If the defendant intends to call a codefendant it may not be a sufficient basis to sever trials. To prevail the movant need show (1) the sufficiency of the showing that the codefendant would testify at a severed trial and waive his or her Fifth Amendment privilege; (2) the degree to which the exculpatory testimony would be cumulative; (3) the counter arguments of judicial economy; and (4) the likelihood that the testimony would be subject to substantial, damaging impeachment. United States v. Solomon, 1996 WL 399814 (S.D.N.Y. 1996). The defendant may also need to show that a joint trial would cause him "clear, manifest or undue" prejudice. United States v. Hose, 163 F.3d 608 (9th Cir. 1998).

§ 7.35. *What about suppression of statements?*

As to incriminating statements, at least one court holds that the "inevitable discovery" rule does not apply. Though aliens would eventually have to make statements to immigration officials, nothing guarantees the statements would be the same and therefore this rule does not justify the statement's admission. United States v. De Reyes, 149 F.3d 192 (3d Cir. 1998) (all statement evidence obtained after the illegal stop should have been suppressed).

C. Evidentiary matters

§ 7.36. *What evidence is allowed in marriage fraud cases?*

Allowing into evidence the defendant's first wife's own fraudulent marriage, and, more specifically, the fact that the defendant and his first wife never intended to end the first marriage was admissible under Federal Rule of Evidence 404(a) to show the defendant's scheme to remain in the country. United States v. Shalom, 113 F.3d 1236 (6th Cir.), *cert. denied*, 522 U.S. 890, 118 S. Ct. 226 (1997). This court also allowed evidence of other crimes not related to marriage fraud as well as evidence of the defendant's attempt to bribe a government official. *See also* United States v. Dedhia, 134 F.3d 802 (6th Cir.), *cert. denied*, 523 U.S. 1145, 118 S. Ct. 1844 (1998).

Also, evidence of what was said and done before the marriage as well as the parties' conduct and their statements after they returned to the United States is admissible for the jury to decide whether the marriage was a sham. United States v. Lutwak, 195 F.2d 748 (7th Cir. 1952), *cert. granted*, 344 U.S. 809, 73 S. Ct. 13, *aff'd*, 344 U.S. 604, 73 S. Ct. 481, *reh'g denied*, 345 U.S. 919, 73 S. Ct. 726 (1953).

Evidence of defendant's divorce was relevant, because it confirmed testimony of alien defendant and her husband as to what they had originally intended and agreed upon. United States v. Rubenstein, 151 F.2d 915 (2d Cir.), *cert. denied*, 326 U.S. 766, 66 S. Ct. 168 (1945).

§ 7.37. *What evidence is not allowed in marriage fraud cases?*

Erroneous admission of an INS officer's notes of interview with the defendant was reversible error in prosecution for marriage fraud and false statements. United States v. Orellana-Blanco, 294 F.3d 1143 (9th Cir. 2002) (though jury could have concluded that though wife never intended a genuine marriage, defendant did, even if his motivation for marriage was love for a green card rather than love for wife).

§ 7.38. *What about evidence that the defendant can claim other relief?*

The court will generally not allow this evidence. Why a defendant illegally enters the country and the circumstances surrounding his application for political asylum are irrelevant in a marriage fraud prosecution. United States v. Chowdhury, 169 F.3d 402 (6th Cir. 1999).

D. Jury Instructions

§ 7.39. *How must the court instruct the jury on intent?*

Instructions need only include that the jury need find beyond a reasonable doubt that the defendant knew or had reason to know he violated the law. Additional language on intent that the defendant's sole purpose was not to evade the U.S. immigration laws is not necessary. United States v. Chowdhury, 169 F.3d 402 (6th Cir. 1999); United States v. Al-Kurna, 808 F.2d 1072 (5th Cir.) (alien not entitled to instruction on his subjective intent to enter into valid marriage where alien was only convicted of falsely stating that he was residing with his wife), *cert. denied*, 481 U.S. 1023, 107 S. Ct. 1909 (1987). Rather, the statute merely requires proof that the defendant entered into the marriage to evade immigration laws. United States v. Miah, 182 F.3d 919 (6th Cir. 1999) (defendant's argument that he intended to remain married and that he married his wife for a number of reasons, including obtaining LPR status, did not justify instruction with broader intent); United States v. Vickerage, 921 F.2d 143 (8th Cir. 1990), *reh'g en banc denied*, 1991 U.S. App. LEXIS 555 (8th Cir. Jan. 14, 1991); United States v. Yum, 776 F.2d 490 (4th Cir. 1985) (instruction proper that if jury found no mutuality between parties to marriage to establish a life together there was no marriage).

§ 7.40. *What about when there are multiple defendants?*

When there are multiple defendants, courts must instruct the jury as to the elements for each defendant. United States v. Tagalicud, 84 F.3d 1180, 1184 (9th Cir. 1996).

E. Prosecutorial Misconduct

§ 7.41. *Can a prosecutor refer to the defendant's religion?*

When a prosecutor argues the tenets of the defendant's religion as to divorce, the trial court's overruling of defense objections has been upheld. United States v. Shalom, 113 F.3d 1236 (6th Cir.), *cert. denied*, 522 U.S. 890, 118 S. Ct. 226 (1997). In *Shalom*, however, the defendant first raised the issue of his religious faith and the fact that he had not obtained a divorce under Jewish custom from his first wife.

VII. Sentencing

§ 7.42. *Can a defendant receive concurrent sentences?*

Yes, in conspiracy cases or cases involving more than one marriage. United States v. Amahia, 825 F.2d 177 (8th Cir. 1987) (evidence supported sentencing defendant to concurrent three-year terms of imprisonment on convictions of conspiracy to arrange fraudulent marriage); United States v. Ramos, 605 F. Supp. 277 (S.D.N.Y. 1985) (concurrent five-year sentences on each count of conspiring to make false statements/documents and counts of knowingly using false documents allowed because of defendant's knowing participation in scheme).

§ 7.43. *What Guideline applies to the crime of fraudulent marriage?*

Federal Sentencing Guideline § 2L2.1 applies to trafficking in immigration benefits including "Fraudulent Marriage to Assist Alien to Evade Immigration Laws." This Guideline has a base offense level of 11 with several Specific Offense Characteristics including a possible three-level decrease if the defendant committed the offense "other than for profit" or if the offense involved "the defendant's spouse or child."

If the defendant was not trafficking, the marriage fraud Guideline at § 2L2.2 applies for "Fraudulent Marriage by Alien to Evade Immigration Law" with a base offense level of eight. This Guideline also has several Specific Offense Characteristics.

§ 7.44. *What other sentencing issues and sanctions apply?*

A marriage fraud defendant has the right of allocution. United States v. Chowdhury, 169 F.3d 402 (6th Cir. 1999) (trial court conformed to requirements of Federal Rule of Criminal Procedure 32(c)(3)(C) and defendant declined the court's invitation to speak). Conditions of probation that defendant not again violate immigration laws are valid. United States v. Mercedes-Mercedes, 851 F.2d 529 (1st Cir. 1988). Also, in a military prosecution, marriage fraud can result in a bad service discharge. United States v. Soto, 1990 WL 96347 (A.F.C.M.R. 1990).

CHAPTER 8

ALIEN SMUGGLING AND HOSTAGE TAKING

Other Resources:

William G. Phelps, Annotation, *Validity, Construction, and Application of 274(a)(1)(A)(iii) of Immigration and Nationality Act (8 U.S.C. § 1324(a)(1)(A)(iii)), Making It Unlawful to Harbor or Conceal Illegal Alien*, 137 A.L.R. FED. 255 (1997 & 2004 Supp.).

William G. Phelps, Annotation, *Validity, Construction, and Application of 274(a)(1)(A)(ii) of Immigration and Nationality Act (8 U.S.C. § 1324(a)(1)(A)(ii), Making It Unlawful to Transport Alien Who Has Entered the United States in Violation of Law*, 133 A.L.R. FED. 139 (1996 & 2004 Supp.).

Ivy C. Lee & Mie Lewis, *Human Trafficking From a Legal Advocate's Perspective: History, Legal Framework and Current Anti-Trafficking Efforts*, 10 U.C. DAVIS J. INT'L L. & POL'Y 169 (2003).

Mohamed Y. Mattar, *Trafficking in Persons: An Annotated Legal Bibliography*, 96 LAW LIB. J. 669 (2004).

Note, *The Trafficking Victims Protection Act*, 118 HARV. L. REV. 2180 (2005).

Introduction

This chapter covers the crimes of alien smuggling, transporting, harboring, and concealing in violation of 8 U.S.C. § 1324 as well as human trafficking offenses. Despite the increased penalties and enforcement, the drive of illegal aliens to come to the United States remains as strong as ever. *See generally* Ana Guillén, *Traveling North: A Chronicle of an Undocumented Journey*, 35:2 NACLA REPORT ON THE AMERICAS 36 (Sept./Oct. 2001). Moreover, the tactics of the alien smugglers have changed to adjust to both law enforcement and their market. *See generally* Terry McCarthy, *The Coyotes Gain*, TIME, June 11, 2001, at 56. Because human smuggling has become so lucrative, many drug smugglers have switched to it, bringing their violent tactics with them.

See generally Theresa Barone, *The Trafficking Victims Protection Act of 2000: Defining the Problem and Creating a Solution*, 17 TEMP. INT'L & COMP. L.J. 579 (2003); Elizabeth M. Bruch, *Models Wanted: The Search for an Effective Response to Human Trafficking*, 40 STAN. J. INT'L L. 1 (2004).

I. "Pollos" and "Coyotes"

§ 8.1. *How do they say it at the border?*

The multitude of slang terms surrounding the crime of trafficking in human beings illustrates something of the exploitation occurring:

- **Alambrista** — Someone who crawls under the wire, "el alambre," into the United States. This is the Spanish for the derogatory "scrapeback," referring to an alien who crawled under the wire.
- **Bajadores** — A group that preys on loads of smuggled aliens, i.e., one smuggling gang stealing the "pollos" of another.
- **Bajapollos** — "Border bandits," those who prey on illegal aliens — robbing them and raping women in border towns.
- **Cajuela** — The Mexican term for car trunk, and a "cajuelazo" refers to a trunk load of either illegal aliens or drugs.
- **Clavo** — Hidden compartments in a car or truck or in the spare tire or a stash house. This has lead to the verb "Clavar," "to nail or hammer" being used to say "to stash or to hide."
- **Contrabandistas** — Alien or drug smugglers.
- **Coyote** — Refers to a smuggler. In some areas, smugglers are also known as "polleros," or "chicken herders."
- **Enganchadores** — "Alien Brokers," people in border towns that connect those hoping to cross the border with smugglers.
- **Merca** — Short for "mercancia," "merchandise," and can refer either to illegal aliens or drugs.
- **Mero, mero** — The head of the operation of a criminal operation, "the boss" or "big guy."
- **Mojado/Wetback** — The derogatory "wetback" has a Spanish equivalent, "mojado." This term originally referred to aliens who swam across the Rio Grande or Rio Bravo into the United States. In a play on words, an illegal alien is often called a "mojarra" (a marine bass) in an attempt to cover up illegal activity. (The words "mojado" and "mojarra" sound similar in Spanish).
- **Pateros** — On the Texas/Mexico border at the Rio Grande and Rio Bravo, smugglers are known as "pateros" because the raft used to transport the aliens across the rivers is a "pato" (duck).
- **Pollo** — Spanish for chicken and is a slang term on the Mexican border for people being smuggled into the United States.
- **Quemar** — Literally to "burn" a car or driver, i.e., to drive a car across the border checkpoint before crossing the load of drugs or "pollos." It also can mean to send a decoy person to swim across the river to see if the border patrol will respond.
- **Snakehead** — The head of a Chinese smuggling operation. The "snakehead" is far away in China, with the smuggling

operation, i.e., the length of the snake, far from him extending all the way into the United States.

- **Yola** — Slang related to alien smuggling in Puerto Rico district cases describes a smuggling boat from the Dominican Republic as a "yola," the English translation of "yawl." This would make a yawl passenger a "yolero."

§ 8.2. *How will the translation change a case?*

As the Ninth Circuit ruled, "an incorrect or incomplete translation is the functional equivalent of no translation." Perez-Lastor v. INS, 208 F.3d 773, 778 (9th Cir. 2000).

For example, in Mexican Spanish the passenger in the front seat is called "el ayudante" or helper/assistant regardless of whether he even knows the driver or has anything to do with the smuggling operation. Thus, with the wrong translation a "pollo" will find himself charged as a "coyote."

Mistranslations include the subtleties of regional dialects; for example, on the border someone may say that he met an "amigo," normally translated as "friend." In northern Mexico and in some border areas, however, "amigo" more often denotes an acquaintance or someone just met. People from this region generally use a term like "compadre" to denote a "friend." This has great relevance if a defendant states that a "friend" provided him a truck that was later found to contain drugs.

II. Elements of the Offense

§ 8.3. *What are the elements of 8 U.S.C. § 1324?*

The elements of alien smuggling follow with a brief explanation. *See* **X. *In Limine*, Trial Issues and Defenses,** *infra*, for a more detailed treatment of these elements:

- First, that the defendant brought (or transported or harbored or concealed) an alien into the United States at a place other than a designated port of entry or other than designated by a United States immigration official.

  This element focuses on the place of entry. *See* United States v. Barajas-Montiel, 185 F.3d 947, 951 (9th Cir. 1999), *cert. denied*, 531 U.S. 849, 121 S. Ct. 123 (2000).
- Second, the defendant knew that the person was an alien or showed a reckless disregard for this fact.

Reckless disregards means deliberate indifference to facts that, if considered and weighed in a reasonable manner, indicate the highest probability that the alleged aliens were aliens unlawfully in the United States. United States v. Zlatogur, 271 F.3d 1025 (11th Cir. 2001) (taking reckless disregard definition from United States v. Uresti-Hernandez, 968 F.2d 1042, 1046 (10th Cir. 1992)), *cert. denied*, 535 U.S. 946, 122 S. Ct. 1338 (2002).

- Third, the defendant acted with the intent to violate the United States immigration laws by assisting the person entering the United States at a time or place other than as designated by the United States immigration official, or to otherwise elude United States immigration officials.

  Accordingly, the government must prove specific intent to violate U.S. immigration laws. Both the alien's status and defendant's knowledge of the status as well as the alien's knowing and intentional furtherance of the violation are essential to this element. United States v. Hernandez-Franco, 189 F.3d 1151 (9th Cir. 1999), *cert. denied*, 530 U.S. 1206, 120 S. Ct. 2203 (2000); United States v. Diaz, 936 F.2d 786 (5th Cir. 1991). The defendant does not have the requisite mental state if he or she merely intends to assist the alien in obtaining legal status. Rather, the defendant must have the specific intent to further the alien's unlawful presence. United States v. Rivera, 879 F.2d 1247 (5th Cir.), *cert. denied*, 493 U.S. 998, 110 S. Ct. 554 (1989).

- Fourth, the government must prove that the alien has "entered."

  To be guilty of 8 U.S.C. § 1324, the alien being brought into the United States must have actually "entered" the country. United States v. Bunker, 532 F.2d 1262 (9th Cir. 1976). "Entry" is a term of art under immigration law. *See* **Chapter 2, II.C: "Entry" and "Admission"**. However, the government need not prove that the alien was free from the restraint. United States v. Gonzalez-Torres, 309 F.3d 594 (9th Cir. 2002).

- Fifth, the Government must prove that the smuggled person is an alien.

See generally MANUAL OF MODEL CRIMINAL JURY INSTRUCTIONS FOR THE DISTRICT COURTS OF THE NINTH CIRCUIT, Instruction 9.1.3–9.1.6 (1997 ed.); *see also* EDWARD J. DEVITT, CHARLES B. BLACKMAR, &

KEVIN F. O'MALLEY, 2 FEDERAL JURY PRACTICE AND INSTRUCTIONS: CIVIL AND CRIMINAL §§ 1b.01–51b.09 (1998 Supplement).

§ 8.4. *Is "financial gain" an element?*

It is an element only if the government wishes the three-year mandatory minimum to apply. The statute at § 1324(a)(2)(A)(ii) prescribes a statutory mandatory minimum three-year sentence for unlawfully bringing or attempting to bring an alien to the United States for "financial gain," making this an element of the offense. Financial gain issues are not relevant when the government charges under an aiding/abetting theory because under such a theory financial gain is immaterial. United States v. Nolasco-Rosas, 286 F.3d 762 (5th Cir. 2002).

III. The Statute in General

§ 8.5. *What is "alien smuggling"?*

Alien smuggling is bringing any alien into the United States at a place other than a designated port of entry. This statute also punishes transporting or concealing an alien, 18 U.S.C. § 1324, and thus is divided into three parts:

- Subsection (A) penalizes knowingly "bringing in";
- Subsection (B) penalizes the "transport" of any alien "knowing or in reckless disregard of the fact that an alien has come to, entered or remains in the United States in violation of law"; and
- Subsection (C) penalizes anyone who "conceals, harbors, or shields from detection," an alien in "knowing or reckless disregard of the fact."

§ 8.6. *Does it include lesser offenses?*

It appears not. Aiding and abetting the illegal entry of another in violation of 8 U.S.C. § 1325 and 18 U.S.C. § 2 is not a lesser-included offense of 8 U.S.C. § 1324, alien smuggling. United States v. Pruitt, 719 F.2d 975 (9th Cir.), *cert. denied*, 464 U.S. 1012, 104 S. Ct. 536 (1983). This is because illegal entry occurs only at the time of entry and is not a continuing offense. *Id.* at 978 (citing United States v. Rincon-Jimenez, 595 F.2d 1192 (9th Cir. 1979)). Thus, the elements of illegal entry are not contained within the elements of the smuggling statute. Indeed, the Ninth Circuit has recently ruled that there is not a separate offense of aiding and abetting in alien smuggling cases because activity that would constitute aiding and abetting are just a different means to commit the underlying alien smuggling. United States v. Garcia, 400 F.3d 816 (9th Cir.), *remanded by subsequent appeal,* 133 Fed. Appx. 430 (9th Cir. 2005).

The courts, however, have not considered whether the second part of the illegal entry statute, 8 U.S.C. § 1325(a)(2), which punishes eluding examination and inspection, when combined with the aiding and abetting statute at 18 U.S.C. § 2, might provide a lesser-included offense to 8 U.S.C. § 1324.

§ 8.7. *How does aiding and abetting compare with smuggling?*

A defendant can aid and abet under 18 U.S.C. § 2 even though Congress specifically included aiding and abetting wording in the alien smuggling statute at 8 U.S.C. § 1324(a)(1). *See* United States v. Ramirez-Martinez, 273 F.3d 903 (9th Cir. 2001), *cert. denied,* 537 U.S. 930, 123 S. Ct. 330 (2002). Though aiding and abetting cannot be charged after a completed offense, actions that are part of a concerted effort and the defendant's role of bringing aliens into the United States can be charged as aiding and abetting. However, charging the offense and then charging attempt to complete the offense is duplicitous. United States v. Angwin, 263 F.3d 979 (9th Cir.), *amended by* 2001 U.S. App. LEXIS 24951 (9th Cir. Nov. 21, 2001), *cert. denied,* 535 U.S. 966, 122 S. Ct. 1385 (2002).

§ 8.8. *Can a person alien smuggle/transport with a public conveyance?*

Yes. One who uses a public conveyance to bring an alien into the United States or transports one while here may still be convicted of alien smuggling or transporting. United States v. Washington, 471 F.2d 402, 404–05 (5th Cir.), *cert. denied,* 412 U.S. 930, 93 S. Ct. 2759 (1973).

§ 8.9. *Can a person alien smuggle from outside the United States?*

Yes. A person can violate § 1324 even when the acts to encourage the alien to come into the United States take place outside the United States. United States v. Beliard, 618 F.2d 886, 887 (1st Cir.

1980); United States v. Castillo-Felix, 539 F.2d 9, 13 (9th Cir. 1976); United States v. Williams, 464 F.2d 599 (2d Cir. 1972). The offense occurs when the defendant induces the alien to enter the United States, even if the alien ultimately does not end up entering the country. *Castillo-Felix*, 539 F.2d at 12 n.3; United States v. Narvaez-Granillo, 119 F. Supp. 556, 560 (S.D. Cal. 1954).

§ 8.10. *Is it illegal to just drive a car with an illegal alien?*

No. A person is only guilty of transporting illegal aliens if the transportation was "in furtherance of such violation of law," not merely a ride for some other purpose. United States v. Moreno, 561 F.2d 1321, 1322–23 (9th Cir. 1977) (ranch foreman not guilty of "transporting" aliens when he drove them in the "ordinary and required course of his employment as a foreman.... [T]here must be a direct or substantial relationship between that transportation and its furtherance of the alien's presence in the United States."). *See also* United States v. Chavez-Palacios, 30 F.3d 1290 (10th Cir. 1994); United States v. Esparza, 876 F.2d 1390 (9th Cir. 1989); United States v. One 1984 Ford Van, 873 F.2d 1281 (9th Cir. 1989); United States v. One 1984 Ford Van, 826 F.2d 918 (9th Cir. 1987); United States v. Moreno-Duque, 718 F. Supp. 254 (D.Vt. 1989); *but see* United States v. Barajas-Chavez, 162 F.3d 1285 (10th Cir. 1999) (en banc) (the "in furtherance of" element is not limited solely to those who support the presence of illegal aliens through smuggling operations), *cert. denied*, 528 U.S. 826, 120 S. Ct. 76 (1999).

It may be a violation, however, to transport illegal aliens to employment opportunities. United States v. Gonzalez-Hernandez, 534 F.2d 1353, 1354 (9th Cir. 1976).

IV. RICO and Wiretaps

§ 8.11. *Does RICO apply to alien smuggling?*

Yes. The Anti-Terrorism and Effective Death Penalty Act of 1996 (Terrorism Act) amended 18 U.S.C. § 1961(1) to add certain immigration offenses to the list of crimes to which the Racketeer Influenced and Corrupt Organizations Act (RICO) applies. The Terrorism Act provision gives federal prosecutors additional tools to prosecute alien smuggling rings. Offenses include crimes relating to alien smuggling; fraud in connection with identification documents; false statements in the application for and use of passports;

forgery or false use of passports; fraud or misuse of visas, permits, or other documents; peonage and slavery; and retaliation against a witness or informant. IIRAIRA further changed the RICO statute to eliminate the requirement for financial gain from these immigration offenses.

§ 8.12. *What about wiretapping in an alien smuggling case?*

Section 434 of the Terrorism Act changed the federal wiretap laws to allow federal prosecutors to wiretap during the investigation of most alien smuggling crimes. 18 U.S.C. § 2516(1).

V. Hostage Taking and Alien Smuggling

§ 8.13. *Can the government charge both alien smuggling and hostage taking?*

Yes. Alien smuggling can constitute hostage taking. *See* United States v. Lopez-Flores, 63 F.3d 1468 (9th Cir. 1995), *cert. denied*, 516 U.S. 1082, 116 S. Ct. 794 (1996).

§ 8.14. *What are the elements of hostage taking?*

The elements of hostage taking are as follows:

1. A seizure or detention,
2. A threat to kill, injure, or continue to detain, and
3. With the purpose of compelling a third person or governmental entity to act in some way or refrain from acting.

18 U.S.C. § 1203(a).

§ 8.15. *What is the distinction between hostage taking and alien smuggling?*

With alien smuggling, the aliens have contracted to be with the smugglers. With hostage taking, conversely, the aliens are compelled to stay with the smugglers by force or violence. Thus, from the time the defendants hold the aliens in a manner that is not contemplated in the alien smuggling agreement, hostage taking has occurred. United States v. Sierra-Velasquez, 310 F.3d 1217 (9th Cir. 2002), *cert. denied*, 538 U.S. 952, 123 S. Ct. 1640, 540 U.S. 819, 124 S. Ct. 102 (2003), *motion granted by* 104 Fed. Appx. 667, 2004 U.S. App. LEXIS 16798 (9th Cir. 2004).

§ 8.16. *Does the hostage taking statute have a specific intent requirement?*

Yes. Although not expressly spelling out an intent requirement, the statute does require detention to be undertaken to compel a third person to do something. Thus, the statute contemplates a specific intent. United States v. Xue Fei Lin, 139 F.3d 1303 (9th Cir.), *supplemented*, 141 F.3d 1180 (9th Cir.), *cert. denied*, 525 U.S. 904, 119 S. Ct. 238 (1998).

§ 8.17. *What about the equal protection clause?*

Even though the Hostage Taking Act at 18 U.S.C. § 1203 criminalizes conduct that would not be illegal if a U.S. citizen committed it, the statute does not violate the equal protection clause. United States v. Wang Kun Lue, 134 F.3d 79 (2d Cir. 1997); United States v. Chen De Yian, 905 F. Supp. 160 (S.D.N.Y. 1995), *aff'd*, 134 F.3d 79 (2d Cir. 1997) (alienage classification in Hostage Taking Act reasonably furthers legitimate, if not compelling, foreign policy interest).

§ 8.18. *Does payment matter?*

No. The Act does not differentiate between various motivations that might prompt a person to take hostages to compel action. United States v. Lin, 101 F.3d 760 (D.C. Cir. 1996), *remanded by* 1998 U.S. App. LEXIS 1975 (D.C. Cir. Jan. 13, 1998).

§ 8.19. *How is hostage taking punished?*

The Federal Sentencing Guidelines allow for separate punishment for each victim. *See* United States v. Melchor-Zaragoza, 351 F.3d 925 (9th Cir. 2003) (making 23 separate groups for sentencing to account for 23 victims was proper).

VI. Smuggling of Aggravated Felons: 8 U.S.C. § 1327

§ 8.20. *What if the defendant smuggles an aggravated felon?*

Under 8 U.S.C. § 1327, a person who knowingly aids or assists an alien who is inadmissible because the alien has an aggravated felony can face a statutory maximum of 10 years.

§ 8.21. *What is the scienter requirement?*

This is a bit unclear. Under the statutes, the defendant's knowledge of the alien's felony conviction is not an element of the offense. The government need only prove that the accused smuggler knew that the alien was inadmissible/excludable. United States v. Flores-Garcia, 198 F.3d 1119, 1122–23 (9th Cir. 2000). The statute does not require proof that the defendant knew of the alien's prior conviction as the basis for exclusion. United States v. Figueroa, 165 F.3d 111, 119 (2d Cir. 1998).

VII. Material Witnesses

For a good resource on material witnesses and deposition practice, *see generally* DENNIS R. SUPLEE & DIANA S. DONALDSON, THE DEPOSITION HANDBOOK (4th ed. 2003).

A. Deposing Material Witnesses

§ 8.22. *Which is harder to defend, an alien smuggling or a drug smuggling case?*

Alien smuggling: the evidence talks.

§ 8.23. *What is a "material witness"?*

Federal Rule of Criminal Procedure 15(a) provides for the deposition of a "material witness" if there is a chance that the witness will not be present at trial. The government generally wants to deport aliens well before the alien smuggling trial. For this reason, the alien smuggling statute, 8 U.S.C. § 1324(d), specifically allows for admissibility at trial of depositions of the alien witnesses, as long as the defendant had the chance to cross-examine the aliens and the testimony complies with the Federal Rules of Evidence. This includes administering an oath before witness testimony. FED. R. EVID. 603. These provisions apply when the alien witness is detained. 18 U.S.C. § 3144.

§ 8.24. *Must the government detain an alien material witness to assure testimony?*

Not necessarily. The government or defense may seek the alien's continued presence in the United States for criminal process by a procedure called "parole." A witness paroled in the United States for testimony has not legally "entered." They can, however, obtain work authorization. *See* **Chapter 12: Getting Witnesses and Evidence from Abroad**.

§ 8.25. *Does the witness gratuity statute apply to material witnesses?*

Yes, as it would to any witness. *See* 18 U.S.C. § 201(c)(2). However, the prosecutor's writing letters recommending asylum for testifying alien witnesses and agreeing to release on bond does not run afoul of the gratuity statute. Courts recognize that the government can give incentives for truthful testimony. United States v. Feng, 277 F.3d 1151 (9th Cir.), *supplemented*, 25 Fed. Appx. 635 (9th Cir.), *cert. denied*, 537 U.S. 897, 123 S. Ct. 195 (2002).

§ 8.26. *What are due process concerns?*

Title 18 U.S.C. § 3161(c)(2) gives the defendant the right to have a trial "not commence less than 30 days from the date from which the defendant first appears." Often, the prosecutor uses Federal Rule of Criminal Procedure 15(a) to take the video deposition of the alien witness within a week of charging the case. The taking of such a video deposition violates the defendant's right to 30 days to prepare for the trial, because all or any part of the video deposition may be admissible at trial under federal law. *See* 18 U.S.C. § 3161(c)(2); 8 U.S.C. § 1324(d); United States v. Santos-Pinon, 146 F.3d 734 (9th Cir. 1998) (8 U.S.C. § 1324(d)) (allowing videotaped testimony in alien smuggling cases is constitutional).

Moreover, taking a deposition could violate the defendant's rights of due process and confrontation. In *Crawford v. Washington*, 541 U.S. 36, 124 S. Ct. 1354 (2004), the Supreme Court held that out-of-court statements by witnesses that are testimonial are barred, under the Confrontation Clause, unless witnesses are unavailable and defendants had prior opportunity to cross-examine the witnesses, regardless of whether such statements are "reliable." Under Rule 15(a), defense counsel will not have the chance to cross-examine the alien with information that he may obtain after the depositions, which could violate *Crawford*.

B. Video Depositions

§ 8.27. *What allows for taking material witness depositions?*

Federal Rule of Criminal Procedure 15 allows for the taking of a witness deposition under the supervision of the magistrate judge if "exceptional circumstances of the case is in the interests of justice that the testimony of a prospective witness of a party be taken and preserved for trial." Title 18 U.S.C. § 3503(b) allows the defendant to move for an extension of time for taking the deposition.

§ 8.28. *Why do prosecutors want depositions of material witnesses?*

Prosecutors often depose aliens who were smuggled to provide a nonhearsay basis for establishing that the defendant brought in, transported, harbored, or concealed aliens. Also, the aliens' statements establish the fact that they are aliens, an element of the offense. Depositions, however, may not always be necessary because the statements of witnesses as to alienage and citizenship are admissible hearsay. United States v. Olafson, 213 F.3d 435 (9th Cir. 2000).

§ 8.29. *Are videotape depositions admissible at trial?*

Yes. Title 8 U.S.C. § 1324(d) allows for the admission of videotaped depositions for a witness "who has been deported or otherwise expelled from the United States, or is otherwise unable to testify ... if the witness was available for cross examination and the deposition otherwise complies with the Federal Rules of Evidence." This statute works in conjunction with Federal Rule of Criminal Procedure 15(e) governing the admission of depositions in criminal proceedings. United States v. Aguilar-Tamayo, 300 F.3d 562 (5th Cir. 2002); United States v. Santos-Pinon, 146 F.3d 734 (9th Cir. 1998) (allowing videotaped testimony constitutional).

§ 8.30. *What procedures are used for the depositions?*

District standing orders or local rules usually exist defining the practice, with wide variations among districts and even within the same district. In some districts, a magistrate judge presides over the depositions. At others, the depositions are conducted with the prosecutor, defense attorney, and a court reporter. They may be videotaped. Both prosecutors and defense attorneys need to object to questions to preserve the objection for later ruling if the case goes to trial. This is true regardless of whether a judge is present at the deposition.

These differing practices may open an equal protection claim. *See* United States v. Sierra-Hernandez, 192 F.3d 501 (5th Cir. 1999) (court declines review of equal protection claim with no evidence of different procedures in two divisions), *cert. denied*, 528 U.S. 1178, 120 S. Ct. 1213 (2000).

§ 8.31. *What procedural objections exist?*

Objections can include the following if appropriate:

- No transcript was made as Rule 15(a)(2) requires;
- The government failed to provide the deponents' statements for use at the deposition as Rule 15(e)(3) requires;
- The deposition officer is not qualified under Rule 28(c);
- The deposition officer failed to certify the deposition as Federal Rule of Civil Procedure 30(f) requires;
- The deposition officer did not actually attend the deposition or leaves the deposition after swearing in the witness;
- The deposition is invalid for lack of a certified interpreter;
- The witness did not testify under oath as Federal Rule of Evidence 601 requires.

§ 8.32. *What does "unavailable" mean in this context?*

Rule 15(e) provides that deposition testimony "'so far as [it is] otherwise admissible under the rules of evidence, may be used if the witness is unavailable, as unavailability is defined in rule 804(a) of the Federal Rules of Evidence.' Federal Rule of Evidence 804(a)(5) defines unavailability as being 'absent from the hearing and the proponent of [his] statement has been unable to procure [his] presence by process or other reasonable means.'" Usually, the Confrontation Clause bars statements where the defendant cannot cross-examine the witness at trial. United States v. Aguilar-Tamayo, 300 F.3d 562, 565 (5th Cir. 2002) (citing Ohio v. Roberts, 448 U.S. 56, 100 S. Ct. 2531 (1980)). To establish "unavailability" the government must show that it took reasonable steps to procure the testimony. *Id.* While the government need not engage in "futile" efforts, it must take some steps to secure the witness's live testimony. *Id. See* United States v. Allie, 978 F.2d 1401 (5th Cir. 1992) (government used reasonable means to procure witness by (1) providing witness fees and travel costs, (2) giving the witness a subpoena to facilitate entry, (3) calling witness in Mexico and receiving assurances that he would return, and (4) telling border inspectors of the witness's expected arrival), *cert. denied,* 507 U.S. 1011, 113 S. Ct. 1662 3668 (1993); *cf. Aguilar-Tamayo,* 300 F.3d at 566 (government failed to use "reasonable means" to secure witness's presence).

§ 8.33. *How does the alien's prior statement affect the deposition?*

Because a deposition can be likened to trial testimony, either side can impeach the alien with a prior statement. Often the material witness will disavow initial statements. *See, e.g.,* United States v. Perez, 217 F.3d 323 (5th Cir.) (INS agent with 12 years experience in anti-smuggling testified that in the initial interview "approximately ninety percent of undocumented aliens apprehended do not give a truthful and accurate account of events that led up their arrest"), *cert. denied,* 531 U.S. 973, 121 S. Ct. 416 (2000). The witness's different language or the language skills of the interrogator may be a factor.

C. Exculpatory Witnesses

§ 8.34. *Does the government detain all aliens to preserve testimony?*

No. When there are several illegal aliens, the prosecutor (actually, the border patrol or ICE) often detains only one or two of the witnesses and deports the others. By doing this, the government may cause the loss of exculpatory evidence. *See* United States v. Carreno, 363 F.3d 883 (9th Cir. 2004) (government's deportation of witnesses though "unbecoming" did not violate Fifth or Sixth Amendment), *cert. granted, vacated and remanded by* 125 S. Ct. 1000 (2005).

§ 8.35. *Does it matter how many other aliens the government deports?*

Usually it does not. United States v. Perez, 217 F.3d 323 (5th Cir.) (removal of 19 out of 24 aliens before defense interviewed them allowed when charge was harboring even though removed witnesses told INS no one at house was a coyote), *cert. denied,* 531 U.S. 973, 121 S. Ct. 416 (2000).

§ 8.36. *What defense motions are possible regarding material witnesses?*

The deportation of alien witnesses gives rise to a potential motion from the defense to dismiss the indictment under the Compulsory Process Clause of the Sixth Amendment and the Due Process Clause of the Fifth Amendment. The Supreme Court dealt with this issue in *United States v. Valenzuela-Bernal,* 458 U.S. 858, 102 S. Ct. 3440 (1982), holding that the deportation or voluntary return of aliens whose testimony would be both "material and favorable" to the defendant violates the above-mentioned clauses. However, "[although] the defendant cannot be expected to render a detailed description of [the] lost testimony," the defense must make "a plausible showing that the testimony of the deported witnesses would have been material and favorable to [the] defense, in ways not merely cumulative of testimony of available witnesses." *Id.* at 867.

§ 8.37. *Does it matter if the witnesses were deported or voluntarily returned?*

No. Whether potential defense witnesses were deported or voluntarily returned is irrelevant under *United States v. Valenzuela-Bernal,* 458 U.S. 858, 102 S. Ct. 3440 (1982). United States v. Morales-Quinones, 812 F.2d 604, 608–09 (10th Cir. 1987) (INS facilitation of voluntary departure equivalent to deportation).

§ 8.38. *How are Valenzuela-Bernal claims evaluated?*

Courts "strictly evaluate" the requirements of *United States v. Valenzuela-Bernal,* 458 U.S. 858, 102 S. Ct. 3440 (1982). United States v. Sierra-Hernandez, 192 F.3d 501, 502 (5th Cir. 1999) (listing cases), *cert. denied,* 528 U.S. 1178, 120 S. Ct. 1213 (2000). *See also* United States v. Nesbitt, 852 F.2d 1502, 1519 (7th Cir. 1988) (noting "the strict standard of materiality set forth in *Valenzuela-Bernal*"), *cert. denied,* 488 U.S. 1015, 109 S. Ct. 808 (1989); United States v. Ginsberg, 758 F.2d 823 (2d Cir. 1985) (speculating on testimony most favorable to defendant does not satisfy *Valenzuela-Bernal*). Courts frequently reject *Valenzuela-Bernal*-based claims of due process violations). Indeed, the Ninth Circuit requires the defendant to show prosecutorial bad faith. United States v. Dring, 930 F.2d 687, 693 (9th Cir. 1991), *cert. denied,* 506 U.S. 836, 113 S. Ct. 110 (1992).

§ 8.39. *How can the defense support this motion?*

The defense should try at least two things:

1. Review reports of *all* deportable aliens, even those not brought to court. These reports usually are found in a document called an I-213.
2. If at all possible, interview any of the aliens who were deported or otherwise sent back to Mexico to learn of favorable information.

At the deposition, counsel should cross-examine the material witnesses about the border patrol's investigation and the failure to explore mitigating evidence. Success for the defense will often hinge on the defendant's ability to show the testimony would have been material to a valid defense. *See, e.g.*, United States v. Romero-Cruz, 201 F.3d 374 (5th Cir.) (testimony not material that would have only impeached second alien's testimony on collateral matter), *cert. denied*, 529 U.S. 1135, 120 S. Ct. 2017 (2000); United States v. Sierra-Hernandez, 192 F.3d 501, 503 (5th Cir. 1999) (testimony that defendant was not hired to cross aliens immaterial to whether defendant transported aliens), *cert. denied*, 528 U.S. 1178, 120 S. Ct. 1213 (2000).

D. Representing Material Witnesses

§ 8.40. *Do material witnesses have the right to a lawyer?*

Yes. Generally, the government agrees not to prosecute material witnesses for illegally entering the country. 8 U.S.C. § 1325. Because of Fifth Amendment implications, however, alien material witnesses are afforded counsel under the Criminal Justice Act. 8 U.S.C. § 3006A.

For good articles related to representing material witnesses in the context of a terrorism case but also applicable to an alien smuggling case, *see* Kent V. Anderson, Jonathon E. Hawley, & Richard A. Parson, *Challenging the Detention of a Client Who Has Been Declared a Material Witness or the Incommunicado Detention of Any Client*, THE CHAMPION, Mar. 2003 at 14 *and* Richard A. Parson, Kent V. Anderson & Jonathon E. Hawley, *Part II: Ways To Challenge the Detention of your Client Who Has Been Declared a Material Witness or the Incommunicado Detention of Any Client*, THE CHAMPION, Apr. 2003 at 34.

§ 8.41. *What about conflicts of interest among material witnesses?*

One lawyer often is assigned to represent all material witnesses in an alien smuggling case despite the potential conflicts among the witnesses. The most obvious scenario is where a witness is really a smuggler and the others are afraid to identify him.

§ 8.42. *Do material witnesses have a right to release?*

Yes. The court can release or detain the material witness under the Bail Reform Act. 18 U.S.C. § 3144. The Act directs the judge to release material witnesses unless they pose a "serious risk" of flight. 18 U.S.C. § 3142(f)(2)(A). In addition, in order to detain a witness the court must specifically find that no conditions can reasonably assure the person's appearance. 18 U.S.C. § 3142(f). The government must prove there are no reasonable conditions of release. *See* United States v. Motamedi, 767 F.2d 1403 (9th Cir. 1985).

§ 8.43. *Is there a challenge to the material witness detention statute?*

Yes. As part of the Comprehensive Crime Control Act of 1984, Congress enacted 18 U.S.C. § 3144, which, along with Federal Rule of Criminal Procedure 46(b), purports to give government agents authority to arrest and detain material witnesses without prior notice. It appears from the legislative history that Congress relied exclusively on a Ninth Circuit case, *Bacon v. United States*, 449 F.2d 933 (9th Cir. 1971), to support its passage. The Supreme Court has never spoken on this issue, and indeed the reasoning of the *Bacon* case and, thus, the statute itself could be amenable to challenge. The Constitution allows detention only when there is probable cause to believe a person has committed a crime, not when the person is merely a witness to a crime. Cutting against this argument, however, is that the alien witness himself has committed the crime of illegal entry under 8 U.S.C. § 1325.

§ 8.44. *Can material witnesses move for an immediate deposition?*

Yes. If the court orders the detention of material witnesses, it should order the deposition as soon as possible. The Bail Reform Act mandates that detention is not authorized where video depositions can be taken. 18 U.S.C. § 3144. Rule 15(a) of the Federal Rule of Criminal Procedure expressly allows for taking video depositions of material witnesses upon the witness's written motion. *See* Torres-Ruiz v. United States Dist. Ct., So. Dist. of Cal., 120 F.3d 933 (9th Cir. 1997) (relying on Aguilar-Ayala v. Ruiz, 973 F.2d 411 (5th Cir. 1992)). This, of course, may run against the right of the accused to ask for 30 days to prepare for trial testimony under the Speedy Trial Act, 18 U.S.C. § 3161, and the Fifth and Sixth Amendments.

The Mexican consulate and consulates of other countries often have agreements with the U.S. Marshal or the U.S. Attorney to process material witness depositions within 72 hours.

§ 8.45. *Will the material witness be released after the deposition?*

Often, neither the government nor the defense has an interest in the continued presence of material witnesses after depositions. Thus, they are released to ICE for eventual immigration proceedings. At the request of one of the parties, the aliens can be kept in custody in the United States or "paroled into" the country until their testimony is needed at trial. Being "paroled in" means that the alien is released from custody and given the status of a "parolee." *See* **Chapter 12: Getting Witnesses and Evidence from Abroad.**

The prosecutor, not the court, retains power to parole material witnesses back into the United States for trial testimony, even if the government deported them earlier. *See* 8 U.S.C. § 1182(d)(5)(A). Specifically, federal law vests the Attorney General with the power to parole illegal aliens "for reasons deemed strictly in the public interest." *Id.* (*See* **Chapter 7: Marriage Fraud.**) Thus, it should be considered unjust to allow material witnesses who are not judged a flight risk to be held in custody so that they can testify on the government's behalf. The government itself has the power to rectify the situation temporarily by paroling the witnesses into the country for their testimony. Most material witnesses, however, just want to be sent back to their country, without taking the time to fight the issue.

§ 8.46. *Would a material witness have the chance for an immigration benefit?*

Yes, victims of trafficking may seek a T-visa if they can show they will suffer "extreme hardship involving unusual and severe harm" if deported. *See generally* Dina Francesca Haynes, *Used, Abused, Arrested and Deported: Extending Immigration Benefits to Protect the Victims of Trafficking and to Secure the Prosecution of Traffickers*, 26 HUM. RTS. Q. 221 (2004). Also, if the witnesses was otherwise a victim of crime he may have the right to ask for a U-visa. *See generally* Lory Diana Rosenberg, *Consideration of (Not So) New "T" and "U" Visas and How They Work*, 8:20 BENDER'S IMMIGR. BULL. 1628 (Oct. 15, 2003); Greta D. Stoltz, *The U Visa: Another Remedy for Battered Immigrant Women*, 7 SCHOLAR 127 (2004).

§ 8.47. *How can lawyers help the witnesses after release?*

When alien witnesses go to ICE custody, counsel can do several things to help them. Counsel can call the consulate of the relevant country to alert it to the alien's situation and provide a fax of the federal magistrate judge's order of release. The ICE acts quickly if a consulate calls and has the order, which ensures that the aliens do not have to wait a week or more while paperwork is processed through normal channels. The consulate might also provide money for material witnesses to return home after being abandoned by ICE at the other side of the border.

VIII. Motions to Suppress Statements

§ 8.48. *What about suppression of statements?*

ICE has the power to ask anyone his immigration status without providing *Miranda* warnings. However, if ICE brings a criminal charge against the defendant, the statements are inadmissible unless they were proceeded by *Miranda* warnings and a valid waiver. United States v. Mata-Abundiz, 717 F.2d 1277, 1279 (9th Cir. 1983) ("[c]ivil as well as criminal interrogation of in-custody defendants by INS investigators should generally be accompanied by the *Miranda* warnings"). *See also* United States v. Gonzalez-Sandoval, 894 F.2d 1043 (9th Cir. 1990); United States v. Perez-Castro, 606 F.2d 251 (9th Cir. 1979).

§ 8.49. *What about when the government does not advise the alien of his right to contact his consulate?*

This is ground for suppression under the Vienna Convention on Consular Relations. Most foreign consulates certify that they will inform arrested nationals of their constitutional and other rights, in the alien's native language. They are usually willing to provide an affidavit to this effect for a suppression hearing. Major law enforcement agencies generally have notice of the right of a foreign national to contact the consulate. *See generally* United States v. Lombera-Camorlinga, 206 F.3d 882 (9th Cir.) (en banc), *cert. denied*, 531 U.S. 991, 121 S. Ct. 481 (2000).

IX. Motions Regarding Roving Border Stops

§ 8.50. *What are "roving border stops"?*

These are stops the Border Patrol conducts, often well away from the border, usually at points, roads, or intersections that alien smugglers commonly frequent. *See* **Chapter 3: Border Stops**.

§ 8.51. *How are roving border stops legally justified?*

The border patrol agent must be aware of specific articulable facts that reasonably warrant "suspicion to believe that criminal activity may be afoot." United States v. Arvizu, 534 U.S. 266, 273, 122 S. Ct. 744, 750 (2002) (internal quotations omitted). This language derives from *Terry v. Ohio*, 392 U.S. 1, 88 S. Ct. 1868 (1968). Reasonable suspicion must support any roving stop, even one those that take place on roads notorious for alien smuggling near the border. United States v. Granado, 302 F.3d 421 (5th Cir.), *reh'g denied*, 2002 U.S. App. LEXIS 20533 (5th Cir. Sept. 12, 2002); United States v. Lopez-Valdez, 178 F.3d 282 (5th Cir. 1999).

§ 8.52. *What are factors relevant to this determination?*

In *United States v. Brignoni-Ponce*, 422 U.S. 873, 95 S. Ct. 2574 (1975), the Supreme Court set out the following factors:

1. Known characteristics of a particular area;
2. Previous experience of the arresting agents with criminal activity;
3. Proximity of the area to the border;
4. Usual traffic patterns of that road;
5. Information about recent illegal trafficking in aliens or narcotics in the area;
6. Behavior of the vehicle's driver;
7. Appearance of the vehicle; and
8. Number, appearance, and behavior of the passengers.

Under *Arvizu*, courts must look at the "totality of circumstances" of each case to see whether the detaining officer has a "particularized and objective basis" for suspecting legal wrongdoing. United States v. Arvizu, 534 U.S. 266, 122 S. Ct. 744 (2002) (rejecting a "divide and conquer" style of analysis).

§ 8.53. *What does the location of the border have to do with it?*

Proximity to the border can be a crucial fact. Courts scrutinize with greater care roving border patrol stops occurring at more than 50 miles from the border. United States v. Rodriguez-Rivas, 151 F.3d 377 (5th Cir. 1998); United States v. Ortega-Serrano, 788 F.2d 299 (5th Cir. 1986) (stop improper based on uneven paint job, fact that occupants were Hispanic and appeared "dirty" and "nervous," when stop was 300-400 miles north of the border); United States v. Lamas, 608 F.2d 547 (5th Cir. 1979) (agent not justified in stopping vehicle 190 miles from border even though the car was heavily loaded, had out-of-state plates yet did not appear to be a "typical tourist's car," and the passengers appeared to avoid eye contact with the agents).

X. *In Limine*, Trial Issues, and Defenses

§ 8.54. *What are the potential hearsay issues?*

Arguably, hearsay statements of material witnesses who have been deported or failed to appear for trial should be excluded. These statements may be offered under Federal Rule of Evidence 804(a)(5) on the ground that the witnesses are "unavailable." Countering this, however, is the fact that the witnesses are not "unavailable" because the absence of the witnesses is actually attributed to the proponent of the statement, the U.S. government. *See* United States v. Pena-Gutierrez, 222 F.3d 1080 (9th Cir.) (error, though harmless, for trial court to admit hearsay of "unavailable" material witness when government had witness's address and never sought to contact him to testify), *cert. denied*, 531 U.S. 1057, 121 S. Ct. 670 (2000); United States v. Pluta, 176 F.3d 43 (2d Cir.) (any error from hearsay as to alien's statements of citizenship was harmless), *cert. denied*, 528 U.S. 906, 120 S. Ct. 248 (1999).

§ 8.55. *What does the alienage of the person smuggled have to do with it?*

One of the elements of the offense is that the person smuggled was "an alien." An alien is "any person not a citizen or national of the United States." 8 U.S.C. § 1101(a)(3). Thus, the government must have evidence, such as the alien's statement or a birth certificate, that the person smuggled was an alien. United States v. Alvarado-Machado, 867 F.2d 209, 212 (5th Cir. 1989). Typically, proof of alienage is established through the alien's videotaped depositions under 8 U.S.C. § 1324(d). To prove alienage, the government may not merely introduce the final judgment of the alien's conviction for an immigration status crime. United States v. Diaz, 936 F.2d 786, 788 (5th Cir. 1991).

§ 8.56. *Must the government prove that the alien was unlawfully present?*

Yes. The possibility that the alien may be eligible to stay in the United States under something like asylum, bond, parole, or adjustment of status does not alter the alien's unlawful status. United States v. Alvarado-Machado, 867 F.2d 209 (5th Cir. 1989); United States v. Rodriguez-Rodriguez, 840 F.2d 697 (9th Cir. 1988); United States v. Pereira-Pineda, 721 F.2d 137 (5th Cir. 1983). *But see* United States v. Medina-Garcia, 918 F.2d 4, 7 (1st Cir. 1990) (transporter of a alien with a 30-day parole under a form I-210 did not violate law, though he could be prosecuted for conspiracy).

§ 8.57. *Must the defendant know the alien was unlawfully present?*

Yes. The defendant's knowledge of the alien's illegal status is an essential element of the offense. United States v. Williams, 132 F.3d 1055, 1059 (5th Cir. 1998). Usually the circumstances surrounding the offense prove this state of mind. *See* United States v. Shaddix, 693 F.2d 1135 (5th Cir. 1982); *but see* United States v. Diaz, 936 F.2d 786 (5th Cir. 1991) (evidence insufficient where defendant stopped at 1:30 a.m. after leaving rest stop a few miles north of checkpoint with six illegal aliens).

§ 8.58. *Is the defendant's religious or humanitarian motivation a defense?*

No. The defendant's religious motivation is irrelevant as a trial defense. United States v. Aguilar, 883 F.2d 662 (9th Cir. 1989), *cert.*

denied, 498 U.S. 1046, 111 S. Ct. 751 (1991), *overturned (superceded by statute as stated in)*, United States v. Gonzalez-Torres, 273 F.3d 1181 (9th Cir. 2001). In part, this is because harboring an unlawful alien does not require specific intent to aid the alien's presence. The *Aguilar* case, which involved the "Sanctuary Movement," also found that defendants were not entitled to a "necessity" defense instruction. *But see* United States v. Merkt, 764 F.2d 266 (5th Cir.) (worker at sectarian shelter for refugees drove aliens from border to San Antonio so they could apply for political asylum), *reh'g denied en banc*, 772 F.2d 904 (5th Cir. 1985).

§ 8.59. *What is the intent element?*

Title 8 U.S.C. § 1324 requires that the defendant know or have reckless disregard of the fact that the person is an alien. The prosecutor must also prove criminal intent regarding "bringing" the alien into the country. United States v. Nguyen, 73 F.3d 887, 895 (9th Cir. 1995). Where a person is merely transporting aliens at the direction of another out of personal fear, he would not be guilty of alien smuggling because he lacks criminal intent. *See Nguyen* at 889–90. The government must prove criminal intent beyond a reasonable doubt.

§ 8.60. *Can experts testify on whether the defendant is a smuggler?*

Generally not. Federal Rule of Evidence 704(b) does not allow government experts to testify on this point. This goes to the ultimate issue, which is the jury's decision. *See* United States v. Wang, 49 F.3d 502, 504 (9th Cir. 1995); *see also* United States v. Kinsey, 843 F.2d 383 (9th Cir.), *cert. denied*, 487 U.S. 1223, 108 S. Ct. 2882 (1988), *overruled on other grounds by* United States v. Nordby, 225 F.3d 1053 (9th Cir. 2000). Such an opinion necessarily requires the expert to infer about the defendant's state of mind, which Rule 704(b) prohibits.

Under Federal Rule of Criminal Procedure 16(a)(1)(G), upon request, the government must "give to the defendant a written summary of any testimony that the government intends to use under Rules 702, 703, or 705 of the Federal Rules of Evidence during its case-in-chief at trial." Moreover, "the summary must describe the witness's opinions, the bases and reasons for those opinions, and the witness's qualifications." Failure to disclose will result in reversal on appeal if the "expert adversely affected [the defendant's] ability to present a defense." United States v. Tinoco, 304 F.3d 1088, 1119 (11th Cir.) (quoting United States v. Chastain, 198 F.3d 1338, 1348 (11th Cir. 1999)), *cert. denied sub nom.* Hernandez v. United States, 538 U.S. 909, 123 S. Ct. 1484 (2003).

The court may, however, permit such testimony if it helps the jury place evidence and events in context, which, in smuggling cases, may take the form of opinions concerning the way alien smuggling organizations work.

§ 8.61. *What about evidence like Western Union records?*

The business record exception to the hearsay rule in Federal Rule of Evidence 803(6) does not permit the introduction of statements made by customers of Western Union unless the employee was responsible for verifying the statements. Western Union records relating to "send money" forms are not verified and, therefore, should be excluded, while information on "to receive" money forms, which are verified, can be admitted. United States v. Arteaga, 117 F.3d 388 (9th Cir. 1997), *relief denied*, 58 Fed. Appx. 374 (9th Cir. 2003).

§ 8.62. *What types of other prior bad act evidence may come into evidence?*

Under Federal Rule of Evidence 404(b), evidence of a defendant's prior alien smuggling conviction may show that he was acting with the requisite intent. The propriety of such evidence turns on the facts of the case. The Fifth Circuit, for example, in *United States v. Hernandez-Guevara*, 162 F.3d 863, 870 (5th Cir. 1998), *cert. denied*, 526 U.S. 1059, 119 S. Ct. 1375 (1999) and *United States v. Beechum*, 582 F.2d 898, 911 (5th Cir. 1978), *cert. denied*, 440 U.S. 920, 99 S. Ct. 1244 (1979) states that Rule 404(b) calls for a two-step test before admitting evidence of prior alien smuggling:

1. whether the extrinsic evidence is relevant on a matter other than the defendant's character, and
2. whether the evidence possess probative value not substantially outweighed by prejudicial effect.)

Prior act evidence may be used, for example, to rebut a defendant's claim that he happened to be at the wrong place at the wrong time. *Hernandez-Guevera*, 162 F.3d at 870; United States v. Robles-Vertiz, 155 F.3d 725, 730 (5th Cir.) (evidence of prior smuggling admissible to show lack of mistake as to alienage), *reh'g denied*, 1998 U.S. App. LEXIS 29645 (5th Cir. Oct. 23, 1998).

§ 8.63. *What about when the defendant is an alien but not a smuggler?*

This is a valid defense, especially considering that there is often confusion when several people are arrested in an alien smuggling case. Sometimes a person is just carrying the passenger tickets for the others and becomes the defendant as a result. *See, e.g.*, United States v. Perez-Robles, 718 F.2d 700 (5th Cir. 1983), *cert. denied*, 465 U.S. 1031, 104 S. Ct. 1297 (1984).

§ 8.64. *Does the "official restraint" doctrine apply in alien smuggling cases?*

In a reentry after deportation case, the government must prove that the defendant was free from "official restraint." *See* **Chapter 10: Illegal Entry and Reentry — Pretrial and Trial.** In an alien smuggling case, however, the government need not prove that the aliens being smuggled were ever free from the official restraint. Thus, the Official Restraint Doctrine no longer applies to an alien smuggling case. United States v. Gonzalez-Torres, 309 F.3d 594 (9th Cir. 2002), *overturning (stating supercession by statute)* United States v. Aguilar, 883 F.2d 662 (9th Cir. 1989), *cert. denied*, 498 U.S. 1046, 111 S. Ct. 751 (1991). Congress' changing one word in the statute succeeded in eliminating this doctrine as a defense in the Ninth Circuit. *See also* United States v. Hernandez-Garcia, 284 F.3d 1135 (9th Cir.), *amended, reh'g en banc denied*, 2002 U.S. App. LEXIS 8929 (9th Cir. May 9, 2002), *cert. denied*, 537 U.S. 932, 123 S. Ct. 335 (2002).

This defense would also not apply to transporting aliens under 18 U.S.C. § 1324(A)(1)(ii) because the offense makes it illegal to "come to" the country. Thus, so long as the aliens were transported in this country and the defendant knew they were aliens an offense has occurred.

XI. Plea Bargaining

§ 8.65. *What is the most common plea agreement?*

The most common plea is to "accessory after the fact" of the illegal entry of another, in violation of 8 U.S.C. § 1325 and 18 U.S.C. § 3.

This avoids the defendant's being classed as an aggravated felon under 8 U.S.C. § 1101(a)(43)(N) and negates the basis of deportation under 8 U.S.C. § 1227(a)(1)(E)(i). *See generally* United States v. Taylor, 322 F.3d 1209 (9th Cir.) (accessory after the fact only occurs when a person assists an offender but the person committing accessory is not the offender himself), *cert. denied*, 541 U.S. 939, 124 S. Ct. 1653 (2004). The maximum punishment is three months imprisonment, and removal is highly unlikely. Also, even if the alien is deported and illegally returns, without the aggravated felony conviction he stands a better chance at sentencing under the new reentry after deportation charge. *See* United States v. Monjares-Castaneda, 190 F.3d 326 (5th Cir.) (affirming 16-level increase in illegal reentry case for transporting illegal aliens following a conviction for aggravated felony), *reh'g denied*, 1999 U.S. App. LEXIS 30735 (5th Cir. Tex. Oct. 20, 1999), *cert. denied*, 528 U.S. 1194, 120 S. Ct. 1254 (2000).

Another plea is to have the defendant admit to aiding the illegal entry of another in violation of 8 U.S.C. § 1325. The first conviction is a misdemeanor, with a possible six-month penalty; subsequent convictions are felonies. With these, the defendant is sentenced under Federal Sentencing Guideline § 2L1.2 for unlawful entry or remaining in the United States. If the defendant is an alien, this provides a basis for deportation under 8 U.S.C. § 1227.

§ 8.66. *What about the defendant who is worried about immigration status?*

If a person pleads to violating the alien smuggling statute under 8 U.S.C. § 1324, he is an aggravated felon under 8 U.S.C. § 1101(a)(43)(N) and *will be deported* (*see* **Chapter 4: Immigration Consequences of Criminal Convictions** *and* **Chapter 5: Aggravated Felonies**) regardless of whether he is a legal permanent resident. It does not matter whether the alien smuggler did not smuggle for profit — the government will deport him as an aggravated felon nonetheless. The only exception to the aggravated felony definition occurs if the person smuggled was a spouse, child, or other close family member of the smuggler. *See* 8 U.S.C. § 1101(a)(43)(N).

If a person avoids the alien smuggling conviction but pleads to aiding and abetting the illegal entry of another under 8 U.S.C. § 1325, the person is "deportable" under 8 U.S.C. § 1227(a)(1)(E)(i) (*see* **Chapter 4: Immigration Consequences of Criminal Convictions**). Interestingly, under this statute, smuggling or "bringing in" is a basis for deportation, but transporting is not. It is, however, an aggravated felony for deportation purposes under 8 U.S.C. § 1101(a)(43)(N). The same exception exists for persons who transport a spouse, child, or other close family member. *See* 8 U.S.C. § 1227(a)(1)(E)(ii).

XII. Sentencing Issues

A. Statutory Penalties

§ 8.67. *What are the statutory penalties for alien smuggling?*

The penalty provisions are found at 8 U.S.C. § 1324(a)(1)(B) and include mandatory minimums of three to 10 years for a first or second violation, or five to 15 years for a third or subsequent violation. Also, smuggling an alien whom the smuggler knows will commit a felony, or for financial gain, carries a 10-year maximum sentence, with a three-year mandatory minimum for the first or second offense, and a 15-year maximum sentence with a five-year mandatory minimum for subsequent offenses. § 1324(a)(1)(B)(iii). In all other cases, the penalty for alien smuggling for financial gain is 10 years. 8 U.S.C. § 1324(a)(1)(B)(i) (with Federal Sentencing Guideline § 2L1.1 controlling the actual sentence). Transportation, concealment, encouragement, or aiding and abetting without financial gain has a five-year statutory maximum. 8 U.S.C. § 1324(a)(1)(B)(ii).

In addition to imprisonment, the law provides for the seizure and forfeiture of the conveyance used to transport the undocumented aliens. 8 U.S.C. § 1324(b).

There are still calls for increasing the penalties. *See, e.g.*, Statement of Paul K. Charlton, United States Attorney, District of Arizona, before the Subcommittee on Crime, Corrections and Victims' Rights Committee on the Judiciary, United States Senate, concerning human trafficking and illegal immigrants smuggling presented on July 25, 2003, at http://judiciary.senate.gov/print_testimony.cfm?id=873&wit_id=2465.

§ 8.68. *What special considerations apply if an alien dies?*

If "during and in relation to" the violation the defendant "causes serious bodily injury ... to, or places in jeopardy the life of, any person" the maximum penalty jumps to 20 years. 8 U.S.C. § 1324(a)(1)(B)(iii). If a death resulted during the smuggling, the smuggler upon conviction can receive capital punishment or life imprisonment. 8 U.S.C. § 1324(a)(1)(B)(iv). *See* United States v. Garcia-Guerrero, 313 F.3d 892 (5th Cir. 2002) (death in desert); United States v. Cuyler, 298 F.3d 387 (5th Cir. 2002) (aliens riding in bed of pickup truck); *see also* U.S. SENTENCING GUIDELINES MANUAL § 2L1.1(b)(4)–(6).

§ 8.69. *Can a defendant be punished for both "bringing in" and "transporting"?*

No. When the underlying criminal conduct consists of a single act or transaction of bringing an undocumented person into the United States, it does not result in multiple punishments. United States v. Sanchez-Vargas, 878 F.2d 1163 (9th Cir. 1989). Thus, a court cannot impose consecutive sentences for multiple counts. United States v. Candelario-Cajero, 134 F.3d 1246 (5th Cir. 1998).

B. The Federal Sentencing Guidelines

Starting with *Blakely v. Washington*, 542 U.S. 296, 124 S. Ct. 2531 (2004) through *United States v. Booker/United States v. Fanfan*, 125 S. Ct. 738 (2005), the entire concept of federal sentencing has shifted. The Guidelines are for now, truly "guidelines" and "advisory." They are just one factor among several that the courts must consider in imposing a sentence that is "sufficient but not greater than necessary" to achieve the purposes of 18 U.S.C. § 3553(a)(2). Thus, the following sections outline a sentencing scheme that will yield the advisory sentence and not what was formerly a mandatory sentence allowing only for departures in "rare" cases outside the "heartland" of typical cases. *See* **Ch 11, II.B: Departures from the Sentencing Guidelines**.

1. Base Offense Level and General Considerations

§ 8.70. *What is the base offense level for alien smuggling?*

The base offense level under Guideline § 2L1.1 is 12. If the defendant is convicted of smuggling an aggravated felon alien, the base offense level is 23.

2. Number of Aliens Adjustment

§ 8.71. *How does the number of aliens affect the sentence?*

Guideline § 2L1.1 adds levels for the number of aliens smuggled: six to 24 aliens adds three levels, 25 to 99 aliens adds six levels; and 100 or more aliens adds nine levels to the calculation. *See* United States v. Cabrera, 288 F.3d 163 (5th Cir. 2002) (approving estimating of number of aliens to fix range).

§ 8.72. *For more than 100 aliens, can the court add more than nine levels?*

No. The Ninth Circuit in United States v. Nagra, 147 F.3d 875 (9th Cir. 1998), held that the Guideline allows for the addition of only nine levels; an upward departure/adjustment was disallowed in a case involving 180 aliens.

§ 8.73. *What factors become relevant regarding alien numbers?*

Given that the Guideline punishes for the number of people smuggled, the question becomes one of attribution. For example, several aliens smuggled by several different coyotes may be sent to the same drop house, but the coyote charged may have smuggled only a fraction of the number of people in the house. The sentence should be enhanced for only the number of aliens with whom he was involved. The government has the burden to establish this Guideline enhancement factor under § 2L1.2(b)(2).

3. Other Adjustments

§ 8.74. *Who has the burden of establishing an adjustment?*

The party who gains from an adjustment must show the adjustment applies. United States v. Krcic, 186 F.3d 178 (2d Cir. 1999) (defendant must show entitlement to not-for-profit reduction); United States v. Alfaro, 919 F.2d 962, 965 (5th Cir. 1990). *See also* United States v. Trinidad-Lopez, 979 F.2d 249, 251 (1st Cir. 1992) (discussing burden of proof rulings); United States v. Howard, 894 F.2d 1085, 1089 (9th Cir. 1990) (discussing the burden of proof rulings in the Third and Fourth Circuits; agreeing with these Circuits that "under the Guidelines the party seeking to adjust the offense level should be required to persuade the court that such an adjustment is merited").

§ 8.75. *By what standard of proof must a party establish an adjustment?*

Although *Blakely v. Washington*, 542 U.S. 296, 124 S. Ct. 2531 (2004), indicated that the standard of proof for all sentencing factors or enhancements must be proof beyond a reasonable doubt, *United States v. Booker/United States v. Fanfan*, 125 S. Ct. 738 (2005) seems to have taken these issues to the preponderance standard. This conforms to the Guideline statement at § 6A1.3, comment, that the proponent of an adjustment must show a preponderance of the "relevant and sufficiently reliable evidence" to support an adjustment.

This issue is obviously still in play at the Supreme Court and with Congress.

§ 8.76. *Under the Guideline can a vulnerable victim adjustment apply?*

Potentially, although by definition the persons being smuggled are often vulnerable, precluding this adjustment under Guideline § 3A1.1. United States v. Williams, 291 F.3d 1180, 1195–96 (9th Cir. 2002); United States v. Castaneda, 239 F.3d 978, 980–81 (9th Cir. 2001). The adjustment could apply adding two points to a defendant's calculation if the victims were unusually vulnerable relative to the normal smuggled alien. Immigration status, low education, and language difficulties may all factor into this analysis. *See* United States v. Veerapol, 312 F.3d 1128, 1132–33 (9th Cir. 2002), *cert. denied*, 538 U.S. 981, 123 S. Ct. 1785 (2003).

§ 8.77. *What if the defendant lacked a profit motive?*

The Guideline allows that if the defendant committed the offense for motive other than profit there can be a three level decrease. U.S. SENTENCING GUIDELINES MANUAL § 2L1.1(b)(1). The commentary states that the phrase means there was no payment or "expectation of payment." U.S. SENTENCING GUIDELINES MANUAL § 2L1.2 cmt. n.1. "Payment" and "expectation of payment," can refer to something other than money, such as the forgiveness of a debt to a coyote. United States v. Juan-Manuel, 222 F.3d 480, 485 (8th Cir. 2000) (reduction disallowed where defendant committed offense to avoid paying smuggling fees). The defendant has the burden of establishing lack of profit. United States v. White, 1 F.3d 13 (D.C. Cir. 1993), *cert. denied*, 510 U.S. 1111, 114 S. Ct. 1053, *reh'g denied*, 511 U.S. 1047, 114 S. Ct. 1580 (1994).

§ 8.78. *What if the defendant smuggled a family member?*

There is a three level decrease if the offense involved the defendant's spouse or child. U.S. SENTENCING GUIDELINES MANUAL § 2L1.1(b)(1).

§ 8.79. *What about when the defendant was a "leader"?*

The court can add points for this, but the adjustment cannot be made if the defendant merely translated for the rest of the co-conspirators, because a translator is akin to a middleman between a buyer and a supplier. United States v. Lopez-Sandoval, 146 F.3d 712 (9th Cir. 1998).

4. Reckless Endangerment or Death

§ 8.80. *What is the mental state for the reckless endangerment adjustment?*

The defendant must have some intent to create the danger or to subject the persons transported to a danger. United States v. Rodriguez-Cruz, 255 F.3d 1054, 1059 (9th Cir. 2001). Arguably then, the adjustment should only apply to defendants with a reckless mental state requiring an awareness of circumstances that present a danger to others' safety. *Black's Law Dictionary, Sixth Edition* (West 1990) (defining "reckless"). *See also* U.S. SENTENCING GUIDELINES MANUAL § 2A1.4 application note n.1 (defining "reckless" for purposes of involuntary manslaughter Guideline, referring "to a situation in which the defendant was aware of the risk created by his conduct and the risk was of such a nature and degree that to disregard that risk constituted a gross deviation from the standard of care that a reasonable person would exercise in such a situation"). Thus, a single act of endangerment should not trigger this adjustment. United States v. Lopez-Garcia, 316 F.3d 967 (9th Cir. 2003).

§ 8.81. *What if the "coyote" faced the same dangers as the "pollos"?*

That the coyote defendant shared the same dangers as the alien that died does not protect him from the death adjustment. United

States v. Herrera-Rojas, 243 F.3d 1139 (9th Cir. 2001). Even if the alien smuggler leaves the aliens to find help or assists in other ways it would not prevent the Guidelines being increased because death occurs. *See* United States v. Rodriguez-Cruz, 255 F.3d 1054 (9th Cir. 2001). This is because if the smugglers did not prepare the aliens with adequate food and water, they assume the risk if death occurs. *See* United States v. Hernandez-Guardado, 228 F.3d 1017 (9th Cir. 2000). A specific intent is not required when death actually results. *See also* United States v. Matus-Leva, 311 F.3d 1214 (9th Cir. 2002) (intent element for smuggling same if death occurs and trial need not be bifurcated on the issues), *cert. denied*, 540 U.S. 925, 124 S. Ct. 331 (2003).

§ 8.82. *Does Apprendi apply to the enhancement when death results?*

No. *Apprendi v. New Jersey*, 530 U.S. 466, 120 S. Ct. 2348 (2000), does not preclude a Guideline sentencing enhancement/adjustment for recklessly creating a risk of death or serious injury, despite its not being charged in the indictment or proved. United States v. Hernandez-Guardado, 228 F.3d 1017 (9th Cir. 2000). Because the sentence was under the ten-year maximum, *Apprendi* did not apply. *Id.* In the post-*Blakely*, post-*Booker/Fanfan* world, however, this argument may have credence. *See* United States v. Booker/United States v. Fanfan, 125 S. Ct. 738 (2005); Blakely v. Washington, 542 U.S. 296, 124 S. Ct. 2531 (2004).

5. Departures

§ 8.83. *Are there other bases for departure?*

Yes, for dangerous or inhumane treatment. *See* U.S. SENTENCING GUIDELINES MANUAL § 2L1.1 application note n.6. *See also* United States v. Velasquez-Mercado, 872 F.2d 632, 637 (5th Cir.) (transporter demanded sexual favors), *reh'g denied*, 1989 U.S. App. LEXIS 7793 (5th Cir. June 1, 1989), *cert. denied*, 493 U.S. 866, 110 S. Ct. 187 (1989); United States v. Salazar-Villarreal, 872 F.2d 121 (5th Cir. 1989) (reckless flight resulting in death).

CHAPTER 9

IMMIGRATION DOCUMENT FRAUD AND FALSE STATEMENTS

Introduction

I. Basis of Congressional Power

II. General Issues

- A. Materiality
- B. Third-Party Liability
- C. RICO and Wiretaps

III. General False Statement Statutes in the Immigration Context

- A. Perjury
- B. Conspiracy
- C. General False Statements, 18 U.S.C. § 1001

IV. Specific Immigration False Statement Crimes

- A. False Statements upon Entry, Fraud with Visas, Permits, and Other Documents: 18 U.S.C. § 1546
  - 1. Section 1546 in General
  - 2. Section 1546 and Entry
- B. False Passports
- C. Impersonating Another for an Immigration Benefit
- D. False Statements as to Convictions and Crimes
- E. False Statements as to Prior Deportations
- F. False Claims as to Citizenship: 18 U.S.C. § 911
- G. Fraud and Identity Documents: 18 U.S.C. § 1028
- H. False Statements in Voting
- I. False Claims for Welfare Benefits

V. Prosecutions and Trial Issues

- A. Indictment
- B. Admissibility of Evidence
- C. Defenses

VI. Sentencing and Forfeiture

Other Resources:

Howard J. Alperin, Annotation, *Validity and Construction of Federal Statute (18 U.S.C. § 1546) Making Fraud and Misuse of Visas, Permits, and Other Entry Documents A Criminal Offense*, 3 A.L.R. FED. 623 (1970 & 2004 Supp.).

Stephen Yale-Loehr, *New Developments to Combat Alien Smuggling and Document Fraud*, 2:1 BENDER'S IMMIGR. BULL. 3 (Jan. 1, 1997).

Introduction

This chapter focuses on false statements and documents in the immigration context, mainly under 18 U.S.C. § 1546. Several other statutes punish related conduct:

- Title 18 U.S.C. § 1621 applies to perjury generally;
- Title 18 U.S.C. § 911 prohibits false claims to citizenship;
- Title 8 U.S.C. § 1306(c) proscribes false statements in an alien registration application;
- Title 8 U.S.C. § 1325 applies to an alien entering the United States by false representation;
- Title 18 U.S.C. § 1542 applies to false passports;
- Title 18 U.S.C. § 1543 applies to forgery of a passport;
- Title 18 U.S.C. § 1544 applies to the misuse of a passport;
- Title 22 U.S.C. § 1203 applies to perjury in a foreign consular office;
- Title 18 U.S.C. § 1001 applies to false statements to the United States government generally.

See **Chapter 6: Alien Employment Crimes** and **Chapter 7: Marriage Fraud** regarding false statements in the context of alien employment and marriage.

I. Basis of Congressional Power

§ 9.1. *What is the basis of congressional power?*

Uttering a materially false statement affronts United States' sovereignty, having a "deleterious influence" on valid governmental interests. Rocha v. United States, 288 F.2d 545 (9th Cir.), *cert. denied*, 366 U.S. 948, 81 S. Ct. 1902 (1961). Immigration fraud statutes are "necessary and proper for carrying into execution" the congressional power over foreign relations. United States v. Pizzarusso, 388 F.2d 8 (2d Cir.), *cert. denied*, 392 U.S. 936, 88 S. Ct.

2306 (1968). The national government has a legitimate interest in knowing the background of those seeking admission to the United States and Congress can make any law necessary to execute a "Uniform Rule of Naturalization" at U.S. CONST. ART. 1, § 8, cl. 4. *See* Note, *Federal Jurisdiction Over Crimes Committed Abroad by Aliens*, 13 STAN. L. REV. 155, 157–58 (1960).

II. General Issues

A. Materiality

§ 9.2. *What if the statement is not material?*

If the statement is not materially harmful to the United States, the defendant may have a defense. United States v. Khalje, 658 F.2d 90 (2d Cir. 1981) (phrase "any such false statement" refers back only to phrase "any false statement with respect to a material fact"); United States v. Diogo, 320 F.2d 898 (2d Cir. 1963) (§ 1546 violations, like common law perjury, require proof of knowing falsity); Clarke v. Landon, 139 F. Supp. 113 (D.C. Mass.) (word "material" should be inserted between the word "any" and "false"), *vacated on other grounds*, 239 F.2d 631 (1st Cir. 1956).

§ 9.3. *What about concealment of material facts?*

Willful concealment of material facts constitutes immigration fraud. United States v. Rubenstein, 151 F.2d 915 (2d Cir.), *cert. denied*, 326 U.S. 766, 66 S. Ct. 168 (1945). In 1996 congress amended 18 U.S.C. § 1546, changing "knowingly presenting a document that contains a false statement" to "knowingly presenting a document that fails to contain any reasonable basis in fact or law."

B. Third-Party Liability

§ 9.4. *What about makers of false immigration documents?*

"Knowingly and willfully" preparing or concealing one's role in preparing, for a fee or other remuneration, a false application for benefits under the immigration laws is a crime. 8 U.S.C. § 1324c(e). Convicted defendants can be jailed for up to five years and are barred from preparing any such application. *See* 8 U.S.C. § 1325(c). A convicted defendant who later prepares or assists in preparing an application for immigration benefits, for a fee or not, can be jailed for up to 15 years.

§ 9.5. *Can the government prosecute a U.S. citizen?*

Yes, because even citizens can get benefits from fraudulent immigration conduct. *See, e.g.*, United States v. Knight, 514 F.2d 1286 (5th Cir. 1975) (citizen who impersonated another when applying for admission prosecutable).

§ 9.6. *What about employer's preparing false immigration documents?*

This is a crime under 18 U.S.C. § 1546. United States v. de Cruz, 82 F.3d 856 (9th Cir. 1996). *See* **Chapter 6: Alien Employment Crimes.**

C. RICO and Wiretaps

§ 9.7. *Is document fraud a RICO violation?*

Yes, under 18 U.S.C. § 1961(1).

§ 9.8. *Can the government use wiretaps to investigate document fraud?*

Yes, under 18 U.S.C. § 2516(1).

III. General False Statement Statutes in the Immigration Context

A. Perjury

§ 9.9. *Does the general perjury statute apply?*

Yes, the immigration perjury statute refers to the general perjury statute at 18 U.S.C. § 1621 and empowers immigration officers and employees to administer oaths:

> [A]ny person to whom such oath has been administered (or who has executed an unsworn declaration, certificate, verification, or statement under penalty of perjury ...), ... who shall knowingly or willfully give false evidence or swear ... to any false statement concerning any matter referred to in this sub-

> section shall be guilty of perjury and shall be punished as provided by section 1621 of Title 18.

8 U.S.C. § 1357(b).

§ 9.10. *What about perjury in specific immigration proceedings?*

Title 22 U.S.C. § 4221 authorizes certain embassy and consular officials to administer oaths, and allows the government to prosecute any person who "willfully and corruptly" commits perjury or "by any means procure[s] any person to commit perjury."

§ 9.11. *Does a perjury charge preclude other false document charges?*

No, the government can charge a person with perjury as well as the other false documents charges. Given the demanding proofs for a perjury conviction, prosecutors often charge the defendant under other statutes.

B. Conspiracy

§ 9.12. *Does the general conspiracy statute apply?*

Yes. Shimi Miho v. United States, 57 F.2d 491 (9th Cir. 1932). The general federal conspiracy statute, 18 U.S.C. § 371, is another way the government can prosecute immigration false statements, misrepresentations, and other fraud:

> If two or more persons conspire either to commit any offense against the United States, or to defraud the United States, or any agency thereof in any manner or for any purpose, and one or more of such persons do any act to effect the object of the conspiracy, each shall be fined not more than $10,000 or imprisoned not more than five years, or both.

18 U.S.C. § 371. Under the terms of § 371, if the conspired offense is a misdemeanor the punishment must not exceed the maximum misdemeanor punishment.

§ 9.13. *Can the government charge both conspiracy and the substantive offense?*

Yes. Pereira v. United States, 347 U.S. 1, 74 S. Ct. 358 (1954) (conspiracy often easier to prove than substantive crime).

C. General False Statements, 18 U.S.C. § 1001

§ 9.14. *What is the general false statement statute?*

Title 18 U.S.C. § 1001 covers any materially untruthful statement anyone makes to a government official:

> [W]hoever, in any matter within the jurisdiction of the executive, legislative, or judicial branch of the Government of the United States, knowingly and willfully (1) falsifies, conceals, or covers up by any trick, scheme, or device a material fact; (2) makes any materially false, fictitious, or fraudulent statement or representation; or (3) makes or uses any false writing or document knowing the same to contain any materially false, fictitious, or fraudulent statement or entry; shall be fined under this title or imprisoned not more than 5 years, or both.

§ 9.15. *Does 18 U.S.C. § 1001 apply in the immigration context?*

Yes. *See, e.g.*, United States v. Rodriguez-Rodriguez, 840 F.2d 697 (9th Cir. 1988) (§ 1001 conviction upheld because of defendant's material misstatement to border patrol that alien passengers were United States citizens); United States v. Diogo, 320 F.2d 898 (2d Cir. 1963) (false statements in visa application violates 18 U.S.C. § 1001).

§ 9.16. *Is there an argument that 18 U.S.C. § 1001 is overbroad?*

Yes but it will probably not win as the statute has withstood an overbreadth attack under the First Amendment. United States v. Esparza-Ponce, 193 F.3d 1133, 1137–38 (9th Cir. 1999).

§ 9.17. *Can an "exculpatory no" violate 18 U.S.C. § 1001?*

Yes. The Eleventh Circuit holds there is no "exculpatory no" defense in 18 U.S.C. § 1001 cases to false claims of U.S. citizenship. United States v. Lopez-Iraeta, 129 F.3d 1206 (11th Cir. 1997) (rejecting defense that person merely answered interrogation questions rather than affirmatively misrepresented his citizenship), *reh'g en banc denied*, 136 F.3d 143 (11th Cir. Fla. 1998); Brogan v. United States, 522 U.S. 398, 118 S. Ct. 805 (1998) (rejecting "exculpatory no" defense in § 1001 cases).

IV. Specific Immigration False Statement Crimes

A. False Statements upon Entry, Fraud with Visas, Permits, and Other Documents: 18 U.S.C. § 1546

§ 9.18. *What is immigration document or statement fraud?*

Under 18 U.S.C. § 1546, the government can prosecute any statement of material fact in any immigration document a person makes for an immigration benefit including the following:

1. To forge, alter, or create a document for immigration purposes;
2. To use, possess, obtain, accept, or receive any such document for immigration purposes;
3. To use someone else's document for an immigration benefit;
4. To accept someone else's document to comply with employment verification requirements;
5. To prepare, file, or assist another person in filing an application for an immigration benefit with knowledge, or in reckless disregard of the fact, that the application is false; or
6. To present to a carrier a document that relates to the alien's eligibility to enter the United States but fail to present such document to an immigration officer upon Unite States arrival.

See United States v. Montemayor, 712 F.2d 104 (5th Cir. 1983) (false statement after arrest for deportation hearing, on immigration affidavits forms, sustained conviction); United States v. Carrillo-Colmenero, 523 F.2d 1279 (5th Cir. 1975) (prosecution not limited to persons applying for entry documents); United States v. O'Connor, 158 F. Supp. 2d 697 (E.D. Va. 2001) (knowing false statements in visa applications).

§ 9.19. *How has Congress changed the statute?*

Congress passed 18 U.S.C. § 1546 in 1948, replacing a similar predecessor statute from 1924 at 8 U.S.C. § 220 (1940 ed.). In 1996, Congress expanded the types of entry documents the statute covered.

At least one court notes that the statute "is certainly not a model of good draftsmanship; a better description would be that it is a masterpiece of obfuscation, a not uncommon fault of federal statutes." United States v. Tamayo, 427 F.2d 1072, 1073 (9th Cir. 1970).

1. Section 1546 In General

§ 9.20. *What about nonentry immigration documents?*

By its express terms 18 U.S.C. § 1546 is not limited to entry documents. United States v. Carrillo-Colmenero, 523 F.2d 1279 (5th Cir. 1975).

§ 9.21. *Does the alien have to enter with the false document?*

No. Under 18 U.S.C. § 1546 entry is not an element of the offense. United States v. Pizzarusso, 388 F.2d 8 (2d Cir.), *cert. denied*, 392 U.S. 936, 88 S. Ct. 2306 (1968). The government, however, usually cannot prosecute unless the alien enters the country.

§ 9.22. *What is the mens rea for an 18 U.S.C. § 1546 violation?*

"Knowingly and willfully" is the *mens rea*. This is satisfied if defendant acted with reckless disregard of whether statements made were true or with conscious effort to avoid learning the truth. United States v. Sarantos, 455 F.2d 877 (2d Cir. 1972).

§ 9.23. *What is the statute of limitations?*

Generally, 10 years. *See* United States v. Alameh, 341 F.3d 167 (2d Cir. 2003) (prosecution for knowingly obtaining citizenship was timely if brought within applicable ten-year statute of limitations).

§ 9.24. *When is the crime completed?*

The false statement itself completes the crime. United States v. Pizzarusso, 388 F.2d 8 (2d Cir.) (perjury in visa application was completed in foreign country), *cert. denied*, 392 U.S. 936, 88 S. Ct. 2306 (1968).

§ 9.25. *What if the document does not fool the government?*

The false statement still violates the statute. United States v. Diogo, 320 F.2d 898 (2d Cir. 1963) (courts look to defendant's intended meaning rather than to immigration authorities' interpretation).

§ 9.26. *Is a Social Security card an "immigration document"?*

No. A Social Security card is not an immigration document under 18 U.S.C. § 1546. United States v. Tyson Foods, Inc., 258 F. Supp. 2d 809 (E.D. Tenn.), *dismissed in part,* 2003 U.S. Dist. LEXIS 20174 (E.D. Tenn. Jan. 28, 2003).

§ 9.27. *What if the alien does not make the statement under oath?*

It does not matter because under 18 U.S.C. § 1546 materially false statements are illegal regardless of whether the individual swears to them. United States v. Khalje, 658 F.2d 90 (2d Cir. 1981).

§ 9.28. *Does 18 U.S.C. § 1546 apply to statements at deportations?*

Yes, § 1546 covers not only false statements a defendant makes at entry, but also those he makes after arrest for a deportation hearing. United States v. Montemayor, 712 F.2d 104 (5th Cir. 1983).

§ 9.29. *Does 18 U.S.C. § 1546 cover conduct outside the United States?*

Yes. Congress intended for the statute to have extraterritorial jurisdiction. United States v. Pizzarusso, 388 F.2d 8 (2d Cir.) (the section is constitutionally valid even when the defendant commits the crime outside the United States), *cert. denied,* 392 U.S. 936, 88 S. Ct. 2306 (1968); Rocha v. United States, 288 F.2d 545 (9th Cir.), *cert. denied,* 366 U.S. 948, 81 S. Ct. 1902 (1961); United States v. Rodriguez, 182 F. Supp. 479 (S.D. Cal. 1960), *aff'd in part, rev'd in part on other grounds,* 288 F.2d 545 (9th Cir.), *cert. denied,* 366 U.S. 948, 81 S. Ct. 1902 (1961); *see also* United States v. Khalje, 658 F.2d 90 (2d Cir. 1981); Note, *Federal Jurisdiction Over Crimes Committed Abroad by Aliens,* 13 STAN. L. REV. 155 (1960).

2. Section 1546 and Entry

§ 9.30. *What entry documents does the statute cover?*

The criminal statute, 18 U.S.C. § 1546, applies to any document used to gain entry into the United States, including a visa or entry permit. United States v. Ryan-Webster, 353 F.3d 353 (4th Cir. 2003) (Congress intended to broaden reach of statute by now prohibiting such documents "required for entry" to include documents "prescribed by statute or regulation for entry"), *post-conviction relief denied*, 2005 U.S. App. LEXIS 19656 (4th Cir. Sept. 12, 2005). *Cf.* United States v. Campos-Serrano, 404 U.S. 293, 92 S. Ct. 471 (1971) (mere possession of counterfeit alien registration card not punishable under § 1546).

§ 9.31. *What is a "visa, permit, or other entry document"?*

This broad phrase in 18 U.S.C. § 1546 does not limit the statute to solely visas or entry permits. Before Congress passed § 1546, neither citizenship papers nor alien registration cards fell under the definition because these had no function in facilitating initial entry. United States v. Campos-Serrano, 404 U.S. 293, 92 S. Ct. 471 (1971) (statute only applies to "documents whose primary *raison d'etre* is the facilitation of entry into the country."). *Cf.* McFarland v. United States, 19 F.2d 807 (6th Cir. 1927) (prior § 220 did not apply to act of impersonation not related to a visa or permit).

§ 9.32. *Does 18 U.S.C. § 1546 include unlawful sale of entry document?*

Yes. United States v. Castro, 476 F.2d 750 (9th Cir. 1973) (defendant guilty under 18 U.S.C. § 1546 for bribes to issue immigration documents to Mexican citizens).

B. False Passports

§ 9.33. *How does the government prosecute false passports?*

Title 18 U.S.C. § 1543 prohibits the intentional use or making of a false, forged, counterfeit, mutilated, or altercated passport or any instrument purporting to be a passport. This statute also prohibits attempting to furnish or furnishing to another a false passport.

§ 9.34. *Can the government also prosecute false passports under 18 U.S.C. § 1546?*

Now, yes. A prior version of the statute did not allow a conviction for possession of a fraudulent passport. United States v. Fox, 766 F. Supp. 569 (N.D. Tex. 1991); United States v. Vargas, 380 F. Supp. 1162 (E.D.N.Y. 1974) (defendant's sale of Columbian passport to undercover agent of U.S. Bureau of Customs not prosecutable under § 1546). In 1986 Congress amended 18 U.S.C. § 1546 to allow prosecution for counterfeit passports. United States v. Rahman, 189

F.3d 88, 118–19 (2d Cir. 1999) (a foreign counterfeit passport prosecutable — distinguishing *Vargas*, *Fox* and *United States v. Campos-Serrano*, 430 F.2d 173 (7th Cir. 1970), *aff'd*, 404 U.S. 293, 92 S. Ct. 471 (1971), as pre-1986 Act cases). *See also* United States v. Osiemi, 980 F.2d 344 (5th Cir. 1993) (§ 1546 applies to fraudulent passport even where it did not contain a visa); United States v. Dangdee, 616 F.2d 1118 (9th Cir. 1980) (18 U.S.C. § 1546 also concerns passports, to extent "other documents of entry" can be interpreted to encompass passports); United States v. Mouyas, 42 F.2d 743 (S.D.N.Y. 1930) (one who uses a passport to impersonate another and thereby gains entry should not be freed from prosecution).

§ 9.35. *What about making a false impression in a passport?*

Title 18 U.S.C. § 1543 punishes making a false impression in a passport. "Impression" as used in statute, however, is a mark produced by impressing, and merely possessing a rubber stamp to make the forbidden mark is not an "impression." United States v. Naaman, 813 F.2d 1577 (9th Cir. 1987). Moreover, using such a rubber stamp would not constitute a fraud in reproduction of visas. United States v. Hammoude, 51 F.3d 288 (D.C. Cir.) (use of multiple-piece rubber stamp glued to paper not printed in passport was not counterfeit under statute criminalizing fraud in reproduction of visas), *cert. denied*, 515 U.S. 1128, 115 S. Ct. 2290 (1995).

§ 9.36. *What about false foreign passports?*

Both 18 U.S.C. § 1543 and § 1546 allow for the prosecution of a person carrying a false passport from any country, not just the United States. United States v. Osiemi, 980 F.2d 344 (5th Cir. 1993) (foreign passport is a document "prescribed by statute or regulation"); United States v. Dangdee, 616 F.2d 1118, 1119 (9th Cir. 1980); United States v. Restrepo-Granda, 575 F.2d 524 (5th Cir.) (foreign passport is a document "prescribed by statute or regulation"), *cert. denied*, 439 U.S. 935, 99 S. Ct. 331 (1978), *reh'g denied*, 439 U.S. 1104, 99 S. Ct. 885 (1979); United States v. Simo, 68 F. Supp. 2d 706 (E.D. Va. 1999), *aff'd*, 230 F.3d 1355 (4th Cir. 2000). *But cf.* United States v. Fox, 766 F. Supp. 569 (N.D. Tex. 1991) (purported "passport" from nonexistent county not a "document" under statute).

§ 9.37. *What about making a false statement to get a passport?*

Making a false statement in a passport application is illegal under 18 U.S.C. § 1542. United States v. Suarez-Rosario, 237 F.3d 1164 (9th Cir. 2001) (government need not prove defendant's identity, only that he used a false statement to get a passport).

C. Impersonating Another for an Immigration Benefit

§ 9.38. *What does "impersonate another" mean in immigration law?*

The term "impersonate another" includes misrepresentation of imaginary, as well as specific individuals. United States v. Mouyas, 42 F.2d 743 (S.D.N.Y. 1930). Thus, one may "impersonate" by misrepresenting his own image as a citizen as well as by representing himself to be someone else who is a citizen. Shimi Miho v. United States, 57 F.2d 491 (9th Cir. 1932). Impersonating another for an immigration benefit is a crime. United States v. Carrillo-Colmenero, 523 F.2d 1279 (5th Cir. 1975) (alien's using citizen's identity properly convicted); United States v. Santelises, 476 F.2d 787 (2d Cir. 1973), 509 F.2d 703 (2d Cir. 1975) (per curiam) (receiving a visa for another named person by fraud constitutes a crime); *Shimi Miho v. United States* (applicant's signing his own name did not preclude conviction for false impersonation). *Cf.* McFarland v. United States, 19 F.2d 807 (6th Cir. 1927) (indictment charging alien with impersonating another by presenting citizenship papers did not constitute offense under former § 220); United States v. Birnbaum, 55 F. Supp. 356 (S.D.N.Y. 1944) (indictment insufficient under former § 201 et seq. that failed to allege visas issued out of turn on waiting list).

§ 9.39. *Can the government charge a person with both false impersonation and the false document?*

Yes. Charges of false impersonation and presentment of a visa application containing false statements are not duplicitous. United States v. Khalje, 658 F.2d 90 (2d Cir. 1981) (impersonation crime requires proof of a different fact than presentment provision).

D. False Statements as to Convictions and Crimes

§ 9.40. *Do alien's denials of criminal convictions violate the law?*

Yes, denying a criminal conviction violates 18 U.S.C. § 1546. *See* United States v. Kong Yin Chu [Chu Kong Yin], 5 F.3d 1244 (9th Cir. 1993) (applicant for permanent residency who misstated that he had no conviction for crime involving moral turpitude violated statute).

§ 9.41. *What about denials of criminal activity?*

A misrepresentation denying criminal activity can be a material false statement even if the defendant was not convicted. In these cases a jury will decide if the denial of criminal activity is a false statement. United States v. Posada-Rios, 158 F.3d 832 (5th Cir. 1998), *cert. denied,* 526 U.S. 1031, 119 S. Ct. 1280; 526 U.S. 1080, 119 S. Ct. 1487; 526 U.S. 1137, 119 S. Ct. 1792 (1999).

E. False Statements as to Prior Deportations

§ 9.42. *Are denials of prior deportations material?*

Yes. A defendant's false "no" to whether he had ever been deported constitutes a material false statement. United States v. Wiggan, 673 F.2d 145 (6th Cir.), *cert. denied,* 456 U.S. 1011, 102 S. Ct. 2306 (1982).

§ 9.43. *What if the deportation is later overturned?*

It does not matter as the statement that he was not deported is false. United States v. Wiggan, 673 F.2d 145 (6th Cir.), *cert. denied,* 456 U.S. 1011, 102 S. Ct. 2306 (1982).

F. False Claims as to Citizenship: 18 U.S.C. § 911

§ 9.44. *What are the elements to false claim to citizenship?*

The government must prove three essential elements:

1. The defendant was an alien at the time alleged in the indictment;
2. The defendant falsely represented himself to be a citizen;
3. The defendant made such false representation willfully.

18 U.S.C. § 911. *See* United States v. Romero-Avila, 210 F.3d 1017 (9th Cir.) (rejecting the defense that the exact identity of the person lied to is an element of the offense), *cert. denied*, 531 U.S. 899, 121 S. Ct. 233 (2000).

§ 9.45. *What does "willfully" mean under 18 U.S.C. § 911?*

Willfully means only that the misrepresentation was voluntary and deliberate; the government need not prove the misrepresentation was for a fraudulent purpose. Chow Bing Kew v. United States, 248 F.2d 466 (9th Cir. 1957) (§ 911 amended a prior statute that required fraudulent purpose). *See also* United States v. Franklin, 188 F.2d 182 (7th Cir. 1951); De Pratu v. United States, 171 F.2d 75 (9th Cir. 1948).

§ 9.46. *Must the defendant specifically claim citizenship?*

Yes, a defendant must specifically state "I am a United States citizen" or present a false birth certificate. United States v. Rodriguez-Serrate, 534 F.2d 7 (1st Cir. 1976) (false birth certificate); Rodriguez v. United States, 433 F.2d 964, 965 (9th Cir. 1970); Smiley v. United States, 181 F.2d 505 (9th Cir.), *cert. denied*, 340 U.S. 817, 71 S. Ct. 48 (1950). *Cf.* United States v. Garcia, 739 F.2d 440 (9th Cir. 1984) (statement that defendant was "born in McAllen, Texas" not a violation of 18 U.S.C. § 911).

§ 9.47. *What is the penalty for false claim to U.S. citizenship?*

Under 18 U.S.C. § 911, any person who falsely and willfully represents her/himself to be a United States citizen may be fined and imprisoned for not more than three years. The Federal Sentencing Guidelines control the real sentence a given defendant faces. *See* **VI: Sentencing and Forfeiture**, *infra*.

§ 9.48. *What is the best defense?*

American citizenship is, of course, a complete defense to 18 U.S.C. § 911. Citizenship may be acquired by birth, naturalization, special act of Congress, or derivatively. *See* **Chapter 2, III: Citizenship and Naturalization**.

G. Fraud and Identity Documents: 18 U.S.C. § 1028

§ 9.49. *Is 18 U.S.C. § 1001 the only false statement statute an alien faces?*

No. An undocumented alien may also face prosecution under 18 U.S.C. § 1028, prohibiting fraud and related activity in connection with identification documents.

§ 9.50. *What conduct does 18 U.S.C. § 1028 punish?*

If a defendant uses, possesses, or assists others to use or possess a false government identification document it violates § 1028. The government can charge this offense as a felony or a misdemeanor, depending on circumstances.

§ 9.51. *What does the government need to prove?*

The government must prove "a sufficient connection between the defendant and the contraband to support the inference that the defendant exercised dominion and control over the substance." United States v. Barajas-Montiel, 185 F.3d 947, 955–56 (9th Cir. 1999) (conviction reversed where documents found in vase in defendant's bedroom that other persons occupied), *cert. denied*, 531 U.S. 849, 121 S. Ct. 123 (2000).

§ 9.52. *Does the statute cover fraudulent foreign documents?*

Yes, 18 U.S.C. § 1028's prohibitions include knowingly using a fraudulent foreign, international, or generic governmental identification.

§ 9.53. *What is the penalty?*

The penalty under 18 U.S.C. § 1028(b) may be 15 years or 20 if the defendant uses a false identity document to facilitate a drug crime and 25 to facilitate terrorism. The Federal Sentencing Guidelines control the real sentence a given defendant faces. *See* **VI: Sentencing and Forfeiture**, *infra*.

H. False Statements in Voting

§ 9.54. *Is it a crime for an alien to vote in a U.S. election?*

Yes, 18 U.S.C. § 611 makes it unlawful for an alien to vote in a federal election.

§ 9.55. *Is there a defense?*

Yes, under the following:

1. Defendant's parents were or are citizens;
2. Defendant permanently resided in the United States before age 16; and
3. Defendant reasonably believed at the time of voting that he was a citizen.

This exception applies retroactively to persons prosecuted on or after Sept. 30, 1996 unless criminal proceedings were concluded before Oct. 30, 2000.

I. False Claims for Welfare Benefits

§ 9.56. *What if an alien claims U.S. citizenship to get welfare?*

Under 18 U.S.C. § 1015(e) and § 1015(f), the government can prosecute aliens who make false claims of U.S. citizenship to receive a federal benefit.

V. Prosecutions and Trial Issues

A. Indictment

§ 9.57. *Must the indictment quote the false statement?*

No. The Fifth Amendment does not require that the indictment quote the purported misrepresentation. United States v. Bartle, 835 F.2d 646 (6th Cir. 1987), *cert. denied*, 485 U.S. 969, 108 S. Ct. 1245 (1988).

§ 9.58. *Must the indictment allege the alien entered the country?*

No, under most statutes the crime is complete when the person makes the false statement and therefore the indictment does not need to allege that the alien entered the country. United States v. Pizzarusso, 388 F.2d 8 (2d Cir.), *cert. denied*, 392 U.S. 936, 88 S. Ct. 2306 (1968).

B. Admissibility of Evidence

§ 9.59. *What document fraud evidence is admissible?*

Courts have allowed the accused's admissions as to his birthplace, United States v. Montemayor, 712 F.2d 104 (5th Cir. 1983), as well as evidence of prior similar conspiracy involving a codefendant to show *modus operandi*. United States v. Castro, 476 F.2d 750 (9th Cir. 1973). Moreover, evidence of an immigration official's ordinary procedure when taking statements is admissible. United States v. Kong Yin Chu [Chu Kong Yin], 5 F.3d 1244 (9th Cir. 1993). Courts have even allowed expert medical testimony to show that defendant and alien did not engage in sexual relationship to undermine the government's theory that defendants committed immigration fraud to import women for sex. United States v. Rushing, 313 F.3d 428 (8th Cir. 2002).

§ 9.60. *What about evidence of foreign convictions?*

At least one court holds that admitting evidence of defendant's alleged foreign convictions violates the Confrontation Clause. United States v. Kong Yin Chu [Chu Kong Yin], 935 F.2d 990 (9th Cir. 1991).

C. Defenses

§ 9.61. *Does an alien have the right to Miranda warnings?*

Yes, even noncitizens have Fifth Amendment rights under the Constitution. Thus, immigration agents have a duty to warn aliens of their constitutional rights before asking them a second time about their statements on immigration documents. United States v. Campos-Serrano, 430 F.2d 173 (7th Cir. 1970), *aff'd*, 404 U.S. 293, 92 S. Ct. 471 (1971).

§ 9.62. *What if the alien is ignorant of immigration law?*

This is not a valid defense. United States v. de Cruz, 82 F.3d 856 (9th Cir. 1996) (ignorance of law was not defense to knowingly receiving and accepting forged immigration documents). Moreover, the government may have the right to an instruction on deliberate indifference. *Id.*

§ 9.63. *Is there a justification defense?*

The justification defense is, of course, available when not committing the crime would cause a greater harm than committing the crime. This is not easy to show in the context of a false statement or document case. *See* United States v. Khalje, 658 F.2d 90 (2d Cir. 1981).

VI. Sentencing and Forfeiture

§ 9.64. *What are the penalties for immigration document fraud?*

The various statutes treated in this chapter present a range of statutory maximums, fines, and penalties. More pertinent, however, are the Federal Sentencing Guidelines. In response to Congress' increasing the statutory maximum sentences, the Sentencing Commission in 1997 increased the base offense level for immigration document fraud at §§ 2L2.1 and 2L2.2 by two offense levels. The Guidelines also added a specific offense characteristic for defendants who have one or more prior convictions for the same or similar conduct, and adjusted the current specific offense characteristics.

§ 9.65. *What about trafficking in immigration documents?*

Federal Sentencing Guideline § 2L2.1 provides for a base offense level of 11 but increases the offense level for the number of false documents as follows:

- 6-24 documents, 3 levels;
- 25-99 documents, 6 levels;
- 100 or more documents, 9 levels.

The Guideline also provides increases for the following:

- 4 levels if the defendant knew that the document was used for another, nonimmigration, crime;
- 2 levels if the defendant has a prior felony immigration conviction;
- 4 levels if he has two or more immigration felonies from separate prosecutions.

Guideline § 2L2.1 does provide for a decrease of three levels if the defendant did not commit the offense "for profit." United States v. Buenrostro-Torres, 24 F.3d 1173 (9th Cir. 1994) (evidence justified denial of reduction in defendant's sentencing offense level for producing false documents).

§ 9.66. *How is possession of false immigration documents punished?*

Federal Sentencing Guideline § 2L2.2 provides for a base offense level of eight. If the government had deported the defendant, add two levels. If the defendant has a prior immigration felony conviction, add two levels or, if he has two or more immigration felonies from separate prosecutions, add four levels.

§ 9.67. *What about civil forfeiture issues and document fraud?*

Title 18 U.S.C. § 982(a) now provides that a person convicted of 18 U.S.C. §§ 1425–27, 1541–44, 1546, or 18 U.S.C. § 1082, if committed in connection with passport or visa fraud, forfeits any conveyance he used during the crime. In addition, the defendant's real or personal property that he intended to use to facilitate the violation, and property traceable to the proceeds of the violation, are forfeited. 18 U.S.C. § 982(a)(6).

PART IV

REENTRY AFTER DEPORTATION AND ILLEGAL ENTRY

CHAPTER 10

ILLEGAL ENTRY AND REENTRY: PRETRIAL AND TRIAL

C. Challenging the Deportation Documents

D. Duress, Necessity, Corpus Delicti, Insanity

Other Resources:

DAN KESSELBRENNER & LORY D. ROSENBERG, IMMIGRATION LAW AND CRIME (2000).

Kurtis Kemper, Annotation, *Illegal Re-entry Under § 276 of Immigration and Nationality Act (8 U.S.C. § 1326) of Alien Who Has Been Denied Admission, Excluded, Deported, or Removed or Has Departed the United States by Order of Exclusion, Deportation, or Removal is Outstanding*, 177 A.L.R. FED. 459 (2002).

Introduction

§ 10.1. *What is this chapter about?*

This chapter focuses on pretrial and trial issues of federal prosecutions for violations of 8 U.S.C. § 1326, illegal reentry after deportation and, to a lesser extent, 8 U.S.C. § 1325, illegal entry. Federal prosecutors and defense attorneys will be most interested in this chapter, but, given the changes in immigration policy, even state criminal lawyers should review these crimes. *See* Carol Nagengast, *Militarizing the Border Patrol*, XXXII: 32:3 NACLA REPORT ON THE AMERICAS 37 (Nov./Dec. 1998).

The genesis of this chapter is Robert J. McWhirter & Jon Sands, *A Primer for Defending a Criminal Immigration Case*, 8 GEO. IMMIGR. L.J. 23 (1994).

§ 10.2. *What has changed in the government?*

What used to be the Immigration and Naturalization Service (INS) in the Department of Justice is now primarily Immigration and Customs Enforcement (ICE) in the Department of Homeland Security (DHS). *See* **Chapter 2, I, § 2.6. *How was the INS chopped up?*.** Generally, this chapter will use the ICE label except when referring to case law with the INS title. Also, this chapter uses the terms "removal" and "deportation" interchangeably, though in most circumstances the correct legal term is now "removal."

§ 10.3. *What has changed in border crime and prosecution?*

This book's first edition noted a drastic increase in reentry prosecutions. *See generally Caseloads Swamp Border Courts*, 31:10 NEWSLETTER OF FED. CTS., ADMIN. OFF. U.S. CTS. (Oct. 1999); Michael O'Connor & Celia Rumann, *The Death of Advocacy in Reentry After Deportation Cases*, THE CHAMPION, Nov. 1999, at 42 (citing statistics and outlining ethical problems attendant to prosecuting the large numbers of these cases). This increase has been the trend since the Illegal Immigration Reform and Immigrant Responsibility Act of 1996 (IIRAIRA).

In fiscal year 2000, U.S. Attorney offices received 16,495 referrals with suspected immigration offenses as the most serious charge — more than double from 1985. THE BUREAU OF JUSTICE STATISTICS SPECIAL REPORT, UNITED STATES DEPARTMENT OF JUSTICE, OFFICE OF JUSTICE PROGRAMS, August 2002, NCJ 191745. (There has also been a corresponding increase in the number of noncitizens the government charged with other offenses, particularly drug trafficking offenses, from 1,799 in 1985 to 7,803 in 2000. *Id.*). Roughly 75% of this increase between 1996 and 2000 were in the five states along the Mexican border. *Id.* Also, the number of immigration law enforcement officers increased from 12,403 to 17,654 with the border patrol receiving almost two-thirds of the additional officers. *Id.* Also, in the various border patrol sectors programs have been implemented across the southwest border including *Operation Gatekeeper* in San Diego and Imperial Valley, *Operation Safeguard* in Arizona, *Operation Hold the Line* in El Paso, and *Operation Rio Grande* in South Texas. Consequently, reentry cases flooded federal courts — for example, making up 35.4% of the Ninth Circuit's fiscal year 2001 docket.

Fifty-seven percent of suspected immigration offenders were Mexicans, seven percent U.S. citizens, three percent Chinese, and 28% all other nationalities. The government most often charged Mexicans (87%) and Chinese (93%) with unlawful entry or reentry and U.S. citizens (64%) with alien smuggling. *Id.*

I. Elements and Statutory Application

§ 10.4. *What are the elements of illegal entry?*

For illegal entry, 8 U.S.C. § 1325, the government must prove the defendant is the following:

1. An alien;
2. Who entered or attempted to enter the United States at a time or place other than that designated by immigration officers;
3. Who made false or misleading representations and/or concealed a material fact.

§ 10.5. *What are the elements of reentry after deportation?*

For reentry after deportation, 8 U.S.C. § 1326, the government must prove the defendant was the following:

1. An alien;
2. Previously arrested and lawfully deported, excluded, or removed (with proof that he left while an order or deportation was outstanding);
3. Found in the United States;
4. Without the consent of the Department of Homeland Security.

Section 1326 provides three different statutory maximums:

1. A two-year maximum for defendants who reenter after deportation with no felony convictions;
2. A 10-year maximum for defendants who reenter after a felony conviction or three misdemeanor convictions for crimes against a person or drug crimes; and
3. A 20-year maximum for defendants who reenter after an aggravated felony conviction defined at 8 U.S.C. § 1101(a)(43).

See United States v. Rivera-Sillas, 376 F.3d 887 (9th Cir.) (reentry is general intent crime meaning intent element satisfied with defendant's commission of a voluntary act), *amended by* 417 F.3d 1014 (9th Cir. 2004); 2005 U.S. App. LEXIS 18302 (9th Cir. Aug. 25, 2005).

Currently, the prosecutor need not prove prior felonies at trial because they are sentencing enhancements, Almendarez-Torres v. United States, 523 U.S. 224, 118 S. Ct. 1219 (1998), though the Supreme Court's decision in *Apprendi v. New Jersey*, 530 U.S. 466, 120 S. Ct. 2348 (2000) specifically called this holding into question as does the recent holding in *Blakely v. Washington*, 542 U.S. 296, 124 S. Ct. 2531 (2004).

§ 10.6. *How does illegal entry differ from the reentry statute?*

Illegal entry and reentry after deportation are closely related crimes and share common elements such as alienage. The two statutes, however, define different offenses requiring proofs of distinct *actus reus* and *mens rea*. Under the illegal entry statute, 8 U.S.C. § 1325, the government must prove the defendant's entry was illegal. Under the reentry after deportation statute, 8 U.S.C. § 1326, the government need prove only that the defendant was "found in" the United States. *See, e.g.*, United States v. Ebolum, 72 F.3d 35 (6th Cir. 1995) (applicable sentencing guidelines are those in effect when the defendant was "found in" the United States, rather than when he illegally reentered).

§ 10.7. *How are the statutes enforced?*

The government can charge with illegal entry any alien caught entering the United States without inspection or by fraud. The first conviction is a misdemeanor but later convictions are felonies. 8 U.S.C. § 1325. *See* United States v. Arambula-Alvarado, 677 F.2d 51 (9th Cir. 1982) (in felony § 1325 prosecution, government must prove prior conviction not merely just illegal entry).

Although the government could prosecute any alien who enters illegally, it does not criminally prosecute the vast majority. Rather, the Bureau of Immigration and Customs Enforcement (ICE) (the former INS), the Executive Office of Immigration Review (which include immigration courts), and the Board of Immigration Appeals (BIA) administratively handle the case through various civil mechanisms including "voluntary return" and deportation. Deportations are "civil," even though they may result "in loss of both property and life; or of all that makes life worth living." Ng Fung Ho v. White, 259 U.S. 276, 284, 42 S. Ct. 492 (1922).

§ 10.8. *What about appointed counsel with a misdemeanor 8 U.S.C. § 1325 charge?*

Alabama v. Shelton, 535 U.S. 654, 122 S. Ct. 1764 (2002), clarified that even defendants charged with misdemeanors have a right to court appointed counsel. *Shelton* raises the question as to whether prior uncounseled § 1325 misdemeanor convictions can later "felonize" an illegal entry prosecution as well as whether such a conviction can add criminal history points under Federal Sentencing Guideline § 4A1.1(b)-(e).

§ 10.9. *When does reentry after deportation begin and end?*

Reentry after deportation is a "continuing offense" starting when the defendant "enters" the country and is not completed until the defendant is "found in" the United States. United States v. Mendez-Casillas, 272 F.3d 1199 (9th Cir. 2001); United States v. Ramirez-Valencia, 202 F.3d 1106, 1110 (9th Cir.), *cert. denied*, 531 U.S. 892, 121 S. Ct. 218 (2000).

§ 10.10. *If an alien is deported for a specific number of years, does he still violate 8 U.S.C. § 1326 if he enters after that time?*

Yes. If the alien who was deported enters without the consent of the Department of Homeland Security, regardless of when he enters, he can be charged with reentry after deportation. *But see* United States v. Idowu, 105 F.3d 728 (D.C. Cir. 1997) (possible jury defense in the defendant's mistaken belief that he could reenter after the five-year period of his deportation); *contra* Eric H. Singer, United States v. Idowu: *Inadmissibility and Unlawful Reentry After Deportation — Still Confused After All These Years*, 29 SW. U. L. REV. 301 (2000).

§ 10.11. *Can the government charge a U.S. citizen or U.S. national with these crimes?*

No. Both illegal entry in violation of 8 U.S.C. § 1325 and reentry after deportation in violation of 8 U.S.C. § 1326 have "alienage" as an element. An alien is any person who is not a national or citizen of the United States. 8 U.S.C. § 1101(a)(3). A national is a person owing permanent allegiance to the United States, even though not a citizen. 8 U.S.C. § 1101(a)(21), (22). *See* **Chapter 2: Immigration Law for Criminal Lawyers**. A defendant in a reentry case does not have the right to a jury instruction that a "national" is not an alien or to a definition of national to the jury. United States v. Sotelo, 109 F.3d 1446 (9th Cir. 1997).

As an aside, 8 U.S.C. § 1358 guarantees the right of Native Americans born in Canada to enter the United States so long as they have 50 percent blood of an American Indian tribe.

II. Detention Issues

§ 10.12. *Can an immigration defendant be released on bail?*

Yes. The Bail Reform Act of 1984 controls. 18 U.S.C. § 3041 (1985). A defendant will be released unless the government proves he is either (1) a danger to the community by clear and convincing evidence, or (2) a serious flight risk by a preponderance of the evidence. 18 U.S.C. §§ 3142(d)(1)(B), 3142(d)(2). Criminal immigration cases do not change, at least officially, the presumption that the court should release a defendant pending trial. Defendants charged with immigration crimes, however, are usually detained as a flight risk because they lack "contacts with the community." In practice, therefore, a systemic presumption detains the defendant, which arguably violates the Bail Reform Act. *See* United States v. Townsend, 897 F.2d 989, 994 (9th Cir. 1990) ("That the defendant is an alien may be taken into account, but alienage does not by itself 'tip the balance either for or against detention'."), *quoting* United States v. Motamedi, 767 F.2d 1403, 1408 (9th Cir. 1985); *Motamedi*, 767 F.2d at 1408 ("alienage ... may be taken into account, but it does not point conclusively to a determination [of] a serious risk of flight"); *see also* United States v. Adomako, 150 F. Supp. 2d 1302 (M.D. Fla. 2001) (district court decision to release a criminal defendant under Bail Reform Act supercedes the INS' authority to take defendant into custody).

§ 10.13. *What is a "lodged detainer"?*

Often, the court may deny the defendant's release because ICE has lodged a detainer or "hold" on the defendant. If the defendant is released from federal custody, the government can take him into ICE custody and he will spend his time in an ICE detention center pending immigration proceedings. In ICE custody, however, the defendant can often post bond. IRA J. KURZBAN, KURZBAN'S IMMIGRATION LAW SOURCEBOOK (9th ed. 2004).

§ 10.14. *What if the immigration judge denies the defendant's release?*

The defendant has the option of a habeas corpus action to federal court. Although 8 U.S.C. § 1226(c) authorizes ICE to detain aliens, in the context of aliens charged with federal crimes, this statute appears to conflict with the Bail Reform Act, 18 U.S.C. § 3142(d).

ICE's use of § 1226(c) to detain aliens released under the Bail Reform Act is a substantive violation of due process because the federal criminal court has already determined that a defendant released on bond is not a flight risk or danger to the community.

There may even be a separation of powers argument given that ICE, like the United States attorney, is an executive branch agency. Thus, by detaining the defendant it is unconstitutionally interfering with the judiciary's ability to perform its duty under the Bail Reform Act.

§ 10.15. *If the habeas corpus action is not practical, what benefit is there for a defendant to get released to an ICE hold?*

An ICE detention center arguably offers better lifestyle than jail. In addition, having a defendant released to ICE custody can prove a windfall to the alien, because defendants in ICE custody are sometimes deported. When this happens, the government really has no choice but to dismiss the original charge of illegal entry or reentry after deportation. One argument is that the government has deprived itself of *in personam* jurisdiction. *See* Pennoyer v. Neff, 95 U.S. 714 (5 Otto), 24 L.Ed. 565 (1878).

One concern, however, is that the defendant may have trouble getting credit for time served if he is in ICE instead of federal criminal custody.

§ 10.16. *What is an aggravated felon's chance of release?*

Not very good, as aggravated felons almost certainly get detained. If the federal court releases the defendant who is an aggravated felon as defined at 8 U.S.C. § 1101(a)(43), ICE generally will take him into custody and hold him without bond. Barring a habeas action explained *supra*, an attempt to gain federal criminal court release is usually futile.

If, however, the defendant's aggravated felony is old, it might not preclude release on immigration bond, unless the defendant was recently released from custody for that crime. *See* Pastor-Camarena v. Smith, 977 F. Supp. 1415, 1417 (W.D. Wash. 1997) (statute precluding release of aggravated felons by ICE "applies immediately after release from incarceration, not to aliens released many years earlier"). But in another context the Supreme Court has held that Congress could require an alien's detention for removal proceedings without an individualized determination as to flight risk. Demore v. Hyung Joon Kim, 538 U.S. 510, 123 S. Ct. 1708 (2003), *rev'g* 276 F.3d 523 (9th Cir. 2002) (legal permanent resident cannot be categorically denied bail without individualized determination).

III. Trial Preparation and the Preliminary Hearing

§ 10.17. *What is special about investigating a criminal immigration case?*

In many districts the Assistant U.S. Attorney will offer the defendant an "open file" for waiving the preliminary hearing. *See* FED. R. CRIM. P. 16. Generally, this is not a bad idea for both sides, because cases involving illegal entry and reentry after deportation are essentially "paper cases." The defense attorney, however, can obtain the relevant evidence from other sources, such as the immigration court.

§ 10.18. *What information is important from the beginning?*

The most important information to obtain in the early stages is the defendant's ICE alien number, or "A" number. ICE uses the A number to classify aliens under its jurisdiction. The A number is often contained in the statement of probable cause connected with the criminal complaint, or the attorney can ask it of the prosecutor or ICE agent. (Keep in mind that a defendant can have more than one "A" number/file.) Using this number, the defense attorney can independently obtain much of the information necessary to defend the case.

§ 10.19. *What information is in the A-file?*

The A-file may indicate identification problems such as whether ICE failed to maintain fingerprints and other data to connect the defendant to the crime or record. It may also hold evidence that would support a good faith belief in citizenship or the right to remain in the United States, such as an application for permanent resident status.

§ 10.20. *What about information from the immigration court hearing?*

As outlined in **Chapter 2: Immigration Law for Criminal Lawyers,** during a deportation hearing ICE presents the case to the immigration judge. Using the A-number, counsel can obtain the immigration court documents and tape of the hearing to review whether there was any legal problem with the deportation. Sometimes, immigration courts display the same lethargy as the rest of ICE. In such a case, the defense attorney should wait until indictment and then subpoena the documents and tape from immigration court. *See* FED. R. CRIM. P. 17(c).

Tapes of the proceedings will reveal such things as the number of aliens present at a "Master Calendar Hearing" and may also reveal potential problems with the translation of the immigration judge's statements and the aliens' responses. These are the types of deficiencies that might demonstrate a fundamental unfairness in the deportation and thus constitute a defense to the charge.

§ 10.21. *What should a lawyer consider at the preliminary hearing?*

The testifying ICE officer is usually not the same person who arrested the defendant. His testimony comes from reading reports of other agents and the A-file. After laying this foundation, the defense attorney has the right to view reports from those agents and may have the right to view the A-file. *See* FED. R. CRIM. P. 26.2(a).

§ 10.22. *What about records of prior criminal convictions?*

If the defendant's charge is reentry as a felon or aggravated felon, 8 U.S.C. § 1326(b)(1), (2), the attorney should send for or subpoena *all* records and transcripts of the defendant's prior conviction(s). First, if the convictions are somehow invalid and the defendant was deported because of them, there is a basis to collaterally attack the deportation. Second, discovered defects in the prior convictions may preclude their use for a later sentencing enhancement.

IV. Pretrial Motions

A. Motions to Suppress

1. Statements

§ 10.23. *Who can border patrol and immigration agents question?*

Border patrol agents have authority to question anyone they believe an illegal alien. They generally request biographical data regarding citizenship and manner of entry while filling out form I-213, Record of Deportable Alien. To obtain the alien's statements, the agents generally will give the alien administrative/immigration court warnings that look like *Miranda* warnings but differ in several key aspects. Agents will often use these administrative warnings when they make jail sweeps under the Criminal Alien Return Program (C.A.R.P.), looking for criminal aliens who are then charged with immigration crimes and put in removal proceedings.

§ 10.24. *Do ICE agents have to give Miranda warnings?*

Not for the deportation hearing. Statements the alien makes during the administrative investigation are admissible during an alien's deportation hearing but cannot be used in a later criminal trial unless the alien was *Mirandized* and the statements were voluntary. United States v. Gonzalez-Sandoval, 894 F.2d 1043, 1047 (9th Cir. 1990); United States v. Mata-Abundiz, 717 F.2d 1277, 1280 (9th Cir. 1983).

In a strange distinction, the Ninth Circuit has held that an ICE officer need not give *Miranda* warnings to a defendant in jail on unrelated state charges so long as the questions go to the administrative action; but that if the defendant later reenters the statements can be used against him in this later criminal proceeding. United States v. Salgado, 292 F.3d 1169 (9th Cir.), *cert. denied,* 537 U.S. 1011, 123 S. Ct. 479 (2002).

§ 10.25. *How is "custody" determined for Miranda analysis?*

The law seems unclear on the question of when an alien is in custody for purposes of *Miranda* analysis. In *United States v. Galindo-Gallegos,* 244 F.3d 728 (9th Cir.), *amended by* 255 F.3d 1154 (9th Cir. 2001), the court held that aliens caught near the border are not in custody. In *United States v. Beraun-Panez,* 812 F.2d 578, 580–82 (9th Cir.), *modified by* 830 F.2d 127 (9th Cir. 1987), the court found on nearly identical facts that the aliens were in custody.

§ 10.26. *What about when the alien gets more than one set of warnings?*

A defendant must understand *Miranda* rights to validly waive them. If ICE gives administrative warnings, which among other things tells the defendant that he cannot have a court appointed lawyer, and then later gives the defendant full-fledged *Miranda* warnings, it may create great confusion for an unsophisticated defendant. Thus, if the agent gives the defendant both warnings and does not clarify the confusion by telling the defendant to ignore the administrative warnings or explain that the *Miranda* warnings supercede, there is not a valid waiver of the right to remain silent. *See* United States v. San Juan-Cruz, 314 F.3d 384 (9th Cir. 2002).

§ 10.27. *What about statements during deportation hearings?*

Prosecutors will naturally seek to admit the defendant's deportation hearing statements in addition to documents such as the Order to Show Cause (now called Notice to Appear) and Order of Deportation (now Order of Removal). These statements and documents should be suppressed at a later criminal trial because the "immigration judge" is not a judge but a "special inquiry officer" with the same delegated authority from the attorney general as a border patrol officer or immigration agent. See 8 C.F.R. § 3.16. The Ninth Circuit, with little reasoning, ruled that the Fifth Amendment does not require *Miranda* warnings at a deportation hearing, despite the fact that the defendant may incriminate himself. United States v. Solano-Godines, 120 F.3d 957 (9th Cir.), *supplemented*, 1997 U.S. App. LEXIS 18904 (9th Cir. July 21, 1997).

§ 10.28. *What happens if the defendant's statements are suppressed?*

The alien's statements often are the only of evidence the prosecutor has on the alienage element. *See* United States v. Meza-Soria, 935 F.2d 166 (9th Cir. 1991). If these statements are suppressed, then the case is likely to be dismissed.

2. Defendant's Body/Identity

§ 10.29. *Can a defendant's identity be suppressed?*

This may be an emerging issue. In *United States v. Garcia-Beltran*, 389 F.3d 864 (9th Cir. 2004), the court held that while the simple fact of who the defendant is cannot be excluded, a court may suppress other evidence showing identity such as fingerprints if the police obtained them "to pursuer a criminal immigration violation." Thus, if the alien was arrested illegally, evidence of his identity that resulted from the arrest may be suppressible. Because the government must prove the defendant was "found in" the United States, it stands to reason that if he was "found" by some government misconduct the court should suppress this evidence. *Garcia-Beltran* distinguished *United States v. Guzman-Bruno*, 27 F.3d 420, 422–23 (9th Cir.) (presently no Fourth Amendment right to suppress the body), *cert. denied*, 513 U.S. 975, 115 S. Ct. 451 (1994), and other cases that had been unreceptive to this issue. *See* United States v. Del Toro Gudino, 376 F.3d 997 (9th Cir. 2004) (defendant's identity is not suppressible even if stop or arrest was illegal), *cert. denied*, 125 S. Ct. 1356 (2005); United States v. Parga-Rosas, 238 F.3d 1209 (9th Cir.), *cert. denied*, 534 U.S. 942, 122 S. Ct. 319 (2001); *cf.* Muehler v. Mena, 125 S. Ct. 1465 (2005) (immigration authorities do not need reasonable suspicion during detention to justify questioning).

The theory that a defendant's identity may be suppressed may run afoul of dicta in *INS v. Lopez-Mendoza*, that "[t]he 'body' or identity of a defendant or respondent in a criminal or civil proceeding is never itself suppressible as a fruit of an unlawful arrest, even if it is conceded that an unlawful arrest, search, or interrogation occurred." 468 U.S. 1032, 1039, 104 S. Ct. 3479 (1984). *Lopez-Mendoza* did state, however, that its holding was "[c]onsistent with the civil nature of the [deportation] proceeding ..." and that "various protections that apply in the context of a criminal trial do not apply in a deportation hearing." 468 U.S. at 1038. However, in dicta from *Hiibel v. Sixth Judicial District Court of Nevada*, 542 U.S. 177, 124 S. Ct. 2451, *reh'g denied*, 125 S. Ct. 18 (2004), the Supreme Court suggests that the Fifth Amendment may furnish the right to suppress an identity:

> [A] case may arise where there is a substantial allegation that furnishing identity at the time of a stop would have given the police a link in the chain of evidence needed to convict the individual of a separate offense. In that case, the court can then consider whether the privilege applies, and, if the Fifth Amendment has been violated, what remedy must follow.

Hiibel, 124 S. Ct. at 2461. *See also* Florida v. Perkins, 760 So. 2d 85 (Fla.), *cert. denied*, 531 U.S. 1029, 121 S. Ct. 606 (2000). This issue may have more currency if the seizure is motivated by something like race or other egregious agent misconduct. *See generally* Daniel P. Blank, *Suppressing Defendant's Identity and Other Strategies for Defending Against a Charge of Illegal Re-entry after Deportation*, 50 STAN. L. REV. 139 (1997).

B. Motions to Dismiss

1. Statute of Limitations and Speedy Trial

§ 10.30. *How does the statute of limitations work?*

Neither crime of illegal entry or reentry has its own statute of limitations as both rely on the general five-year statute. *See* 18 U.S.C. § 3282. For illegal entry, however, the five years begins when the defendant actually entered the United States, because 8 U.S.C. § 1325 is not a continuing offense after the alien has entered. Conversely, for reentry after deportation, the statute does not begin until the alien is "found in" the United States. United States v. Rincon-Jimenez, 595 F.2d 1192 (9th Cir. 1979). This is because the offense is "continuing" until the defendant is "found in the United States United States v. Rivera-Ventura, 72 F.3d 277 (2d Cir. 1995). An alien is "found in" when his presence is first noted by the immigration authorities. United States v. DiSantillo, 615 F.2d 128 (3d Cir. 1980). Thus, if ICE has notice of an alien's presence and does nothing for five years, the statute has run.

§ 10.31. *When does the Speedy Trial Act run?*

Although ICE may detain a defendant, the Speedy Trial Act is not triggered until the U.S. Marshal executes a warrant pursuant to the illegal reentry indictment. United States v. Vasquez-Escobar, 30 F. Supp. 2d 1364 (M.D. Fla. 1998) (under Speedy Trial Act defendant "arrested" when federal government detained him specifically for illegally reentering the United States). Conversely, if the government uses deportation detentions as "'mere ruses to detain a defendant for later criminal prosecution'" the Speedy Trial Act applies. United States v. Drummond, 240 F.3d 1333, 1336 (11th Cir. 2001), *quoting* United States v. Noel, 231 F.3d 833, 836 (11th Cir. 2000), *cert. denied*, 531 U.S. 1200, 121 S. Ct. 1208 (2001). To invoke the exception, the defendant must establish that the "primary or exclusive purpose ... was to hold him for future prosecution." *Drummond*, 240 F.3d at 1336, *quoting Noel*; United States v. Restrepo, 59 F. Supp. 2d 133 (D. Mass 1999) (Speedy Trial Act may apply if ICE detains an alien longer than necessary for deportation to develop criminal case for the same conduct).

2. Collateral Attacks on Deportation

This section will outline the legal basis for a collateral attack of a deportation, present the procedural defect and prejudice prong of the attack, and treat other related issues.

a. Legal Basis

§ 10.32. *What is the legal basis of a collateral attack on the deportation?*

In *United States v. Mendoza-Lopez*, 481 U.S. 828, 837, 838 n.15, 107 S. Ct. 2148 (1987), the Supreme Court held that a deportation order can establish an element of a crime only if the alien had the opportunity to obtain meaningful judicial review. *Mendoza-Lopez* did not refer to the Board of Immigration Appeals but rather Article III courts. Thus, if the tape of the deportation hearing or any other document shows the defendant did not have the chance to appeal the deportation judge's order, that deportation cannot form the basis of the charge of reentry after deportation. *See, e.g.*, Barker v. Wingo, 407 U.S. 514, 525, 92 S. Ct. 2182, 2189–90 (1972) (court should indulge every reasonable presumption against waiver); United States v. Proa-Tovar, 945 F.2d 1450, 1452 (9th Cir. 1991), *reh'g en banc*, 975 F.2d 592 (9th Cir. 1992). Prior authority on this issue included *United States v. Rangel-Gonzales*, 617 F.2d 529 (9th Cir. 1980) and *United States v. Calderon-Medina*, 591 F.2d 529 (9th Cir. 1979).

§ 10.33. *Why raise a challenge to the deportation in a pretrial motion?*

Despite the fact that a lawful deportation is the basis of reentry after deportation, a judge decides this question. United States v. Alvarado-Delgado, 98 F.3d 492, 493 (9th Cir. 1996) (en banc), *cert. denied*, 519 U.S. 1155, 117 S. Ct. 1096 (1997), *overruling* United States v. Ibarra, 3 F.3d 1333 (9th Cir. 1993), *cert. denied*, 510 U.S. 1205, 114 S. Ct. 1327 (1994). *See also* 8 U.S.C. § 1252(b)(7)(A)). There may be a chance to argue, however, that a unique factual issue relating to the deportation exists that requires jury determination. The law before was ambiguous on when to raise the challenge. *See, e.g.*, United States v. Bejar-Matrecios, 618 F.2d 81 (9th Cir. 1980).

§ 10.34. *Aside from dismissal, what other remedies exist?*

The district court can remand the case for another deportation hearing, "with instructions to apply the law as it existed at the time" of the original hearing. United States v. Castillo-Perez, 212 F.3d 518, 528 (9th Cir. 2000).

§ 10.35. *What establishes a collateral attack of the deportation?*

To collaterally attack a deportation the defendant must establish two prongs: (1) The deportation was procedurally defective; (2) the defendant was prejudiced.

The first prong, procedural defect, comes from *United States v. Mendoza-Lopez*, 481 U.S. 828, 107 S. Ct. 2148 (1987).

The second prong, defendant's prejudice, is not in *Mendoza-Lopez*, but most of the circuits read *Mendoza-Lopez* as requiring the defendant to show prejudice. *Compare* United States v. Proa-Tovar, 945 F.2d 1450 (9th Cir. 1991) (defendant need not show prejudice) *with* United States v. Proa-Tovar, 975 F.2d 592 (9th Cir. 1992) (en banc) (defendant must show prejudice from the deportation hearing); *see also* United States v. Arrieta, 224 F.3d 1076, 1079 (9th Cir. 2000); United States v. Fares, 978 F.2d 52, 57 (2d Cir. 1992); United States v. Campbell, 967 F.2d 20 (2d Cir. 1992); United States v. Encarnacion-Galvez, 964 F.2d 402, 407 (5th Cir.), *cert. denied*, 506 U.S. 945, 113 S. Ct. 391 (1992); United States v. Holland, 876 F.2d 1533 (11th Cir. 1989).

Even before *Mendoza-Lopez*, the Ninth Circuit had adopted a "two-step test to determine whether a violation of the given regulation invalidated the deportation" which outlined the need to show procedural defect and prejudice. United States v. Rangel-Gonzales, 617 F.2d 529 (9th Cir. 1980); United States v. Calderon-Medina, 591 F.2d 529 (9th Cir. 1979) (citing 8 C.F.R. § 242-2E (1979); INS failure to advise a defendant of his right to consult with the Mexican consulate created a procedural defect). *See also* United States v. Gasca-Kraft, 522 F.2d 149 (9th Cir. 1975)

§ 10.36. *Who has the burden of proving the collateral attack?*

Several recent cases have held that the defendant bears the burden of proving that he was prejudiced from the defect that occurred in his deportation hearing. *See, e.g.,* United States v. Leon-Leon, 35 F.3d 1428 (9th Cir. 1994). These cases do not explore this question in great depth and older case law states that the defendant only has the burden of demonstrating a *prima facie* showing and then the burden shifts back to the government to prove the validity of the deportation. *See* United States v. Rangel-Gonzales, 617 F.2d 529 (9th Cir. 1980); United States v. Calderon-Medina, 591 F.2d 529 (9th Cir. 1979).

§ 10.37. *Has Congress tried to change collateral attack law?*

Yes. With the Anti-Terrorism and Effective Death Penalty Act of 1996, Congress amended 8 U.S.C. § 1326(d) to state that a collateral attack is prohibited on the underlying deportation or removal order unless the alien could prove (1) all other administrative remedies for relief had been sought; (2) the deportation proceedings deprived the alien of judicial review; and (3) the deportation was fundamentally unfair. This provision incorporates part of the *Mendoza-Lopez* standard but adds other requirements that contravene the *Mendoza-Lopez* standard. *See* United States v. Mendoza-Lopez, 481 U.S. 828, 107 S. Ct. 2148 (1987). Moreover, this particular provision conflicts with another part of the Terrorism Act at 8 U.S.C. § 1252(a)(2)(C), stating that no court may even hear a collateral attack on the deportation based on certain criminal convictions. *But see* United States v. Arce-Hernandez, 163 F.3d 559 (9th Cir. 1998), *amended, reh'g denied*, 1999 U.S. App. LEXIS 3823 (9th Cir. Cal. Mar. 11, 1999).

§ 10.38. *Did Congress try to eliminate judicial review of deportations?*

It appears so. In 1996 Congress modified 8 U.S.C. § 1252(a)(2)(C) to statutorily eliminate judicial review of deportations based on most criminal convictions:

> Not withstanding any other provision of law, no court shall have jurisdiction to review any final order of removal against an alien who is removable by reason of having committed a criminal offense covered in § ...1227(a)(2)(A)(3), (b) ....

This contradicts *United States v. Mendoza-Lopez*, 481 U.S. 828, 107 S. Ct. 2148 (1987), which guarantees that a deportation cannot form the basis of the reentry charge unless the alien had the right to "meaningful judicial review."

The only way to give effect to both 8 U.S.C. § 1326(d), allowing collateral attacks, and 8 U.S.C. § 1252(a)(2)(C), prohibiting collateral attacks, is to read § 1252(a)(2)(C) as applying to "an alien who is removable by reason of having committed a criminal offense ...," meaning § 1326(d) only applies to aliens not deported for a criminal conviction.

§ 10.39. *What about aliens deported on old aggravated felonies?*

An alien should win a collateral attack on his deportation because of an old criminal conviction if the conviction was for a felony that later became an aggravated felony. Thus, if the defendant alien pled to a crime that was not an aggravated felony and later was deported because it became one, the alien can challenge the deportation at his reentry. United States v. Ubaldo-Figueroa, 364 F.3d 1042 (9th Cir. 2003) (applying INS v. St. Cyr, 533 U.S. 289, 121 S. Ct. 2271 (2001)).

b. Procedural Defect

§ 10.40. *What is a "procedural defect?*

Under *Mendoza-Lopez* a procedural defect occurs when the deportation denies the alien "meaningful review":

> Our cases establish that where a determination made in an administrative proceeding is to play a critical role in the subsequent imposition of a criminal sanction, there must be *some* meaningful judicial review of the administrative proceeding.

United States v. Mendoza-Lopez, 481 U.S. 828, 837–38, 107 S. Ct. 2148 (1987) (emphasis in original). *Mendoza-Lopez* was based on the Due Process Clause of the Constitution. Thus, where what occurred in the prior deportation denied the alien of judicial review the hearing was procedurally defective.

Various examples of procedural defects follow but for a more complete listing of immigration court procedures and requirements *see* **Chapter 2: Immigration Law for Criminal Lawyers**.

§ 10.41. *What are an alien's rights to notice?*

Due process requires that ICE serve notice to the potential deportee in a manner reasonably calculated to advise him of the proceedings. Farhoud v. INS, 122 F.3d 794, 796 (9th Cir. 1997). The notice must inform him of the consequences resulting from a deportation order. Walters v. Reno, 145 F.3d 1032, 1042–43 (9th Cir. 1998), *cert. denied*, 526 U.S. 1003, 119 S. Ct. 1140 (1999). Under ICE regulations the alien has the responsibility to keep ICE advised of a valid address. Thus, sending the notice to the last known address is permissible and ICE need not show that the notice was actually received. Arrieta v. INS, 117 F.3d 429 (9th Cir. 1997). *See In re* Grijalva, 21 I&N Dec. 27 (BIA 1995) (en banc). If notice never reached the address, however, the immigration court should hold a hearing. *Arrieta v. INS.* The immigrant cannot waive an in-person hearing simply by failing to request one. United States v. Contreras, 63 F.3d 852, 856 (9th Cir. 1995). Thus, if there was no deportation hearing, counsel should see if the alien waived the hearing knowingly, voluntarily, and intelligently. *Walters*, 145 F.3d at 1037. *See* **Chapter 2: Immigration Law for Criminal Lawyers.**

§ 10.42. *What is the alien's right to counsel at a deportation hearing?*

Under the INA at 8 U.S.C. § 1229a(b)(4)(A) and the Fifth Amendment, an alien has the right to counsel at his deportation hearing, but not free counsel. *See* United States v. Lara-Aceves, 183 F.3d 1007, 1012 (9th Cir. 1999), *cert. denied*, 528 U.S. 1095, 120 S. Ct. 836 (2000); *see generally* NATIONAL LAWYERS GUILD, IMMIGRATION LAW AND DEFENSE Chapter 7 (2000 ed.) (explaining right to counsel at deportation). Although counsel is not free to the alien, the immigration judge has the duty to advise the respondent of his right to representation, including the availability of pro bono legal services. 8 C.F.R. § 240.10(a). The alien has several other guarantees connected with the right to counsel. *See, e.g.*, 8 C.F.R. § 3.29 (alien has the automatic right to one continuance to obtain counsel); 8 C.F.R. § 240.6 (right to further continuances to obtain counsel upon a showing of good cause); Escobar-Grijalva v. INS, 206 F.3d 1331, 1335 (9th Cir.) (reversal of deportation where immigration judge failed to clarify whether the immigrant had consented to representation by the lawyer present), *amended by* 213 F.3d 1221; 216 F.3d 807 (9th Cir. 2000).

§ 10.43. *What are the alien's rights to effective assistance?*

"'Ineffective assistance of counsel in a deportation proceeding is a denial of due process under the Fifth Amendment if the proceeding was so fundamentally unfair that the alien was prevented from reasonably presenting his case.'" Ortiz v. INS, 179 F.3d 1148, 1153 (9th Cir. 1999) (quoting *Lopez v. INS*, 775 F.2d 1015, 1017 (9th Cir. 1985)), *subsequent appeal remanded by* Ortiz v. Ashcroft, 95

Fed. Appx. 862 (2004). *See also* Ontiveros-Lopez v. INS, 213 F.3d 1121 (9th Cir. 2000); *In re* Lozada, 19 I&N Dec. 637 (BIA), *rev. denied by* Lozada v. INS, 857 F.2d 10 (1st Cir. 1988) (defining BIA's requirements of specific procedures for appeals of deportation orders based on ineffective assistance of counsel).

For example, "where an alien is prevented from filing an appeal in an immigration proceeding due to counsel's error, the error deprives the alien of the appellate proceeding entirely," creating presumption of prejudice because "'the adversary process itself' has been rendered 'presumptively unreliable.'" Dearinger ex rel. Volkova v. Reno, 232 F.3d 1042, 1045 (9th Cir. 2000) (quoting Roe v. Flores-Ortega, 528 U.S. 470, 120 S. Ct. 1029, 1038 (2000)). *See generally* Gregory G. Sarno, Annotation, *Adequacy of Counsel's Representation of Alien in Deportation Proceedings*, 91 A.L.R. FED. 394 (2004).

§ 10.44. *What about translators at the deportation hearing?*

Aliens in deportation hearings have the right to competent translation. Hartooni v. INS, 21 F.3d 336, 340 (9th Cir. 1994). *See* Perez-Lastor v. INS, 208 F.3d 773, 778 (9th Cir. 2000) (defective translation includes evidence of incorrectly translated words, witness' unresponsive answers, and a witness' difficulty understanding).

§ 10.45. *What are the immigration judge's duties?*

The immigration judge must require the alien to state on the record whether he wants a lawyer. Montilla v. INS, 926 F.2d 162 (2d Cir. 1991). Moreover, immigration judges must ensure the potential deportee has the chance to present evidence. Colmenar v. INS, 210 F.3d 967, 971 (9th Cir. 2000); Campos-Sanchez v. INS, 164 F.3d 448, 450 (9th Cir. 1999). Also, the immigration judge can only find the deportee incredible if he has a "legitimate articulable basis to question [the immigrant's] credibility, and must offer a specific, cogent reason for any stated disbelief." Hartooni v. INS, 21 F.3d 336, 342 (9th Cir. 1994). *See also* Osorio v. INS, 99 F.3d 928, 931 (9th Cir. 1996). Also, an immigration judge's biases can violate due process and invalidated the removal order. *See, e.g.*, Reyes-Melendez v. INS, 342 F.3d 1001 (9th Cir. 2003) (immigration judge's moral judgments about respondent's many sexual relationships that producing numerous children took over role of prosecuting agency and denied due process). "A neutral judge is one of the most basic due process protections." Castro-Cortez v. INS, 239 F.3d 1037, 1049 (9th Cir. 2001). *See* **Chapter 2: Immigration Law for Criminal Lawyers**.

§ 10.46. *Can immigration judges accept the alien's waiver of rights?*

Yes, but the immigration judge must ensure that the alien only waives rights knowingly, intelligently, and intentionally. *See* United States v. Zarate-Martinez, 133 F.3d 1194, 1197 (9th Cir.), *cert. denied*, 525 U.S. 849, 119 S. Ct. 123 (1998). The immigration judge cannot presume a waiver of appeal without the alien's affirmative act. *Id.* at 1198. The immigrant must have received sufficient information regarding the charges and procedures of the deportation before a waiver of rights may be considered knowing and intelligent. *See* Walters v. Reno, 145 F.3d 1032 (9th Cir. 1998), *cert. denied*, 526 U.S. 1003, 119 S. Ct. 1140 (1999). Waivers of appeal are invalid if the immigration judge fails to inform the potential deportee of any deportation relief. United States v. Arrieta, 224 F.3d 1076, 1079 (9th Cir. 2000). *See* Lory Diana Rosenberg, *Rules to Follow: An Immigration Judge's Responsibilities*, 8:10 BENDER'S IMMIGR. BULL. 851 (May 15, 2003).

§ 10.47. *What if the alien has potential relief from deportation?*

If any evidence "raises a reasonable possibility that [the alien] may be eligible for relief, the [immigration judge] must advise the alien of this possibility and give him the opportunity to develop the issue." Moran-Enriquez v. INS, 884 F.2d 420, 423 (9th Cir. 1989). *See In re* Cordova, 22 I&N Dec. 966 (BIA 1999) (en banc) (emphasizing the absolute duty of an immigration judge to inform aliens of any relief they are statutorily eligible to receive); *see also* 8 C.F.R. § 240.11(a)(2) (1999) (requiring immigration judges to inform aliens of apparent eligibility for all "benefits enumerated in this chapter"); United States v. Leon-Paz, 340 F.3d 1003 (9th Cir. 2003); United States v. Arce-Hernandez, 163 F.3d 559, 563 (9th Cir. 1998), *amended, reh'g denied*, 1999 U.S. App. LEXIS 3823 (9th Cir. Cal. Mar. 11, 1999).

Though an immigration judge has a duty to inform a potential deportee of any rights to relief from deportation, the Due Process Clause does not require him to inform the alien of potential constitutional challenges to immigration laws. United States v. Garza-

Sanchez, 217 F.3d 806 (9th Cir. 2000), *cert. denied,* 531 U.S. 1180, 121 S. Ct. 1159 (2001).

By definition though, if the alien had some claim to relief from deportation, it will also establish the prejudice prong of the collateral attack. United States v. Arrieta, 224 F.3d 1076, 1079 (9th Cir. 2000). *See* Agyeman v. INS, No. 01-16910 (9th Cir. June 23, 2003); United States v. Muro-Inclan, 249 F.3d 1180 (9th Cir. 2001).

§ 10.48. *What are other procedural defects?*

Several immigration court practices are procedurally defective. *See, e.g.,* United States v. Ahumanda-Aguilar, 189 F.3d 1121 (9th Cir. 1999) (conviction for reentry after deportation reversed because of the following due process violations: rights to be represented by counsel was not individually waived at the underlying group deportation hearing, and right to appeal was not validly waived based on immigration judge's erroneous interpretation of consequences resulting from deportation), *vacated, remanded by, motion granted by* 533 U.S. 913, 121 S. Ct. 2518 (2001); United States v. Contreras, 63 F.3d 852, 856–57 (9th Cir. 1995) (telephonic deportation hearing not allowed as alien has a right to in-person hearing); United States v. Lopez-Vasquez, 1 F.3d 751 (9th Cir. 1993) ("mass silent waivers" do not comport with due process because they incorrectly presume the waiver); *see generally* C. GORDON, S. MAILMAN, & S. YALE-LOEHR, IMMIGRATION LAW AND PROCEDURE § 9.06 (rev. ed. 1998).

§ 10.49. *What about the validity of new deportation proceedings?*

Using removal under procedures from the 1996 acts as a basis for a later charge of reentry after deportation raises several constitutional problems. Most of these procedures, such as *in absentia* deportation proceedings, expedited removals, and reinstatements of prior removal orders, allow for no meaningful judicial review by an Article III court as *United States v. Mendoza-Lopez,* 481 U.S. 828, 107 S. Ct. 2148 (1987), requires. *But see* United States v. Martinez-Vitela, 193 F.3d 1047 (9th Cir. 1999) (reinstatement of defendant's deportation proceeding satisfied due process and was properly used as the predicate deportation under 8 U.S.C. § 1326 charge), *opinion withdrawn by* 213 F.3d 1205 (9th Cir.), *substituted by* 225 F.3d 665 (9th Cir. 2000).

§ 10.50. *What about a deportation for an invalid criminal conviction?*

This is a procedural error and, depending on the defendant's circumstances, may show prejudice. ICE must have specifically listed the alien's conviction on the Order to Show Cause or Notice to Appear. The definition of a conviction in the immigration statutes is found at 8 U.S.C. § 1101(a)(48)(A). *See* Chowdhury v. INS, 249 F.3d 970 (9th Cir. 2001) (INS must allege within the Order to Show Cause the specific subsection of 8 U.S.C. § 1101(a)(43) that supports its theory that alien was convicted of an aggravated felony and may not substitute alternate theories on appeal not specifically alleged); MacLeod v. INS, 327 F.2d 453 (9th Cir. 1964) (Order to Show Cause must list all factual allegations upon which INS alleges deportability); *In re* A-P, 22 I&N Dec. 468 (BIA 1999) (en banc) (immigration judges must articulate the precise subsection of the aggravated felony definitional statute at issue); *In re* Fortiz-Zelaya, 21 I&N Dec. 1199 (BIA 1998) (en banc) (aggravated felony bars are only applicable if the alien was actually charged with being deportable on that ground); *accord* Choeum v. INS, 129 F.3d 29, 33 (1st Cir. 1997) (INS may not substitute alternative grounds for deportation after deportation hearing).

§ 10.51. *What about an alien deported for an expunged conviction?*

This will often be an invalid basis of deportation, meaning that the deportation can be attacked in a later prosecution for illegal entry. *See* Lujan-Armendariz v. INS, 222 F.3d 728 (9th Cir. 2000) (aliens with drug offenses "expunged" under federal First Offender Act or similar state provision not "convicted" under 8 U.S.C. § 1101(a)(48)).

§ 10.52. *What if ICE deports someone before his appeal?*

When the immigration service removes an alien while his deportation appeal is pending, he has not been "deported" for purposes of a § 1326 prosecution. United States v. Fermin-Rodriguez, 5 F. Supp. 2d 157 (S.D.N.Y. 1998). This circumstance may also indicate that there is no need to show prejudice because the defendant alien was not even "deported."

c. Prejudice

§ 10.53. *What is "prejudice" in the deportation context?*

As stated *supra*, to prevail in a collateral attack of the deportation a defendant must demonstrate that the violations in the deportation prejudiced him. United States v. Proa-Tovar, 975 F.2d 592 (9th Cir. 1992) (en banc). In the Ninth Circuit, a defendant is "prejudiced" if he had "plausible grounds for relief from deportation." United States v. Esparza-Ponce, 193 F.3d 1133, 1136 (9th Cir. 1999). *See also* United States v. Muro-Inclan, 249 F.3d 1180, 1184 (9th Cir. 2001); United States v. Arrieta, 224 F.3d 1076, 1079 (9th Cir. 2000) (defendant "does not have to show that he actually would have been granted relief"); United States v. Arce-Hernandez, 163 F.3d 559, 563 (9th Cir. 1998), *amended, reh'g denied,* 1999 U.S. App. LEXIS 3823 (9th Cir. Cal. Mar. 11, 1999); United States v. Jimenez-Marmolejo, 104 F.3d 1083 (9th Cir. 1996).

The Fifth and Eighth Circuits require a somewhat greater showing, holding that "prejudice means 'there was a reasonable likelihood that but for the errors complained of the defendant would not have been deported.'" United States v. Benitez-Villafuerte, 186 F.3d 651, 659 (5th Cir. 1999), *cert. denied,* 528 U.S. 1097, 120 S. Ct. 838 (2000) and United States v. Perez-Ponce, 62 F.3d 1120, 1122 (8th Cir. 1995) (quoting United States v. Encarnacion-Galvez, 964 F.2d 402, 407 (5th Cir.), *cert. denied,* 506 U.S. 945, 113 S. Ct. 391 (1992)).

§ 10.54. *Is there prejudice if the alien was denied relief retroactively?*

Perhaps. In 1996, Congress took away nearly all forms of deportation relief from aliens with aggravated felonies and drug convictions. ICE has sought to apply this retroactively to all aggravated felon aliens regardless of when they received their criminal conviction. The circuits are split on the validity of this retroactive application. *Compare* Henderson v. INS, 157 F.3d 106 (2d Cir. 1998) (such denials not applied retroactively to aliens with older convictions), *cert. denied,* 526 U.S. 1004, 119 S. Ct. 1141 (1999), *affirming in part* Mojica v. Reno, 970 F. Supp. 130 (E.D.N.Y. 1997); *with* Vasquez v. Reno, 233 F.3d 688 (1st Cir. 2000), *cert. denied,* 534 U.S. 816, 122 S. Ct. 43 (2001); Jurado-Gutierrez v. Greene, 190 F.3d 1135 (10th Cir. 1999), *amended by* 1999 U.S. App. LEXIS 30710 (10th Cir. Nov. 29, 1999), *cert. denied,* 529 U.S. 1041, 120

S. Ct. 1539 (2000); LaGuerre v. Reno, 164 F.3d 1035 (7th Cir. 1998), *reh'd en banc denied,* 1999 U.S. App. LEXIS 11418 (7th Cir. Apr. 9, 1999), *cert. denied,* 528 U.S. 1153, 120 S. Ct. 1157 (2000); Richardson v. Reno, 162 F.3d 1338 (11th Cir. 1998), *vacated and remanded,* 526 U.S. 1142, 119 S. Ct. 2016, (1999), *reaff'd in part,* 180 F.3d 1311 (11th Cir. Fla. 1999), *cert. denied,* 529 U.S. 1036, 120 S. Ct. 1529 (2000); Duldulao v. INS, 90 F.3d 398 (9th Cir. 1996) (statute denying judicial review of deportation for aliens convicted of firearms offense applied retroactively and did not offend separation of powers or due process).

§ 10.55. *Is there any time when prejudice need not be shown?*

Yes. Some 50 years ago the Supreme Court held that prejudice may not be necessary to invalidate the deportation. *See* Accardi v. Shaughnessy, 347 U.S. 260, 74 S. Ct. 499 (1954) (deportation order vacated without a showing of prejudice because INS failed to follow its own regulations), *superceded by statute as stated in* LaGuerre v. Reno, 164 F.3d 1035 (7th Cir. 1998). Since *Accardi,* several circuits have noted "there may well be times when the administrative proceedings were so flawed that effective judicial review will be foreclosed," making a showing of prejudice unnecessary. United States v. Proa-Tovar, 975 F.2d 592, 595 (9th Cir. 1992) (en banc). *See also* Walters v. Reno, 145 F.3d 1032, 1044 n.8 (9th Cir. 1998) (questioning whether a showing of prejudice necessary where alien was completely deprived of adequate hearing), *cert. denied,* 526 U.S. 1003, 119 S. Ct. 1140 (1999); Waldron v. INS, 17 F.3d 511, 517–18 (2d Cir.) ("We conclude, therefore, that when a regulation is promulgated to protect a fundamental right derived from the Constitution or a federal statute, and the INS fails to adhere to it, the challenged deportation proceeding is invalid and remand to the agency is required."), *cert. denied,* 513 U.S. 1014, 115 S. Ct. 572 (1994); United States v. Cerda-Pena, 799 F.2d 1374, 1377 n.3 (9th Cir. 1986) ("an outright refusal to allow an alien the opportunity to obtain representation may be such an egregious violation of due process so as to not require any further showing of prejudice"); Castaneda-Delgado v. INS, 525 F.2d 1295, 1300 (7th Cir. 1975) (structural error in immigration proceeding violated right too fundamental to be circumscribed by prejudice test); Garcia-Guzman v. Reno, 65 F. Supp. 2d 1077 (N.D. Cal. 1999) (violation of alien's right to counsel per se prejudicial error); *but see* United States v. Garcia-Martinez, 228 F.3d 956, 964 (9th

Cir. 2000) (court fails to accept argument that prejudice should be presumed because deportation hearing officer had been institutionally biased against defendant), *cert. denied,* 531 U.S. 1179, 121 S. Ct. 1158 (2001).

d. Exhaustion of Administrative Remedies

§ 10.56. *What is "exhaustion of administrative remedies"?*

In 1996 as part of IIRAIRA, Congress codified *United States v. Mendoza-Lopez,* 481 U.S. 828, 107 S. Ct. 2148 (1987), but added the requirement that before a defendant could collaterally attack his prior deportation he must show that he has "exhausted administrative remedies." 8 U.S.C. § 1326(d). *See* INA § 242(a)(2)(C), 8 U.S.C. § 1252(a)(2)(C), effective April 1, 1997. The statute did not define "exhaustion of remedies" but presumably it refers to the appeal process to the Board of Immigration Appeals. *See* **Chapter 2: Immigration Law for Criminal Lawyers**. Given that *Mendoza-Lopez*'s basis is the Due Process Clause, Congress arguably lacked the authority to put this requirement on defendants in their collateral attacks.

§ 10.57. *What if the defendant waived his appeal of the deportation?*

According to at least one case in the Ninth Circuit, an alien may not collaterally challenge the deportation that forms the basis of a prosecution under 8 U.S.C. § 1326 "'if he validly waived the right to appeal that order' during the underlying deportation proceedings"; the waiver of the appeal, however, is not valid when "the record contains an inference that the petitioner is eligible for relief from deportation, but the Immigration Judge fails to 'advise the alien of this possibility and give him the opportunity to develop the issue.'" United States v. Muro-Inclan, 249 F.3d 1180, 1182 (9th Cir. 2001) (quoting United States v. Arrieta, 224 F.3d 1076, 1079 (9th Cir. 2000)).

§ 10.58. *What if the defendant did not "exhaust administrative remedies"?*

As stated, the "exhaustion" requirement may be irrelevant under *United States v. Mendoza-Lopez,* 481 U.S. 828, 107 S. Ct. 2148

(1987). Moreover, the defendant may have been coerced by the fact that immigration detainees can expect to wait months or years before the Board of Immigration Appeals can hear their case. Thus, the waiver may have been coerced and itself violative of the Due Process Clause. Also, the alien's failure to exhaust administrative remedies may have been from ineffective assistance of counsel at the deportation hearing. *See* United States v. Jimenez-Marmolejo, 104 F.3d 1083, 1085 (9th Cir. 1996) (waiver of right to appeal was "not the result of considered judgment" though alien was represented by counsel); United States v. Leon-Leon, 35 F.3d 1428 (9th Cir. 1994).

e. Attacking *In Absentia*, Reinstated, Administrative, and Expedited Deportations

i. *In Absentia* Deportations

§ 10.59. *What about deportation proceedings held in the absence of alien?*

These proceedings can be valid for later use in a § 1326 charge. Celis-Castellano v. Ashcroft, 298 F.3d 888 (9th Cir. 2002) (articulating the "exceptional circumstances" defense for aliens who fail to attend removal proceedings); United States v. Dekermenjian, 508 F.2d 812 (9th Cir. 1974) (deportation proceedings held *in absentia* do not per se violate due process if alien had reasonable opportunity to be present and failed to attend without reasonable cause). The record must show that ICE sent the alien notice. Before 1997 this had to have been by certified mail, *see In re* Grijalva, 21 I&N Dec. 27 (BIA 1995) (en banc), but the current statute now allows ICE to use regular mail. *See* 8 U.S.C. § 1229(a)(1) (1998); *see also In re* G-Y-R-, 23 I&N Dec. 181 (BIA 2001) (en banc); *but see* Salta v. INS, 314 F.3d 1076 (9th Cir. 2002) (service by regular mail is not entitled to the presumption of delivery of service by certified mail); *In re* Meiia-Andino, 23 I&N Dec. 533 (BIA 2002) (en banc) (ruling that, in most cases, service on a minor will be effective only when the Notice To Appear is provided to the parents).

§ 10.60. *What if the alien had relief from deportation?*

This is generally grounds for reopening the *in absentia* deportation. "The INS should not deny reopening of an *in absentia* deportation order where the denial leads to the unconscionable result of deporting an individual eligible for relief from deportation." Singh v. INS, 295 F.3d 1037, 1040 (9th Cir. 2002), *cert. denied*, 539 U.S. 941, 123 S. Ct. 2605 (2003). *See also* Chowdhury v. INS, 241 F.3d 848 (7th Cir. 2001).

ii. Reinstated Deportations

§ 10.61. *What are "reinstated deportations"?*

Since 1996 ICE can merely reinstate prior orders of deportation without giving the alien a new deportation hearing. 8 U.S.C. § 1231(a)(5). A reinstated removal's legality is predicated on the validity of the original deportation hearing and order. *See* 8 U.S.C. § 1231(a)(5).

§ 10.62. *What is the validity of a reinstated removal?*

The Ninth Circuit has recently ruled that the reinstatement procedure done without an immigration judge is invalid because INA § 240(a) states that an immigration judge shall conduct all proceedings on admissibility or deportability. Morales-Izquierdo v. Ashcroft, 388 F.3d 1299 (9th Cir. 2004), *vacated for reh'g en banc*, Morales-Izquierdo v. Gonzales, 2005 U.S. App. LEXIS 19582 (9th Cir. Sept. 12, 2005). *Morales-Izquierdo* followed other cases from the Ninth Circuit suggesting that reinstated orders do not comport with "full and fair hearing" requirements and raise due process concerns. *See* Castro-Cortez v. INS, 239 F.3d 1037, 1050 (9th Cir. 2001) ("we have serious doubts as to the constitutionality of these procedures"); *but cf.* Alvarenga-Villalobos v. Ashcroft, 271 F.3d 1169, 1174 (9th Cir. 2001) (reinstatement of a removal order does not violate due process).

§ 10.63. *What if the reinstated removal is after the aggravated felony?*

An alien can be subject to the enhanced sentence based on a prior aggravated felony even when his removal was "subsequent to" — i.e., after — the aggravated felony conviction regardless of whether the removal was merely a reinstatement. United States v. Luna-Madellaga, 315 F.3d 1224 (9th Cir.), *cert. denied*, 540 U.S. 853, 124 S. Ct. 142 (2003). Thus, even if a person is not deported for an aggravated felony, he is still subject to the enhanced penalty under

8 U.S.C. § 1326(b)(2) and Guideline § 2L1.2(b)(1)(A). United States v. Nava-Perez, 242 F.3d 277 (5th Cir.), *cert. denied*, 533 U.S. 923, 121 S. Ct. 2537 (2001), *petition for cert. filed* Aug. 5, 2002. *But cf.* Alvarez-Portillo v. Ashcroft, 280 F.3d 858 (8th Cir. 2002) (reinstatement procedural framework retroactive but substantive provisions are not); Castro-Cortez v. INS, 239 F.3d 1037 (9th Cir. 2001) (impermissible to apply reinstatement provision to aliens who entered before April 1, 1997).

§ 10.64. *Are reinstated deportations subject to collateral attack?*

Yes. The attack would focus on the original, not the reinstated, deportation. Because the alien was not deported as an aggravated felon, but later became one, he may have had relief from deportation. Thus, this alien may be able to show "prejudice" under the plausible grounds standard of *United States v. Jimenez-Marmolejo*, 104 F.3d 1083, 1085 (9th Cir. 1996).

iii. Expedited Deportations

§ 10.65. *What are expedited deportations?*

In 1996 Congress allowed border patrol officers to deport at the border a person whom they determine is inadmissible. 8 U.S.C. § 1225(b)(1). An alien can be inadmissible for a number of reasons but most often because he has an aggravated felony conviction. About the only defense to this deportation is if the alien can establish claim to political asylum or fear of persecution or torture. Despite the fact there is no judicial review of this procedure, the circuit courts have upheld the expedited removal regulations. *See, e.g.*, American Immigration Lawyer's Ass'n v. Reno, 199 F.3d 1352, 1356–57 (D.C. Cir. 2000). Also, the courts have not invalidated the use of administrative deportations as the basis of the illegal reentry prosecution because the defendants have not shown prejudice. *See* United States v. Garcia-Martinez, 228 F.3d 956 (9th Cir. 2000) (prejudice cannot be presumed just because of the nature of the proceeding and the lack of unbiased adjudicator), *cert. denied*, 531 U.S. 1179, 121 S. Ct. 1158 (2001); United States v. Benitez-Villafuerte, 186 F.3d 651 (5th Cir. 1999) (expedited removal process affords noncitizens adequate due process so long as INS comports with all applicable regulations), *cert. denied*, 528 U.S. 1097, 120 S. Ct. 838 (2000).

§ 10.66. *What is the legal validity of an expedited removal?*

The Ninth Circuit has recently ruled that the reinstatement procedure done without an immigration judge is invalid. Although *Morales-Izquierdo v. Ashcroft*, 388 F.3d 1299 (9th Cir. 2004), *vacated for reh'g en banc*, Morales-Izquierdo v. Gonzales, 2005 U.S. App. LEXIS 19582 (9th Cir. Sept. 12, 2005), applied to reinstated deportations, the reasoning would also apply to any expedited removal without an immigration judge. Again, an immigration judge does not conduct the expedited removal, which runs afoul of INA § 240(a) stating that an immigration judge shall conduct all proceedings on admissibility or deportability.

Thus, these administrative orders present a host of special concerns and potential challenges. Counsel should examine the alien's criminal history. As stated, aliens with aggravated felony convictions are subject to administrative removal. 8 U.S.C. § 1228 (Supp. 2001). If ICE incorrectly determined that the alien's conviction was an aggravated felony, the administrative removal is invalid. In addition, such a proceeding clearly deprived the alien of any chance for judicial review, much less the meaningful judicial review required by *United States v. Mendoza-Lopez*, 481 U.S. 828, 107 S. Ct. 2148 (1987). *But see* Brumme v. INS, 275 F.3d 443 (5th Cir. 2001) (judicial review of expedited removal limited under IIRAIRA to whether order issued and alien is same person subject to the order); Meng Li v. Eddy, 259 F.3d 1132 (9th Cir. 2001) (judicial review of removal limited), *vacated by* 324 F.3d 1109 (9th Cir. 2003).

3. Constitutional Issues, Disparity, Treaty Violations

§ 10.67. *Have there been constitutional attacks on the reentry statute?*

Yes but none have succeeded so far. Defendants have failed on the following grounds: (1) Eighth Amendment, United States v. Ayala, 35 F.3d 423 (9th Cir. 1994), *cert. denied*, 514 U.S. 1019, 115 S. Ct. 1365 (1995); United States v. Cupa-Guillen, 34 F.3d 860, 864 (9th Cir. 1994), *cert. denied*, 513 U.S. 1120, 115 S. Ct. 921 (1995); (2) vagueness, United States v. Ortiz-Gutierrez, 36 F.3d 80 (9th Cir. 1994) (*but see* United States v. Canals-Jimenez, 943 F.2d 1284, 1289 (11th Cir. 1991) (court expressed concern that statute may be vague)); and (3) double jeopardy, United States v. Flores-Peraza, 58 F.3d 164 (5th Cir. 1995), *cert. denied,* 516 U.S. 1076, 116 S. Ct. 782 (1996); United States v. Ramirez-Aguilar, 455 F.2d 486 (9th Cir. 1972). Moreover, 8 U.S.C. § 1326 is not an unconstitutional status offense because the defendants committed the affirmative act of entering and being "found in" the United States. United States v. Parga-Rosas, 238 F.3d 1209 (9th Cir.), *cert. denied,* 534 U.S. 942, 122 S. Ct. 319 (2001).

§ 10.68. *Is there dismissal for disparity in prosecutorial practices?*

Probably not. In a decision upholding disparate prosecution practices between adjoining districts, the Ninth Circuit held "[l]ike the district court, we find absolutely nothing wrong (and, quite frankly, a great deal right) with such a practice." United States v. Estrada-Plata, 57 F.3d 757, 761 (9th Cir. 1995).

§ 10.69. *What about deportations that violate treaties?*

A deportation that potentially violates a United States treaty obligation should be subject to collateral attack during the illegal reentry prosecution. In *Beharry v. Reno,* 183 F. Supp. 2d 584 (E.D.N.Y. 2002), *rev'd on other grounds,* 329 F.3d 51 (2d Cir. 2003), the court conducted a detailed analysis of, among other sources, the INA, international law, the Supremacy Clause at Article IV of the Constitution, the International Convention on Civil and Political Rights, and the Convention on the Rights of the Child. *Beharry* concludes that under international law and treaties, alien parents of U.S. citizen children should have the right to relief from deportation even if they were deported as aggravated felons. Though *Beharry* dealt with a legal permanent resident and relief under INA § 212(h), the opinion conceivably applies to any alien who is the parent of a citizen child. *See* Parastou Hassouri, *Decision in* Beharry v. Reno *Presents Innovative Avenue of Relief for Aggravated Felons,* 7:6 BENDER'S IMMIGR. BULL. 308 (March 15, 2002); Ryan J. Moore, *Reinterpreting the Immigration and Nationality Act's Categorical Bar to Discretionary Relief for "Aggravated Felons" in Light of International Law: Extending* Beharry v. Reno, *(183 F. Supp. 2d 584, E.D.N.Y. 2002,* rev'd on other grounds, *329 F.3d 51, 2d Cir. 2003),* 21 ARIZ. J. INT'L & COMP. L. 535 (2004); *but see* Gonzalez-Polanco v. INS, No. 02 Civ. 2734 (S.D.N.Y. Aug. 5, 2002) (court declines to extend *Beharry* to nonlegal permanent resident without potential § 212(h) relief).

V. Trial Issues

A. Criminal Intent

§ 10.70. *What is the mens rea for illegal entry?*

In a § 1326 prosecution, the government does not have to charge or prove willfulness or a specific intent to commit a crime. *See, e.g.*, United States v. Torres-Echavarria, 129 F.3d 692 (2d Cir. 1997), *cert. denied*, 522 U.S. 1153, 118 S. Ct. 1177 (1998); Pena-Cabanillas v. United States, 394 F.2d 785 (9th Cir. 1968) (entry and found in offenses are general intent crimes). Rather, the government must show that the defendant had a general intent to do the prohibitive act and that his entry was voluntary. United States v. Espinoza-Leon, 873 F.2d 743, 746 (4th Cir.), *cert. denied*, 492 U.S. 924, 109 S. Ct. 3257 (1989). In a prosecution under 8 U.S.C. § 1326, "the voluntariness of the return is an element of the crime and, as such, must be proved beyond a reasonable doubt by the prosecution." United States v. Quintana-Torres, 235 F.3d 1197, 1200 (9th Cir. 2000), *cert. denied*, 532 U.S. 953, 121 S. Ct. 1427 (2001).

Even attempted reentry is a general intent crime. United States v. Gracidas-Ulibarry, 192 F.3d 926 (9th Cir. 1999), *opinion substituted by* 231 F.3d 1188 (9th Cir. 2000), *cert. denied*, 535 U.S. 1069, 122 S. Ct. 1944 (2002).

§ 10.71. *What if the defendant did not even know he was in the United States?*

This may be a defense to the charge. United States v. Carlos-Colmenares, 253 F.3d 276, 279 (7th Cir.) (defendant must "knowingly return" and he did not have "express consent" to be guilty), *cert. denied*, 534 U.S. 914, 122 S. Ct. 258 (2001), *overturning* United States v. Anton, 683 F.2d 1011 (7th Cir. 1982); Pena-Cabanillas v. United States, 394 F.2d 785, 790 (9th Cir. 1968) ("Obviously if appellant was drugged and carried across the line, he would not be guilty of this offense.").

B. Evidentiary Issues

§ 10.72. *Are there any foundation challenges to A-file documents?*

Yes, the documents in an A-File are subject to challenges for authenticity, personal knowledge, and signatures. Also, counsel should look for hearsay within hearsay, *see* United States v. Orellana-Blanco, 294 F.3d 1143 (9th Cir. 2002), and ask for redactions when appropriate. *Crawford v. Washington* may give added weight to these challenges. 541 U.S. 36, 124 S. Ct. 1354 (2004) (holding out-of-court statements not admissible even if "reliable" and within a "firmly rooted hearsay exception"). *But see* United States v. Bahena-Cardenas, 411 F.3d 1067 (9th Cir. 2005) (*Crawford* held not to apply to warrant of deportation); *cf.* United States v. Hernandez-Herrera, 273 F.3d 1213 (9th Cir. 2001) (rejecting Confrontation Clause challenge to immigration document admission but case is pre-*Crawford*), *cert. denied*, 537 U.S. 868, 123 S. Ct. 272 (2002); United States v. Hernandez-Rojas, 617 F.2d 533, 534–35 (9th Cir.), *cert. denied*, 449 U.S. 864, 101 S. Ct. 170 (1980).

§ 10.73. *Are A-file documents hearsay?*

Some are, and a potential hearsay objection is available. Several are not hearsay because they are public records under Federal Rule of Evidence 803(8). United States v. Loyola-Dominguez, 125 F.3d 1315 (9th Cir. 1997). *See also* United States v. Hernandez-Herrera, 273 F.3d 1213 (9th Cir. 2001), *cert. denied*, 537 U.S. 868, 123 S. Ct. 272 (2002). Again, *Crawford v. Washington*, 541 U.S. 36, 124 S. Ct. 1354 (2004), changes the analysis and consul need consider its application to documents such as the Certificate of Nonexistence of Record.

C. Alienage Element

§ 10.74. *What is "alienage"?*

"An alien" is "any person not a citizen or national of the United States." 8 U.S.C. § 1101(a)(3). This is an element of illegal entry and reentry after deportation that the government must prove to the jury beyond a reasonable doubt. *Alien Re-Entry of Deported Alien (8 U.S.C. § 1326)*, in MANUAL OF MODEL CRIMINAL JURY

INSTRUCTIONS FOR THE DISTRICT COURTS OF THE NINTH CIRCUIT § 9.01(a) (1997 ed.); United States v. Meza-Soria, 935 F.2d 166, 168 (9th Cir. 1991). If the government offers the jury nothing more than the immigration judge's finding that the defendant is an alien, this is legally insufficient to sustain its burden of proof. United States v. Ortiz-Lopez, 24 F.3d 53 (9th Cir. 1994). This is because the immigration judge does not make findings under the standard of proof beyond a reasonable doubt. *See* **Chapter 2: Immigration Law for Criminal Lawyers**. Put another way, collateral estoppel does not apply and the government cannot argue that prior judicial alienage findings are res judicata. United States v. Arnett, 353 F.3d 765 (9th Cir. 2003) (government cannot use collateral estoppel when it has burden of proof), *cert. denied*, 541 U.S. 1091, 124 S. Ct. 2828, *reh'g denied*, 125 S. Ct. 15 (2004); United States v. Gallardo-Mendez, 150 F.3d 1240 (10th Cir. 1998) (refusing to apply collateral estoppel in 8 U.S.C. § 1326 case); United States v. Pelullo, 14 F.3d 881 (3d Cir.) (rejecting collateral estoppel that precludes defendant from relitigating prior issue), *reh'g en banc denied*, 1994 U.S. App. LEXIS 5413 (3d Cir. Mar. 22, 1994); United States v. Harnage, 976 F.2d 633, 636 (11th Cir. 1992) (refusing to apply collateral estoppel in 8 U.S.C. § 1326 case).

§ 10.75. *How would the government prove alienage?*

Evidence for the jury's consideration might include testimony of persons who knew where the defendant was born, the defendant's own statements, paperwork including birth, death and baptismal records, affidavits of neighbors, voter registration records, employment records, Social Security records, and even old telephone directories.

§ 10.76. *Can a person born outside the United States be a citizen?*

Yes, through the law of derivative citizenship when a parent is a citizen. *See* 8 U.S.C. § 1401 et seq. Even if an immigration court determined that the defendant was not a citizen, it does not preclude a trial defense of derivative citizenship. United States v. Meza-Soria, 935 F.2d 166, 168 (9th Cir. 1991). The law on derivative citizenship is confusing because it depends not only on the defendant's date of birth but on such factors as whether his parents were married. These facts also must comply with the immigration act in force at the time. *See* NATIONAL LAWYER'S GUILD,

IMMIGRATION LAW AND DEFENSE §§ 11.9–11.11 & app. J (3d ed. 1995) (a useful outline of the law on derivative citizenship).

Also, a child may become a citizen when a parent becomes a citizen under several conditions. *Id.*

§ 10.77. *What if the defendant has a prior 8 U.S.C. § 1325 or 8 U.S.C. § 1326 conviction?*

A prior conviction for illegal entry or reentry after deportation may preclude the alienage defense, barring a show of new facts. *See* Hernandez-Uribe v. United States, 515 F.2d 20 (8th Cir. 1975) (defendant collaterally estopped from denying alienage after guilty plea in prior prosecution under 8 U.S.C. § 1326), *cert. denied,* 423 U.S. 1057, 96 S. Ct. 791 (1976). This question has also been defined in terms of res judicata. *See* Pena-Cabanillas v. United States, 394 F.2d 785 (9th Cir. 1968). The trend now is to allow a defendant to raise the claim of derivative citizenship regardless of prior guilty pleas. *See e.g.,* United States v. Barragan-Cepeda, 29 F.3d 1378, 1381 (9th Cir. 1994) (suggesting collateral estoppel of guilty plea conviction inappropriate); United States v. Pelullo, 14 F.3d 881, 886 (3d Cir.) (same), *reh'g en banc denied,* 1994 U.S. App. LEXIS 5413 (3d Cir. Mar. 22, 1994); United States v. Harnage, 976 F.2d 633, 636 (11th Cir. 1992) (same). The Tenth Circuit does not allow collateral estoppel arguments regarding alienage where the defendant pleaded guilty without a trial on this issue. United States v. Gallardo-Mendez, 150 F.3d 1240, 1242 (10th Cir. 1998).

§ 10.78. *Can an alien claim "de facto" citizenship?*

No. This is not a defense to a reentry charge even when the alien's entire life has been spent in the United States. United States v. Serna-Vargas, 917 F. Supp. 711 (C.D. Cal. 1996) (rejecting "de facto" citizenship as an affirmative defense). This can still be a valid basis for downward departure at sentencing for "cultural assimilation." *See* **Chapter 11, II.B.2.a: Cultural Assimilation**.

D. The "Found In" Element

§ 10.79. *What constitutes the "found in" element?*

An alien is "found in" the United States when his presence is first noted by immigration authorities. United States v. DiSantillo, 615 F.2d 128 (3d Cir. 1980); United States v. Lopez-Flores, 275 F.3d

661 (7th Cir. 2001). At least one circuit has held that local police can "find in" a previously deported alien. United States v. Jimenez-Borja, 378 F.3d 853 (9th Cir. 2004). In a § 1326 prosecution, the government must prove this element beyond a reasonable doubt.

§ 10.80. *Must the defendant be deported to be "found in"?*

Yes. The defendant must have been physically deported (not just ordered deported) before he can be "found in." United States v. Romo-Romo, 246 F.3d 1272 (9th Cir. 2001) (§ 1326 prosecution requires showing the defendant actually left U.S. soil before being found); United States v. Ruiz-Lopez, 234 F.3d 445 (9th Cir. 2000) (same), *amended by* 2001 Cal. Daily Op. Service 124, 2001 D.A.R. 157 (9th Cir. Jan. 3, 2001); United States v. Quintana-Torres, 224 F.3d 1157 (9th Cir.) (jury instruction erroneous that alien could be presumed deported), *amended by* 235 F.3d 1197 (9th Cir. 2000), *cert. denied*, 532 U.S. 953, 121 S. Ct. 1427 (2001).

§ 10.81. *What does "found in" have to do with completing the crime?*

A § 1326 offense begins with entry but not is completed until the defendant is "found in." United States v. Rivera-Ventura, 72 F.3d 277 (2d Cir. 1995); United States v. Rincon-Jimenez, 595 F.2d 1192 (9th Cir. 1979). Thus, the defendant's conduct does not complete this element. Rather, "'being found' is an element of the offense [but] it is a passive state, not requiring proof of a voluntary act." United States v. Salazar-Robles, 207 F.3d 648, 650 (9th Cir.), *cert. denied*, 531 U.S. 859, 121 S. Ct. 145 (2000). *See also* Nyirenda v. INS, 279 F.3d 620 (8th Cir. 2002) (setting forth the components of an entry under immigration law). In a sense, it is the government that completes the crime by "finding" the defendant.

§ 10.82. *Does the government have to prove the "found in" date?*

No, as the government need only prove that the defendant was here and not the exact time at which he was found. *See* United States v. Godinez-Rabadan, 289 F.3d 630, 632 (9th Cir.) ("The exact date on which Godinez was found in the United States is not an element of a § 1326 violation."), *cert. denied*, 537 U.S. 917, 123 S. Ct. 339 (2002); *but see* United States v. Herrera-Ochoa, 245 F.3d 495 (5th Cir. 2001) (government must prove defendant was present in the United States upon date specified in the indictment regardless of fact that defendant was present at trial). Not requiring the government to allege the exact date, however, is inconsistent with cases stating that the statute of limitations runs from when the defendant is "found," not when he reentered.

§ 10.83. *If the alien originally entered legally, can he still be "found in"?*

Yes. For example, in *United States v. Pina-Jaime*, 332 F.3d 609 (9th Cir. 2003), the defendant was paroled into the United States legally to attend a child custody hearing but he illegally stayed an additional 29 months. His subsequent conviction for illegal reentry stood despite his argument that he was not "found in" illegally because he entered the country with permission.

§ 10.84. *What about if the defendant entered through a port of entry?*

This does not change whether he is amenable to prosecution. United States v. Gay, 7 F.3d 200, 202 (11th Cir. 1993) (defendant can be "found in" under the statute even though he had entered the country through recognized port of entry and not surreptitiously), *cert. denied*, 511 U.S. 1130, 114 S. Ct. 2141 (1994).

§ 10.85. *What about venue issues when the alien is "found"?*

Generally, venue for a reentry case is where the defendant illegally entered or where he was apprehended. United States v. Guzman-Bruno, 27 F.3d 420, 422–23 (9th Cir.), *cert. denied*, 513 U.S. 975, 115 S. Ct. 451 (1994). A given defendant is not "found" in a district just because the government takes him there. United States v. Hernandez, 189 F.3d 785 (9th Cir. 1999) (case analyzes how venue is intertwined with constitutional rights of trial — defendant cannot be "found" over and over again in different districts), *cert. denied*, 529 U.S. 1028, 120 S. Ct. 1441 (2000). Issues as to venue may be important given that some districts have better plea policies than others. Venue, however, is not an element of the offense and the government need only prove it by a preponderance. United States v. Powell, 498 F.2d 890, 891 (9th Cir.), *cert. denied*, 419 U.S. 866, 95 S. Ct. 121 (1974).

E. Attorney General's Consent to Reenter

§ 10.86. *Must the government demonstrate lack of consent?*

Yes. The reentry statute lists as an element that the defendant did not receive the Attorney General's consent to return to the United States. The government usually offers a "Certificate of Non-Existence of Record." United States v. Oris, 598 F.2d 428, 430 (5th Cir.) ("the jury could reasonably assume that any expression of the Attorney General's consent would appear in the INS files"), *reh'g denied*, 602 F.2d 992 (5th Cir.), *cert. denied*, 444 U.S. 945, 100 S. Ct. 304 (1979). Generally, the law views the Certificate of Non-Existence of Record under seal as a self-authenticating document. United States v. Mateo-Mendez, 215 F.3d 1039 (9th Cir.), *cert. denied*, 531 U.S. 983, 121 S. Ct. 437 (2000). Thus, a government employee does not have to attest to it at trial. *See* Federal Rule of Evidence 902.

§ 10.87. *How would the alien get the consent?*

The reentry after deportation statute gives direction regarding how to attain permission from the Attorney General to reapply for admission. *See* United States v. Morales-Tovar, 37 F. Supp. 2d 846 (W.D. Tex. 1999). Under 8 C.F.R. § 212.2, the permission can be obtained two ways:

First, the alien may file at the United States Consulate in his country a form I-212, Application for Permission to Reapply for Admission into the United States After Deportation or Removal, requesting permission before entering. *See* 8 C.F.R. § 212.2(b)(1). If the form I-212 is filed with the consulate, the consular officer has discretion to not accept it.

Second, the alien may file a form I-212 at a port of entry. The ICE district director handles the request. 8 C.F.R. § 212.2(f). The district director must accept and process the application. If a request is granted, it will be retroactive to when the defendant embarked from outside the United States. 8 C.F.R. § 212.2(i)(1)(I).

§ 10.88. *Who can grant the consent?*

Now it is the Department of Homeland Security. *See* **Chapter 2: Immigration Law for Criminal Lawyers**. Thus, if the defendant enters, even if he has been deported with no chance to legally enter, and he requests permission to enter, he may have a defense to the charge of reentry after deportation. This is because the port of entry itself has the authority to grant such a waiver. 8 C.F.R. § 2.1. Likewise, 8 C.F.R. § 212.2 grants a person previously deported or removed the right to apply for permission to be admitted at the port of entry. *See* United States v. Morales-Tovar, 37 F. Supp. 2d 846 (W.D. Tex. 1999); *see also* United States v. Cabral, 252 F.3d 520 (1st Cir. 2001).

Before, the Attorney General through the INS Commissioner granted the consent with a form I-212. 8 C.F.R. § 2.1.

§ 10.89. *What if the alien has reasonable belief that he had consent?*

This is not a defense. "An alien who has been deported reenters this country at his peril. He had better make certain that he has the Attorney General's express consent to enter, because if he does not he is guilty of a felony." United States v. Carlos-Colmenares, 253 F.3d 276, 278 (7th Cir.), *cert. denied*, 534 U.S. 914, 122 S. Ct. 258 (2001), *overturning* United States v. Anton, 683 F.2d 1011 (7th Cir. 1982).

§ 10.90. *How does ICE recordkeeping problems relate to consent?*

In 2002, ICE contracted with a private records management service at the ICE regional processing center at Laguna, California. Several employees found a creative way to deal with the huge backlog of filings — a document shredder. *Backlog Problem Solved: Fire Up the Shredder*, 8:5 BENDER'S IMMIGR. BULL. 371 (Mar. 1, 2003). Among other euphemisms, the shredding was called "Special Searches." The documents included ICE Notices of Action, birth and marriage certificates, foreign passports, ICE Employment Authorization documents, return mail, ICE approval and rejection notices, checks and money orders. Thus, it may now be hard for the government to prove that the defendant did not make an application using the "Certificate of Non-Existence of Record."

VI. Trial Defenses

A. No "Entry" Free from "Official Restraint"

§ 10.91. *What does it mean to "enter" the United States?*

To "enter" the United States is a term of art. *See* **Chapter 2, II.C: "Entry" and "Admission"**. If an alien is under surveillance from the moment he passes through the port of entry or crosses the border until arrest, he has not "entered" as he is still under "official restraint." United States v. Pacheco-Medina, 212 F.3d 1162 (9th Cir. 2000); United States v. Angeles-Mascote, 206 F.3d 529 (5th Cir. 2000); *Ex parte* Chow Chok, 161 F. 627, 628–29 (C.D.N.Y.), ("enter" means more than the mere act of the crossing the border and is aimed at preventing aliens from going freely about the United States), *aff'd*, 163 F. 1021 (2d Cir. 1908). Thus, aliens who attempt to enter and are taken immediately into custody never were at large and had not violated the statute. *See also* Yang v. Maugans, 68 F.3d 1540, 1549–50 (3d Cir.), *reh'g en banc denied*, 1995 U.S. App. LEXIS 37147 (3d Cir. Dec. 27, 1995); United States v. Kavazanjian, 623 F.2d 730, 736–37 (1st Cir. 1980); *In re* Pierre, 14 I&N Dec. 467 (1973).

§ 10.92. *What then does it take to be "free from official restraint"?*

Not much. If there is any break in surveillance allowing the alien to exercise his will by being at large, he is free from official restraint. In *United States v. Hernandez-Herrera*, 273 F.3d 1213 (9th Cir. 2001), *cert. denied*, 537 U.S. 868, 123 S. Ct. 272 (2002), a "still watch" agent watched suspected aliens scaling the border fence. Agents arrested all the suspects but two who fled into thick brush and were then arrested. The escape into the brush constituted a sufficient break of official restraint, even though the area the defendant fled into had no exit. *See also* United States v. Bello-Bahena, 411 F.3d 1083 (9th Cir. 2005); United States v. Ramos-Godinez, 273 F.3d 820 (9th Cir. 2001) (defendant and others crossed over the All-American Canal where surveillance was sufficiently interrupted to break official restraint), *cert. denied*, 537 U.S. 910, 123 S. Ct. 253 (2002); United States v. Castellanos-Garcia, 270 F.3d 773 (9th Cir. 2001) (defendant walking yards from the border with significant periods not under surveillance made him free from official restraint), *cert. denied*, 535 U.S.

1067, 122 S. Ct. 1939 (2002); United States v. Martin-Plascencia, 532 F.2d 1316 (9th Cir.) (defendant managed to pass through two border fences without detection, which, though brief, was sufficient to break official restraint), *cert. denied*, 429 U.S. 894, 97 S. Ct. 255 (1976).

§ 10.93. *Does the official restraint doctrine apply to 8 U.S.C. § 1325 cases?*

Yes. *See* United States v. Gonzalez-Torres, 273 F.3d 1181 (9th Cir. 2001) (official restraint doctrine applied to § 1325 prosecution), *opinion and substituted by* 309 F.3d 594 (9th Cir. 2002), *cert. denied*, 538 U.S. 969, 123 S. Ct. 1768 (2003).

§ 10.94. *When should this defense be presented?*

Generally, the defendant will present this issue at the end of the government's case unless pretrial proceedings establish the facts. Often video tapes from the border will establish the facts. Both the defense and prosecution must attend to evidentiary issues on this question. *See* United States v. Castellanos-Garcia, 270 F.3d 773 (9th Cir. 2001) (trial court properly precluded cross-examination about sensors or detecting devices after agent testified that he did not rely on them for arrest), *cert. denied*, 535 U.S. 1067, 122 S. Ct. 1939 (2002).

§ 10.95. *Does the "official restraint" defense apply to attempted reentry?*

No. Attempted entry is a different crime than reentry, which requires physical presence and freedom from official restraint. United States v. Leos-Maldonado, 302 F.3d 1061 (9th Cir. 2002) (crime of attempted reentry after deportation requires specific positive proof of a specific intent); United States v. Berrios-Centeno, 250 F.3d 294 (5th Cir.) (being found in the United States after deportation is a general intent offense and an indictment charging the defendant with having been deported and subsequently found in the United States sufficiently alleges the general intent *mens rea*), *cert. denied*, 534 U.S. 928, 122 S. Ct. 288 (2001); United States v. Cardenas-Alvarez, 987 F.2d 1129, 1133 (5th Cir. 1993) ("to graft 'freedom from official restraint' onto the crime of attempted entry would make that crime synonymous with actual entry").

§ 10.96. *If defendant "entered," can he be charged with attempted entry?*

Yes. A defendant can be convicted of attempted reentry even if he successfully completes the reentry after deportation crime. Essentially, a defendant can be charged with trying to do something even if he successfully did it. United States v. Rivera-Relle, 333 F.3d 914, 920 (9th Cir.), *cert. denied*, 540 U.S. 977, 124 S. Ct. 459 (2003).

§ 10.97. *Can the alien attempt reentry from outside the United States?*

Yes. For example, when the defendant is arrested on the high seas while on his way to the United States, the government can prosecute him for attempted reentry under 8 U.S.C. § 1326. *See* United States v. Ayala, 35 F.3d 423 (9th Cir. 1994), *cert. denied*, 514 U.S. 1019, 115 S. Ct. 1365 (1995).

§ 10.98. *Is attempted entry a specific intent crime?*

Yes, the government must allege the "attempt" in the indictment. "[T]he crime of attempted illegal reentry into the United States includes the common law element of specific intent." United States v. Gracidas-Ulibarry, 231 F.3d 1188, 1190 (9th Cir. 2000), *cert. denied*, 535 U.S. 1069, 122 S. Ct. 1944 (2002). *See also* United States v. Pernillo-Fuentes, 252 F.3d 1030 (9th Cir. 2001) (conviction for attempted reentry invalid where indictment did not allege specific intent).

B. Good Faith Defenses

§ 10.99. *What about an alien's "good faith" belief that he can return?*

This is a possible defense. ICE often advises a person he cannot reenter for five years. If the alien believes that this allows him to enter after five years, this could be a valid jury defense. *See* United States v. Idowu, 105 F.3d 728 (D.C. Cir. 1997); *contra* Eric H. Singer, United States v. Idowu*: Inadmissibility and Unlawful Reentry After Deportation — Still Confused After All These Years*, 29 SW. U. L. REV. 301 (2000).

The other circuits that have addressed this issue have generally held that the alien's mistaken belief that he could reenter is not a defense. *See, e.g.*, United States v. Torres-Echavarria, 129 F.3d 692 (2d Cir. 1997), *cert. denied*, 522 U.S. 1153, 118 S. Ct. 1177 (1998); United States v. Champegnie, 925 F.2d 54 (2d Cir. 1991) (deported aliens who reenter "do so at their peril" as subjective belief is irrelevant).

The reasoning in these cases seems to contravene the Supreme Court's holding on intent in *Staples v. United States*, 511 U.S. 600, 114 S. Ct. 1793 (1994). *See also* Alan Michaels, *Constitutional Innocence*, 112 HARV. L. REV. 828 (1999) (exploring the concept of strict liability in criminal law and the Supreme Court's limitations on such power, so that the legislature can criminalize only intentional acts leading up to the offense).

§ 10.100. *What about an "entrapment by estoppel" defense?*

The courts have generally rejected the argument that the government should be estopped from prosecuting the defendant alien when he reentered believing that it was legal after the five years as is stated in the I-294 form. *See, e.g.*, United States v. Ramirez-Valencia, 202 F.3d 1106 (9th Cir.) (no defense even if INS [current ICE] gives the wrong information about alien's right to return), *cert. denied*, 531 U.S. 892, 121 S. Ct. 218 (2000); United States v. Trevino-Martinez, 86 F.3d 65 (5th Cir. 1996) (no error in court refusal to instruct jury on entrapment by estoppel), *cert. denied*, 520 U.S. 1105, 117 S. Ct. 1109 (1997). However, if the government assures the defendant, beyond just giving him the I-294 form, that certain conduct is lawful and the defendant relies on this assurance he may have a claim to this defense. United States v. Aquino-Chacon, 109 F.3d 936 (4th Cir.), *cert. denied*, 522 U.S. 931, 118 S. Ct. 335 (1997).

C. Challenging the Deportation Documents

§ 10.101. *What about challenging the government's documents?*

Documents in any trial can be challenged on foundation or other evidentiary grounds such as authentication, lack of personal knowledge, signatures, and hearsay within hearsay. Also, the defense can ask for redactions of irrelevant or prejudicial information. Generally, however, documents from the A-file are not hearsay as public records under Federal Rule of Evidence 803(8). United States v. Hernandez-Herrera, 273 F.3d 1213 (9th Cir. 2001) (rejecting a Confrontation Clause challenge to admission of documents), *cert. denied*, 537 U.S. 868, 123 S. Ct. 272 (2002); United States v. Loyola-Dominguez, 125 F.3d 1315 (9th Cir. 1997).

§ 10.102. *What if the government cannot prove actual deportation?*

This defense is closely related to the pretrial motion issue of whether the defendant was "found in" discussed *supra*. The government must prove the defendant was taken to the border and set foot in the country of deportation. 8 C.F.R. §§ 243.7, 237.5; United States v. Meza-Villarello, 602 F.2d 209, 210 (9th Cir.), *cert. denied*, 444 U.S. 968, 100 S. Ct. 460 (1979). This information is recorded on the back of the Warrant of Deportation showing that the warrant was "executed." Without this executed warrant, a prosecution for reentry after deportation should be difficult to maintain. In fact, 8 U.S.C. § 1326 requires the Warrant of Deportation to be served on the alien. Without proof of this service, there is no notice to the defendant of his deportation. United States v. Bahena-Cardenas, 70 F.3d 1071 (9th Cir. 1995) (rejecting government argument that any self-deported alien would be free to reenter without consequence because the government can always arrest the defendant and execute the deportation order with proper service).

§ 10.103. *What about the Vienna Convention on Consular Relations?*

How about a rabbit out of the hat! Generally overlooked, the Vienna Convention on Consular Relations guarantees the right of an accused to be advised of the right to seek assistance from the consul of his country. The Vienna Convention on Consular Relations, Apr. 24, 1963, 21 U.S.T. 77. *See generally* Faulder v. Johnson, 81 F.3d 515, 520 (5th Cir.), *cert. denied*, 519 U.S. 995, 117 S. Ct. 487 (1996). This treaty remains largely unenforced, despite the fact that the U.S. State Department mails notices about the treaty every few years to the states and major cities. The treaty may provide a basis to challenge the prior deportation, a prior § 1326 conviction, or prior criminal conviction. *See generally* Logene L. Foster & Stephen Doggett, *Vienna Convention: New Tool for Representing Foreign Nationals in the Criminal Justice System*, THE CHAMPION, Mar. 1997, at 2; John Carry Sims & Linda E. Carter, *Emerging Importance of the Vienna Convention on Consular Relations as a Defense Tool*, THE CHAMPION, Sept./Oct. 1998, at 8; Cara Drinan, Note, *Ar-*

ticle 36 of the Vienna Convention on Consular Relations: Private Enforcement in American Courts After LaGrand [Germany v. United States], 54 STAN. L. REV. 1303 (2002).

D. Duress, Necessity, Corpus Delicti, Insanity

§ 10.104. *What about the duress defense?*

The risk of great financial loss is insufficient to provide a duress defense. United States v. Palmer, 458 F.2d 663 (9th Cir. 1972). Also, an alien's claim to political asylum did not provide a duress defense to a reentry after deportation charge. United States v. Polanco-Gomez, 841 F.2d 235 (8th Cir.), *cert. denied,* 1988 U.S. App. LEXIS 6373 (8th Cir. Apr. 26, 1988). But, if the defendant can show that he had a well-founded fear of immediate bodily harm or death, the defense is available *Id. See also* United States v. Meraz-Valeta, 26 F.3d 992 (10th Cir. 1994) (defense only available for aliens with no legal alternatives). With this in mind, a possible defense could be that the defendant had to enter the country to procure medication for a child, or a similar plea, it could also be coupled with a claim for political asylum in a collateral attack on the prior deportation.

§ 10.105. *What about the necessity defense?*

Generally, this is not going to be a successful defense to a reentry charge. To successfully raise a necessity defense, the defendant must show: (1) there was no legal alternative to violating the law; (2) the harm to the defendant was imminent; and (3) there was a direct causal relationship reasonably anticipated to exist between the defendant's action and the avoidance of harm. *See* United States v. Smith, 160 F.3d 117, 123 & n.3 (2d Cir. 1998); United States v. Meraz-Velata, 26 F.3d 992, 995 (10th Cir. 1994). Generally, the defendant must show "he was faced with the choice of evils and chose the lesser evil." United States v. Aguilar, 883 F.2d 662, 693 (9th Cir. 1989), *cert. denied,* 498 U.S. 1046, 111 S. Ct. 751 (1991), *overturned (superceded by statute as stated in),* United States v. Gonzalez-Torres, 273 F.3d 1181 (9th Cir. 2001); United States v. Nwene, 20 F. Supp. 2d 716 (D.N.J. 1998) (defendant asserted he could not even come out of hiding to claim political asylum before he was arrested for reentry), *summarily aff'd,* 213

F.3d 629 (3d Cir.), *cert. denied,* 531 U.S. 864, 121 S. Ct. 157 (2000).

§ 10.106. *Is this issue subject to a motion in limine?*

Yes. A district judge may preclude a necessity defense by granting a motion *in limine*. United States v. Arellano-Rivera, 244 F.3d 1119 (9th Cir. 2001) (defendant's attempts to mount a "necessity defense" rejected though the defendant had suffered from AIDS because he could have petitioned the Attorney General for entry for treatment), *cert. denied,* 535 U.S. 976, 122 S. Ct. 1450 (2002); United States v. Aguilar, 883 F.2d 662, 693 (9th Cir. 1989) (defendants not entitled to necessity defense for supporting illegal entry of Central American immigrants in the face of INS improprieties), *cert. denied,* 498 U.S. 1046, 111 S. Ct. 751 (1991), *overturned (superceded by statute as stated in),* United States v. Gonzalez-Torres, 273 F.3d 1181 (9th Cir. 2001); United States v. Polanco-Gomez, 841 F.2d 235, 238 (8th Cir.) (finding defendant was not entitled to a necessity defense to charges of illegal reentry, despite alleged persecution in his home country, because he could not show that he had attempted to apply for political asylum), *cert. denied,* 1988 U.S. App. LEXIS 6373 (8th Cir. Apr. 26, 1988).

§ 10.107. *What about corpus delicti?*

Often, the prosecution in both illegal entry and reentry after deportation cases relies heavily on the defendant's own statements to meet its burden of proof. If the prosecution has failed to corroborate the defendant's admissions, the defense should move for judgment of acquittal under Federal Rule of Criminal Procedure 29 at the close of the government's case and at the close of evidence. United States v. Lopez-Garcia, 683 F.2d 1226 (9th Cir. 1982), *cert. denied,* 459 U.S. 1174, 103 S. Ct. 822 (1983).

§ 10.108. *What about insanity?*

This is a valid defense to an illegal entry or reentry after deportation charge. Under federal law, the defendant has the burden of proving with clear and convincing evidence that "at the time of the commission of the acts constituting the offense, [he], as a result of mental disease or defect, was unable to appreciate the nature and quality or the wrongfulness of his acts." 18 U.S.C. § 17. *See generally* W. E. Shipley, Annotation, *Presumption of Continuing Insanity as Applied to Accused in Criminal Case,* 27 A.L.R. 2D 121 (1953).

After arraignment, the defense must give notice of intent to rely on an insanity defense. *See* FED. R. CRIM. P. 12.2(a).

CHAPTER 11

ILLEGAL ENTRY AND REENTRY: PLEAS AND SENTENCING

Introduction

The number of immigrants serving federal prison sentences increased from 1,593 during 1985 to 13,676 during 2000 and the average time they served in federal prisons increased from four months to 21 months. THE BUREAU OF JUSTICE STATISTICS SPECIAL REPORT, UNITED STATES DEPARTMENT OF JUSTICE, OFFICE OF JUSTICE PROGRAMS, August 2002, NCJ 191745. An interesting question is whether the Supreme Court's decisions starting with *Blakely v. Washington*, 542 U.S. 296, 124 S. Ct. 2531 (2004) through *United States v. Booker/United States v. Fanfan*, 125 S. Ct. 738 (2005) will affect this trend.

I. Plea Bargaining and Proceedings

§ 11.1. *Are there standard pleas in criminal immigration cases?*

Yes. Starting under Attorney General Janet Reno and continuing under Attorney General John Ashcroft and Alberto Gonzales, several districts, mostly along the Mexican border, produced "standard" or "fast-track" plea policies to resolve the large numbers of reentry cases and induce early resolution. In the District of Arizona, for example, these pleas have reduced time from complaint to sentencing in 8 U.S.C. § 1326 cases by 50%. Though resolution can occur quickly, various ethical problems exist under these fast-track policies — primarily for defense counsel but also for prosecutors. *See* Michael O'Connor & Celia Rumann, *The Death of Advocacy in Re-entry After Deportation Cases*, THE CHAMPION, Nov. 1999, at 42. Moreover, various districts have different policies, creating a wide disparity in sentencing between districts. *See* Erin T. Middleton, *Fast Track to Disparity: How Federal Sentencing Policies Along the Southwest Border Are Undermining the Sentencing Guidelines and Violating Equal Protection*, 2004 UTAH L. REV. 827.

§ 11.2. *What about discrepancies between districts with and without "fast track"?*

The courts have allowed different pleas practices in different districts to stand. United States v. Estrada-Plata, 57 F.3d 757 (9th Cir. 1995), *following* United States v. Cupa-Guillen, 34 F.3d 860, 864 (9th Cir. 1994), *cert. denied*, 513 U.S. 1120, 115 S. Ct. 921 (1995). Thus, the fact that a defendant cannot get the plea from even an adjacent district is legal.

§ 11.3. *What are other plea resolutions?*

An alien charged with simple reentry after deportation under 8 U.S.C. § 1326 could plead to illegal entry under 8 U.S.C. § 1325 because a first conviction under 8 U.S.C. § 1325 is a misdemeanor. A subsequent § 1325 conviction is a felony with a two-year statutory maximum. If the government wishes to "stack" § 1325 convictions for a plea offer, it must make sure to allege the prior § 1325 conviction to assure the second will be a felony. United States v. Rodriguez-Gonzales, 358 F.3d 1156 (9th Cir. 2004).

If the defendant has a prior felony conviction and the government has charged him under 8 U.S.C. § 1326(b)(1) or (2), the parties may consider allowing the defendant to plead to illegal entry, 8 U.S.C. § 1325, or simple reentry after deportation, 8 U.S.C. § 1326(a). This provides the defendant a cap of 24 months (the two-year statutory maximum). United States v. Arias-Granados, 941 F.2d 996 (9th Cir. 1991), *overruled in part,* Almendarez-Torres v. United States, 523 U.S. 224, 118 S. Ct. 1219 (1998). Other possible resolutions involve manipulating the Guideline calculations or agreeing to a stipulated cap within presumed Guideline ranges.

§ 11.4. *Can the U.S. Attorney bind ICE with a plea?*

Yes, if the U.S. Attorney has ICE's written consent. 28 C.F.R., pt. O.

§ 11.5. *Can magistrate judges take pleas in reentry cases?*

Yes, with the defendant's consent under the Federal Magistrates Act, 28 U.S.C. § 636 (2000). Some circuits require some form of district court *de novo* review. In *United States v. Reyna-Tapia,* 328 F.3d 1114 (9th Cir.) (en banc), *cert. denied,* 540 U.S. 900, 124 S. Ct. 238 (2003), the court held that there will only be a district court *de novo* review if the defendant requests. *See also* United States v. Torres, 258 F.3d 791, 796 (8th Cir. 2001); United States v. Dees, 125 F.3d 261, 265 (5th Cir. 1997), *cert. denied,* 522 U.S. 1152, 118 S. Ct. 1174 (1998); United States v. Ciapponi, 77 F.3d 1247, 1251 (10th Cir.) (no review of magistrate's Rule 11 proceedings unless a defendant demands it under Federal Rule of Criminal Procedure 32(d)), *cert. denied,* 517 U.S. 1215, 116 S. Ct. 1839 (1996), *opinion corrected* (March 7, 1996).

II. Sentencing

§ 11.6. *What are the statutory penalties for reentry after deportation?*

Under 8 U.S.C. § 1326, aliens who have been convicted of "three or more misdemeanors involving drugs, crimes against the person, or both" shall be treated as felons. The penalty for a felon who reenters the country after deportation is now 10 years; for the aggravated felon, defined at 8 U.S.C. § 1101(a)(43), the penalty is now 20 years.

See generally James P. Fleissner & James A. Shapiro, *Federal Sentences for Aliens Convicted of Illegal Reentry Following Deportation: Who Needs the Aggravation?*, 9 GEO. IMMIGR. L.J. 451 (1995).

§ 11.7. *How were these enhancements considered in the past?*

Before 1998, the Ninth Circuit described the offense of illegally reentering as "simple re-entry after deportation" with a maximum penalty of two years. *United States v. Arias-Granados*, 941 F.2d 996, 997 (9th Cir. 1991), *overruled in part*, Almendarez-Torres v. United States, 523 U.S. 224, 118 S. Ct. 1219 (1998). *See also* United States v. Campos-Martinez, 976 F.2d 589, 590–92 (9th Cir. 1992); United States v. Gonzalez-Medina, 976 F.2d 570, 572–73 (9th Cir. 1992). Other circuits held that 8 U.S.C. § 1326(b) was a sentencing enhancement that did not create a separate criminal offense and the defendant could be charged by indictment only with the elements of § 1326(a) but could be punished up to the 20 year maximum specified in § 1326(b). United States v. Vasquez-Olvera, 999 F.2d 943, 944–47 (5th Cir. 1993), *cert. denied*, 510 U.S. 1076, 114 S. Ct. 889 (1994). *See also* United States v. Valdez, 103 F.3d 95, 97–99 (10th Cir. 1996); United States v. Haggerty, 85 F.3d 403, 405 (8th Cir.), *reh'g en banc denied*, 1996 U.S. App. LEXIS 17508 (8th Cir. July 15, 1996); United States v. De Leon-Rodriguez, 70 F.3d 764, 767 (3d Cir. 1995), *cert. denied*, 517 U.S. 1115, 116 S. Ct. 1343 (1996); United States v. Palacios-Casquete, 55 F.3d 557, 560 (11th Cir. 1995), *cert. denied*, 516 U.S. 1120, 116 S. Ct. 927 (1996); United States v. Munoz-Cerna, 47 F.3d 207, 211 n.6 (7th Cir. 1995); United States v. Smith, 36 F.3d 128, 132 (1st Cir.), *cert. denied*, 513 U.S. 1008, 115 S. Ct. 529 (1994); United States v. Cole, 32 F.3d 16, 19 (2d Cir.), *cert. denied*, 513 U.S. 993, 115 S. Ct. 497 (1994); United States v. Crawford, 18 F.3d

1173, 1178 (4th Cir.), *cert. denied*, 513 U.S. 860, 115 S. Ct. 171 (1994); United States v. Forbes, 16 F.3d 1294, 1297–1300 (1st Cir. 1994).

§ 11.8. *How are these enhancements now considered?*

The Supreme Court in *Almendarez-Torres v. United States*, 523 U.S. 224, 118 S. Ct. 1219 (1998), held that subsection (b)(2) of 8 U.S.C. 1326 is a penalty provision that does not create a separate crime. Thus the government need not charge the fact of an earlier conviction in the indictment. United States v. Anglin, 284 F.3d 407 (2d Cir. 2002) (Second Circuit holds that fact of prior conviction is sentencing factor, not separate element of offense); United States v. Moreno-Arredondo, 255 F.3d 198 (5th Cir.) (prior aggravated felony is not an element of illegal reentry and is merely a sentencing factor), *cert. denied*, 534 U.S. 1008, 122 S. Ct. 491 (2001).

§ 11.9. *Did Apprendi change the status of these sentencing factors?*

No. In *Apprendi v. New Jersey*, 530 U.S. 466, 489, 120 S. Ct. 2348 (2000), the Supreme Court stated in dicta that "it is arguable that *Almendarez-Torres* was incorrectly decided." *See* Almendarez-Torres v. United States, 523 U.S. 224, 118 S. Ct. 1219 (1998). Although defendants have argued that the sentencing enhancements under 8 U.S.C. § 1326 should fall outside the scope of *Almendarez-Torres*, generally, the circuits have foreclosed such arguments. *See, e.g.*, United States v. Bahena-Cardenas, 411 F.3d 1067, 1073 (9th Cir. 2005) ("Section 1326 does not violate the rule of *Apprendi* ...."); United States v. Santiago, 268 F.3d 151 (2d Cir. 2001), *cert. denied*, 535 U.S. 1070, 122 S. Ct. 1946 (2002); United States v. Arellano-Rivera, 244 F.3d 1119 (9th Cir. 2001) (*Apprendi* did not overrule *Almendarez-Torres*), *cert. denied*, 535 U.S. 976, 122 S. Ct. 1450 (2002); United States v. Martinez-Villalva, 232 F.3d 1329 (10th Cir. 2000) (*Apprendi* does not apply to 16-level enhancement because prior felony conviction is not an element of the offense but instead is a sentencing factor).

§ 11.10. *What about Booker/Fanfan?*

Following *Blakely v. Washington*, 542 U.S. 296, 124 S. Ct. 2531 (2004), *United States v. Booker/United States v. Fanfan*, 125 S. Ct. 738 (2005) could radically change all aspects of federal sentencing including reentry cases and could spell the end of *Almendarez-Torres v. United States*, 523 U.S. 224, 118 S. Ct. 1219 (1998):

> [T]he "statutory maximum" for *Apprendi* [*v. New Jersey*, 530 U.S. 466, 120 S. Ct. 2348 (2000)] purposes is the maximum sentence a judge may impose *solely on the basis of facts reflected in the jury verdict or admitted by the defendant.* In other words, the relevant "statutory maximum" is not the maximum sentence a judge may impose after finding additional facts, but the maximum he may impose *without* any additional findings.

Blakely, 124 S. Ct. at 2537 (citations omitted) (emphasis in original). This holding indicates that *Almendarez-Torres* was wrongly decided.

§ 11.11. *What does the government need to prove prior convictions?*

The government can use uncertified copies of prior conviction records to prove sentencing enhancements. United States v. Chavaria-Angel, 323 F.3d 1172 (9th Cir.), *cert. denied*, 540 U.S. 887, 124 S. Ct. 217 (2003).

§ 11.12. *Can the government enhance the sentence with old convictions?*

Yes. However, if the defendant entered into a plea for a crime that was not an aggravated felony at the time but one that Congress later defined as an aggravated felony he may have an argument that it should not count. *See* United States v. Magana-Pizano, 200 F.3d 603, 614 (9th Cir. 1999) (alien entered a guilty plea for the prior conviction "in reliance upon the relief afforded by INA § 212(c) [8 U.S.C. § 1182(c)]"); Kathleen M. Sullivan, *Commentary on* Magana-Pizano, 5:2 BENDER'S IMMIGR. BULL. 75 (Jan. 15, 2000); *see also* INS v. St. Cyr, 533 U.S. 289, 121 S. Ct. 2271 (2001); Restrepo v. McElroy, 369 F.3d 627 (2d Cir. 2004), *on remand, writ of habeas corpus denied*, 354 F. Supp. 2d 254 (E.D.N.Y. 2005); United States v. Leon-Paz, 340 F.3d 1003 (9th Cir. 2003).

A. The Guidelines Today

The Federal Sentencing Guidelines control sentencing in federal immigration cases. *See* U.S. SENTENCING GUIDELINES MANUAL

(1993). Immigration offenses are referenced under part 2L. For a general discussion of Guideline sentencing, see THOMAS HUTCHISON & DAVID YELLEN, FEDERAL SENTENCING LAW AND PRACTICE (1989 & 1992 Supp.); GERALD MCFADDEN, JUDY CLARKE & JEFFREY STANIELS, FEDERAL SENTENCING MANUAL (1993 & Supp.); Judy Clark, *Sentencing Options and Procedures Under the Sentencing Reform Act of 1984*, in DEFENDING A FEDERAL CRIMINAL CASE (1992 ed.).

§ 11.13. *How have Booker/Fanfan affected sentencing in § 1326 cases?*

Starting with *Blakely v. Washington*, 542 U.S. 296, 124 S. Ct. 2531 (2004), through *United States v. Booker/United States v. Fanfan*, 125 S. Ct. 738 (2005), the entire concept of federal sentencing has shifted. The Guidelines are, for now, truly "guidelines" and "advisory." They are just one factor among several that the courts must consider in imposing a sentence that is "sufficient but not greater than necessary" to achieve the purposes of 18 U.S.C. § 3553(a)(2). Thus, the following sections outline a sentencing scheme that will yield the advisory sentence and not what was formerly a mandatory sentence only allowing departures in "rare" cases outside the "heartland" of typical cases. *See* **II.B: Departures from the Sentencing Guidelines**, *infra*.

For an interesting and well-crafted application of *Booker/Fanfan* to a § 1326 sentencing, *see* United States v. Galvez-Barrios, 355 F. Supp. 2d 958 (E.D. Wis. 2005). (In the interests of full disclosure, it should be noted that Judge Adelman in *Galvez-Barrios* cited extensively and quoted from this author's other published work pointing out the arbitrariness and other limitations of Guideline § 2L1.2).

§ 11.14. *Which Guidelines apply?*

The Guidelines in effect when the defendant is "found in" apply unless the Guideline at sentencing is more lenient. United States v. Ebolum, 72 F.3d 35 (6th Cir. 1995) (applicable sentencing guidelines are those in effect when the defendant was "found in" the United States, rather than when he illegally reentered); United States v. Rodriguez, 26 F.3d 4 (1st Cir. 1994) (same).

For definition of "found in" see **Chapter 10: Illegal Entry and Reentry — Pretrial and Trial.**

1. Offense Level Calculations

a. General Application Issues

§ 11.15. *How did the old Guideline work?*

Before the 2002 edition, Guideline § 2L1.2(a) set a base offense level of eight with a 16-level enhancement for aggravated felonies and a four-level enhancement for "regular" felonies. If a defendant had a prior nonimmigration felony conviction, the Guideline increased the offense level by 4. *Id.* If the felony was an "aggravated felony," the increase was 16 levels. *Id.* Thus, the offense level, depending on a defendant's prior felonies, was 8, 12, or 24. *Id.* To determine an aggravated felony, one looked to 8 U.S.C. § 1101(a)(43) and interpreted case law.

Now, the Guideline bases increases in offense level, i.e., punishment, on the types of the defendant's prior convictions. Although better for many defendants, the Guideline is now much more complicated. *See generally* Linda Drazga Maxfield, *Aggravated Felonies and § 2L1.2 Immigration Unlawful Reentry Offenders: Simulating the Impacts of Proposed Guideline Amendments*, 11 GEO. MASON L. REV. 527 (2003).

§ 11.16. *Why did the sentencing commission change the Guideline?*

The new Guideline "responds to concerns raised by a number of judges, probation officers, and defense attorneys, particularly in districts along the southwest border between the United States and Mexico, that § 2L1.2 (unlawfully entering or remaining in the United States) sometimes resulted in disproportionate penalties because of the 16-level enhancement provided in the Guideline for a prior conviction for an aggravated felony." U.S. SENTENCING GUIDELINES MANUAL app. C, amendment 632 (2001).

§ 11.17. *Does the Guideline define "felony"?*

Yes. "Felony means any federal, state, or local offense punishable by imprisonment for a term exceeding one year." Application Note 1(B)(iv). *See also* Application Note 3(A) defining "misdemeanor." This includes punishment available for the crime itself, not enhanced punishment available under separate recidivism statutes. *See* United States v. Corona-Sanchez, 291 F.3d 1201, 1209–11 (9th Cir. 2002) (en banc).

§ 11.18. *How will courts interpret a record of conviction?*

Sentencing courts use a "modified categorical approach" when looking at the defendant's prior conviction to see if it is a deportable conviction.

First, the judge will look to see if the statute of conviction categorically establishes an aggravated felony or felony. United States v. Tighe, 266 F.3d 1187, 1196 (9th Cir. 2001); United States v. Bonat, 106 F.3d 1472 (9th Cir.), *cert. denied*, 522 U.S. 874, 118 S. Ct. 192 (1997); Lory Diana Rosenberg, *Separate Opinion — The Immigration Consequences of a "Crime as Defined": How to Analyze and Assess a Criminal Conviction*, 8:5 BENDER'S IMMIGR. BULL. 373 (Mar. 1, 2003).

Second, only if the statute is unclear will the judge "modify" the categorical approach and look to the judicially-noticeable documents. United States v. Sandoval-Venegas, 292 F.3d 1101 (9th Cir. 2002); United States v. Rivera-Sanchez, 247 F.3d 905, 909 (9th Cir. 2001) (en banc); United States v. Palmer, 68 F.3d 52, 55–56 (2d Cir. 1995) ("'if the statutory description ... blankets both violent and non-violent crimes, the court may peek beneath the coverlet'") (quoting United States v. Winter, 22 F.3d 15, 18 (1st Cir. 1994)). The judicially noticeable documents include "the indictment, the judgment of conviction, jury instructions, a signed guilty plea, or the transcript from the plea proceedings," United States v. Casarez-Bravo, 181 F.3d 1074, 1077 (9th Cir. 1999), but not a California Abstract of Judgment. United States v. Navidad-Marcos, 367 F.3d 903 (9th Cir. 2004), *overturning* United States v. Velasco-Medina, 305 F.3d 839 (9th Cir. 2002).

§ 11.19. *Who has the burden of proving prior convictions?*

The government has the burden of proving a prior conviction with clear and convincing evidence. United States v. Bonilla-Montenegro, 331 F.3d 1047, 1049 (9th Cir. 2003), *cert. denied*, 540 U.S. 1210, 124 S. Ct. 1487 (2004). The district court cannot shift the burden to the defense. *See* United States v. Guzman, 318 F.3d 1191, 1197–98 (10th Cir. 2003); United States v. Mezas de Jesus, 217 F.3d 638, 645 (9th Cir. 2000); *see generally* Mitchell v. United States, 526 U.S. 314, 327–30, 119 S. Ct. 1307 (1999) (defendant retains privilege against self-incrimination at sentencing and cannot be forced to provide the proof for sentencing enhancers).

§ 11.20. *How do probation/parole revocations count?*

If the revocation was before the defendant alien's deportation, the courts count the revocation time. Conversely, if the revocation was after deportation, the revocation time is not counted. *See* United States v. Jimenez, 258 F.3d 1120, 1125–26 (9th Cir. 2001), *cert. denied*, 534 U.S. 1151, 122 S. Ct. 1115 (2002); United States v. Guzman-Bera, 216 F.3d 1019, 1021 (11th Cir. 2000) ("Although [defendant's] 1995 conviction may have become an aggravated felony after his reentry into the United States and he received the 18-month prison sentence, it was not one when he was deported and when he reentered ....").

b. Offense Levels for Priors

§ 11.21. *How do a defendant's priors count?*

Guideline § 2L1.2 graduates punishment based on the nature of the prior conviction adding points as follows:

A. 16 levels for various listed crimes of violence including "drug trafficking offenses" with a sentence of 13 months or more;
B. 12 levels for a "drug trafficking offense" with a sentence of 13 months or less;
C. 8 levels for an "aggravated felony" not covered in A. and B.;
D. 4 levels for non-aggravated felonies and four misdemeanors for drug trafficking offenses or crimes of violence.

§ 11.22. *So who gets the 16-level increase under the new Guideline?*

Defendant aliens with the following convictions:

1. "Drug trafficking" with a sentence of 13 months;
2. Crime of violence;
3. Firearms offense;
4. Child pornography offense;
5. National security or terrorism offense;
6. Human trafficking offense;
7. Alien smuggling committed for profit.

§ 11.23. *Can a non-aggravated felony get the 16-levels?*

Yes. Under the former § 2L1.2 the 16-level increase was only for aggravated felonies defined at 8 U.S.C. § 1101(a)(43). Under the new § 2L1.2, the Guideline definition controls and therefore even if a crime is not an § 1101(a)(43) aggravated felony the 16-level increase may apply. United States v. Pimentel-Flores, 339 F.3d 959 (9th Cir. 2003).

§ 11.24. *So what is a "drug trafficking" offense?*

A drug trafficking offense is an offense under federal, state, or local law that prohibits the manufacture, export, distribution, or dispensing of a controlled substance (or a counterfeit substance) or the possession of a controlled substance (or a counterfeit substance) with intent to manufacture, import, export, distribute, or dispense." Application Note 1(B)(iii).

§ 11.25. *Are the 13 months based on time served or time imposed?*

Time actually served. Application Note (1)(A)(iv) states that the following:

> If all or any part of a sentence of imprisonment was probated, suspended, deferred, or stayed, "sentence imposed" refers only to the portion that was not probated, suspended, deferred, or stayed.

This note is at odds with the definition of "conviction" at 8 U.S.C. § 1101(a)(48)(B), which counts the time imposed. *See* **Chapter 4: Immigration Consequences of Criminal Convictions**. This new definition is for determining sentences under § 2L1.2; the ICE and immigration court will still use 8 U.S.C. § 1101(a)(48)(B) for deportability questions.

But, the amendment effective November of 2003 deletes Note (1)(A)(iv) and adds (1)(B)(vii) giving the following definition:

> "Sentence of imprisonment" has meaning given in App. Note 2 and § 4A1.2(b), without regard to date of conviction."

Thus, the length of the sentence will now include any term of imprisonment given upon revocation. *See* United States v. Ruiz-Gea, 340 F.3d 1181 (10th Cir. 2003); United States v. Compian-Torres, 320 F.3d 514 (5th Cir. 2003); United States v. Moreno-Cisneros, 319 F.3d 456 (9th Cir.), *cert. denied*, 540 U.S. 1061, 124 S. Ct. 840 (2003); United States v. Hidalgo-Macias, 300 F.3d 281 (2d Cir. 2002); United States v. Jimenez, 258 F.3d 1120, 1125–26 (9th Cir. 2001), *cert. denied*, 534 U.S. 1151, 122 S. Ct. 1115 (2002).

§ 11.26. *What is a "crime of violence"?*

"Crime of violence" means an offense under federal, state, or local law that has as an element the use, attempted use, or threatened use of physical force against the person of another, and includes murder, manslaughter, kidnapping, aggravated assault, forcible sex offenses (including sexual abuse of a minor), robbery, arson, extortion, extortionate extension of credit, and burglary of a dwelling." Application Note 1(B)(ii).

§ 11.27. *Do the two parts of this "crime of violence" definition diverge?*

On certain points, yes. An open question is whether all listed crimes at Application Note (1)(B)(ii)(II) are "crimes of violence" if they do not have an element of force. For example, Commentary 1(B)(ii)(II) states that "forcible sex offenses (including sexual abuse of a minor)" is a crime of violence even though statutory rape usually lacks the element of "force." *See, e.g.*, 18 U.S.C. § 2243. Thus, under Commentary 1(B)(ii)(I) no element of force means this crime is not a crime of violence but under Commentary 1(B)(ii)(II) it may be. *See* United States v. Medina-Maella, 351 F.3d 944 (9th Cir. 2003) (lewd act upon child constitutes "sexual abuse of a minor" under § 2L1.2(b)(1)(A) regardless of whether conduct involved force or threat), *cert. denied*, 124 S. Ct. 2927 (2004); United States v. Pereira-Salmeron, 337 F.3d 1148 (9th Cir. 2003) (carnal knowledge offense even without force is crime of violence); *but see* United States v. Calderon-Pena, 383 F.3d 254 (5th Cir. 2004), *cert. denied*, 125 S. Ct. 932 (2005); United States v. Vargas-Duran, 356 F.3d 598 (5th Cir.) (en banc) (child endangerment conviction without element of force or threat not crime of violence), *cert. denied*, 541 U.S. 965, 124 S. Ct. 1728, *cert. denied, motion granted by* 125 S. Ct. 494 (2004).

§ 11.28. *Must a crime of violence include the intentional use of force?*

The circuits are split with some holding that the term "use of force" under either the Guideline or 18 U.S.C. § 16(b) means the intentional use of force. *See, e.g.*, United States v. Lucio-Lucio, 347 F.3d 1202, 1205–06 (10th Cir. 2003) ("use of force" in § 16(b) "carries a connotation of at least some degree of intent"); Bazan-Reyes v. INS, 256 F.3d 600 (7th Cir. 2001). Conversely, other circuits hold that the Guideline definition does not contain a volitional element.

United States v. Gonzalez-Lopez, 335 F.3d 793 (8th Cir.), *cert. denied,* 540 U.S. 1027, 124 S. Ct. 591 (2003); United States v. Bonilla-Montenegro, 331 F.3d 1047 (9th Cir. 2003) ("reckless" intent satisfies element), *cert. denied,* 540 U.S. 1210, 124 S. Ct. 1487 (2004).

§ 11.29. *Is felony driving under the influence a crime of violence?*

Under the aggravated felony definition at 8 U.S.C. § 1101(a)(43), felony DUI is not a crime of violence in several circuits and therefore will probably not be under § 2L1.2. *See* Montiel-Barraza v. INS, 275 F.3d 1178 (9th Cir. 2002) (per curiam) (state DUI with multiple DUI priors not crime of violence and aggravated felony); United States v. Trinidad-Aquino, 259 F.3d 1140 (9th Cir. 2001) (California conviction for driving under influence with injury to another was not "crime of violence"); United States v. Chapa-Garza, 243 F.3d 921 (5th Cir. 2001) (overturning United States v. Camacho-Marroquin, 188 F.3d 649 (5th Cir. 1999), *on rehearing, opinion withdrawn, petition dismissed, stay lifted, motion granted by* 222 F.3d 1040 (5th Cir. 2000)). The reason for this is that drunk driving does not involve the intent to use force. This is at odds with the Tenth and Eleventh Circuits. *See* Tapia-Garcia v. INS, 237 F.3d 1216 (10th Cir. 2001); Le v. Attorney General, 196 F.3d 1352 (11th Cir. 1999).

§ 11.30. *Is burglary a "crime of violence" under this Guideline?*

The Guideline states that "burglary of a dwelling" is a crime of violence. This provision narrows the definition of "burglary" to that in *United States v. Taylor,* 495 U.S. 575, 110 S. Ct. 2143 (1990), and *Sareang Ye v. INS,* 214 F.3d 1128 (9th Cir. 2000) and distinguishes the definition from many state "burglary" statutes. However, if the defendant has a conviction for burglary of a dwelling it is a crime of violence. *See* United States v. Rodriguez-Rodriguez, 364 F.3d 1142 (9th Cir. 2004) (aiding and attempts included in definition of crime of violence at § 2L1.2), *opinion amended and superceded on denial of reh'g by* 393 F.3d 849 (9th Cir. 2005), *cert. denied,* 125 S. Ct. 2280 (2005).

§ 11.31. *What assaults are "crimes of violence"?*

Under the new § 2L1.2, felony assault is a "crime of violence" regardless of the sentence imposed. This appears to be different from the definition of assault under the aggravated felony statute at 8 U.S.C. § 1101(a)(43), which states that assault is an aggravated felony if "the term of imprisonment [is] at least one year." This divergence appears incompatible with the Commission's goal in modifying the aggravated felony enhancement because "a defendant who previously was convicted of murder, for example, receives the same 16-level enhancement as a defendant previously convicted of simple assault."

§ 11.32. *Which "firearms offenses" add 16-levels?*

A trafficking of a firearm or explosive device defined at 18 U.S.C. § 921 and 18 U.S.C. § 841(c), possession of a firearm or explosive device defined at 26 U.S.C. § 5845(a) and 18 U.S.C. § 841(c), violations of 18 U.S.C. §§ 844(h), 924(c), 929(a), and analogous state statutes all cause the 16-level adjustment to apply.

§ 11.33. *What other convictions add 16-levels?*

Child pornography offenses, national security or terrorism offenses, human trafficking offenses, and alien smuggling committed for profit all are predicates for the 16-level adjustment. *See* Title 18, United States Code.

§ 11.34. *Is the 16-level increase cruel and unusual?*

No. Even though the 16-level increase for the crime of reentering the country illegally after a prior aggravated felony makes the crime equivalent under the Guidelines to committing voluntary manslaughter, it is not cruel and unusual punishment. United States v. Estrada-Plata, 57 F.3d 757 (9th Cir. 1995), *following* United States v. Cupa-Guillen, 34 F.3d 860, 864 (9th Cir. 1994), *cert. denied*, 513 U.S. 1120, 115 S. Ct. 921 (1995).

§ 11.35. *Who gets 12 levels under the new Guidelines?*

A defendant alien with a "drug trafficking conviction" who received a sentence of 13 months or less gets 12 levels added to the base offense level.

§ 11.36. *Who gets eight levels under the new Guidelines?*

"For purposes of subsection (b)(1)(c), 'aggravated felony' has the meaning given that term in 8 U.S.C. § 1101(a)(43), without regard to the date of conviction of the aggravated felony." Application

Note 2. This statements invokes all the case law from all the circuits and the BIA on what constitute aggravated felonies under 8 U.S.C. § 1101(a)(43). *See* **Chapter 5: Aggravated Felonies.**

§ 11.37. *Who gets four levels under the new Guidelines?*

All other felons as well as persons with three or more misdemeanors for crimes of violence or drug trafficking offenses get the four levels. The new definitions of "crimes of violence" and "drug trafficking offenses" in the Guideline application notes affect this. *See supra.*

§ 11.38. *Does a prior for simple possession of drugs get eight or four levels?*

Under *United States v. Ibarra-Galindo,* 206 F.3d 1337 (9th Cir. 2000), *cert. denied,* 531 U.S. 1102, 121 S. Ct. 837 (2001), "simple possession" was an aggravated felony because it is a "drug trafficking" crime. United States v. Garcia-Olmedo, 112 F.3d 399, 400 (9th Cir. 1997). However, the Ninth Circuit has conflicting opinions depending on the context of whether simple drug possession constitutes an aggravated felony under 8 U.S.C. § 1101(a)(43). *Compare* Cazarez-Gutierrez v. Ashcroft, 356 F.3d 1015 (9th Cir.), *opinion withdrawn,* 366 F.3d 736 (9th Cir.), *reh'g,* 382 F.3d 905 (9th Cir. 2004) (simple drug possession is not an aggravated felony under § 1101(a)(43) for immigration purposes), *on rehearing, judgment entered (case transferred to district court for consideration as petition for habeas corpus), with United States v. Ibarra-Galindo* (simple drug possession is an aggravated felony under § 1101(a)(43) for sentencing purposes). Moreover, the Ninth Circuit's rulings on various state drug provisions are confusing. *Compare* United States v. Robles-Rodriguez, 281 F.3d 900 (9th Cir. 2002) (Arizona conviction for drug possession not aggravated felony because under Arizona Proposition 200, incarceration was not authorized) *with* United States v. Arellano-Torres, 303 F.3d 1173 (9th Cir. 2002) (under Nevada Proposition 36, conviction for first possession was an aggravated felony for sentencing purposes), *cert. denied,* 538 U.S. 915, 123 S. Ct. 1502 (2003).

As of this writing, the Ninth Circuit's interpretation of new § 2L1.2 is that such a prior still is an aggravated felony using the definition of 8 U.S.C. § 1101(a)(43)(B), meaning the eight-level enhancement under § (b)(1)(C) applies. *United States v. Arellano-Torres. See also* U.S. SENTENCING GUIDELINES MANUAL § 2L1.2 n.2

(2001). This interpretation differs, however, from the definition of "drug trafficking offense" at Note 1(B)(iii), indicating a simple possession conviction may be excludable from the definition of "aggravated felony," thus requiring only a four-level adjustment under § (b)(1)(D).

2. Criminal History

§ 11.39. *For criminal history points, is the relevant date when the defendant entered illegally or when he was "found in"?*

When the defendant entered. Under Guideline § 4A1.1(d) and (e), a defendant gets points added to his criminal history for committing the illegal entry offense within two years following release from another imprisonment and for being under criminal justice supervision. *See* United States v. Reyes-Pacheco, 248 F.3d 942, 946 (9th Cir. 2001) ("being found in" is a continuing offense that "'commences with the illegal entry, but is not completed until discovery'") (quoting United States v. Ruelas-Arrequin, 219 F.3d 1056, 1061 (9th Cir.), 531 U.S. 1024, 121 S. Ct. 594 (2000)). This ruling is despite the fact that the statute of limitations does not begin to run until the defendant is "found in."

§ 11.40. *Can a defendant's priors be used for both the offense level and criminal history category?*

Using a prior conviction for both the offense level and to add points for criminal history category is not "double counting" under the Guidelines. United States v. Carrasco, 313 F.3d 750 (2d Cir. 2002); United States v. Luna-Herrera, 149 F.3d 1054 (9th Cir. 1998), *cert. denied*, 525 U.S. 1128, 119 S. Ct. 916 (1999); United States v. Torres-Echavarria, 129 F.3d 692 (2d Cir. 1997), *cert. denied*, 522 U.S. 1153, 118 S. Ct. 1177 (1998); United States v. Crawford, 18 F.3d 1173 (4th Cir.), *cert. denied*, 513 U.S. 860, 115 S. Ct. 171 (1994); United States v. Adeleke, 968 F.2d 1159 (11th Cir. 1992); United States v. Campbell, 967 F.2d 20 (2d Cir. 1992).

§ 11.41. *But what about when the prior cannot count as criminal history?*

Even if a prior does not count for assessing criminal history points under Guideline § 4A1.2, the court can still use the conviction to determine the offense level. United States v. Lara-Aceves, 183 F.3d 1007 (9th Cir. 1999), *cert. denied*, 528 U.S. 1095, 120 S. Ct. 836 (2000).

3. Multiple Punishment Issues

§ 11.42. *Can there be punishment for 8 U.S.C. § 1325 and 8 U.S.C. § 1326 at the same time?*

No. A defendant cannot receive consecutive sentences for violating the illegal entry statute, § 1325, and the reentry after deportation statute, § 1326. United States v. Ortiz-Martinez, 557 F.2d 214, 216–17 (9th Cir. 1977) ("Congress enacted two closely related statutes at the same time in order to discourage by equally harsh punishment two kinds of violations of immigration laws. Congress did not express an intent to pyramid the punishment of the alien who violated both statutes in a single transaction.").

§ 11.43. *Are two separate illegal reentry acts grouped?*

According the Seventh Circuit, no. In *United States v. Bahena-Guifarro*, 324 F.3d 560 (7th Cir. 2003), the court found that two separate acts of illegal reentry into the United States should not be grouped under the Sentencing Guidelines because the defendant's offenses did not constitute a single composite harm and he did not provide the court with any evidence that the crimes were committed as part of a common scheme or plan. This was despite the fact that the two counts involved the same victim, society at large, and were connected by a common criminal objective, the alien's desire to be in the United States near his family. The court reasoned that the illegal reentries were separate in time and each caused the government to incur separate costs of processing and deporting.

§ 11.44. *What about fines, special assessments, or restitution?*

Sentencing courts generally do not impose these in reentry or illegal entry cases. The vast majority of persons charged with these crimes are indigents and there is not a specific identifiable victim other than society at large. Statutes do provide for a $100 special assessment against every criminal defendant and this has been applied to reentry after deportation defendants. The government can consider remitting this $100 special assessment especially for sentences under 18 months because it costs more to review and open a file than to remit the special assessment.

4. Supervised Release Issues

§ 11.45. *What about defendants already on supervised release?*

In addition to being sentenced under higher criminal history categories, the defendant who reenters after a reentry conviction may face a petition to violate supervised release. Most reentry after deportation sentences have a supervised release term that requires defendants to not illegally reenter the country. Thus, when they come back in the country, they not only violate the reentry after deportation statute, they have violated supervised release. *See* United States v. Ortega-Brito, 311 F.3d 1136 (9th Cir. 2002) (informing alien of supervised release orally sufficient as it gave the alien actual notice even though there is not a written condition), *cert. denied*, 539 U.S. 950, 123 S. Ct. 2627 (2003); United States v. Felix, 994 F.2d 550 (8th Cir. 1993) (same).

§ 11.46. *Does supervised release raise any Apprendi concerns?*

No. Supervised release is generally considered part of a criminal conviction, which carries with it the possibility of further incarceration. United States v. Gomez-Gonzales, 295 F.3d 990 (9th Cir. 2002). However, *Blakely v. Washington*, 542 U.S. 296, 124 S. Ct. 2531 (2004) may now open the question. *See Apprendi v. New Jersey*, 530 U.S. 466, 120 S. Ct. 2348 (2000).

§ 11.47. *Does the time the alien spends out of the country count?*

In most circuits while the alien is out of the country during the supervised release, usually three years, the term runs. United States v. Juan-Manuel, 222 F.3d 480 (8th Cir. 2000) (district court lacks authority to toll supervised release during time when defendant is outside the United States or illegally in the United States when his whereabouts are unknown to the probation officer); United States v. Balogun, 146 F.3d 141 (2d Cir. 1998) (Congress did not provide for suspension of supervised release upon deportation). *But see* United States v. Isong, 111 F.3d 428 (6th Cir.) (18 U.S.C. § 3583(d) gave sentencing court authority to suspend supervised release upon deportation), *cert. denied*, 522 U.S. 883, 118 S. Ct. 212 (1997).

B. Departures from the Sentencing Guidelines

1. In General

§ 11.48. *What are departures from the Guidelines?*

Departures are those factors that allow a court to sentence either above or below a Guideline range. "The Commission intends the sentencing courts to treat each guideline as carving out a 'heartland,' a set of typical cases embodying the conduct that each guideline describes." U.S. SENTENCING GUIDELINES MANUAL ch. 1 pt. A4(b). If something is outside the "heartland" a departure may be warranted.

§ 11.49. *Do the Guidelines list departures?*

Yes. The Guidelines list several departure grounds such as for over- or under-representation of criminal history. *See* U.S. SENTENCING GUIDELINES MANUAL §§ 5K1.1, 5K2.0; *see also* 18 U.S.C. § 3553(b); U.S. SENTENCING GUIDELINES MANUAL §§ 5H1.1-10, 5K1.1, 5K2. Other grounds for departure the defense should consider are for coercion and duress under § 5K2.12.

§ 11.50. *Are there departures the Guidelines do not mention?*

Yes. The Supreme Court in *United States v. Koon*, 518 U.S. 81, 116 S. Ct. 2035 (1996), approved such departures, holding that "the Commission did not adequately take into account cases that are, for one reason or another, 'unusual.'" *Koon*, 518 U.S. at 93, 116 S. Ct. at 2044. *See* United States v. Sanchez-Rodriguez, 161 F.3d 556 (9th Cir. 1998) (en banc) (applying *Koon* to a § 1326 case). Thus, circuit courts cannot preclude downward departures unless specified in the Federal Sentencing Guidelines. *See generally* Jason Bent, *Sentencing Equality for Deportable Aliens: Departures from the Sentencing Guidelines on the Basis of Alienage*, 98 MICH. L. REV. 1320 (2000).

§ 11.51. *Under Koon, what is the relevant issue for Guideline departures?*

United States v. Koon, 518 U.S. 81, 116 S. Ct. 2035 (1996), established that the relevant inquiry for deciding whether a departure applies is fact-based. "The relevant question, however, is not, as the Government says, whether a particular factor is within the 'heartland' as a general proposition, but whether the particular factor is within the heartland given all the facts of the case." *Koon*, 518 U.S. at 99–100, 116 S. Ct. at 2047 (internal quotations omitted).

§ 11.52. *How does Koon define such a fact-based inquiry?*

Koon directs sentencing courts to four questions:

1. What features of this case, potentially, take it outside the Guidelines' 'heartland' and make it a special, or unusual, case?
2. Has the Commission forbidden departures based on those features?
3. If not, has the Commission encouraged departures based on those features?
4. If not, has the Commission discouraged departures based on those features?

United States v. Koon, 518 U.S. 81, 95, 116 S. Ct. 2035, 2045 (1996) (quoting United States v. Rivera, 994 F.2d 942, 949 (1st Cir. 1993)).

2. Specific Types of Departures

a. Cultural Assimilation

§ 11.53. *What is "cultural assimilation"?*

United States v. Lipman, 133 F.3d 726, 731 (9th Cir. 1998), recognized that an alien with long ties to the United States may have a ground for downward departure. "[C]ultural assimilation may be relevant to sentencing under U.S.S.G. § 2L1.2 if a district court finds that a defendant's unusual cultural ties to the United States — rather than ordinary economic incentives — provided the motivation for the defendant's illegal reentry or continued presence in the United States." *See also* United States v. Rodriguez-Montelongo, 263 F.3d 429 (5th Cir. 2001); United States v. Sanchez-Valencia,

148 F.3d 1273, 1274 (11th Cir. 1998); *but see* United States v. Bautista, 258 F.3d 602, 607 (7th Cir. 2001) (no downward departure for cultural assimilation as "[h]ere, there is nothing extraordinary about Bautista's relationship with his mother and siblings, or his separation from them upon his incarceration and deportation.")

§ 11.54. *What are the factors of cultural assimilation?*

Cultural assimilation applies when the alien has the following:

- Significant ties to the United States;
- Youth at time of entry into the United States;
- Long history of continuous residence in the United States;
- Attendance at U.S. schools;
- Married to or parent of U.S. citizen;
- English principal language.

United States v. Rivas-Gonzalez, 365 F.3d 806, 811 (9th Cir.), *amended by* 384 F.3d 1034 (9th Cir. 2004), *cert. denied,* 125 S. Ct. 1353 (2005), limited the cultural assimilation downward departure to "cases for persons brought to the United States as children, who had adapted to American culture in a strong way and who, after deportation, returned to the United States for cultural rather than economic reasons." The alien's mere "desire to secure and enjoy a higher standard of living" does not justify this departure. *Id.* at 812. *See generally* Kay L. Levine, *Negotiating the Boundaries of Crime and Culture: A Sociologic Perspective on Culture Defense Strategies,* 28 LAW & SOC. INQUIRY 39 (2003).

b. Criminal History and Mitigating Nature of Prior

§ 11.55. *What about criminal history downward departures?*

Former Application note 5 to § 2L1.1 authorized a downward departure for over-representation of criminal history as follows:

> Aggravated felonies that trigger the adjustment from subsection (b)(1)(A) vary widely. If subsection (b)(1)(A) applies, and (A) the defendant has previously been convicted of only one felony offense; (B) such offense was not a crime of violence or firearms offense; and (C) the term of imprisonment imposed for such offense did not exceed one year, a downward departure

may be warranted based on the seriousness of the aggravated felony.

This departure followed cases such as *United States v. Cuevas-Gomez*, 61 F.3d 749 (9th Cir. 1995) (holding that district courts can downward depart despite Guideline mandate of 16-level increase for over-representation of criminal history). The question now is whether the new Guideline precludes such a departure. Under *United States v. Koon*, 518 U.S. 81, 116 S. Ct. 2035 (1996), this basis should still be available because "[a]fter *Koon*, federal courts can no longer categorically proscribe a basis for departure — unless the Commission has proscribed, as a categorical matter, consideration of the factor." United States v. Cubillos, 91 F.3d 1342, 1344 (9th Cir. 1996). The trend appears to follow this reasoning from *Koon* to allow such departures. *See* United States v. Lopez-Zamora, 392 F.3d 1087 (9th Cir. 2004) (2001 Guideline amendments did not bar downward departure consideration for truly minor past offenses characterized as aggravated felonies), *opinion withdrawn*, 2005 U.S. App. LEXIS 16038 (9th Cir. Aug. 4, 2005), *opinion substituted by* 2005 U.S. App. LEXIS 16249 (9th Cir. Cal. Aug. 4, 2005); *but see* United States v. Machiche-Duarte, 286 F.3d 1153 (9th Cir. 2002) (no note 5 departures unless the defendant meets the three listed criteria).

§ 11.56. *What about the mitigating nature of the prior?*

The mitigating nature and circumstances of a prior "aggravated felony" conviction may provide a downward departure. *See, e.g.*, United States v. Castillo-Casiano, 204 F.3d 1257 (9th Cir. 2000) (defendant allowed to raise *Sanchez-Rodriguez* issue between sentencing and appeal); United States v. Sanchez-Rodriguez, 161 F.3d 556, 558–63 (9th Cir. 1998) (en banc); *see also* United States v. Cruz-Guevara, 209 F.3d 644 (7th Cir. 2000); United States v. Diaz-Diaz, 135 F.3d 572, 579–82 (8th Cir. 1998).

c. Consent to Deportation

§ 11.57. *What about consent to deportation with no government agreement?*

Yes. "With respect to the issue of governmental consent, we conclude that, although consent is relevant to a sentencing court's decision whether to depart from the guidelines, the absence of such consent does not constitute an absolute and categorical bar to departure." United States v. Rodriguez-Lopez, 198 F.3d 773, 777 (9th Cir. 1999). Arguably, however, this departure is only open to those aliens with a possible defense to deportation. *Cf.* United States v. Galvez-Falconi, 174 F.3d 255 (2d Cir. 1999). Moreover, 8 U.S.C. § 1231(a)(5) provides for reinstatement of prior removal orders regardless of what an alien defendant does. *See also* United States v. Clase-Espinal, 115 F.3d 1054, 1057–60 (1st Cir.), *cert. denied*, 522 U.S. 957, 118 S. Ct. 384 (1997); United States v. Cruz-Ochoa, 85 F.3d 325 (8th Cir. 1996).

d. Treatment of Aliens in the Federal Bureau of Prisons

§ 11.58. *What about treatment of aliens in the Federal Bureau of Prisons?*

Several cases recognize a downward departure for alien status in non-§ 1326 prosecutions because the Federal Bureau of Prisons does not allow aliens to spend the last six months of their sentences in halfway houses, to get high-paying prison jobs, and to qualify for "low" security classification. *See, e.g.*, United States v. Davoudi, 172 F.3d 1130 (9th Cir. 1999); United States v. Farouil, 124 F.3d 838, 845–47 (7th Cir. 1997); United States v. Charry-Cubillos, 91 F.3d 1342, 1343–45 (9th Cir. 1996); United States v. Smith, 27 F.3d 649, 651–56 (D.C. Cir. 1994); *see also* United States v. Gonzalez-Portillo, 121 F.3d 1122, 1123–25 (7th Cir. 1997), *cert. denied*, 522 U.S. 1061, 118 S. Ct. 720 (1998); United States v. Veloza, 83 F.3d 380 (11th Cir. 1996); United States v. Ebolum, 72 F.3d 35, 38–39 (6th Cir. 1995); United States v. Restrepo, 999 F.2d 640, 645–47 (2d Cir.), *cert. denied*, 510 U.S. 954, 114 S. Ct. 405 (1993). In § 1326 prosecutions, however, courts do not allow this departure because alienage is part of the offense and therefore the Guidelines take it into account. United States v. Cardosa-Rodriguez, 241 F.3d 613 (8th Cir. 2001); United States v. Martinez-Ramos, 184 F.3d 1055 (9th Cir. 1999). This is despite the holding in *United States v. Koon*, 518 U.S. 81, 116 S. Ct. 2035 (1996), that a downward departure basis is valid unless the Commission proscribed it. *See also* McClean v. Crabtree, 173 F.3d 1176 (9th Cir. 1999) (aliens ineligible for one-year reduction of sentence from BOP drug treatment program because they cannot fulfill the halfway house component), *amended by* 1999 U.S. App.

LEXIS 14016 (9th Cir. June 25, 1999), *cert. denied*, 528 U.S. 1086, 120 S. Ct. 814 (2000).

e. Disparity in Plea Practices

§ 11.59. *What about disparity in prosecutorial plea practices?*

Although various U.S. Attorneys offices have "fast-track" policies granting relatively favorable pleas to defendants in § 1326 cases, others do not. But, "[e]ven if differing prosecutorial policies could be considered a mitigating circumstance within the meaning of the statute, the Guidelines themselves would preclude granting a downward departure based on disparity of this nature." United States v. Banuelos-Rodriguez, 215 F.3d 969. 973 (9th Cir. 2000) (en banc). *See also* United States v. Armenta-Castro, 227 F.3d 1255 (10th Cir. 2000); United States v. Bonnet-Grullon, 212 F.3d 692 (2d Cir.), *cert. denied*, 531 U.S. 911, 121 S. Ct. 261 (2000).

f. Good Motives or Necessity

§ 11.60. *What about aliens who return for good reasons?*

The Guidelines at § 5K2.11 allow a downward departure for lesser harms. At least one court has applied this to a reentry defendant who returned to help his girlfriend get surgery. United States v. Barajas-Nunez, 91 F.3d 826 (6th Cir. 1996). *See also* United States v. Singh, 224 F. Supp. 2d 962 (E.D. Pa. 2002) (departure justified for defendant who reentered to see dying mother with intent to stay one week as airline ticket evidenced).

g. Credit for Time Served Immigration Detention

§ 11.61. *What about aliens that spent time in immigration custody?*

These aliens may have a basis for downward departure. When the alien spent time in immigration custody before ICE (formerly INS) referred him to the U.S. Attorney for the § 1326 prosecution, the court can downward depart to account for the time spent. United States v. Camejo, 333 F.3d 669 (6th Cir. 2003); United States v.

Montez-Gaviria, 163 F.3d 697 (2d Cir. 1998); United States v. Ogbondah, 16 F.3d 498 (2d Cir. 1994).

h. Pre-Indictment Delay

§ 11.62. *What about prejudicial pre-indictment delay?*

This is a basis for downward departure such as when it precludes a defendant's chance for concurrent time. United States v. Sanchez-Rodriguez, 161 F.3d 556, 563–64 (9th Cir. 1998) (en banc) (delay in federal charges prejudiced defendant by eliminating chance for concurrent sentence); United States v. Garcia. 165 F. Supp. 2d 496 (S.D.N.Y. 2001).

PART V

ALIEN WITNESSES AND DEFENDANTS

CHAPTER 12

GETTING WITNESSES AND EVIDENCE FROM ABROAD

Other Resources:

MICHAEL ABBELL, OBTAINING EVIDENCE ABROAD IN CRIMINAL CASES (2003).

Department of State website, http://travel.state.gov/law/info/judicial/judicial_702.html. Within this site are the Department of State circulars "Service of Process Abroad," "Service Provisions of the Foreign Sovereign Immunities Act," "Operation of the Hague Service Convention," "Operation of the Inter-American Convention on Service," and "Preparation of Letters Rogatory."

Introduction

§ 12.1. *A hypothetical.*

You are preparing for trial. Luckily, you know a good witness. Unluckily, he is outside the United States. Worse still, he may not be a United States citizen or entitled to enter the United States. What do you do now?

§ 12.2. *Scope.*

This chapter covers getting witnesses and evidence abroad for use in the United States. To get evidence in the United States to use in another country see 28 U.S.C. § 1782. This statute provides a straightforward and effective way for criminal defendants in other countries to get depositions or items from persons or organizations in the United States. On questions of how to effect service of process on another country, consult Rule 4(j)(1) of the Federal Rules of Civil Procedure. This rule provides for service of process on a foreign country under 28 U.S.C. § 1608. Check this statute and the State Department web site listed *supra* for details on which countries accept service by mail or otherwise.

For an extensive review of how prosecutors can obtain evidence under Mutual Legal Assistance Treaties (MLATs), see the U.S. DEPARTMENT OF JUSTICE, UNITED STATES ATTORNEY'S CRIMINAL RESOURCES MANUAL (U.S. ATTORNEY'S CRIMINAL RESOURCES MANUAL) at Sections 266–286. The U.S. government contends that MLATs are only for the use of the prosecution and no case has yet contradicted this. *See* http://travel.state.gov/law/info/judicial/judicial_690.html ("Generally, the remedies offered by the treaties are only available to the prosecutors. The defense must usually proceed with the methods of obtaining evidence in criminal matters under the laws of the host country which usually involves letters rogatory.").

I. Subpoenas to U.S. Citizens and LPRs Abroad

§ 12.3. *Who can be subpoenaed by a United States court?*

Under 28 U.S.C. § 1783 a United States court can subpoena citizens and legal permanent residents living or traveling abroad. *See* Blackmer v. United States, 284 U.S. 421, 436, 52 S. Ct. 252 (1932).

§ 12.4. *How can a litigant counsel subpoena a U.S. citizen in another country?*

Get your subpoena ready under Federal Rule of Criminal Procedure 17(e)(2), which states, "[a] subpoena directed to a witness in a foreign country shall issue under the circumstances and in the manner and be served as provided in 28 U.S.C. § 1783." This statute allows the court to issue the subpoena and defines the manner of service. *See* Gary E. Davidson, *Congressional Extraterritorial Investigative Powers: Real or Illusory?*, 8 EMORY INT'L L. REV. 99 (1994). Rule 4(f) of the Federal Rules of Civil Procedure provides for service in a foreign country. Check with the State Department if the country permits foreigners to serve legal documents.

If you are in state court, refer to state rules of criminal procedure.

§ 12.5. *What criterion will the court use?*

The court may issue a subpoena if it finds that the "particular testimony or the production of the document or other thing ... is necessary in the interest of justice." 28 U.S.C. § 1783(a).

§ 12.6. *Who pays for service?*

The person serving the subpoena must tender to the person being subpoenaed his estimated travel and attendance expenses. The court will decide the amount and state it in the order issuing the subpoena. 28 U.S.C. § 1783(b).

§ 12.7. *What if the citizen refuses to submit to process?*

The court may hold the witness in contempt. The witness must "show cause at a designated time" why he should not be held in contempt. As a punishment, the court may levy or seize any of the witness' property in the United States to satisfy a contempt judgment. 28 U.S.C. § 1784. *See also* United States v. Lansky, 496 F.2d 1063, 1068 (5th Cir.), *reh'g denied*, 502 F.2d 1168 (5th Cir. Fla. 1974). Citizens owe permanent allegiance to the United States and are subject to subpoena. Blackmer v. United States, 284 U.S. 421, 436, 52 S. Ct. 252 (1932) (U.S. law binds American in France). *See also* 28 U.S.C. § 1784.3; *Lansky*, 496 F.2d at 1068.

§ 12.8. *What about legal permanent residents?*

A legal permanent resident alien (LPR) is subject to process. Under 28 U.S.C. § 1783, an LPR may be subject to subpoena while in another country. Also, Federal Rule of Civil Procedure 4(f) defines how to serve the subpoena and requires that it state estimated travel costs and expenses for the witness. 28 U.S.C. § 1783(b). *See* U.S. ATTORNEY'S CRIMINAL RESOURCES MANUAL, § 1-14.311 (2000).

II. "Paroling" Foreign Witnesses for Testimony and Cooperating Witness Visas

§ 12.9. *How do I get a non-U.S. citizen witness here?*

If the alien is willing to come and can get proper documentation such as a regular visitor's visa to enter the country, it eliminates a lot of hassle. Just arrange transportation and get your subpoena ready. The consulate of the witness's country will often help find and bring the witness if necessary and can also help with medical, criminal, or other records.

§ 12.10. *What if the witness cannot get documentation to enter the United States?*

Things get more complicated. For the defense, about the only choice is to get the Department of Homeland Security to "parole" your client in the country. Prosecutors, and defense counsel representing cooperating witnesses have the option of parole or seeking a visa for testimony designated as an "S," "T," or "U" visa.

§ 12.11. *What if the government does not get a known foreign witness?*

At least one court has held that such a witness is not "unavailable" under Federal Rule of Evidence 804(a). United States v. Pena-Gutierrez, 222 F.3d 1080 (9th Cir.), *cert. denied*, 531 U.S. 1057, 121 S. Ct. 670 (2000). This means that either side must get the witness as in any criminal proceeding.

§ 12.12. *What about when the government has deported the witness?*

This does not necessarily give the defense a claim under the Due Process Clause of the Fifth Amendment or the Compulsory Process Clause of the Sixth Amendment, even though the deportation may prevent the defense from reaching the witness. Unless the deportation was not in "good faith," the defense must make "some showing that the evidence lost would be both material and favorable to the defense." United States v. Valenzuela-Bernal, 458 U.S. 858, 873, 102 S. Ct. 3440 (1982).

A. Paroling Witnesses

§ 12.13. *What is "parole" of a witness?*

The Secretary of Homeland Security has authority to grant parole for anyone to come to the United States to testify without being admitted in immigration status. 8 U.S.C. § 1182(d)(5); 6 U.S.C. § 551(d)(2). Specifically, regulations provide for the granting of parole to a person who "will be a witness in judicial, administrative or legislative proceedings." 8 C.F.R. § 212.5(b)(4). The witness must present neither a security risk nor risk of absconding. 8 C.F.R. § 212.5(b). Preclusion of witnesses raises due process concerns where the government is both prosecuting and preventing the testimony of a potential defense witness.

§ 12.14. *What about the alien witness's family?*

Under 8 C.F.R. § 212.14(a)(1) the alien's family members may also be granted parole.

§ 12.15. *Does the alien receive witness fees?*

No. An alien who has been paroled into the United States to testify for the prosecution is ineligible for witness fees or statutory allowances. 28 U.S.C. § 1821(e). The witness, however, may get work authorization from ICE.

§ 12.16. *Are there other types of parole for aliens?*

Yes. DHS has set out categories of aliens subject to detention under 8 C.F.R. § 235.3(b), (c), whom it will consider paroling, but only on a case-by-case basis for "urgent humanitarian reasons" or "significant public benefit" under the following categories:

- aliens with serious medical conditions, 8 C.F.R. § 212.5(b)(1);
- women medically certified as pregnant, 8 C.F.R. § 212.5(b)(2);
- juvenile aliens certified under 8 C.F.R. § 236.3(a) following the guidelines at 8 C.F.R. § 212.5(3)(i)-(iii) and 8 C.F.R. § 236.3(a);
- when the district director or chief patrol agent decides that an alien's continued detention is not in the public interest. 8 C.F.R. § 212.5(b)(5).

These criteria, however, do not guarantee parole and instead only provide conditions under which a district director may exercise his discretion. Bedredin v. Sava, 627 F. Supp. 629 (S.D.N.Y. 1986).

§ 12.17. *How does counsel get an alien witness paroled?*

Contact the your local Bureau of Customs and Border Protection Office for form I-131, Application for Travel Document. Check the box on Part 1 stating "I am outside the United States and am applying for an advance parole." CBP will maintain contact with you regarding the exact dates of the proposed testimony. After you know when and where the alien witness will enter, CBP will fax a special pass to the relevant border patrol station. CBP will usually request a copy of your court subpoena as well. Only Parts 1, 2, and 4 of form I-131 need to be completed to obtain the witness' parole.

§ 12.18. *What are the duties of law enforcement?*

A federal or state agent must do the following to parole in a witness:

- Certify that the alien's parole is essential to an investigation or prosecution, is in the national interest, and is requested under 8 U.S.C. § 1182(d)(5). 8 C.F.R. § 212.14(a)(1)(v).
- Establish its intention to file, within 30 days after the alien's arrival in the United States, a completed form I-854, Inter-Agency Alien Witness and Informant Record, with the Assistant Attorney General, Criminal Division, Department of Justice, under the instructions of the form. 8 C.F.R. § 212.14(a)(1)(i).
- Assume responsibility for the alien while in the United States. 8 C.F.R. § 212.14(a)(1)(ii).
- Advise DHS if the alien does not report quarterly any criminal conduct or other activity constituting excludability or deportability. 8 C.F.R. § 212.14(a)(1)(iii).
- Be responsible for the alien's departure when parole ends. 8 C.F.R. § 212.14(a)(1)(iv).
- Agree to make no promises that the alien will or may (1) remain in the United States in parole status or any other nonimmigrant classification; (2) adjust status to that of lawful permanent resident; or (3) try to remain beyond the authorized parole. 8 C.F.R. § 212.14(a)(1)(vi).

§ 12.19. *What must the alien do for parole?*

He and any family member over 18 must sign an acknowledgment that the parole is only temporary and does not convey immigration benefits. 8 C.F.R. § 212.14(a)(1)(vi).

§ 12.20. *Does the witness have any immigration status while under parole?*

No, a parole is not "an admission" into the country. 8 U.S.C. § 1182(d)(5); Leng May Ma v. Barber, 357 U.S. 185, 78 S. Ct. 1072 (1958). For this reason, if an alien overstays his parole the government can charge him with illegal entry or reentry after deportation. This is because he will still be "found in" regardless of the fact that the United States gave him permission to come in, but not "enter." *See* United States v. Pina-Jaime, 332 F.3d 609 (9th Cir. 2003).

§ 12.21. *What happens after the application for parole is authorized?*

After approving the parole, the Secretary of Homeland Security will notify the Assistant Attorney General, Criminal Division. 8 C.F.R. § 212.14(a)(2)(i). At this point, the law enforcement agent will advise the Secretary of the alien's arrival date, time, and place, 8 C.F.R. § 212.14(a)(2)(ii), so the Secretary can coordinate the alien's arrival in parole status with the port director. 8 C.F.R. § 212.14(a)(2)(ii).

§ 12.22. *How long is the parole?*

Thirty days beginning with the alien's arrival in the United States when the law enforcement agent will submit a completed form I-854 to the Assistant Attorney General, Criminal Division. 8 C.F.R. § 212.14(a)(2)(iii). Resubmitting this form will extend the parole.

§ 12.23. *Can a prosecutor prevent the witness from being paroled in?*

No. However, ICE sometimes requires a Statement of Concurrence from the Assistant U.S. Attorney to grant the request. This requirement presents disclosure problems under the federal discovery rule, Federal Rule of Criminal Procedure 16, and failure to provide the concurrence would probably be prosecutorial misconduct, i.e., the intentional obstruction of compulsory defense process. *See, e.g.*, United States v. Theresius Filippi, 918 F.2d 244 (1st Cir. 1990).

§ 12.24. *How is parole ended?*

The Secretary of Homeland Security may end the alien's parole in the public interest. 6 U.S.C. § 551(d)(2); 8 C.F.R. § 212.14. A district director may also end parole when circumstances do not allow the case's referral to the Secretary, but must notify the Secretary. *See generally* 8 C.F.R. § 212.14(b)(1) (specifying means and requirements for parole termination).

§ 12.25. *Can the decision to end parole be appealed?*

No. Neither the alien nor law enforcement can appeal the decision to end parole. 8 C.F.R. § 212.14(b)(1).

§ 12.26. *How is the alien's departure effected after parole?*

Upon the ending of parole, the law enforcement agent will inform the district director where the alien last lived of the alien's departure. 8 C.F.R. § 212.14(c). The district director may oversee the alien's departure and will notify the Secretary of Homeland Security. 6 U.S.C. § 551(d)(2). The agent or district director must notify the Secretary if the alien fails to depart after parole. 8 C.F.R. § 212.14(c).

B. Visas for Cooperating Witnesses

§ 12.27. *What are the visas for cooperating witnesses?*

These are designated the "S," "T," and "U" visas. The S-visa, a.k.a. "Snitch" visa, is available for cooperating witnesses in both federal and state cases. T- and U-visas are for witnesses who have been victims of crime and provide protection against removal. *See* MARY E. KRAMER, IMMIGRATION CONSEQUENCES OF CRIMINAL ACTIVITY: A GUIDE TO REPRESENTING FOREIGN-BORN DEFENDANTS, *Chapter 8 — Visas for Cooperating Witnesses* (2003); Lory Diana Rosenberg, *Consideration of (Not So) New "T" and "U" Visas and How They Work*, 8:20 BENDER'S IMMIGR. BULL. 1628 (Oct. 15, 2003).

§ 12.28. *What statute defines the "S" visa?*

Title 8 U.S.C. § 1101(a)(15)(S) defines the requirements of an S-visa. The witness's information must be critical and reliable to an investigation of a criminal organization or enterprise and the witness must be essential to the prosecution. An agent may file a request for an S-nonimmigrant visa classification to be approved by the Secretary under 8 C.F.R. § 214.2(t). The Secretary can (1) end the parole; (2) determine eligibility for waivers; and (3) admit the alien in S-nonimmigrant classification under 8 U.S.C. § 1101(a)(15)(S) and 8 C.F.R. § 214.2(t). *See* 8 C.F.R. § 212.14(b)(2).

§ 12.29. *How many S-visas are there each year?*

Title 8 U.S.C. § 1184(k)(1) allows for only 200 S-visas a year, including 50 for terrorist cases.

§ 12.30. *Can immigration status adjustment be made for the S-visa recipient?*

After completing testimony or other prosecutorial assistance, the witness can receive the reward of LPR status. Under 8 U.S.C. § 1255(j), the Attorney General can grant this status, which could lead to eventual citizenship for the alien and his family.

§ 12.31. *What is a "T" visa?*

The T-visa defined at 8 U.S.C. § 1101(a)(15)(T) is for victims of "severe" human trafficking who cooperate with law enforcement. This is for cases involving commercial sex workers or forced labor. The regulations are at 8 C.F.R. § 214.11.

§ 12.32. *What is a "U" visa?*

The U-visa provides a three year permission to stay in the United States for victims of various types of "criminal activity" defined at 8 U.S.C. § 1101(a)(15)(U)(iii). After the three years the victim/alien may apply for permanent resident status. The statute defines "criminal activity" as a violation of a state or federal law involving rape, torture, trafficking, incest, domestic violence, sexual assault, abusive sexual contact, prostitution, sexual exploitation, female genital mutilation, being held hostage, peonage, involuntary servitude, slave trade, kidnapping, abduction, unlawful criminal restraint, false imprisonment, blackmail, extortion, manslaughter, murder, felonious assault, witness tampering, obstruction of justice, perjury, or attempt, conspiracy, or solicitation to commit any of the above mentioned crimes.

III. Compelling Foreign Witnesses or Taking Foreign Depositions and Foreign Documents

§ 12.33. *What about an alien who does not want to testify?*

Generally, a U.S. court cannot compel an alien to appear, because aliens owe no allegiance to the United States. United States v. Theresius Filippi, 918 F.2d 244, 247 (1st Cir. 1990) (court has no subpoena power over non-U.S. citizen outside the United States);

Gillars v. United States, 182 F.2d 962 (D.C. Cir. 1950). *See also* U.S. ATTORNEY'S CRIMINAL RESOURCES MANUAL § 1-14.321 (2000). However, there may be a "treaty of mutual assistance" that the attorney can use to compel foreign testimony, or the option of a letter rogatory (explained below).

§ 12.34. *If the parole does not work or the witness refuses, what then?*

Consider taking the deposition of the witness in the foreign country. Federal Rule of Criminal Procedure 15(a) and 18 U.S.C. § 3503 allow for taking depositions in "exceptional circumstances." *See* United States v. Sanchez-Lima, 161 F.3d 545 (9th Cir.) (trial court erred under Sixth Amendment by refusing to admit sworn videotaped testimony of deported Mexican witness), *amended by* 98 Cal. Daily Op. Service 9038, 98 D.A.R. 12651 (9th Cir. Cal. Dec. 11, 1998), *amended, rehearing en banc denied,* 1998 U.S. App. LEXIS 31063 (9th Cir. Aug. 19, 1998); United States v. Sines, 761 F.2d 1434 (9th Cir. 1985). Specifically, Rule 15(a) allows the court to order a deposition "[w]henever due to exceptional circumstances of the case it is in the interests of justice that the testimony of a prospective witness of a party be taken and preserved for use at trial."

As with any deposition with a witness speaking another language, a good interpreter is a must. *See* Nina Ivanichvili, *A Lawyer's Guide to Cross-Cultural Depositions,* 32 COLO. LAW. 81 (2003).

§ 12.35. *What constitutes "exceptional circumstances"?*

In *United States v. Drogoul,* 1 F.3d 1546, 1552 (11th Cir. 1993), the court defined exceptional circumstances as follows:

> [E]xceptional circumstances exist within the meaning of Rule 15(a) when the prospective deponent is unavailable for trial and the absence of his or her testimony would result in an injustice. The principal consideration guiding whether the absence of a particular witness's testimony would produce injustice is the materiality of that testimony to the case. When a prospective witness is unlikely to appear at trial and his or her testimony is critical to the case, simple fairness requires permitting the moving party to preserve that testimony — by deposing the witness — absent significant countervailing factors which would render the taking of the deposition unjust.

(Citations omitted.) The witness must be generally unavailable, although Rule 15 and 18 U.S.C. § 3503 do not require any conclusive showing of "unavailability" before the deposition. Unavailability may be shown "through affidavits or otherwise." United States v. Alvarez, 837 F.2d 1024, 1029 (11th Cir.), *cert. denied*, 486 U.S. 1026, 108 S. Ct. 2003 (1988). Also, final admissibility of the testimony is not relevant to whether the court should order the deposition. United States v. Sines, 761 F.2d 1434, 1439 (9th Cir. 1985). However, the testimony must be material to the case. *See, e.g.*, United States v. Berger, 990 F. Supp. 1051 (C.D. Ill. 1997), *rev'd and remanded sub nom.* United States v. Ladd (*In re* AP), 162 F.3d 503 (7th Cir. 1998), *subsequent proceeding rev'd and remanded sub nom.* United States v. Ladd, 218 F.3d 701 (7th Cir. 2000); United States v. Trout, 633 F. Supp. 150 (N.D. Cal. 1985); *see also* United States v. Johnpoll, 739 F.2d 702, 709 (2d Cir.) (deposition of foreign national using letters rogatory justified as exceptional circumstance given witness's refusal to travel or demand of unreasonable compensation to testify), *cert. denied*, 469 U.S. 1075, 105 S. Ct. 571 (1984).

§ 12.36. *What about if the government agent would be in danger?*

The court considers whether the safety of U.S. officials is compromised by the foreign location. United States v. Olafson, 213 F.3d 435, 442 (9th Cir. 2000) ("conditions in Mexico were unsafe for American prosecutors"); United States v. Omene, 143 F.3d 1167, 1169–70 (9th Cir. 1998).

§ 12.37. *Does the defendant have the right to be present?*

Rule 15(c) of the Federal Rules of Criminal Procedure generally guarantees the defendant's right to be present at a deposition, although courts have modified this right for foreign depositions. For example, the host government may not allow the defendant to be present at the deposition. Thus, parties usually provide the defendant with two telephones — one to listen to testimony and one to confer with his attorney. *See, e.g.*, United States v. Kelly, 892 F.2d 255, 260 (3d Cir. 1989) (Belgium refused United States request to allow detainees to enter), *cert. denied*, 497 U.S. 1006, 110 S. Ct. 3243 (1990); United States v. Salim, 855 F.2d 944 (2d Cir. 1988) (defendant given two telephone lines for deposition because U.S. Marshal's office has no authority to "keep him in custody in

France"). The government must still make "diligent efforts" to secure the defendant's presence at the deposition. *See, e.g.*, United States v. Gifford, 892 F.2d 263, 265 (3d Cir. 1989), *cert. denied*, 497 U.S. 1006, 110 S. Ct. 3243 (1990).

§ 12.38. *Is a foreign deposition admissible at trial?*

Rule 15(a) provides that a deposition may be used at trial "so far as otherwise admissible under the Rules of Evidence." For deposition testimony to be admissible, Rule 804(b) requires that (1) the witness be "unavailable," (2) the deposition be taken "in compliance with law", and (3) the opposing party have the opportunity to cross-examine the witness. United States v. Kelly, 892 F.2d 255, 262–63 (3d Cir. 1989), *cert. denied*, 497 U.S. 1006, 110 S. Ct. 3243 (1990). *See also* United States v. Salim, 855 F.2d 944, 953 (2d Cir. 1988) (depositions can be used "unless the manner of examination required by the law of the host nation is so incompatible with our fundamental principles of fairness or so prone to inaccuracy or bias as to render the testimony inherently unreliable").

§ 12.39. *What about cross-examination under new Supreme Court rulings?*

Crawford v. Washington changed cross examination law considerably and gives added weight to challenges of this evidence. 541 U.S. 36, 124 S. Ct. 1354 (2004) (holding out-of-court statements not admissible even if "reliable" and within a "firmly rooted hearsay exception"). This most certainly will be relevant in cases involving foreign depositions. Before, courts had specifically ruled that sworn videotape testimony taken in a foreign country with various guarantees of trustworthiness under the catch-all exception of Federal Rule of Evidence 807 is admissible as part of the Sixth Amendment right to a fair trial. United States v. Sanchez-Lima, 161 F.3d 545 (9th Cir.), *amended by* 98 Cal. Daily Op. Service 9038, 98 D.A.R. 12651 (9th Cir. Cal. Dec. 11, 1998), *amended, rehearing en banc denied*, 1998 U.S. App. LEXIS 31063 (9th Cir. Aug. 19, 1998). *See also* Mark A. Godsey, *The New Frontier of Constitutional Confession Law — The International Arena: Exploring the Admissibility of Confessions Taken by U.S. Investigators from Non-Americans Abroad*, 91 GEO. L.J. 851 (2003).

§ 12.40. *What else does Rule 15 provide for foreign depositions?*

- Rule 15(a) may require a deponent to produce nonprivileged information;
- Rule 15(d) provides that the government must pay expenses when it requests the deposition or when the defendant cannot;
- Rule 15(e) describes the manner for taking depositions;
- Rule 15(g) provides that a party objecting to deposition testimony or evidence must state the grounds during the testimony.

§ 12.41. *Are foreign documents admissible?*

Yes, but the requirements of the Federal Rules of Evidence apply as with any document including authentication under Federal Rule of Evidence 902(3).

IV. Letters Rogatory

§ 12.42. *Is taking a foreign deposition as simple as using Rule 15(a)?*

No. Federal Rule of Civil Procedure 28(b)(3) defines the process for taking depositions in both civil and criminal cases. This includes that the deposition be taken under the authority of a letter rogatory. *See* United States v. Steele, 685 F.2d 793, 809 (3d Cir.) (court may issue requests for letters rogatory), *cert. denied*, 459 U.S. 908, 103 S. Ct. 213 (1982).

§ 12.43. *What is a "letter rogatory"?*

A "letter rogatory" is a request from a U.S. court for assistance from a court in another country. The requests are based on specific treaty obligations such as the Hague Convention and Mutual Legal Assistance in Criminal Matters Treaty, or on the concept of "comity" between nations. Several secondary sources explain this in greater detail. *See, e.g.*, WRIGHT AND MILLER, FEDERAL PRACTICE AND PROCEDURE §§ 2083, 1134 (1970) and 1992 Supplement at 206–07. Letters rogatory for international judicial assistance can go to or from foreign countries. *See, e.g.*, *In re* Letter of Request from Amtsgericht Ingolstadt, Federal Republic of Germany [United States v. Morris], 82 F.3d 590 (4th Cir. 1996) (federal district court properly enforced German judicial request for blood sample from U.S. citizen in paternity matter).

Using letters rogatory can be a long process. Try contacting the foreign consulate of the country to see if another procedure or informal arrangement exists.

§ 12.44. *What is the power for the issuance of letters rogatory?*

The principle of comity between nations is the basis of letters rogatory. *See, e.g.*, Philadelphia Gear Corp. v. Philadelphia Gear de Mexico, S.A., 44 F.3d 187 (3d Cir. 1994) (granting of summary judgment abuse of discretion without reference to letter rogatory or factual findings on international comity), *judgment entered on remand*, 1995 U.S. Dist. LEXIS 15629 (E.D. Pa. Oct. 25, 1995); United States v. Zabady, 546 F. Supp. 35, 39 n.9 (M.D. Pa. 1982) (government sought testimony through letters rogatory from witnesses in eight foreign countries); The Signe, 37 F. Supp. 819, 820 (E.D. La. 1941) (letters rogatory allow country to request assistance for the administration of justice from another country).

§ 12.45. *Under what power do federal courts issue letters rogatory?*

Federal courts do so under 28 U.S.C. §§ 1781, 1782, and their "inherent authority." *See* FED. R. CRIM. P. 57; *see, e.g.*, United States v. Reagan, 453 F.2d 165, 171–73 (6th Cir. 1971), *cert. denied*, 406 U.S. 946, 92 S. Ct. 2049 (1972); United States v. Strong, 608 F. Supp. 188 (E.D. Pa. 1985).

§ 12.46. *Can a letter rogatory be used to compel a foreign witness's testimony?*

Yes, but it depends on what is permitted under the procedures of the foreign government. Letters rogatory provide the mechanism for getting the assistance of foreign authorities to compel evidence.

CHAPTER 13
INTERNATIONAL EXTRADITION

Introduction

I. International Extradition In General

II. Constitutional Issues

III. Alternatives to Extradition: Abduction and Immigration Law

IV. Treaties

V. Types of Extradition Requests

- **A. Provisional Arrest and Detention**
- **B. Formal Extradition Requests**
  - **1. Getting the Fugitive Here**
    - **a. General Procedures**
    - **b. Rule of Specialty**
  - **2. Sending the Fugitive There**
    - **a. General Procedures**
    - **b. The Hearing**
    - **c. Legal Standards**
    - **d. Defenses to Extradition**
      - **i. Political Offenses**
      - **ii. Dual Criminality**
      - **iii. Plea Agreements**

VI. Hearings: Appeals and Habeas

Other Resources:

1 MICHAEL ABBELL, INTERNATIONAL EXTRADITION TO AND FROM THE UNITED STATES (2001).

M. CHERIF BASSIOUNI, INTERNATIONAL EXTRADITION: U.S. LAW AND PRACTICE (4th ed. 2002).

International Extradition and Related Matters, in U.S. ATTORNEY'S CRIMINAL RESOURCES MANUAL § 9-15.000 (2d ed. 2000).

Symposium, *International Extradition*, 25 LOY. L.A. INT'L & COMP. L. REV. 369–766 (2003).

John T. Parry, *The Lost History of International Extradition Litigation*, 43 VA. J. INT'L L. 93 (2002).

Introduction

§ 13.1. *What is "extradition"?*

Extradition is a process in international law whereby one country surrenders a person to another country to face prosecution or sentencing. The charging country must demand the surrender. 18 U.S.C. §§ 3181–3196. Every year the United States receives several hundred requests for extradition. *See generally* Ethan A. Nadelmann, *The Evolution of United States Involvement in the International Rendition of Fugitive Criminals*, 25 N.Y.U. J. INT'L L. & POL. 813, 817–18 n.2 (1993).

The extradition statute allows for the arrest of someone for an alleged crime committed in another country. 18 U.S.C. § 3184.

§ 13.2. *Is extradition known by another name?*

"Rendition." Extradition generally refers to the process a treaty defines and is thus a subcategory of rendition that includes both legal and "extralegal" means of bringing a person against his will to a country that wishes to prosecute him. *See generally* M. CHERIF BASSIOUNI, INTERNATIONAL EXTRADITION: U.S. LAW AND PRACTICE 249 (4th ed. 2002).

I. International Extradition in General

§ 13.3. *Is extradition the same as what occurs between states in the United States?*

No. Treaties control international extradition and this process is thus different from the "extradition" between states that Constitution mandates at Article IV, § 2. In international extradition law the term "state" generally refers to countries, not the states of the United States. This chapter, however, will use the term "countries."

§ 13.4. *What branch of the U.S. government extradites?*

The Executive branch. Federal agents execute a warrant of surrender and take the fugitive to officials of another country. The debated question, however, is whether the Executive controls the entire extradition process. *See generally* John T. Parry, *The Lost His-*

tory of International Extradition Litigation, 43 VA. J. INT'L L. 93 (2002).

§ 13.5. *Which office in the Executive branch is charged with extradition?*

The Department of Justice, Criminal Division, Office of International Affairs (OIA) is the office that determines whether extradition is appropriate. This office also decides whether to ask for provisional arrest. *See generally* U.S. ATTORNEY'S CRIMINAL RESOURCES MANUAL § 9-15.200 (2000). The manual recommends that federal prosecutors consult the OIA on any matter relating to extradition because the law of extradition varies between countries and is subject to foreign policy considerations. Both federal and state prosecutors should do this before contacting any foreign official.

§ 13.6. *Are United States citizens extradited?*

Today, yes. *See* 18 U.S.C. § 3196 (2002). In the Nineteenth Century, however, the government usually only extradited aliens. *See* Valentine v. United States ex rel. Neidecker, 299 U.S. 5, 12–18, 57 S. Ct. 100 (1936); Gerald L. Neuman, *Habeas Corpus, Executive Detention, and the Removal of Aliens*, 98 COLUM. L. REV. 961, 994–95 (1998).

§ 13.7. *Is there such a thing as an international arrest warrant?*

No. But, there are Interpol Red Notices that alert governments of an extradition issue when a person is arrested. *See* U.S. ATTORNEY'S CRIMINAL RESOURCES MANUAL § 9-15.035.

§ 13.8. *Is extradition limited to serious crimes?*

The answer depends on what one considers a "serious" crime, but extradition is not limited to violent crimes. A person can be extradited for business, financial, and tax crimes. *See* 4 MICHAEL ABBELL & BRUNO A. RISTAU, INTERNATIONAL JUDICIAL ASSISTANCE 73–74 (1997); CHRISTOPHER L. BLAKESLEY, TERRORISM, DRUGS, INTERNATIONAL LAW, AND THE PROTECTION OF HUMAN LIBERTY 212–17 (1992); Ethan A. Nadelmann, *The Evolution of United States Involvement in the International Rendition of Fugitive Criminals*, 25 N.Y.U. J. INT'L L. & POL. 813, 829–32 (1993). In short, a person can be extradited for any criminal act listed in a given extradition treaty.

§ 13.9. *What about extradition on a capital offense or life without parole?*

Many extradition treaties allow the country to refuse extradition unless the United States assures that there will be no death penalty. *See, e.g.*, Extradition Treaty Between the United States and United Mexican States (Mexico), 31 U.S.T. 5059, T.I.A.S. no. 9656 (1979). This may also apply to potential imposition of a sentence of life without parole. *See generally* Vanessa Maaskamp, Comment, *Extradition and Life Imprisonment*, 25 LOY. L.A. INT'L & COMP. L. REV. 741 (2003); William Schabas, *Indirect Abolition: Capital Punishment's Role in Extradition Law and Practice*, 25 LOY. L.A. INT'L & COMP. L. REV. 581 (2003).

II. Constitutional Issues

§ 13.10. *What is the constitutional basis of extradition?*

Most, though not all, federal courts agree that "extradition is an executive, not a judicial, function. The power to extradite derives from the President's power to conduct foreign affairs. An extradition proceeding is not an ordinary Article III case or controversy. Rather, the judiciary serves an independent review function delegated to it by the Executive and defined by statute." Martin v. Warden, 993 F.2d 824, 828 (11th Cir. 1993).

§ 13.11. *Under what capacity does a judge conduct an extradition hearing?*

Most federal circuit courts hold that when a judge holds an extradition hearing he is not acting as an Article III judge. *See* Lopez-Smith v. Hood, 121 F.3d 1322, 1327 (9th Cir. 1997); Lo Duca v. United States, 93 F.3d 1100, 1105–09 (2d Cir.), *corrected by* 1996 U.S. App. LEXIS 28746 (2d Cir. Aug. 29, 1996), *cert. denied*, 519 U.S. 1007, 117 S. Ct. 508 (1996); *In re* Mackin, 668 F.2d 122, 125–30 (2d Cir. 1981). Other circuits hold otherwise. *See* DeSilva v. DiLeonardi, 125 F.3d 1110, 1113 (7th Cir. 1997); LoBue v. Christopher, 893 F. Supp. 65 (D.D.C. 1995) (extradition statute unconstitutional for allowing executive review of Article III courts), *vacated*, 82 F.3d 1081 (D.C. Cir. 1996); *see also In re* Kirby, 106 F.3d 855, 866 (9th Cir. 1997) (Noonan, J., dissenting); *In re* Smyth, 72 F.3d 1433 (9th Cir. 1996) (Noonan, J., dissenting from denial of rehearing en banc); *see generally* John T. Parry, *The Lost History of International Extradition Litigation*, 43 VA. J. INT'L L. 93 (2002).

§ 13.12. *What about separation of powers issues?*

The separation of powers concept has been applied to extradition. *See, e.g.*, DeSilva v. DiLeonardi, 125 F.3d 1110, 1113 (7th Cir. 1997), *reh'g en banc denied*; LoBue v. Christopher, 893 F. Supp. 65 (D.D.C. 1995) (extradition statute unconstitutional for allowing executive review of Article III courts), *vacated*, 82 F.3d 1081 (D.C. Cir. 1996). This question often centers on historical analysis of the separation of powers doctrine and the early connection of extradition to immigration law. *See, e.g.*, Lopez-Smith v. Hood, 121 F.3d 1322, 1327 (9th Cir. 1997); Lo Duca v. United States, 93 F.3d 1100, 1105–09 (2d Cir.), *corrected by* 1996 U.S. App. LEXIS 28746 (2d Cir. Aug. 29, 1996), *cert. denied*, 519 U.S. 1007, 117 S. Ct. 508 (1996); *In re* Mackin, 668 F.2d 122, 125–30 (2d Cir. 1981). One reading is that "the Executive Branch would retain plenary authority to extradite" based on a similar executive authority in immigration law. *Lo Duca v. United States*, 93 F.3d at 1103. *See also Lopez-Smith v. Hood*, 121 F.3d at 1326; Sidali v. INS, 107 F.3d 191, 194 (3d Cir. 1997), *cert. denied*, 522 U.S. 1089, 118 S. Ct. 879 (1998); Martin v. Warden, 993 F.2d 824, 828 (11th Cir. 1993); Eain v. Wilkes, 641 F.2d 504, 513 & n.13 (7th Cir.), *cert. denied*, 454 U.S. 894, 102 S. Ct. 390 (1981). Other courts and commentators dispute this, arguing that the extradition statute, 18 U.S.C. § 3184, unconstitutionally authorizes the Executive branch to review the court's legal determination of extraditability, in violation of the separation of powers doctrine. *LoBue v. Christopher*; John T. Parry, *The Lost History of International Extradition Litigation*, 43 VA. J. INT'L L. 93, 99–100 (2002).

§ 13.13. *What other constitutional issues exist?*

Litigants have raised other issues. *See, e.g.*, Mainero v. Gregg, 164 F.3d 1199 (9th Cir. 1999) (petitioners raised issue of confessions obtained by torture as grounds to defeat treaty under U.S. Constitution).

III. Alternatives to Extradition: Abduction and Immigration Law

§ 13.14. *When would extradition not work?*

A government may not be able to extradite someone from another country for any number of reasons: the person is a citizen of another country, the crime is not extraditable, or the statute of limitations has run in the foreign country. Also, a country may for whatever reason deny an extradition request. In this situation, governments may seek alternatives to extradition.

§ 13.15. *What are alternatives to extradition?*

As stated, "rendition" is the broad term that includes the use of extradition, abduction, and immigration law to bring a person against his will to a country that wishes to prosecute him. *See generally* M. CHERIF BASSIOUNI, INTERNATIONAL EXTRADITION: U.S. LAW AND PRACTICE ch. 5 (4th ed. 2002). Other forms of rendition include the following:

- Extradite the person from a third country;
- Use a subterfuge to get the person to the United States or international waters or airspace;
- Request the foreign prosecution of the person.

This last option often conflicts with general United States' policy to encourage extradition treaties.

§ 13.16. *What alternatives are there to extradition in the military context?*

Several treaties such as the North Atlantic Treaty Organization's Status of Forces Agreement have "turn over" provisions in which the contracting countries agree to certain rules for turning over military personnel to another contracting country's military authorities. *See generally* Williams v. Rogers, 449 F.2d 513 (8th Cir. 1971), *cert. denied*, 405 U.S. 926, 92 S. Ct. 976 (1972).

§ 13.17. *What "extralegal" means of rendition do countries use?*

Abduction. Abductions occur in two ways: either a country sends its agents to another to capture a person with or without the consent of the other country or the second country's agents capture a person and give him to the first country outside any legal (i.e., treaty) process. M. CHERIF BASSIOUNI, INTERNATIONAL EXTRADITION: U.S. LAW AND PRACTICE 249 (4th ed. 2002). These extralegal means of extradition generally violate international law but most countries have little power to remedy such a violation. The noteworthy case of the Israeli abduction of Adolf Eichmann from Argentina resulted in formal protests to the United Nations but little else. See M. CHERIF BASSIOUNI, INTERNATIONAL EXTRADITION: U.S. LAW AND PRACTICE 253 n.10 (4th ed. 2002); Julie Philippe & Laurent Tristan, *International Law, Extraterritorial Abductions and the Exercise of Criminal Jurisdiction in the United States*, 11 WILLAMETTE J. INT'L L. & DISP. RESOL. 61 (2004).

§ 13.18. *Will courts allow the trial of a person abducted to the United States?*

Yes. In *United States v. Alvarez-Machain*, 504 U.S. 655, 112 S. Ct. 2188 (1992), the Supreme Court held that even if the government abducted the defendant from another country, the government could try him in the United States. The basis of the holding is that claims of abuse of process do not affect a court's personal jurisdiction. *See generally* Ashley Wright Baker, *Forcible Trans-Border Abduction: Defense Versus Offensive Remedies for* Alvarez-Machain, 48 ST. LOUIS U. L.J. 1373 (2004); Stephen Fohn, *Do DEA Field Agents Have the Power to Unilaterally Execute a Trans-Border Abduction?: The Ninth Circuit's Take On ... (*Alvarez-Machain v. United States*, 331 F.3d 604, 9th Cir. 2003 [*Alvarez VII*], cert. granted sub nom. Sosa v. Alvarez-Machain*, 124 S. Ct. 807, 2003),* 27 HOUS. J. INT'L L. 221 (2004).

§ 13.19. *Is abduction a standard practice?*

No. Abducting people from other countries raises sensitive foreign policy problems. Department of Justice policy is to not allow prosecutors to order this without notifying the OIA. Indeed, DOJ encourages prosecutors to notify OIA anytime formal extradition is not used as the method of rendition and the defendant may claim illegality. U.S. ATTORNEY'S CRIMINAL RESOURCES MANUAL § 9-15.610 (2000).

§ 13.20. *What is the relationship between extradition and immigration law?*

Historically they have been closely related and the differences between the two under the law have been confusing. Early extradition cases have arisen "in the immigration context." INS v. St. Cyr, 533 U.S. 289, 305, 121 S. Ct. 2271 (2001) (discussing *In re* Kaine, 55 U.S. (14 How.) 103 (1853)). *See also* Grin v. Shine, 187 U.S. 181, 184, 23 S. Ct. 98 (1902) (describing extradition treaties as "an extension of our immigration laws prohibiting the introduction of persons convicted of crimes by providing for their deportation and return to their own country, even before conviction"); *In re* Ghandtchi, 697 F.2d 1037, 1038 (11th Cir.) (relying on immigration bail procedures to craft a parallel rule for extradition). Also, at least one important early immigration case relied on extradition law. *See* Fong Yue Ting v. United States, 149 U.S. 698, 714, 13 S. Ct. 1016 (1893).

§ 13.21. *Can the government remove aliens instead of extraditing them?*

Yes. Removal is an alternative to extradition if the basis for removal against the alien exists. 4 MICHAEL ABBELL & BRUNO A. RISTAU, INTERNATIONAL JUDICIAL ASSISTANCE 175–76 (1997); M. CHERIF BASSIOUNI, INTERNATIONAL EXTRADITION: UNITED STATES LAW AND PRACTICE 167–216 (3d ed. 1996). The OIA, usually through the Department of State, may ask another country to deport a United States' citizen back to the United States. A variation on this is that the Department of State may revoke the passport of an alien under a federal arrest warrant, which can result in the loss of an alien's legal permanent resident status.

§ 13.22. *What if removal and extradition proceedings are going at the same time?*

The government usually holds back on the removal until it resolves extradition. *See* Barapind v. Reno, 225 F.3d 1100, 1113–14 (9th Cir. 2000).

§ 13.23. *What does immigration law infer about executive authority?*

In immigration law, the political branches have plenary authority often limiting judicial power. *See* INS v. St. Cyr, 533 U.S. 289, 121 S. Ct. 2271 (2001) (current immigration statutes eliminate judicial review but maintain habeas corpus); Gerald L. Neuman, *Jurisdiction and the Role of Law After the 1996 Immigration Act*, 113 HARV. L. REV. 1963 (2000). Courts and commentators, however, dispute Congress' authority to limit judicial review in the immigration context, *see* Richard H. Fallon, Jr., *Of Legislative Courts, Administrative Agencies, and Article III*, 101 HARV. L. REV. 915, 967–70 (1988) (arguing Article III requires federal court review in immigration), and these arguments apply to extradition law. John T. Parry, *The Lost History of International Extradition Litigation*, 43 VA. J. INT'L L. 93, 99 (2002).

IV. Treaties

The Jay Treaty of 1794 (Treaty of Amity Commerce and Navigation) with Great Britain was the first U.S. extradition treaty. The Senate ratified it in 1795.

§ 13.24. *Who can be extradited?*

In most cases the United States can extradite a person only if a treaty exists with the country seeking extradition and federal legislation has implemented the treaty. *See* 18 U.S.C. § 3184 et seq. Title 18 U.S.C. § 3181 lists U.S. extradition treaties. Section 3184 governs extradition of foreign fugitives in the United States. *See also* RESTATEMENT (THIRD) OF FOREIGN RELATIONS LAW § 475 n.5 (1986) (listing multilateral treaties with extradition provisions).

§ 13.25. *Must there always be a treaty for extradition?*

No. Some countries grant extradition without a treaty if there is an offer of reciprocity. Further, 18 U.S.C. §§ 3181 and 3184 permit the United States to extradite without a treaty non-U.S. citizens, nationals or permanent residents who have committed violent crimes against U.S. nationals in other countries where the charge is not politically motivated. *See* 18 U.S.C. § 3181(b).

§ 13.26. *Why are treaties so important for extradition?*

The basic premise of international law is that absent an extradition treaty or specific authority under treaty, a country will not extradite a fugitive. *In re* Chan Kam-Shu, 477 F.2d 333, 338 n.9 (5th Cir.), *cert. denied*, 414 U.S. 847 94 S. Ct. 112 (1973). The Supreme Court, however, has upheld criminal convictions of foreign nationals even after failure to follow extradition treaty provisions. *See*

United States v. Alvarez-Machain, 504 U.S. 655, 112 S. Ct. 2188 (1992). Subsequent courts have declined to extend this holding, instead favoring extradition treaty provisions. *See, e.g.*, Wang Zong Xiao v. Reno, 837 F. Supp. 1506 (N.D. Cal. 1993), *aff'd*, 81 F.3d 808 (9th Cir. 1996). Consequently, the specific language of a treaty determines a court's action.

§ 13.27. *Do treaties control over state law?*

Yes. In the past, states of the United States extradited to foreign countries. *See* Jack L. Goldsmith, *Federal Courts, Foreign Affairs, and Federalism*, 83 VA. L. REV. 1617, 1650 & n.144 (1997). Since then, the Supreme Court has recognized that "[t]he power to provide for extradition is a national power." Valentine v. United States ex rel. Neidecker, 299 U.S. 5, 8, 57 S. Ct. 100 (1936). *See also* United States v. Rauscher, 119 U.S. 407, 412–14, 7 S. Ct. 234 (1886). Treaties, including extradition treaties, are the supreme law of the land under the Supremacy Clause.

V. Types of Extradition Requests

§ 13.28. *What types of extradition requests are there?*

Extradition treaties commonly allow for two types of extradition requests:

1. Provisional arrest requests — this allows arrest under the treaty before all formal documents are ready. The requesting country can go directly to the Department of Justice for a provisional arrest request.
2. Formal requests — these generally occur when the requesting country has all the supporting documents that the treaty requires.

See 18 U.S.C. § 3184; U.S. ATTORNEY'S CRIMINAL RESOURCES MANUAL § 9-15.700 (2000).

A. Provisional Arrest and Detention

§ 13.29. *What is provisional arrest?*

"Provisional" in this context means "temporary." This is the arrest of a fugitive defendant in urgent cases before all the formal treaty requests and documents are ready. Most treaties allow for this.

Counsel for both the government and the defense should keep in mind that all time the fugitive spends under provisional arrest and during extradition proceedings is "dead-time" that will not count against his sentence in the requesting country.

§ 13.30. *What statutes allow for provisional arrest?*

Although a specific treaty may change the time period, 18 U.S.C. § 3183 provides that authorities have three months to hold a foreign fugitive and if the requesting country does not collect the fugitive within this period he may be discharged. Section 3187 provides that when the person is held pursuant to a telegraphic request, the person should be released after 90 days if the government does not produce the necessary documentation from the requesting country.

§ 13.31. *Who decides if the case is "urgent" in the United States?*

The OIA decides whether the case is "urgent" under the relevant treaty. If the defendant is unlikely to flee, the OIA will decide against provisional arrest to allow for more time to prepare the documents for the formal request. Both state and federal prosecutors should contact the OIA on these questions.

§ 13.32. *Can a provisional arrest stand on its own?*

No, it is temporary. The requesting country must submit a formal extradition request with all the documentation that the treaty requires. Moreover, the documents must be certified, authenticated and translated into the receiving country's language. This all must be done within the time the treaty specifies, which is usually from 30 days to three months from arrest, depending on the treaty.

§ 13.33. *What if the requesting country does not conform to the formal treaty requirements?*

If the requesting county does not follow though, the fugitive defendant must be released.

§ 13.34. *Can the accused move for release pending the extradition determination?*

Yes, but as a matter of course the government opposes bond in extradition cases and it must be based upon a showing of special circumstances. *See* **V.A: Provisional Arrest and Detention**, *supra*.

§ 13.35. *Can the court grant the alleged fugitive bail?*

Because extradition is not a criminal proceeding, the Bail Reform Act does not apply. Kamrin v. United States, 725 F.2d 1225, 1227–28 (9th Cir.), *cert. denied*, 469 U.S. 817, 105 S. Ct. 85 (1984). Nevertheless, courts generally have assumed that there is at least a theoretical possibility of bail in extradition cases. Over a century ago, "the Supreme Court recognized that there is a presumption against bail in an extradition case and only 'special circumstances' will justify bail." *In re* Kirby, 106 F.3d 855, 858 (9th Cir. 1996) (quoting Wright v. Henkel, 190 U.S. 40, 63, 23 S. Ct. 781 (1903)). If the extraditees will likely appeal the order of extradition, any unusual delay in that appellate process can be a "special circumstance" that justifies bail. *Kirby*, 106 F.3d at 863. *See also* United States v. Kin-Hong, 83 F.3d 523, 524 (1st Cir. 1996). However, "aside from its broad humanitarian appeal," the fact that the receiving country will not credit the extraditees with time spent in custody in the fugitive country "does not constitute a 'special circumstance.'" *Kirby*, 106 F.3d at 863.

§ 13.36. *What does the alleged fugitive need to show to get bail?*

Only "special circumstances" justify granting bail. Koskotas v. Roche, 931 F.2d 169, 175 (1st Cir. 1991):

> "Special circumstances include the raising of substantial claims upon which the appellant has a high probability of success, a serious deterioration of health while incarcerated, and unusual delay in the appeal process." That the detainee is not a flight risk is not a special circumstance warranting release.

In re Extradition of Rouvier, 839 F. Supp. 537, 539 (N.D. Ill 1993) (quoting Salerno v. United States, 878 F.2d 317, 317, 318 (9th Cir. 1989)).

§ 13.37. *Can an alleged fugitive appeal detention?*

Yes. A federal appellate court has jurisdiction to hear an appeal of a district court's bail determination. *In re* Kirby, 102 F.3d 365 (9th Cir. 1995), *opinion withdrawn, reported at* 1996 U.S. App. LEXIS 33337 (9th Cir. Dec. 16, 1996). Generally, the appeal will be under Federal Rule of Appellate Procedure 27.

§ 13.38. *Does detention time count?*

No. Detention time is "dead time" — the foreign country requesting rendition need not give credit on any underlying sentence for the time the person spends in U.S. custody. If the person has no desire for habeas review then counsel should advise the prosecution and the State Department and request an expedited process.

B. Formal Extradition Requests

1. Getting the Fugitive Here

a. General Procedures

§ 13.39. *How does the United States extradite a fugitive here?*

The federal or state prosecutor contacts the Office of International Affairs, which determines whether extradition is appropriate. The OIA must authorize the extradition. The OIA also makes the decision to ask for provisional arrest. The *U.S. Attorney's Criminal Resources Manual* outlines the exact steps a federal or state prosecutor must follow to complete these requirements. U.S. ATTORNEY'S CRIMINAL RESOURCES MANUAL § 9-15.200 (2000).

§ 13.40. *Why should prosecutors contact the OIA?*

An extradition request that the OIA does not approve may create diplomatic difficulties. Extradition treaties are not uniform. The OIA will advise prosecutors about the chances and procedures for extradition.

§ 13.41. *What documents start extradition?*

The State Department prepares a diplomatic note and transmits it to the foreign government through diplomatic channels. The documents specified in the treaty must accompany the diplomatic note.

§ 13.42. *What documents must support the extradition request?*

The OIA will advise the prosecutor of the documents needed, but the prosecutor must assemble the documents. The prosecutor must also forward the original and four copies to OIA for review, authentication, translation, and transmission to the foreign country thought the State Department. Every treaty is different but all usually require the following:

- The prosecutor's affidavit explaining the case;
- The statutes the fugitive violated and the statute of limitations;
- Certified copies of the arrest warrant and the complaint or indictment;
- If the fugitive has not been convicted, affidavits or grand jury transcripts, establishing the fugitive's identity and that he committed the crime, including sufficient evidence (i.e., photograph, fingerprints, and affidavit of identifying witness) (the Department of Justice recommends avoiding using grand jury transcripts or trial transcripts);
- If the fugitive has been convicted, evidence of identity and a certified copy of the order of judgment and committal and an affidavit stating whether the sentence was partially served and the amount of time remaining to be served.

OIA will provide samples of the required documents.

§ 13.43. *What happens after the documents are assembled?*

Unless the OIA states otherwise, the prosecutor should forward the original and four copies of the entire package to OIA for review and send a copy to the State Department for translation. This can take three weeks even for common languages. The OIA will explain billing and other procedures.

§ 13.44. *What happens in the foreign country?*

The State Department will send the documents and translations to the American Embassy in the foreign country. The embassy will present them with a diplomatic note requesting extradition to the foreign government's appropriate agency, usually the foreign ministry. The country's foreign ministry then forwards the request and documents to the courts or other agency to decide extraditability under treaty and the country's law.

§ 13.45. *How does the foreign country decide?*

Usually by reviewing the request itself and any evidence the fugitive presents. Consequently, the written submission, particularly the United States prosecutor's affidavit, must be as persuasive as possible. This is particularly essential when the case involves unique United States statutes, such as RICO or CCE.

§ 13.46. *How long will it take?*

Although factual defenses are few, the fugitive may delay through procedural challenges or appeal. Thus, predicting when the foreign government will return the fugitive depends on the case and the practice of the foreign country. Again, consult the OIA.

§ 13.47. *How is the fugitive returned?*

After the foreign authorities notify the American Embassy that they will surrender the fugitive, OIA will inform the prosecutor and arrange with the United States Marshals Service to escort the fugitive to the United States. United States Marshals escort even in a state case, though in rare cases state or other federal law enforcement agents may accompany the U.S. Marshals. If the fugitive is an alien, OIA will ask ICE to issue a "parole letter" authorizing the alien's entry. *See* **Chapter 12: Getting Witnesses and Evidence from Abroad**.

b. Rule of Specialty

§ 13.48. *What is the "rule of specialty"?*

Every extradition treaty limits extradition to certain offenses. The doctrine of specialty prevents a requesting country from prosecuting an extradited person for crimes other than those listed in the extradition request. United States v. Baez, 349 F.3d 90 (2d Cir. 2003); United States v. Baramdyka, 95 F.3d 840 (9th Cir. 1996), *cert. denied*, 520 U.S. 1132, 117 S. Ct. 1282 (1997); United States v. Andonian, 29 F.3d 1432 (9th Cir. 1994), *cert. denied*, 513 U.S. 1128, 115 S. Ct. 938 (1995); United States v. Fowlie, 24 F.3d 1059 (9th Cir.), *supplemented*, 24 F.3d 1070 (9th Cir. 1994), *cert. denied*, 513 U.S. 1086, 115 S. Ct. 742 (1995).

§ 13.49. *Are there any exceptions to the rule of specialty?*

Yes. The requesting country can get the permission of the surrendering country to prosecute the alleged fugitive for other crimes. Also, if the defendant commits an offense after extradition or if he remains in the jurisdiction after expiration of a "reasonable time" (usually defined in the extradition treaty) he can be charged with a new crime.

In an interesting case, the Second Circuit ruled that the rule of specialty did not obligate a sentencing court to adhere to the government's interpretation of the diplomatic note's requirements and instead independently reviewed the note in imposing a longer sentence than the government itself believed it was obliged to ask for under the extradition terms. United States v. Baez, 349 F.3d 90, 93 (2d Cir. 2003). The court based its reasoning on several factors including separation of powers considerations as well as the traditional discretion of a sentencing court. *Id.*

§ 13.50. *What if prosecutors wish to charge other charges?*

The *U.S. Attorney's Criminal Resources Manual* recommends that prosecutors contact the OIA for guidance.

§ 13.51. *Does the defendant have standing to raise specialty claims?*

Specialty is not a right of the fugitive/defendant per se but rather the country's right. Some circuits, however, allow a fugitive defendant to raise specialty on his own. *See e.g.*, United States v. Khan, 993 F.2d 1368 (9th Cir.), *amended by* 93 Cal. Daily Op. Service 3436, 93 D.A.R. 5927 (9th Cir. Nev. May 11, 1993), *reported in full at* 1993 U.S. App. LEXIS 10556 (9th Cir. May 11, 1993); United States v. Levy, 905 F.2d 326 (10th Cir. 1990), *cert. denied*, 498 U.S. 1049, 111 S. Ct. 759 (1991); United States v. Herbage, 850 F.2d 1463 (11th Cir. 1988), *cert. denied*, 489 U.S. 1027, 109 S. Ct. 1158 (1989); United States v. Thirion, 813 F.2d 146, 151 (8th Cir. 1987) (the fugitive "may raise whatever objections to his prosecution that [the surrendering country] may have"). Other circuits require the requesting country to initiate the specialty claim. Demjanjuk v. Petrovsky, 776 F.2d 571, 583–84 (6th Cir. 1985), *cert. denied*, 475 U.S. 1016, 106 S. Ct. 1198 (1986).

2. Sending the Fugitive There

a. General Procedures

§ 13.52. *How does the extradition start?*

A country, through its embassy in the United States, submits the extradition request for a fugitive to the State Department. The State Department reviews the request and then forwards it to the Department of Justice, Criminal Division, Office of International Affairs.

§ 13.53. *Who decides to extradite?*

The Secretary of State decides. Under the "Rule of Non-Inquiry" the discretion of the State Department is not reviewable. The courts only decide whether the crime is extraditable and whether probable cause exists and this is subject to limited habeas review. Cornejo-Barreto v. Siefert, 379 F.3d 1075 (9th Cir.), *reh'g en banc granted by* 386 F.3d 938 (9th Cir.), *opinion vacated on rehearing by* 389 F.3d 1307 (9th Cir. 2004).

§ 13.54. *What happens when the OIA receives the request?*

The OIA reviews both types of requests for sufficiency and forwards appropriate ones to the district where the fugitive is thought to be. Federal prosecutors then file a complaint in federal district court asking for the arrest, detention, and extradition of the alleged fugitive. A district judge or magistrate issues an arrest warrant. Upon arrest, the alleged fugitive has a hearing. After the hearing, the OIA advises the requesting country and arranges for the transfer of the fugitive to the requesting country's appointed agents.

§ 13.55. *Can the defendant waive extradition hearings?*

Yes and considering that the time a defendant/fugitive spends in extradition hearings will not count against any potential or already imposed sentence, he may wish to do so. Waivers can be of two types: "General," leaving the defendant open to prosecution for any crime in the requesting country, or "Specific," opening the defendant to prosecution only for the specific offense in the requesting country under the Rule of Specialty.

b. The Hearing

§ 13.56. *How are the courts involved?*

As stated under **II. Constitutional Issues**, *supra*, the role of federal courts, if any, is undefined. Under 18 U.S.C. § 3184, the federal court (usually a magistrate judge) determines whether the arrested person is subject to surrender to the foreign country under terms of the treaty, as well as under U.S. statutes and case law. The court must establish "dual criminality" by probable cause and also find the following: (1) the hearing court has jurisdiction to conduct the extradition hearing and proper jurisdiction over the fugitive; (2) the fugitive is being sought for an offense for which the applicable treaty permits extradition; and (3) there is sufficient evidence to establish that the individual appearing in court is the fugitive sought and committed the offense. *See* Bingham v. Bradley, 241 U.S. 511, 516–17, 36 S. Ct. 634 (1916); McNamara v. Henkel, 226 U.S. 520, 523, 33 S. Ct. 146 (1913).

§ 13.57. *What happens if the court finds the fugitive extraditable?*

If the court finds the evidence sufficient and the offense is within the relevant extradition treaty, it certifies to the Secretary of State, i.e., the State Department, that the person is extraditable. *See* 18 U.S.C. § 3184 (2002). The Secretary of State is "the ultimate decision maker" on whether to issue a warrant of surrender and to extradite. *In re* Howard, 996 F.2d 1320, 1325 (1st Cir. 1993); 6 MARJORIE M. WHITEMAN, DIGEST OF INTERNATIONAL LAW 1027–28, 1046 (1968).

§ 13.58. *Is the magistrate subject to district court review?*

If a magistrate conducts the hearing, the district court has no review. *See* 18 U.S.C. § 3184 (judge or magistrate certifies a favorable extradition ruling directly to Secretary of State). Generally, habeas corpus provides the only review of a magistrate's extradition decision. *See* Lo Duca v. United States, 93 F.3d 1100, 1109 (2d Cir.) (federal courts may delegate to magistrates the non-Article III task of extradition hearings), *corrected by* 1996 U.S. App. LEXIS 28746 (2d Cir. Aug. 29, 1996), *cert. denied*, 519 U.S. 1007, 117 S. Ct. 508 (1996); Austin v. Healy, 5 F.3d 598, 602–04 (2d Cir. 1993) (magistrates have authority to conduct extradition hearings), *cert. denied*, 510 U.S. 1165, 114 S. Ct. 1192 (1994); Ward v. Rutherford, 921 F.2d 286 (D.C. Cir. 1990) (habeas corpus provides only review of extradition), *cert. denied*, 501 U.S. 1225, 111 S. Ct. 2844 (1991).

§ 13.59. *Who represents the country seeking extradition?*

Federal prosecutors usually represent the country seeking extradition. *See* U.S. ATTORNEY'S CRIMINAL RESOURCES MANUAL § 614 (1997) (noting the possibility of private counsel where conflicts of interest arise); John G. Kester, *Some Myths of United States Extradition Law*, 76 GEO. L.J. 1441, 1445 & n.27 (1988) ("On rare occasions, but almost never in recent years, the requesting country appears by private counsel.").

c. Legal Standards

§ 13.60. *Is an extradition proceeding a criminal proceeding?*

No. Consequently, "the rules of evidence and civil [and criminal] procedure that govern federal court proceedings heard under the authority of Article III ... do not apply in extradition hearings that are conducted under the authority of a treaty enacted pursuant to Article II." *In re* Smyth, 61 F.3d 711, 720–21 (9th Cir. 1995), *reh'g denied*, 72 F.3d 1433 (9th Cir. 1996). *See also* FED. R. CRIM. P. 54(b)(5); FED. R. EVID. 1101(d)(3). Moreover, the Fourth, Fifth, and Sixth Amendments of the Constitution do not apply, meaning that the accused has no right to indictment, confrontation of witnesses, speedy trial, or double jeopardy protection.

§ 13.61. *What is the standard of proof for extradition?*

Probable cause. Sufficiency of the evidence or other such questions or standards are not at issue because the foreign court determines these. Fernandez v. Phillips, 268 U.S. 311, 312, 45 S. Ct. 541 (1925); United States v. Barr, 619 F. Supp. 1068, 1071 (E.D. Pa. 1985) ("Probable cause signifies evidence sufficient to cause a person of ordinary prudence and caution to consciously entertain a reasonable belief of the accused's guilt") (quoting Coleman v. Burnett, 477 F.2d 1187, 1202 (D.C. Cir. 1973)). Basically, the magistrate need determine only whether there is competent evidence to justify holding the foreign national for extradition, not whether evidence is sufficient to justify conviction.

However, the magistrate must still have valid evidence and an indication of the actual source of the information in the extradition request. There must be probable cause to believe a crime occurred, not just probable cause to believe that the defendant is charged with a crime. *See* Caltagirone v. Grant, 629 F.2d 739, 747 (2d Cir. 1980).

§ 13.62. *Can the requesting country submit ex parte information?*

Yes, but the arrestee cannot. Thus the requesting country can submit authenticated and certified depositions and other such documents gathered in that country. 18 U.S.C. § 3190.

§ 13.63. *Does the actual guilt of the fugitive matter?*

No, the requesting country need only show probable cause. First Nat'l Bank of N.Y. v. Aristeguieta, 287 F.2d 219, 226–27 (2d Cir. 1960), *vacated as moot,* 375 U.S. 49, 84 S. Ct. 144 (1963); M. CHERIF BASSIOUNI, INTERNATIONAL EXTRADITION. UNITED STATES LAW AND PRACTICE 654–789 (3d ed. 1996).

d. Defenses to Extradition

§ 13.64. *What defenses does the fugitive have at the hearing?*

Precious few. The fugitive cannot introduce contradictory evidence to the requesting country's proof nor evidence of alibi or insanity. Also, a judge will not review whether the proceedings in the requesting country are fair. *See* John Quigley, *The Role of Non-Inquiry and the Impact of Human Rights on Extradition Law,* 15 N.C.J. INT'L L. & COM. REG. 401 (1990); Jacques Semmelman, *Federal Courts, the Constitution, and the Rule of Non-Inquiry in International Extradition Proceedings,* 76 CORNELL L. REV. 1198 (1991). In addition, a magistrate judge doe not have jurisdiction to hear a motion to quash the complaint for provisional arrest. *In re* Extradition of Orozco, 268 F. Supp. 2d 1115 (D. Ariz. 2003) (case cite to § 3187 probably should be to § 3184). Conversely, an extradited person may raise whatever objections the extraditing country is entitled to raise. United States v. Andonian, 29 F.3d 1432 (9th Cir. 1994), *cert. denied,* 513 U.S. 1128, 115 S. Ct. 938 (1995); United States v. Cuevas, 847 F.2d 1417 (9th Cir. 1988), *cert. denied,* 489 U.S. 1012, 109 S. Ct. 1122 (1989). *See generally* Michael D.

Wims, *Re-Examining the Traditional Exceptions to Extraditions*, 62 INT'L REV. PENAL L. 325 (1991).

i. Political Offenses

§ 13.65. *What if the fugitive is charged with a "political offense"?*

The fugitive can contend that the offense is a political offense, such as treason, spying, or possibly common crimes committed for political purposes, and this would be a defense to extradition. *See generally* M. CHERIF BASSIOUNI, INTERNATIONAL EXTRADITION: UNITED STATES LAW AND PRACTICE 594–676 (4th ed. 2002); CHRISTOPHER L. BLAKESLEY, TERRORISM, DRUGS, INTERNATIONAL LAW, AND THE PROTECTION OF HUMAN LIBERTY 264–70 n.2 (1992).

ii. Dual Criminality

§ 13.66. *What is "dual criminality"?*

For extradition to occur, the same act must be criminal in both nations; this is dual criminality. Collins v. Loisel, 259 U.S. 309, 312, 42 S. Ct. 469 (1922). Dual criminality does not require that the charges be identical but only that the acts alleged constitute a crime in both countries. *Id.* (The "law does not require that the name by which the crime is described in the two counties shall be the same; nor that the scope of the liability shall be coextensive ...."). *See also* Clarey v. Gregg, 138 F.3d 764 (9th Cir.) (finding a Mexican statute against "simple homicide" analogous to U.S. statutes on felony murder), *cert. denied*, 525 U.S. 853, 119 S. Ct. 131 (1998). This is the same standard used with prisoner transfers. *See* **Chapter 14: Treaty Transfers — Aliens There and Citizens Here**.

iii. Plea Agreements

§ 13.67. *Can a plea agreement bind the United States from extraditing?*

Possibly. The *U.S. Attorney's Criminal Resources Manual* discourages federal prosecutors from entering into plea agreements with "no extradition" clauses. U.S. ATTORNEY'S CRIMINAL RESOURCES MANUAL § 9-15.800 (2000). The reason is that the United States has a treaty obligation to extradite that could conflict with such a plea agreement. *See In re* Petition of Geisser, 627 F.2d 745 (5th Cir. 1980) (case describing problems of resolving nonextradition clause in plea with extradition treaty), *cert. denied*, 450 U.S. 1031, 101 S. Ct. 1741 (1981). Thus, if such a nonextradition clause exists, it could be a defense to extradition.

Prosecutors who wish to consider entering into nonextradition plea must submit a written request to the OIA for authorization and receive an express written approval from the Assistant Attorney General, Criminal Division.

VI. Hearings: Appeals and Habeas

§ 13.68. *Can an extradition hearing be appealed?*

Courts have asserted appellate jurisdiction based on treaty language though no statute creates appellate jurisdiction. *In re* Smyth, 61 F.3d 711, 713 (9th Cir. 1995), *reh'g denied*, 72 F.3d 1433 (9th Cir. 1996); *In re* Howard, 996 F.2d 1320, 1326 (1st Cir. 1993). Generally, though, there is no appeal from the judge's decision. *See In re* Mackin, 668 F.2d 122, 125–30 (2d Cir. 1981). The no-appeal rule also applies if the judge decides against extradition, although the government is free to file a new complaint. *See In re* Macdonnell, 16 F. Cas. 59, 66 (1873); *In re* Stupp, 23 F. Cas. 296, 302 (1875). Because principles of *res judicata* do not apply in extradition proceedings, the denial of an extradition warrant does not bar a new attempt to obtain the warrant. *See Macdonnell*, 16 F. Cas. at 63; *Ex parte* Schorer, 195 F. 334 (E.D. Wis. 1912); *In re* Kelly, 26 F. 852 (C.C.D. Minn. 1886). For this reason, the Federal Rules of Appellate Procedure generally do not apply. *See In re* Kirby, 106 F.3d 855, 857 n.1 (9th Cir. 1997). However, if the specific extradition treaty allows for appellate review, the Federal Rules of Civil and Appellate Procedure may apply. *See In re Howard*, 996 F.2d at 1326 (quoting treaty language providing for direct appeal and application of federal rules).

§ 13.69. *What about habeas corpus relief?*

Yes, the fugitive may seek habeas relief before or after the Secretary executes the warrant under 28 U.S.C. § 2241. 6 MARJORIE M. WHITEMAN, DIGEST OF INTERNATIONAL LAW 1020–23, 1046 (1968).

§ 13.70. *What usually would be the subject of habeas review?*

Habeas review is generally limited to three questions: whether the court had jurisdiction (including whether the request was timely); whether the offense charged was within the extradition treaty (including the concept of dual criminality); and "whether there was any evidence warranting the finding that there was reasonable ground to believe the accused guilty." Fernandez v. Phillips, 268 U.S. 311, 312, 45 S. Ct. 541 (1925). *See also* Bozilov v. Seifert, 983 F.2d 140 (9th Cir. 1993). Whether the offense is an extraditable crime is reviewed *de novo.*

§ 13.71. *Does time during habeas review count?*

No. Detention, including time during the habeas review, is "dead time" — the foreign country requesting rendition need not give credit on any underlying sentence for the time the person spends in U.S. custody. Generally, the Secretary of State will delay processing the extradition warrant for 30 days to allow for the person to file a Habeas Corpus Petition. If the person has no desire for habeas review then counsel should advise the prosecution and State Department and request expedition of the process.

§ 13.72. *Are there other issues for habeas review?*

Counsel should consider the constitutional issues presented in **II: Constitutional Issues**, *supra.*

CHAPTER 14

TREATY TRANSFERS: ALIENS THERE AND CITIZENS HERE

Other Resources:

MICHAEL ABBELL, INTERNATIONAL PRISONER TRANSFER (2002).

Alan Ellis, *An Introduction to International Prisoner Transfers: Going Home*, THE CHAMPION, July 1999, at 32.

Lara S. Vinnard, *Foreign Convictions, Prisoner Transfer Treaties, and the Federal Sentencing Guidelines*, 13:2 FED. SENT'G REP. 1 (Sept./Oct. 2000).

Proceedings for the Transfer of Offenders To or From Foreign Countries, Administrative Office of the United States Courts, Magistrate Judges Division (Feb. 1997).

Bureau of Prisons Program Statement #5140.29 at www.bop.gov.

The International Prisoner Transfer Unit, Office of Enforcement Operations Criminal Division, United States Department of Justice, P.O. Box 7600, Ben Franklin Station, Washington, D.C. 20044-7600.

Introduction

§ 14.1. *What is a "treaty transfer"?*

A treaty transfer involves either the transfer of a foreign prisoner from a U.S. prison to a prison in his own country, or transfer of a U.S. citizen from a foreign prison to one in the United States. By definition, there needs to be an international treaty between the United States and the other country. The United States has transfer treaties with more than 50 countries. The Department of Justice lists these countries as well as its guidelines for treaty transfers on its website, www.usdoj.gov. Go to the part of the site relating to the Criminal Division at http://www.usdoj.gov/criminal/criminal-home.html.

I. Treaty Transfers in General

§ 14.2. *What are the goals of transfer treaties?*

Transfer treaties aim to (1) promote the prisoner's rehabilitation by allowing him to serve his sentence in his home country closer to family, friends, and counsel, and (2) provide for more humane conditions of confinement than existed in many foreign prisons. *See* David S. Finkelstein, Note, *"Ever Been in a [Foreign] Prison?": The Implementation of Transfer of Penal Sanctions Treaties by U.S. States*, 66 FORDHAM L. REV. 125, 127 (1997).

§ 14.3. *What do transfer treaties require?*

Transfer treaties, like most treaties, are not self-implementing and require legislation to be effective. The United States treaty transfer statute requires an applicable treaty, United States nationality, dual criminality (the prisoner's conduct is punishable in both countries), finality of judgment in sentence, and the prisoner's consent. The Department of Justice reviews whether the prisoner's situation complies with these requirements. 18 U.S.C. § 4100(a)-(d).

§ 14.4. *What legislation is involved?*

The implementing legislation for treaty transfer is 18 U.S.C. §§ 4101–4115, and accompanying regulations at 21 C.F.R. § 527.40. Title 18 U.S.C. § 4107 governs transfer of prisoners from the United States; 18 U.S.C. § 4108 governs the transfer of prisoners to the United States.

§ 14.5. *How do transfer treaties benefit the United States?*

The most obvious benefit is that American citizens convicted of crimes in foreign countries with a transfer treaty may elect to serve their sentence in the United States. Alien prisoners sent back to their country also benefit the United States given the number of incarcerated aliens in both federal and state prisons that taxpayers support.

§ 14.6. *How is the prisoner's sentence calculated?*

Time served is calculated under the laws of the home country, which sometimes results in a shorter sentence. Parole eligibility and good time are calculated using the law of the home country, which may be more favorable to the prisoner.

§ 14.7. *How does the procedure begin?*

The transfer process is relatively simple: both the transferring and the receiving country must agree and the prisoner must consent. *See* Rosado v. Civiletti, 621 F.2d 1179, 1187 (2d Cir.) (discussing mutual agreement and consent), *cert. denied*, 449 U.S. 856, 101 S. Ct. 153 (1980). A transfer hearing is held in the transferring country in front of a judicial officer where the prisoner consents on the record to the transfer.

§ 14.8. *What is "dual criminality"?*

"Dual criminality" assures that the offense is a crime in both countries. *See, e.g.*, 28 C.F.R. § 2.68(a)(4); Treaty on the Execution of Penal Sentences, Nov. 25, 1976, U.S.-Mexico, 28 U.S.T. 7399, art. II, para. 1; Liana E. Olivarez, Comment, *The Mexican-American Prisoner Transfer Treaty: Current Problems and Solutions*, 30 TEX.

INT'L L.J. 395, 397 (1995). If the conduct is not a crime in both countries, there cannot be a treaty transfer. For this reason, prisoners with a conviction for reentry after deportation under 8 U.S.C. § 1326 are not eligible for transfer.

§ 14.9. *What was the first transfer treaty?*

The United States and Mexico entered into the first prisoner transfer treaty and this has been the model for later treaties. *See* Ronald M. Emanuel, Note, *Intervention of Constitutional Powers: The Prisoner Transfer Treaties*, 2 FLA. INT'L L.J. 203, 203 (1986). This treaty followed repeated complaints to the State Department about Americans enduring deplorable conditions, abuse, and torture in Mexican prisons. *See Implementation of Treaties for the Transfer of Offenders to or from Foreign Countries: Hearings Before the Subcomm. on Immigration, Citizenship & Int'l Law of the House Comm. on the Judiciary*, 95th Cong., 1st Sess., at 1 (1977), *cited in* Lara S. Vinnard, *Foreign Convictions, Prisoner Transfer Treaties, and the Federal Sentencing Guidelines*, 13:2 FED. SENT'G REP. 1 n.6 (Sept./Oct. 2000).

§ 14.10. *Which countries have treaty transfer agreements with the United States?*

The United States has bilateral treaties for the transfer of prisoners with Bolivia, Canada, France, Mexico, Panama, Peru, Thailand, and Turkey. *See* Treaty on the Execution of Penal Sentences, Feb. 10, 1978, U.S.-Bolivia, 30 U.S.T. 796; Treaty on the Execution of Penal Sentences, Mar. 2, 1977, U.S.-Canada, 30 U.S.T. 6263; Convention on the Transfer of Sentenced Persons, Jan. 25, 1983, U.S.-France, T.I.A.S. No. 10,823; Treaty on the Execution of Penal Sentences, Nov. 25, 1976, U.S.-Mexico, 28 U.S.T. 7399; Treaty on the Execution of Penal Sentences, Jan. 11, 1979, U.S.-Panama, 32 U.S.T. 1565; Treaty on the Execution of Penal Sentences, July 6, 1979, U.S.-Peru, 32 U.S.T. 1471; Treaty on Cooperation in the Execution of Penal Sentences, Oct. 29, 1982, U.S.-Thailand, T.I.A.S.; Treaty on the Enforcement of Penal Judgments, June 7, 1979, U.S.-Turkey, 32 U.S.T. 3187.

The United States is also party to a multilateral prisoner transfer treaty with the Council of Europe and is a signatory to the Convention on the Transfer of Sentenced Persons of the Organization of American States. *See* Council of Europe Convention on the Transfer of Sentenced Persons, Mar. 21, 1983, T.I.A.S. No. 10,824;

Inter-American Convention on Serving Criminal Sentences Abroad, ratified June 7, 1993, S. Treaty Doc. No. 104-35 (1993); Ralph Ruebner & Lisa Carroll, *The Finality of Judgment and Sentence Prerequisite in the United States-Peru Bilateral Prisoner Transfer Treaty: Calling Congress and the President to Reform and Justifying Jurisdiction of the Inter-American Human Rights Commission and Court*, 15 Am. U. INT'L L. REV. 1071, 1078–79 (2000) (listing countries with which United States has transfer treaties). These conventions expand the treaty transfer benefits and obligations to 59 countries including Austria, Bahamas, Belgium, Bolivia, Bulgaria, Canada, Chile, Costa Rica, Croatia, Cyprus, Czech Republic, Denmark, Federated States of Micronesia, Finland, France, Georgia, Germany, Greece, Hungary, Iceland, Ireland, Israel, Italy, Latvia, Liechtenstein, Lithuania, Luxembourg, Malta. Marshall Islands, Mexico, Netherlands (including Netherlands Antilles and Aruba), Norway, Panama, Peru, Poland, Portugal, Republic of Palau, Romania, Slovakia, Slovenia, Spain, Sweden, Switzerland, Thailand, Trinidad/Tobago, Turkey, Ukraine, and the United Kingdom (including Territories). *See* Alan Ellis, *An Introduction to International Prisoner Transfers: Going Home*, THE CHAMPION, July 1999, at 33 n.1. Defense counsel or the prosecutor should obtain the relevant treaty for specific procedures. For example, France usually proceeds under its own bilateral treaty with the United States, while Canada uses either the Council of Europe convention or the bilateral treaty. *Id.* at 32.

Finally, the United States has informal agreements for the transfer of prisoners with the Marshall Islands and the Federated States of Micronesia. Ralph Ruebner & Lisa Carroll, *The Finality of Judgment and Sentence Prerequisite in the United States-Peru Bilateral Prisoner Transfer Treaty: Calling Congress and the President to Reform and Justifying Jurisdiction of the Inter-American Human Rights Commission and Court*, 15 AM. U. INT'L L. REV. 1071, 1079 n.2 (2000).

II. Transferring Aliens Back to Their Country

A. Timing and General Considerations

§ 14.11. *How does a transfer proceeding begin?*

Generally, the prisoner must request the transfer. The prisoner can receive assistance from his country's consulate or an attorney. The prisoner then receives a request packet from the Federal Bureau of Prisons (BOP) that contains an application, the criminal judgment, the presentence report, information about the prisoner's adjustment to prison, the prisoner's sentencing computation, information regarding the prisoner's ties to the receiving country, and information regarding pending appeals or detainers. The form is the Federal Prison System Transfer Inquiry form (BP-297). *See* 28 C.F.R. §§ 527.43 and 527.44. The warden transmits the completed form to the BOP office in Washington, D.C., for review. MICHAEL ABBELL, INTERNATIONAL PRISONER TRANSFER ch. 7 (2002).

§ 14.12. *Who needs to approve the transfer?*

When a Latin American or Mexican inmate arrives at a federal prison, the BOP holds a transfer orientation that includes copies of relevant forms.

After the BOP review, the request moves to the International Prisoner Transfer Unit, Office of Enforcement Operations, Department of Justice (IPTU), which makes the final determination of the prisoner's eligibility for transfer. An attorney for the prisoner can contact this office at the following address:

The International Prisoner Transfer Unit
Office of Enforcement Operations Criminal Division
United States Department of Justice
P.O. Box 7600, Ben Franklin Station
Washington, D.C. 20044-7600

§ 14.13. *Has the Department of Justice issued guidelines?*

Only generally. In 1999 the IPTU issued "Guidelines for Evaluating Prisoner Applications for Transfer." These guidelines can provide information to the prisoners, his family, or his attorney. MICHAEL ABBELL, INTERNATIONAL PRISONER TRANSFER ch. 7 (2002).

§ 14.14. *What does the IPTU do?*

The attorney evaluating the request contacts interested parties, such as the prosecutor's office, the FBI, or other state or federal law enforcement agencies, for their positions. Although these recommendations have considerable weight, the IPTU makes the final decision on whether transfer will happen. U.S. ATTORNEY'S CRIMINAL RESOURCES MANUAL § 735 (1998). Generally, the main issues for the IPTU are the likelihood of social rehabilitation, law enforcement concerns, and the likelihood of return to the United States, which are incorporated in the following 12 criteria:

1. Nationality — citizenship of the person seeking transfer;
2. Dual criminality — is the offense similar for both countries?;
3. Finality of judgment and sentence — the person is not on appeal and there is no Rule 32 or 18 U.S.C. § 2254 or § 2255 proceeding pending in any federal court or U.S. state equivalent court;
4. Amount of sentence remaining — the prisoner must generally have the greater part of his sentence remaining;
5. Offense cannot be political;
6. Offense cannot be military — includes deserters or individuals fallen from grace after political coups;
7. Offense cannot be related to immigration (due to the requirement for dual criminality: an immigration offense in the United States is unlikely to be an offense in the country to which the prisoner seeks transfer);
8. Sentence cannot require capital punishment;
9. Sentence must be determinate — the remaining sentence can be calculated with some degree of certainty (this is especially easy to do with a federal sentence);
10. Defendant cannot be domiciled in the United States — several of the transfer treaties require this;
11. Prisoner cannot have outstanding fines — if he does, he cannot transfer from the United States until he has either paid the fines or obtained remission or discharge of the fines from the sentencing court upon proof of indigence;
12. Minimum portion of sentence spent in sentencing country. Although the United States has no such requirement, some treaties expressly permit the government to require some part of the sentence be served here as a condition of eligibility to transfer.

The prisoner's family is welcome to write the IPTU regarding these factors.

§ 14.15. *What does the prisoner get from the transfer?*

Generally, a treaty transfer occurs before the alien has finished serving his sentence. This makes treaty transfers distinct from the transfer or movement of prisoners under 18 U.S.C. § 4212, which directs the Bureau of Prisons to deliver aliens to immigration officials for deportation proceedings at the end of their sentences.

§ 14.16. *What are considerations for going back?*

Obviously the prisoner's desire to be near family and culture are key factors as well as possible sentencing reductions. The sentencing benefits for the prisoner's return, however, are not always clear. The State Department is still trying to define an official policy for advising foreign nationals of the benefits of transferring to their home country. One option for counsel, the prisoner, or his family is to contact a lawyer in the home country who understands how sentences are calculated and served. Another is to contact foreign prison officials directly (start by calling the country's U.S. consulate.).

§ 14.17. *What about human rights violations in the home country?*

The prisoner should consider that the prisons and human rights practices in their home country could be substandard. The United States Department of State, Bureau of Democracy, Human Rights and Labor issues a comprehensive report on most countries identifying concerns regarding prison conditions, rights violations, and the justice system. *See* United States Department of State Internet site at www.state.gov.

§ 14.18. *Why would the United States wish transfer instead of deportation?*

When the prisoner is deported, the United States government simply deposits him in his country of origin, which has no control over the prisoner at that point. This has caused law enforcement problems. Conversely, if the prisoner is transferred to his country of origin before he has finished his sentence that country can maintain supervision over him during his reintegration into society. *See, e.g.*, Bruce Zagaris, *Caribbean Governments Complain of Deportation of Nationals*, 16 INT'L ENFORCEMENT L. REP. 587 (Feb. 2000).

§ 14.19. *Has the percentage of transfers to other countries gone up or down?*

Down. As part of a general culture to get "tough on crime," Department of Justice officials and United States Attorneys now tend to advise against transfers more than before. Moreover, after November 1, 1987, the Federal Sentencing Guidelines require the prisoner to serve at least 85 percent of his sentence. Most United States treaty partners require prisoners to serve a smaller percentage of their sentence and this cuts against approving the prisoner transfer. Finally, the government often offers prisoner transfer as an incentive to encourage cooperation, which means that prisoners who have not cooperated are less likely to receive approval of their request. MICHAEL ABBELL, INTERNATIONAL PRISONER TRANSFER ch. 7 (2002).

B. Eligibility

§ 14.20. *Who can receive a treaty transfer?*

Any alien who is not a permanent resident or domiciliary is eligible to apply for transfer to his country of origin. The following applies under most transfer treaties:

- The prisoner must be a national of the country where he is requesting to go;
- There must be dual criminality meaning that the same conduct is punished in both countries;
- The prisoner's judgment and sentence must be final in the United States;
- The prisoner must have a specified minimum sentence remaining;
- The offense must not be a political offense, a military offense, or immigration offense;
- The prisoner in must not be under a capital sentence;
- The sentence must be determinant.

See MICHAEL ABBELL, INTERNATIONAL PRISONER TRANSFER ch. 6 (2002).

§ 14.21. *Can state prisoners apply for transfer?*

Yes, if state laws allow it. *See* 28 C.F.R. § 527.45, *Transfer of State prisoners to other countries*. The following 43 states allow such transfers: Alabama, Alaska, Arizona, Arkansas, California, Colorado, Connecticut, Florida, Hawaii, Idaho, Illinois, Indiana, Iowa, Kansas, Kentucky, Louisiana, Maine, Maryland, Massachusetts, Michigan, Minnesota, Missouri, Montana, Nebraska, Nevada, New Hampshire, New Jersey, New York, North Dakota, Ohio, Oklahoma, Oregon, Pennsylvania, Rhode Island, South Carolina, South

Dakota, Texas, Utah, Vermont (Canadian transfers), Virginia, Washington, Wisconsin, and Wyoming, plus the territory of Northern Marianna Islands. *See* Alan Ellis, *An Introduction to International Prisoner Transfers: Going Home*, THE CHAMPION, July 1999, at 33 n.2. Generally, the IPTU will approve the transfer if the state has. Conversely, if the state denies the prisoner's transfer, he will have no recourse for federal court review because states are not party to the treaties. Hogan v. Koenig, 920 F.2d 6, 8 (9th Cir. 1990).

§ 14.22. *What about a prisoner with a contempt charge, fines, or pending appeal?*

If the prisoner is in custody for civil contempt or has outstanding fines without court permission, the IPTU will deny the transfer request. 18 U.S.C. § 4100(c); 28 C.F.R. § 527.42 *Limitations on transfer of offenders to foreign countries*. The IPTU will also deny transfer if the prisoner has pending proceedings such as an appeal or habeas petition.

§ 14.23. *What about a prisoner who is a witness?*

If a prisoner is a witness the IPTU will not approve the transfer until after the prosecution no longer needs him.

§ 14.24. *What about a prisoner who received a transfer on a prior sentence?*

In this circumstance it is very unlikely that the IPTU will approve another transfer. MICHAEL ABBELL, INTERNATIONAL PRISONER TRANSFER ch. 7 (2002).

§ 14.25. *What if the prisoner has dual nationality?*

The IPTU will evaluate the prisoner's personal history to determine his main social contacts. The IPTU will only consider transferring the prisoner if a substantial preponderance of those contacts are in the foreign country. MICHAEL ABBELL, INTERNATIONAL PRISONER TRANSFER ch. 7 (2002).

C. Procedure

§ 14.26. *Is there any court review of the government's decision not to transfer?*

Apparently not. The prisoner transfer treaty implementing legislation is silent on whether courts can review the Department of Justice's refusal to approve a prisoner transfer. *See generally* 18 U.S.C. § 3244. It would also appear that there is no review under the Administrative Procedure Act or by writ of mandamus. Bagguley v. Bush, 953 F.2d 660 (D.C. Cir. 1991), *cert. denied,* 503 U.S. 995, 112 S. Ct. 1698 (1992). However, "[i]t is well-established that judicial review exists" if there was an unconstitutional basis for denying the transfer. Cheong Wai Wong v. Warden, 171 F.3d 148, 149 (2d Cir. 1999) (per curiam).

§ 14.27. *If the transfer is approved, how is the prisoner's home country notified?*

The IPTU will notify the prisoner's home country for that country's approval, which will usually have its consulate interview the prisoner to verify citizenship and eligibility. After the prisoner's home country approves the transfer, the IPTU submits the case for a consent verification hearing. MICHAEL ABBELL, INTERNATIONAL PRISONER TRANSFER ch. 7 (2002).

D. The Hearing and Prisoner's Consent

§ 14.28. *Who conducts the hearing?*

In 1977, Congress amended the Federal Magistrate Act to authorize magistrate judges to conduct treaty transfers under 18 U.S.C. §§ 4107, 4108, and 4109. A magistrate judge must personally inform the prisoner of the transfer conditions. The magistrate judge verifies the prisoner's consent and the consent of the United States and exchanging country. The magistrate judges division of the court system offers an extensive guide. Proceeding for the Transfer of Offenders To or From Foreign Countries, Administrative Office of the United States Courts, Magistrate Judges Division (Feb. 1997). The judge must verify that the offender voluntarily consented to the transfer with full knowledge of the consequences. *See generally* Allen B. Bickart, *International Prisoner Transfer and Exchange,* THE DEFENDER, Oct. 1994, at 5.

§ 14.29. *Where does the consent hearing usually take place?*

For both federal and state prisoners this usually takes place where the prisoner is incarcerated. Often, however, the U.S. Marshal will bring the prisoner before a federal magistrate rather than having a magistrate go to the institution.

§ 14.30. *Does the prisoner have the right to counsel?*

Yes. The prisoner has the statutory right to counsel in a proceeding to verify the consent. If the prisoner is indigent, the magistrate will appoint counsel. 18 U.S.C. § 4109(a)(1) (1994).

§ 14.31. *Can the government transfer a prisoner without his consent?*

Not currently, but the 1996 Immigration Act allows the president to negotiate treaties for prisoner transfer regardless of the prisoner's request. Because there is no due process right to a transfer, a decision to transfer contrary to the prisoner's wishes may not be subject to review. *See* Marshall v. Reno, 915 F. Supp. 426 (D.D.C. 1996).

§ 14.32. *Why is the prisoner's consent important?*

Prisoner consent is important because of the restrictions treaties impose on the prisoner's right to challenge the conviction after transfer. *See* 18 U.S.C. § 4108(b)(1) ("only the [sentencing court] may modify or set aside the conviction or sentence."); H.R. Rep. No. 720, 95th Cong., 1st Sess. (1977), *reprinted in* 1977 U.S.C.C.A.N. 1346, 3149, 1977 WL 16079.

§ 14.33. *What occurs at the transfer hearing?*

The transfer consent verification hearing is tape recorded or transcribed, *see* 18 U.S.C. § 4107(e); 28 C.F.R. § 0.64-2; the IPTU will retain the recording or transcript. The prisoner has a right to an interpreter. The prisoner will execute at least three original consent verification forms in English plus three forms in his native language. One copy of each form will go to his home country, one will stay with the district court, and one will go to the IPTU.

E. Repatriation

§ 14.34. *When does the alien actually go home?*

After the court has verified the prisoner's consent to the transfer, it becomes irrevocable and the IPTU is responsible for his transfer to his home country. The prisoner will stay in BOP custody until foreign officials take him. *See* 28 C.F.R. §§ 527.44; 527.45. With Canada and Mexico this usually happens at the border. With other countries this happens at the international airport.

§ 14.35. *How is the sentence conveyed?*

Again, the sentence is conveyed under the laws and procedures of the receiving country. The prisoner could receive a shorter sentence but not have it converted to probation or a fine. The prisoner cannot receive a longer sentence than the one the BOP calculated.

III. Transferring American Citizens Back to the United States

A. Starting the Process

§ 14.36. *Why would a United States prisoner transfer back?*

The prisoner has several advantages to coming home, especially when the prisoner is in a country that abuses human rights, resorts to torture, or when prison conditions are substantially worse than in the United States. Sometimes, however, U.S. citizens may have an advantage to serving their sentences where they were convicted. Some countries have better prison conditions such as some Western European countries like Germany. Lara S. Vinnard, *Foreign Convictions, Prisoner Transfer Treaties, and the Federal Sentencing Guidelines*, 13:2 FED. SENT'G REP. 1 (Sept./Oct. 2000).

§ 14.37. *How is a request to get a U.S. citizen home started?*

United States prisoner transfer treaties specify various ways to begin a transfer. Some treaties require the home country to initiate the request while others require the sentencing country to initiate the request. The Canadian treaty specifies that the prisoner must initiate the request with the warden of the Canadian prison. Usually, the United States embassy in the country where the prisoner is located handles the request. Families interested in a prisoner in a foreign country or attorneys for the prisoner should contact the American consular officers responsible for prisoner transfer in those countries. For information, contact the Citizens Emergency Center, Office of Citizens Services, Bureau of Consular Affairs, United States Department of State (tel. 202-647-5225).

§ 14.38. *Where does the request go in the United States?*

The International Prisoner Transfer Unit, Office of Enforcement Operations Criminal Division, United States Department of Justice (IPTU) receives and reviews the requests.

§ 14.39. *Has the Justice Department published a criterion for treaty transfers?*

No, and the courts have upheld this despite arguments that the Congress intended a published criterion. *See* Bagguley v. Bush, 953 F.2d 660, 662–63 (D.C. Cir. 1991), *cert. denied,* 503 U.S. 995, 112 S. Ct. 1698 (1992); Scalise v. Thornburgh, 891 F.2d 640, 644–49 (7th Cir. 1989), *cert. denied,* 494 U.S. 1083, 110 S. Ct. 1815 (1990); *see also* Coleman v. Reno, 91 F. Supp. 2d 130 (D.D.C. 2000). However, most transfer treaties list criteria. *See* Marquez-Ramos v. Reno, 69 F.3d 477 (10th Cir. 1995) (upholding DOJ's denial of treaty transfer request as complying with requirements of Mexican transfer treaty Article IV(4)).

B. Basis of Decision

§ 14.40. *When do foreign countries deny transfer?*

A country makes this decision based on what is in its interest. Thus, if the U.S. citizen committed a particularly egregious crime with a lot of negative publicity, transfer of the prisoner back to the United States is less likely. MICHAEL ABBELL, INTERNATIONAL PRISONER TRANSFER ch. 4 (2002).

§ 14.41. *On what will the United States base its decision?*

The IPTU will decide whether the prisoner is eligible for transfer and whether the transfer fits under United States policy. The IPTU issues "guidelines for evaluating prisoner applications for transfer." This guideline, however, is written more for deciding whether to send a prisoner back to his home country rather than bringing United States citizens home. The issues for consideration on whether to approve a prisoner transfer are the likelihood of social rehabilitation, law enforcement concerns, and the likelihood of return to the United States. The IPTU will also tend to disfavor transfers where the transfer will cause a significantly reduced sentence under the Federal Sentencing Guidelines. MICHAEL ABBELL, INTERNATIONAL PRISONER TRANSFER ch. 4 (2002). The IPTU will also check with investigating agencies in the United States for outstanding warrants and information about a prisoner, including whether the prisoner has relatives in the United States. MICHAEL ABBELL, INTERNATIONAL PRISONER TRANSFER ch. 4 (2002).

§ 14.42. *How do ties to criminal enterprises in the United States affect transfer?*

This could defeat in the prisoner's intention to transfer. In *Scalise v. Thornburgh*, 891 F.2d 640 (7th Cir. 1989), *cert. denied*, 494 U.S. 1083, 110 S. Ct. 1815 (1990), the court upheld the IPTU's refusal to transfer two Americans convicted in a major jewelry robbery in England because of their ties to the Chicago Mafia.

§ 14.43. *How do the family and social ties affect the transfer decision?*

If the prisoner's social ties are actually stronger in the sentencing country, it will cut against transfer.

§ 14.44. *What if the prisoner is needed in the United States as a witness?*

Here, law enforcement interests will favor an expedited transfer process. This will not only encourage fast approval of the transfer but also the prisoner's physical return to the United States. MICHAEL ABBELL, INTERNATIONAL PRISONER TRANSFER ch. 4 (2002).

§ 14.45. *How does the potential for probation affect the transfer decision?*

The general policy of the United States is to encourage monitoring of the prisoner after release from prison. Foreign sentences generally do not allow for supervised release and this cuts in favor of transfer. MICHAEL ABBELL, INTERNATIONAL PRISONER TRANSFER ch. 4 (2002).

§ 14.46. *What happens after the transfer is approved?*

The IPTU informs the U.S. embassy in the sentencing country and the Office of Citizens Emergencies Services, Bureau of Consular Affairs, United States Department of State. The IPTU coordinates the actual physical transfer of the prisoner with the embassy and authorities in the sentencing country as well as with the Administrative Office of the United States Courts to verify that the prisoner consented to the transfer. MICHAEL ABBELL, INTERNATIONAL PRISONER TRANSFER ch. 4 (2002).

§ 14.47. *Is there any review of United States disapproval of the transfer request?*

The implementing legislation allowing returns to the United States is silent on whether courts have authority to review the Department of Justice's transfer decisions. Moreover, because the prisoner is not under United States custody he cannot seek habeas corpus review. Thus, the only possible judicial review is under the Administrative Procedures Act, 5 U.S.C. § 701(a)(2), which allows a federal court to review the administrative decision of a government agency unless a statute precludes it. MICHAEL ABBELL, INTERNATIONAL PRISONER TRANSFER ch. 4 (2002).

C. Bringing the Prisoner Home

§ 14.48. *After legal proceedings, how is the prisoner sent to the United States?*

The United States Bureau of Prisons has the responsibility for handling the actual physical transfer. *See* 28 C.F.R. §§ 0.96b, 527.46; *see also* Federal Bureau of Prisons, Program Statement No. 5140.29, FP 10 (1997), at www.bop.gov. Generally, the Justice Department tries to move the prisoner as soon as possible after verification.

§ 14.49. *Where will the Bureau of Prisons house the prisoner?*

After the prisoner is transferred to the United States, the BOP places him at one of several designated federal prisons such as La Tuna, Texas (for men convicted in Mexico) and Dublin, California (for women convicted in Mexico). Men and women convicted in Thailand go to Los Angeles, California. Lara S. Vinnard, *Foreign Convictions, Prisoner Transfer Treaties, and the Federal Sentencing*

Guidelines, 13:2 FED. SENT'G REP. 1 (Sept./Oct. 2000); telephone interviews with Ronnie M. Scotkin, Special Projects Coordinator, United States Parole Commission (Mar. 14 and 20, 2001).

§ 14.50. *What happens to the prisoner after he goes to a federal prison?*

A federal probation officer in the district where the prisoner is confined interviews the prisoner, does a background investigation, and writes what amounts to a presentence report. 28 C.F.R. § 527.46(c). This report is normally completed within 30 days.

D. Challenging the Foreign Conviction

§ 14.51. *What right does the prisoner have to challenge his foreign conviction?*

None. This is one of the main reasons why the prisoner's consent is important. Each of the treaties, as well as the implementing legislation, eliminates the prisoner's right to challenge the conviction after transfer to the United States. *See* 18 U.S.C. § 4108(b)(1) (prisoner must understand that "only the [sentencing court] may modify or set aside the conviction or sentence.").

§ 14.52. *What was the policy reason for disallowing challenges?*

This limitation protects the judicial process in other countries. The Departments of State and Justice advised Congress as follows:

> [N]either the United States nor any other country which is currently a party or expected to become a party to a treaty for the execution of penal sentences would have acquiesced to a provision that would permit the courts of the [r]eceiving [s]tate to set aside or modify a sentence imposed by the courts of the [t]ransferring [s]tate ... [because] fundamental sovereignty of a nation over crimes committed within its territorial boundaries would be impugned.

See H.R. Rep. No. 720, 95th Cong., 1st Sess. (1977), *reprinted in* 1977 U.S.C.C.A.N. 1346, 3149, 1977 WL 16079.

§ 14.53. *Are there constitutional problems with this?*

Given that many countries have fundamentally different criminal procedures, such as the absence of trial by jury, disallowing any due process challenge to the foreign conviction or sentence raises various concerns. *See, e.g.*, Ronald M. Emanuel, Note, *Intervention of Constitutional Powers: The Prisoner Transfer Treaties*, 2 FLA. INT'L L.J. 203, 203 (1986); David S. Finkelstein, Note, *"Ever Been in a [Foreign] Prison?": The Implementation of Transfer of Penal Sanctions Treaties by U.S. States*, 66 FORDHAM L. REV. 125, 129–34 (1997). Federal courts, however, uphold the constitutionality of the treaties and rule that prisoners who voluntarily consent to transfer are estopped from challenging their convictions in the United States. *See, e.g.*, Rosado v. Civiletti, 621 F.2d 1179, 1199 (2d Cir.), *cert. denied*, 449 U.S. 856, 101 S. Ct. 153 (1980); Pfeifer v. United States Bureau of Prisons, 615 F.2d 873, 876 (9th Cir.), *cert. denied*, 447 U.S. 908, 100 S. Ct. 2993 (1980).

E. The Role of the Parole Commission

§ 14.54. *What entity has jurisdiction over the prisoner and decides release date?*

The U.S. Parole Commission. Title 18 U.S.C. § 4106A(b)(1)(A) instructs the Parole Commission to determine a release date and supervised release for each prisoner as though the prisoner was "convicted in a United States district court of a similar offense." Title 18 § 4106A(b)(1)(B) requires the Commission to consider the U.S. Probation Office's recommendation and any documents from the transferring country. *See also* 28 C.F.R. § 2.68(c). Counsel for the prisoner can object by letter to the Parole Commission. 28 C.F.R. § 2.68(d).

§ 14.55. *Is the Parole Commission like a sentencing court?*

Not exactly. The Parole Commission decides the prisoner's release date based on the already imposed foreign sentence and thus does not act as a sentencing court. *See* Thorpe v. United States Parole Commission, 902 F.2d 291, 292 (5th Cir.) ("Under 18 U.S.C. § 4106A, the Commission is obligated to set a release date and period of supervised release, not to impose a sentence. The offender's obligation to the Government has already been established by the sentence imposed by the foreign court."), *cert. denied*, 498 U.S. 868, 111 S. Ct. 185 (1990).

§ 14.56. *Does the Parole Commission conduct a hearing?*

Yes, unless the prisoner wants to expedite the process. The hearing is a "special transferee hearing," where the prisoner appears before a Parole Commission examiner who questions the prisoner, hears argument from counsel, and recommends a sentence to the Parole Commission. The Parole Commission either modifies or adopts the recommendation for the final sentence. 28 C.F.R. § 2.68(a)(1), (h). This is much like the proceedings in the old federal parole hearings.

§ 14.57. *So why would a prisoner want to expedite the process?*

The prisoner may be eligible for release in the United States because of the time the prisoner has already served in the foreign country. The prisoner will ask for "release on the record" and will waive the probation interview and special transferee hearing, and is sentenced and released after a minimal presentence report and Parole Commission review. 28 C.F.R. § 2.68(e)(1)-(2).

§ 14.58. *Does the date of the offense matter?*

Yes. If the prisoner is convicted of an offense committed before November 1, 1987, he receives the parole hearing under Parole Commission regulations to set his release date. 28 C. F. R. § 2.12(a). If the prisoner committed the offense after November 1, 1987, the Parole Commission still has jurisdiction but takes the background investigation from the U.S. Probation Office and applies the Federal Sentencing Guidelines to determine the release date. 18 U.S.C. § 4106A(b)(1). *See* MICHAEL ABBELL, INTERNATIONAL PRISONER TRANSFER app. I (2002) (reprinting Parole Commission regulations on determining release date under the Federal Sentencing Guidelines).

§ 14.59. *Can the sentence be longer than the original foreign sentence?*

No. The sentence, including any term of supervised release, cannot be longer than the total length of the foreign sentence. 18 U.S.C. § 4106A(b)(1)(B).

F. How the Parole Commission Decides the Release Date

§ 14.60. *How does the Parole Commission decide the release date?*

First, the parole commission analogizes the foreign offense to the most similar offense it can find in the United States. It does this by finding an offense with substantially the same elements as the foreign conviction.

Second, the sentence for the analogous offense must be calculated under the Federal Sentencing Guidelines. Lara S. Vinnard, *Foreign Convictions, Prisoner Transfer Treaties, and the Federal Sentencing Guidelines*, 13:2 FED. SENT'G REP. 1 (Sept/Oct. 2000). Once the Parole Commission finds an analogous offense it simply applies the corresponding Federal Sentencing Guideline.

See U.S. PAROLE COMMISSION RULES & PROCEDURES MANUAL, *Subpart B, Transfer Treaty Prisoners and Parolees*, § 2.68-07(c), at 176 (2001) (PAROLE COMMISSION MANUAL), available online at http://www.usdoj.gov/uspc; *see also* Appendix 9, *Supplementary Instructions for Application of Sentencing Guidelines* (revised Aug. 15, 1996), at 234.

1. Applying the Federal Sentencing Guidelines

§ 14.61. *How does the Parole Commission apply the Sentencing Guidelines?*

The *Parole Commission Manual* lists "internal guidelines." So far, the courts have found these "internal guidelines" nonbinding. *Cf.* Tramel v. United States Parole Commission, 100 F.3d 129, 132–33 (11th Cir. 1996) (improper reliance on internal guidelines may be a meritorious argument in the right case).

§ 14.62. *Does the Parole Commission apply statutory mandatory minimums?*

No. The Commission does not impose the statutory mandatory minimum sentences because Congress did not write the Guidelines with treaty transfers in mind:

> It is the Commission's interpretation of 18 U.S.C. § 4106A that U.S. Code provisions for mandatory minimum terms of imprisonment and supervised release, as well as sentencing guideline provisions implementing such U.S. Code requirements (e.g., § 5G1.1(b) of the sentencing guidelines), were not intended by Congress to be applicable in an 18 U.S.C. § 4106A(b)(1)(A) determination. Alternatively, it is the Commission's position that there is good cause in every transfer treaty case for a departure from any statutorily required minimum sentence provision in the sentencing guidelines, including section 5G1.1(b) of the sentencing guidelines, because Congress did not enact mandatory sentence laws with transferees in mind.

28 C.F.R. § 2.68(a)(7).

§ 14.63. *How does the Parole Commission calculate drug quantity?*

In drug cases, the Parole Commission adjusts downward the base offense level when the drug quantity is on the dividing line between two offense levels and the foreign documents show the gross weight of the drugs included the weight of packaging. Lara S. Vinnard, *Foreign Convictions, Prisoner Transfer Treaties, and the Federal Sentencing Guidelines,* 13:2 FED. SENT'G REP. 1 (Sept./Oct. 2000).

2. Downward Departures

§ 14.64. *How does the Parole Commission treat downward departures?*

As part of its Guideline consideration, the Parole Commission will consider grounds for downward departure "outside the range established by the applicable guideline." § 5K2.0; 18 U.S.C. § 3553(b). *See* Cannon v. United States Parole Commission, 973 F.2d 1190, 1195 (5th Cir. 1992) (Parole Commission can depart downward and "set any release date from incarceration" if the record supports the departure and the total sentence does not exceed the foreign sentence). Moreover, "the very fact that the guidelines were not designed with Commission release date determinations for Treaty prisoners in mind may, without more, support a departure." *Cannon*, 973 F.2d at 1197 (citing § 5K2.0). Theoretically then, there should be much broader ground for departures than in a normal federal sentencing.

§ 14.65. *What are common adjustments and departures in treaty transfers?*

Grounds familiar to federal criminal practitioners include acceptance of responsibility, abuse or torture while in foreign custody under § 5K2.0, and substantial assistance to authorities under § 5K1.1. Adjustments include "safety valve" under Federal Sentencing Guideline § 5C1.2 and minor role under Federal Sentencing Guideline § 3B1.2. Lara S. Vinnard, *Foreign Convictions, Prisoner Transfer Treaties, and the Federal Sentencing Guidelines*, 13:2 FED. SENT'G REP. 1 (Sept./Oct. 2000).

a. Cooperation

§ 14.66. *How does the Commission treat cooperating prisoners?*

"The Commission will treat a request from a foreign or a domestic law enforcement authority as equivalent to a 'motion of the government'." 28 C.F.R. § 2.68(k)(5).

b. Acceptance Of Responsibility

§ 14.67. *How does the Parole Commission treat acceptance of responsibility?*

The *Parole Commission Manual* states that "[a]pplication of § 3E1.1 to transfer treaty cases is made more complicated by the fact that the court procedures in the various transferring countries may be significantly different from those of U.S. Courts." *See* PAROLE COMMISSION MANUAL, *Subpart B, Transfer Treaty Prisoners and Parolees*, § 2.68-07(c), at 176 (2001), available online at http://www.usdoj.gov/uspc; *see also* Appendix 9, *Supplementary Instructions for Application of Sentencing Guidelines* (revised Aug. 15, 1996), at 234. Under the *Parole Commission Manual*, the Commission applies the adjustment differently in two types of cases. First, for countries like Canada and the United Kingdom that allow a defendant to plead guilty rather than have a trial, "the standards set forth in § 3E1.1 are readily adaptable." Second, for countries like Mexico, where every defendant has a trial, the defendant will qualify for acceptance if he "provided self-incriminating information to the police resulting in his conviction." If the prisoner self-incriminated in a timely manner, he will qualify for an additional one-level adjustment.

In most situations, because the treaty transfer itself requires admission of the facts of conviction, the Parole Commission will generally grant the downward adjustment for acceptance.

§ 14.68. *Can the prisoner get acceptance even though he did not cooperate with the foreign country?*

Yes. If the prisoner "promptly accepts responsibility for his offense(s) of conviction (even if only because the law and treaty require it) and there are no countervailing circumstance(s) warranting denial of this adjustment," he can qualify for the adjustment. Appendix 9, *Supplementary Instructions for Application of Sentencing Guidelines* (revised Aug. 15, 1996), at 235.

§ 14.69. *Has the Commission ever rejected applying this adjustment?*

Though the *Parole Commission Manual* implies that a two-level departure should be granted as a matter of course, the Parole Commission has rejected the adjustment in at least one reported case. *See* James v. United States Parole Commission, 159 F.3d 1200 (9th Cir. 1998) (acceptance rejected for prisoner convicted of transporting drugs in undergarments who contended she did not know of drugs), *cert. denied,* 525 U.S. 1186, 119 S. Ct. 1131 (1999).

c. Minor Role

§ 14.70. *Does the Commission grant minor role adjustments?*

Yes, especially because many cases involve drug couriers. Thus, when the prisoner gives a credible explanation of conduct with some corroborating evidence, the Commission will likely grant a minor role adjustment under § 3B1.1. *Cf.* Ajala v. United States Parole Commission, 997 F.2d 651, 657 (9th Cir. 1993) (denial of role reduction upheld where alleged courier's credibility was poor without corroborating evidence or contact information).

d. Abuse or Torture in Foreign Custody

§ 14.71. *How will the Commission treat torture in the foreign country?*

"A commonly asserted ground for departure in the case of transfer treaty prisoners is that the prisoner suffered physical abuse and/or torture while incarcerated in a foreign prison." Tramel v. United States Parole Commission, 100 F.3d 129, 132 (11th Cir. 1996). Moreover, "a downward departure for torture or other severe abuse (including inhumane prison conditions) is taken from the bottom of the guidelines." Appendix 9, *Supplementary Instructions for Application of Sentencing Guidelines* (revised Aug. 15, 1996), at 238. Federal Sentencing Guideline § 5K2.0 provides the basis for this departure given that the Guidelines do not account for unconstitutional conditions like torture except for departures.

§ 14.72. *Must the Commission accept a conviction gained by the prisoner's torture?*

Yes, under the treaty the Commission must accept the foreign court's findings of conviction. Thus, even when the Commission finds the prisoner only confessed under torture, all it can do is grant a downward departure and not overrule the foreign court's findings. Appendix 9, *Supplementary Instructions for Application of Sentencing Guidelines* (revised Aug. 15, 1996), at 236.

§ 14.73. *How is "torture" defined?*

The *Parole Commission Manual* defines "torture" as the "officially-instigated infliction of severe physical or mental pain or suffering upon a prisoner, either to extract a confession, to punish the prisoner unlawfully, to terrorize the prisoner into obedience, or out of wanton cruelty." "Other severe abuse" include "conditions of confinement or conduct (for example, conduct by other prisoners) that inflicts severe physical or mental pain or suffering upon a prisoner, but is not officially instigated or otherwise does not meet the definition of torture." As with torture, severe abuse resulting in permanent physical or psychological injury "may warrant a decision below the guidelines." Appendix 9, *Supplementary Instructions for Application of Sentencing Guidelines* (revised Aug. 15, 1996), at 239.

§ 14.74. *How have reported cases treated this?*

There is a range of reported departures for torture and mistreatment. *See* Tramel v. United States Parole Commission, 100 F.3d 129, 132 (11th Cir. 1996) (no departure where "mistreatment" was not severe); Trevino-Casares v. United States Parole Commission, 992 F.2d 1068 (10th Cir. 1993) (departing 37 months where prisoner suffered permanent physical damage); Thorpe v. United States Parole Commission, 902 F.2d 291 (5th Cir.) (no departure for mere "mistreatment"), *cert. denied*, 498 U.S. 868, 111 S. Ct. 185 (1990).

G. Appealing the Parole Commission

§ 14.75. *Is there internal review?*

Yes. The *Parole Commission Manual* lists special internal procedures to refer the prisoner's case to the General Counsel's Office for review before final determination. PAROLE COMMISSION MANUAL, *Subpart B, Transfer Treaty Prisoners and Parolees*, § 2.68-07(c), at 176 (2001), available online at http://www.usdoj.gov/uspc (requiring referral to General Counsel "[i]f the case involves any substantial sentencing guideline issue, or is otherwise deemed likely to result in appeal (i.e., if the transferee is to serve a substantial prison term)").

§ 14.76. *Can the prisoner then appeal the Parole Commission?*

Yes. If the prisoner does not agree with the Parole Commission's decision on the analogous offense he can appeal. *See, e.g.*, Kleeman v. United States Parole Commission, 125 F.3d 725 (9th Cir. 1997) (Parole Commission's determination that Mexican "simple intentional homicide" with no premeditation was analogized with second-degree murder reversed to voluntary manslaughter for lack of malice); *cf.* Lara v. United States Parole Commission, 990 F.2d 839, 840–41 (5th Cir. 1993) (upholding Parole Commission's determination that transferee's Mexican conviction for simple intentional homicide should be translated into second-degree murder because evidence of transferee's intent was consistent with malice aforethought).

The prisoner can also appeal the Parole Commission's Sentencing Guideline calculation including upward departures. *See* Kleeman v. United States Parole Commission, 142 F.3d 444 (9th Cir. 1998) (unpublished decision) (rejecting Parole Commission's logic that prisoner's mental condition, which formed the basis of voluntary manslaughter finding, was a further basis for upward departure).

§ 14.77. *Where will the prisoner appeal?*

To the United States court of appeals for the circuit were the prisoner is imprisoned at the time of the determination. 18 U.S.C. § 4106A(b)(2).

§ 14.78. *How common are appeals?*

Because many prisoners receive release on the record they do not appeal.

Table of Cases

References are to sections or placement in chapter.
See text for prior and subsequent history of opinion.

C

D

Q

R

V

W

Y

Z

Index

References are to sections or placement in chapter.

B

C

D

E

J

K

L

T

U

V

FROM THE ABA CRIMINAL JUSTICE SECTION